D1505389

YOU CALL IT MADNESS

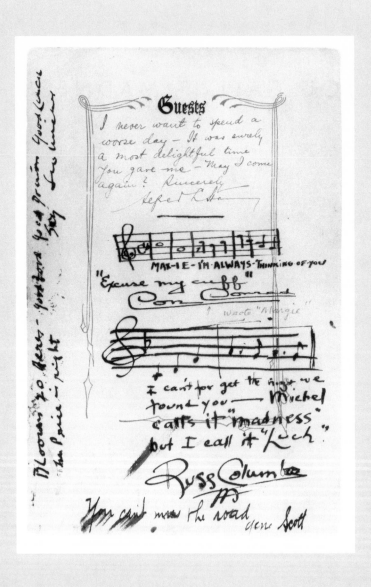

YOU
CALL IT
MADNESS

The Sensuous Song of the Croon

L E N N Y   K A Y E

V I L L A R D

N E W   Y O R K

LIBRARY OF CONGRESS CATALOGING-IN-PUBLICATION DATA
Kaye, Lenny.
You call it madness: the sensuous song of the croon / Lenny Kaye.
p.   cm.
Includes bibliographical references, discography, and index.
ISBN 0-679-46308-9
1. Columbo, Russ, 1908–1934. 2. Singers—United States—Biography. 3. Crooning. I. Title.
ML420.C655K39 2004
782.42164'092—dc22
[B]   2003062162

Villard Books website address: www.villard.com
Printed in the United States of America on acid-free paper
246897531
First Edition
Book design by Jo Anne Metsch

TO THE WOMAN IN MY LIFE.

ALL OF YOU.

CONTENTS

MADNESS

LOVE

I

Madness

Syncopation—shuffling, shuffling, crooning,
*   syncopation . . .*
The jazz tonight has almost roused me to an
*   orgasm.*

ANAÏS NIN,
diary entry, November 10, 1932

THEME SONG

'm cruising along the interstate when I first hear his story. Predawn. We are introduced randomly over the airwaves, radio on the far side of the dial. The hindsight of fate. I could've been on another station, or tuned out; he might have lived.

There are the letters to his mother. His association with Carole. The dark, husky grain of his voice; a nostalgia for a moment I have never known first-hand, have yet to experience. He intrigues me. The in-trigger.

"*I can't forget the night I met you . . .*"

Memory's overwhelming obsession. "*It's all I'm dreaming of.*"

All. What every woman wants.

You c-all it. Heads or tails.

Madness.

Love.

Is there a choice?

HE'S A "baritone with orchestra." *Buh-buh-buh* baritone. The way of the crooner.

He lives for you. There is no existence without your presence. "*I know my heart won't beat again / Until we meet again . . .*" *Auf Wiedersehen*. My dear.

Take a photo. It outlives you. A shot: set and shoot. A match sparking on a cocked hammer. A pair, as dueling pistols go. The complete set.

They're meant for close firing. One on one. Not random protection, or the anonymous carnage of war. This is an intimately twinned weapon, each meant only for the other.

The you of duel. The total absorption; the ultimate mating. Me, you. You, me.

Which is to be who. We could even trade places, across this table that separates us. That is our intention, to penetrate and become you, in much the same way this light becomes you, or that color becomes you. It is the becoming that interests us now.

This could be a smoky nightclub at 3:00 A.M., the Brown Derby or Danny's Hideaway, band choogling in the background, he leaning across the table to ignite her cigarette with a silver lighter. A flared glint. The pinpoint reflection from the lighter intersects the white light flash of a photographer from *Screenland* snapping an exclusive photo. For a moment they're framed by what seems a backlit silver screen, the blinding bulb glare of looking into the mouth of a klieg. A still projected. Neither notices because they're in full linger, time braked until its slowing motion is combusted by the nova-beamed flame edging them each toward their spotlit other.

Dual. He could feel their bloods roaring as he opened his eyes on her. When he sang. He played the gypsy instrument and came from the hot countries; there were three o's in his given name. He had darkened in the gibraltar sun of Hollywood, even as he had lightened under New York's noon moon.

He spoke the romance of Latin, the language of chimera; as in Latin Lover. The Romeo of Song: wherefore art the next Valentino?

The knowing *Ah* before . . . *but I Call It Love*; and then the *ba-dah-dahs*.

The croon. A most sensual singing.

1933

He is his song titles, his movie themes. Every chapter can have its own heading. They all fit.

Broadway Thru a Keyhole. Peeping through a boudoir door with a moon-shaped microphone clutched in his right hand. Got the key to the lock, hovering, ready to insert. His eyebrows are swept back, a comet's tail parting only to let the eye's vein pass through the dark shadow of his upper lids.

But Russ Columbo isn't really looking at anything. He's listening; he's hearing the song come to mind and he's following its melody, humming it in the back of his throat, hoping to tune it clearer. The human radio tube. Pure vacuum. To bring it to the surface so he can sing it.

A pinkie ring. A tuxedo and bow tie. Hair a smooth black sheen brushing backward. He is sleek, like a seal coat.

Broadway Thru a Keyhole is Winchell's baby, a film based on his tell-all tattle. To Russ, it's a trade-off for column inches and a chance to sing for, ironically, his old friends in Hollywood. Back to the movies.

A comeback; that's what the papers like to say. Knocked down but picked himself up off the canvas. Been bounced along the ropes but keeps on bobbing and weaving.

He's come back different, though. He has already lived the life he's playing, perched on a penthouse atop the times squared, and knows his part well. He's The Singer in what *The New York Sun* calls "an old-fashioned gangster, chorus girl, nightclub talkie of the sort that came along when the boom and the gangster films were at their height."

It wasn't just that the picture had a familiar ring, even in November 1933 when Al Capone was nearly on the ferry to Alcatraz. For Russ, it was all too true. Change the setting and everybody's story had a certain constancy. Like his co-star, the lovely Miss Cummings. Read the headlines then; read the deadlines now. The same old lusts and mayhems, murders and trials and freaks of nature and random horrors, strikes, kidnappings, executions, grisly details and center-spread photos, mixed with a lot of everyday life and advertisements.

He lives here, now, back in Californ-I-A. Moved home with the folks. Dad still runs the construction company. Mama isn't well these days. Short of breath, chest pains. And when in Ro*mama* . . .

The family together again, as they all once had been in those last few years before the Great War, in Philadelphia. He was the baby of the Colombos, the dozenth child, and one day there he was, all of *cinque*, Ruggiero Eugenio di Rudolpho sawing away on the Steel Pier in Atlantic City, by the grace of the Lord Jesus and his blessed Mother, playing his violin as if his heart could break.

He loved the instrument. Cradling it under his chin, his wrist quivering to shudder the note just so, drawing out the tone's tensile stretch and making it vanish into air in an imperceptible moment between silence and awareness, he can feel it radiate as he plays. He is forever in pursuit of closing the gap between himself and the violin, to become its dark mahogany wood and shell-like curlicues, sliding up the spine of its neck. A violation: even as he leans in to sing, he can feel himself begin to resemble the violin, waist cinched in (by his cummerbund, no doubt), chest expanding like the fired arch-top of the violin's body, each register of his voice—the tenor, the ethereal soprano, the resonant and smoky bottom—become a different string. His bow the vocal chord.

Even his singing demeanor echoes the violin; head inclined, eyes naturally downcast. His voice gliding along the fingerboard, fingers dancing like a Follies production. This is the era of the chorus girl, the cigarette gal, the taxi and fan dancer.

And for Russ, it is also the lonely college coed; the bored secretary; the middle daughter who couldn't afford to leave home because she had been told that's where she had to stay until marriage, and then after, another house she couldn't afford to leave; the girls who lost loves and those who left them behind; girls who wore the latest fashions, girls who read the fan magazines and placed them tenderly in their hope chests, girls who spun (as in spinsters) and girls who pirouetted before their mirrors and girls giggling and girls fighting back tears and girls sitting on front stoops and porches and in living rooms and bedrooms waiting for a stray signal from the NBC network (at 11:00 P.M. EST) to begin their dreaming.

"The Romeo of Song." Nothing too fast, mind you, all tempos decelerated for slow and sinuous dancing. A music for whispering in ears. For sliding out the slots in the Bakelite, a glowing dial and the warm, crackling static hum of electricity.

Russ didn't know about electric instruments. They hadn't been invented yet, mere rumors and prototypes, if you didn't count the microphone. And he did, because it allowed him to sing softly. To mouth each word as it came out of his mouth, to send it just toward you, you, just the way you always wanted to hear it, and experience it, how you always wished it would be, head back, eyes lidded, hand pressed inside your thigh, to reach that one moment of total real-time bliss in which something meaningful passes back and forth between your heart's flutter, to know how deep love can stick its tongue in your ear.

He knew what it was to have loved, and to have had love taken away. To let the public have their way with him. The morning-after slink from the bed, the knowledge that both he and they had got what they wanted. Fought to a draw. He had given up everything for what his life consisted of now, which to most people was still everything, especially in this time of Depression. He'd spit through more money than he'd ever expected to make, which was how it was supposed to be, since you were who people perceived you to be. You reached for the stars, and then became one. And then found out there were millions of them.

You had to shine brighter. Con Conrad, his manager, had shown him that, standing on the street corner at Broadway and Forty-sixth one fall afternoon two years ago. No way was he going to let Russ Columbo wait for twenty minutes in the rain after he'd just thrilled more than a thousand femme admirers at the Paramount Grill's afternoon milk-benefit, there at the behest of her royal selflessness Mrs. William Randolph Hearst. "More cream" was how they liked to boast at Borden's. That was Con's *operandi*. Maybe it was working. When Russ entered the café, he could sense the intake of breath, the room suddenly drained of oxygen. Chests heaved and tightened. He could hardly breathe. To exhale was to dare break the spell.

Outside, after the autographs and the shy squirm of the young ladies, it had begun to drizzle. As they waited, Conrad paced, fumed. He hated standing there for a cab that might never come. That was no way to treat Russ Columbo, "the biggest name on the radio," or himself, or the two publicity shysters with him, Paul Yawitz and Harry Sobol. He started walking briskly toward the West Side, to Scott & Reilly, dealers in Lincolns. He bought the "biggest damned car you've got," hired a chauffeur, and, fully liveried, glided off to their Central Park overlook. Big front equals big money, that's how Con Conrad bet his horses.

Russ would ask, fret, wonder how they would ever pay for it. Moving from hotel suite to penthouse, the Big Front would make its mark. "Leave that to me, Russ," Conrad would say. "All you've got to worry about is your songs."

He'd heard that one before. Everybody had, but that didn't make it any the less attractive for someone who believed in the song's deep mystery. At that time he was more than content to let Con take care of any business. He didn't really want to deal with the bullshit.

Besides, he was looking for a way out. He'd had enough of all this sob-sister emoting. He wanted to *sing*, to return his mind to the intricacies of the opera, where the actor as vocalist could truly play the instrument of his lines.

He knew that he wasn't born to the talkies. The dialogue seemed artificial on his lips; he would rather move the words into his diaphragm and begin their melody there. Why say "How are you?" when you could sing it, adding the decorative touches of rhythm and grace.

That was the reason, even though his career was going well and upswinging, with Universal almost ready to sign him, with a new record deal with Brunswick in the works, with a new radio hookup awaiting in the new year, he knew it wouldn't last.

He was The Singer. And if that was the case, let it be *Rigoletto*. The Duke of Mantua. *Bella figlia dell' amore* and the pangs of unrequited love.

1931

It is sticky on this late June day in Grand Central Terminal. Paul Yawitz walks through the main concourse; over him, the sky's constellations pinpoint, a Mediterranean winter as seen from beyond our solar system, as if viewed from heaven. Light pours in from the east windows.

He is meeting the Twentieth Century Limited from California. *The Chief.* Track 36. Con Conrad and some Italian singer on board. On the Con-course. Con wants Paul to show up with cameramen and newspaper reporters. That's what publicity flacks are hired for, and he thinks this new boy will be a sensation.

A night letter from Con is folded in Paul's right jacket pocket. "Am bringing an unknown crooner who, with the right publicity, can be built into the biggest thing in the country. Depending on you—don't fail me. It means a fortune."

It means, Paul thinks, shaking out a Chesterfield from a nearly empty pack, lighting it with a book of matches that bears a picture of Carl Hubbell, that he's waiting for them at 8:45 A.M. when the train pulls in. Paul immediately recognizes Con, a songwriter and schemer he had met about the time Conrad had gone belly-up in the Broadway musical business in '28, losing all the money he'd made writing "Margie" and "Ma! (He's Making Eyes at Me)" and Sophie Tucker's "You've Got to See Mamma Ev'ry Night (Or You Can't See Mamma at All)" and scores for shows that never got out of New Haven or their producers' imaginations. He'd left the next year for Hollywood to write for the soundies. *Fox Movietone Follies—"Hey Flap-pers . . . Let's do the*

Break-a-way / Get hot and shake a-way"—and other nonsense. Yawitz liked him, though Con had a tendency never to shut up. Anyway, he was always good for a bottle of wine, and a meal, and maybe a chorus girl introduction.

The kid is compact, muscular, though thin. He takes his handkerchief out of his pocket and mops his forehead. The jet-dark hair rises from his crown in a sharp V, almost devilish. He's not really sweating, but the act of taking the white cloth from his breast pocket, unfolding it, pressing it to his temple once, twice, and beginning its meticulous refold gives him something to do. "Where's the papers?" the kid asks, turning to Con.

Con had promised him there'd be a big crowd waiting to greet them. Con liked to promise, that was what he was hired for.

Yawitz sticks out his hand. First to Con, then to the kid. They see a man with an almost triangular mustache and a nose to match, eyes buried beneath the brim of a large hat. Late twenties, early thirties; younger than Con, who turned forty this month.

"Paul, this is Russ." Conrad waves with a flourish toward his companion. Russ is looking decidedly glum. The conversation awkwardly catches its breath, not sure where it's going. Around them, heels click, bodies brush by, colored redcaps lift bags onto rolling carts. The city swirls around their pause, ignoring them as a thousand other unitings take place.

"Where do you want us to pose for the photographers?"

Con's question arcs in the air. Paul lets it float until it answers itself. What could he tell them? There's plenty of would-be nobodys coming to New York every day, despite what those movie people thought in Hollywood. They believed everything they read in the fan magazines, even if they had written it themselves.

"You can't get those birds to fall for a singer no one ever heard about. Give me a little time; I'll get the ball rolling after I've sized up the situation."

Russ takes in the interchange. Are they talking about him? He can feel his own disappointment, and it bothers him. The future seemed so sure on the train, buoyed by Con's belief in him and the grandiose plans he outlined as they slid down the Great Divide, rolled over the Great Plains, skirted Chicago. Has he traveled three thousand miles to start from scratch? If he had the money, he'd get right back on the train and return to California. But he doesn't, and neither does Con.

In fact, the only person who has any cash is Yawitz. They go out to Vanderbilt Avenue and catch a cab uptown. He pays the taxi to the Warwick, up at Sixth and Fifty-fourth, across the way from Ziegfeld's theater, where Con books them into a four-room suite, four hundred dollars a month. Deluxe.

Built by William Randolph Hearst, the hotel is only four years old. They have a view of Central Park, if they stick their heads out the window and look to the right.

Con believes in the good life. Do unto yourself as you would have others do unto you. He calls up room service and orders caviar, breast of guinea hen *en cocotte*, a quart of 1919 dry Monopole.

Russ slumps in an overstuffed chair, wondering what he's doing here. His flannel trousers ride high above his waist, showing off a pair of gaudy Hollywood sport shoes. Con has ordered him new clothes—"college clothes," he calls them—from Basil Durant and Immerman, by wire from the train.

"We can pay them later," he says, not for the first time.

YOUNG RUSS

BIRTH

He has two births.

The first is the one the public reads about. Born in San Francisco, he begins to emerge from his mother, Julia, during an electrical storm, the twelfth offspring of a twelfth offspring.

January 14, 1908, is the date on which the stories agree, but the actual birthing takes place on the other side of the continent, and he's probably only a single twelfth, counting stillborn, conceived in Camden, New Jersey.

A Colombo. In the original Italian, that is no small matter: a surname to be reckoned with, the Genoan who discovered *Amerigo*, land of opportunity. His father, Nicola, has come here from Naples, where he has met Giulia Peseri, though their marriage will wait until he has established himself in the new world.

The first name, Ruggiero, is harder to pinpoint. By the twelfth child, his folks have run through most of their favorite christenings, paid tribute to the closest relatives. Perhaps they saw, or heard of, fellow *Napoletano* Ruggiero Leoncavallo on his American tour in 1906, conducting *I Pagliacci* and *La Jeunesse de Figaro*. The name was in the air.

The Colombos have been working their way across town since 1901, when Nicholas (Nicola), a stonemason, and Julia (Giulia) surface in East Camden, along a Union Avenue literally the other side of the C&A tracks from opulent Cramer Hill. Now North Twenty-fourth Street—the Colombos live at 130 in 1901, 132 in 1902, when Nicholas describes himself as the more employable "laborer"—Union is around the corner from St. Joe's R.C. church, though the family tends to their spiritual needs at Our Lady of Fatima on South Fourth. The Colombos are familiar figures at its baptismal font.

The dwelling at 130 Union is a small two-story row house, attached, flat front, roofed porch, decorative urnlike finials on top, functional living quarters for a family half their size, much like each successive address as they approach the South Side, where the Italians have a foothold. They move to 306 Spruce, where Nicholas tries his hand at being a grocer and his oldest boy Anthony is a musician. The family shifts to 259 Pine, and finally, perhaps because of Russ's birth, moves to 808 South Ninth in 1908. The numerological portents could hardly have been more promising.

On the eve of his expulsion from the womb, the Rhodes Opera House in Boyertown, Pennsylvania, conflagrates, trapping whole families when panic ensues after an explosion of gas from a motion picture projector. The new medium claims its first casualties.

Camden is feeling the booming effects of technology as well. Downtown, along the waterfront, Eldridge Reeves Johnson is constructing a multibuilding complex to house his Victor Talking Machine Company, cabinetry and spring motors and machining and sound reproduction in one self-contained hive. He is not only making better-sounding lateral recordings by 1908 than Emile Berliner, with whom he has a flat disc partnership, but he has better taste than Thomas Edison. Among the artists recording exclusively for Victor are Enrico Caruso, Antonio Scotti, Emma Calve, and Nellie Melba.

The Italian community are especially proud of Caruso, also *Napoletano*, and the high esteem in which their singing countryman is regarded, but Nicholas Colombo is no fool when it comes to how most people resent these "without-papers" foreigners. Wops. Just this week of Ruggiero's birth, a crew of Italian workmen were stoned while grading sidewalks near the Newton Creek Bridge, and mounted police had to be called. Antonio Coruscini was beaten by unknown assailants as he worked on the Atlantic City Railroad ties. Another *paesano* compatriot, Francisco Leombo, who lived across from the old poet's house on Mickle Street, dropped dead on his way to visit his native soil, steamship ticket in hand, overworked and exhausted. "He no lika da winter," the *Camden Daily Courier* quoted a friend. "He so lika hes own Naples. He lef' all smile and glad."

The Colombos ferry across the Delaware into South Philadelphia's immigrant ghetto in '09. Nicholas has gone back to stonemasonry, and they live at 709 Fulton, near the intersection of Eighth Street just north of Catharine, later relocating three blocks west, to Eleventh Street. The next year they move to 1139 Frankford, northeast from Laurel and Beach. In 1911, Nicholas takes the family farther north, to Laycock Avenue near South Seventy-ninth. Antonio is still a musician; Alphonso is a mason like his dad. In 1912 Alphonso moves to Botanic near Seventy-eighth, and by 1913 the whole family joins up at Botanic near Seventy-ninth Street (southwest from South Forty-eighth). Another of Russell's brothers, John, is a barber.

Now his father is a "contractor" and runs a corner bank. Down the street from where the family lives is Antonio Laveri, originally from Rome. The child Russ studies guitar with him, and the opera of his homeland. It's a musical clan, and the family—his dad on tuba—plays together, impromptu, calling themselves the Colombo Ideal Orchestra.

Before Russ attains double figures, in 1916, his father will go under financially and relocate most of the family to California. Two of his brothers have already passed on (a sister, Florence, will be carried off by the flu in 1919). The Colombos first move to Calistoga in the Napa Valley (where the mud baths seem helpful to the precarious state of his mother's health), then San Francisco (by 1920, he is learning violin from Joseph Czech, a German, appearing at the downtown Imperial Theater in *Land of Make Believe* and as a "wonder violinist of the twentieth century" at the Grenada), and finally Los Angeles. Hollywood. The weather there reminds his father of *Napoli*.

Russ earns money working as a plow-hand in the vineyards, and occupies the first-violin chair at Belmont High. He studies violin and voice "placement" under the operatic coach Alexander Bevani. Nicholas is a "builder"; they live at 1434 Court Street. There are still financial difficulties, and Russ has to give up thoughts of a concert career in order to make the family money, though his duties with the Hollywood Serenaders, playing guitar or violin with Leon Belasco, sometimes teaming up for duets over KFWB radio, seem to his liking.

The 1926 city directory lists him as "Russell, musician." 1322 Tamarind.

This is how he begins.

EARLY BANDS

On the *one*. His first recording opens with a sock cymbal. He's very much a band vocalist, stuck somewhere in the middle of the song like a breakdown, allotted a small solo after the first-verse clarinets while the main theme bides its time to frolic back in.

The Gus Arnheim Orchestra states the refrain and riffs on it, spins it twice over, and he enters. A guitar single-notes along with him in sixteenths, giving the track a sprightly, happy-go-lucky feel. Bpm: 118 clip-clops per minute. Arnheim—thin, black hair parted in the middle before it slicks back, aquiline—likes to get the crowd on his side.

Russ has only a chorus and a half to step in front of the band before the saxophones and trombone dance lithely before him, the tuba takes its squat solo, and the room returns to dancing. His high tenor causes too many heads to turn his way, away from their partner; that's not what a dance band is for.

"Back in Your Own Backyard" dates from April 14, 1928, and is probably his earliest known recorded performance. Al Jolson popularized the song, once called "It's Nobody's Fault But Mine," sliding his name alongside the writer credits of lyricist Billy Rose and melodist Dave Dreyer. The Arnheim Orchestra, and so they are—with strings, brass, and a big kettle drum—foxtrot it along, celebrating the joys of getting back to "where you started from." Kind of hard if you haven't been anywhere yet. *"You can go to the east / You can go to the west. . . ."* There is a violin solo in the last chorus; it's likely Russ in the first chair, all sawing double-stops, Appalachian, as if he were playing with steel instead of gut strings. Swing your partners. Arnheim is not as calm as he looks. The orchestra verges on breaking out, almost *hot*, but he errs on the side of restraint, self-control, too early to risk losing his role as film society's favorite bandleader.

Within Arnheim, Russ grows from boy to man.

His voice changes.

IN 1927, Russ gets a job with George Eckhardt at the Georgian Room in the Mayfair Hotel downtown, then moves to the newly opened Hotel Roosevelt on Hollywood Boulevard with Professor Pryor Moore's Orchestra. It is a perfect vantage point from which to watch the film capital locate its tourist attractions. Sid Grauman's Chinese Theatre will make its bow to the film aristocracy the following year; Joe Musso and Frank Toulet's chophouse has been seating luminaries at their red leather banquettes for almost a decade now. On opening night for the Roosevelt, August 4, the vocalist takes sick, and Russ steps in for the radio broadcast. Can we believe it? Why not! It's every show business story.

By 1928, he has shifted to Arnheim and His Ambassadors. Migrating to Los Angeles as bandleader Abe Lyman's pianist, the twenty-nine-year-old Arnheim had inherited Lyman's coveted residency at the Ambassador Hotel's Cocoanut Grove. It was a large band—a dozen pieces, with an emphasis on instrumental versatility, as when banjoist Vernon Hall takes up his arch-top guitar or violin and puts aside the banjo, and at various times it would include future game show host and drummer Art Fleming and tenor saxist Fred MacMurray.

A tall-seeming Columbo sits at the apex of Arnheim's arrayed crescent of band triangle, in the middle of a string section that consists of another violin, a chording guitar to his right, and the aforementioned Mr. Hall to the left. The rhythm section is split around them, double bass on stage right, the drums, with temple blocks and xylophone adjuncted, stage left. Three saxophones switch easily to clarinets, matched by two trumpets and a trombone. Arnheim reigns in the center at the piano, treble side up.

Three songs are filmed for a *Vitaphone Varieties* short in July 1928. The opening note of the title card is the famous rising swoop of *Rhapsody in Blue*, a hint of sophisticated subliminal even then, suggesting a modulating cadenza of skyscrapers silhouetted against a cathode-ray sky.

The Ambassadors tease with a quote from "I Ain't Got Nobody" and then romp into "If I Can't Have You." Gus tosses it to a counterpointing trombone, then ensembles it until the solo violin. Russ rises to his entrance; from afar, it's as if he is standing on Arnheim's piano. A quick pick-up, count sixteen and he's out, though he uses most of the fourth bar to lower his instrument and place himself within the center of a vocal trio. Three tenors. The voices emanate from pursed lips, Adam's apples bobbing behind their bow ties as they sing the refrain.

Russ juggles back and forth on the balls of his feet. There is no doubt he's buoyant, eagerly wound up. He shifts from foot to foot, twice each beat, his shoulders double-timing. The drummer keeps a rhythm on the cymbal, hardly on the snare, choking it to emphasize the dance steps, a technique that will fall into disuse as the century gets louder and more raucous, only to return in the disco era of the seventies.

When he sings, his violin faces the camera, upright. Along the chin rest is a large taped cloth, where he holds the instrument fast in the crook of his neck. He is not yet styled for the camera; a working musician. Playing several hours a night, you dress your instrument for comfort. Russ is known to break a sweat.

The microphones hide in the shrubbery in the foreground. There is something shameful about their presence, that they must be disguised to preserve an illusion, that they make things seem less real when in actuality they bring them closer, magnified, an ethe-real. Russ is still figuring it out. During the second tune, which begins with a vocal trio two-bar of "Mighty Lak' a Rose"—a familiar 1901 sentimental chestnut (crossed over to the violin via Michel Gusikoff for Victor in 1923)—he sits while the muted trumpet takes its turn. He wonders what to do with himself. He picks at a piece of dust on his trousers, glances down at his bow and right hand, flexes his thumb, takes a deep breath.

The song segues into "There's Something About a Rose (That Reminds Me of You)," and he's up singing again, not really looking out at the audience-that-isn't-there, but tuning in to the other singers, fitting his high harmony atop so the notes blend into a grounded three-pronged chord.

The last track is instrumental, a dixielanding "Tiger Rag" that the band—more band than scripted orchestra at this point—pass around like a hat. The camera cuts to solo turns: New Orleans clarinet, Chicago trombone, K.C. banjo, "Hold That Tiger" tuba, a geography of the music's flow up the Mississippi where it crosses tidewaters with the European migration. When it's Russ, he lets fly a hip-waggling do-your-stuff showboat, raising his eyebrows, flourishing the bow; he's heard Joe Venuti. His gleeful grin, and the band's infectious jollity, give an entertaining inkling why Arnheim was held in such high regard.

Curiously, there is not one close-up of Gus throughout the short, or even any taken solos. When he stands at the end of each song, gesturing at the band, motioning them to rise at the finale, it is done in long shot. Keeping his distance. He prefers to be known by his representatives, his Ambassadors.

THE LOWERING begins in 1929. "Glad Rag Doll," recorded on January 17, broadens Russ's voice even as it searches for a deeper octave. Arnheim attempts to encourage him to explore the cavern of his lungs by positing Hall's high-pitched single-string guitar against him for the second half of the refrain; but the time is too short for Russ to investigate his character, or deviate from the notes of the song.

It's not a throwback like "I Can't Do Without You," recorded for a film short in the next month, where he's once again backgrounded in the vocal trio. At twenty-one, a year makes a big difference. He sings on his own now.

When next he records, on June 18, 1930, again with Arnheim, his voice has found its particular precipice. He's fully enlarged his larynx, though the track—"Peach of a Pair" from a film called *Follow Thru*—moves too fast for him. His diction clips when it trots along. He needs to slow the music down, mold his own sense of timing, the calculus of time as musical space.

He saw it could be done. He had watched the Rhythm Boys as they became the darlings of the bandleaders. Harry Barris, Al Rinker, Jr., and Bing Crosby. Especially Bing. When he sing.

You had to watch out for him. That crazy bastard, he made it look easy.

Russ knew Bing could go off the deep end.

Poco loco. Liable to take off for Mexico and be carried back to L.A. days after the gig. Paul Whiteman had finally given the Rhythm Boys their notice; he was still sore that Bing was in jail when it came time for Crosby to sing "Song of the Dawn" in *The King of Jazz*, and he'd had to use actor John Boles instead. Bing was no stranger to the hoosegow; he had found himself locked up on more than one inebriated occasion, like the night he tried to turn left into the Roosevelt and his car (with blond starlet in tow) was rear-ended, "a few drinks" to the wind. Under the influence.

Arnheim was also about to blow his top. Gus had already started feeling jumpy when on September 28, 1930, a "well-dressed lone bandit" broke into his house on Warner Drive. He and the missus had walked in on him, and the thief had escaped with jewelry worth over two grand. The next day, Bing married Dixie Lee, aspiring Hollywood starlet; Gus took a look at the wedding ring, just to make sure.

He was in no mood to put up with Bing's tomming foolery, though then again, he knew Bing brought in the customers. The Rhythm Boys had a lot of friends from their days at the Montmartre, where Bing had courted Dixie. Harry was the cutup, Al was the stolid right-hand man, but it was Bing who got the girls. Or, in this case, the girl. Maybe she would set him straight.

There was even talk of Bing leaving the Rhythm Boys, going off on his own. Gus himself had utilized him as much as possible in the studio, cutting a dozen or so sides, including a recent Orchestra recording for Victor toward the end of 1930, the double-faced "It Must Be True" / "Fool Me Some More." He even got him to whistle an instrumental break on the A side. It was Bing's specialty.

Crosby's delivery had the curlicues of whistling, the trills and birdcall twitterings, the sudden ascend and descend of notes, whole octaves. That was what Russ liked about Bing's phrasing, its hesitations and inflections and tease of the melody, much as a violin's bow could slur the microtonals between notes, fingers bending the string so slightly and yet so deliberately, implying all the many distinctions between moods. Crosby had an expressiveness of voice that allowed the melody breath and breadth, that soft-focused time, a dance between singer and song, the dip and do-si-do and turnabout.

Russ—like Bing—had spent years watching people swirl in front of him, letting him serenade their parading, their pressing and preening. Pairing. He liked keeping his eye on a couple shimmying near the bandstand, eyes intent on each other, and he, with a shimmer of his violin, could transport himself into their next move. On a slow song, in tune, he could whirl them up into making an overture—an accord, a chord—that might otherwise be shocking, a kiss reaching for a high note, three touching tongues as if they were all in embrace.

Bing could fool you, scaling down a song, making it personal instead of a crowd-pleaser. He was hardly imposing; he took the opposite tack. Easy. He made you think he was singing it for the singular you, your request, tailoring its melodies and word sounds to your ear, my nearest dear, because he knows, oh how he knows, just what you chose, would want to hear if you turned on your receiver, the radio as liquid crystal set. This is "a few pleasurable moments" with Gus Arnheim and His Los Angeles—pronounced with a hard "g"—Ambassador Hotel Cocoanut Grove Hotel Orchestra, playing nightly in southern California, America's "greatest summer playground." Abe Frank, the Grove's manager, had installed a broadcast studio in an upstairs room over the ballroom.

In early 1931, the remote catches Bing joined by Russ on a duet around "Goodnight Sweetheart." Crosby knows he'll ask to leave shortly; Russ is tired of playing second fiddle to Crosby, or whoever comes next. Frank has another vocal trio waiting in the wings, and he's calling them the Three Ambassadors. Russ is tired of fronting for other people.

It's late. The last set. Tuesday at the Grove, the mood playful, as befits a night when only the stars come out to play. The Moroccan desert décor, highlighted with papier-mâché palm trees imported from the set of *The Sheik*, heighten that aspect of L.A. which is Lawrence of Arabian (T.E. would translate admirably and heroically to film). It's an arboretum. Russ and Bing are grouped around the microphone, trading verses, choruses. They're not explicitly friendly, but there is no doubt each has heard the other. Russ has understood Bing's sway with words; Bing respects Russ's sonority, his sensuality with the phrase. Bing's listening is more moral. He is concerned with how to touch the emotion without being swallowed by it. Or rather, swallowing it by the fifth.

He's scared. Bing knows it's all his; he knows that by God's grace he can make people listen, and be his song. He is Everyman. But the freefall of vertigo within him when he opens his emotions is frightening. While he sings "Goodnight Sweetheart," he remembers the Christian prayers of Spokane — "If I die before I wake / I pray the Lord my soul to take" — and feels his own Catholic iniquity. He needs a drink. Despite his seeming ease, inside he's just like a little boy. Can he live up to his own expectations? Can he learn to be a father to himself?

They make a peach of a pair, do Russ and Bing, grazing the edge of croon. Russ's concerns are more maternal; he sings to women. Bing has already opted for the universal, the homogenous, the iconic. "I'm one of the fellas," he'll say in 1972, asked the secret of his success. Russ gesticulates to the gals. Perhaps the song you sing to a woman is the one you originally hum in your mummy's tummy; is the primordial lullaby when breathing locks in tandem, deep in the amniotic sac, and the frequency tunes to the rush of blood and the rhythm of a beating heart, quickening and slowing to the body's metronome of movement. Its racing and resting improvise within the pulse of tempo. Its dance step.

IN THE MOVIES

It was raining in L.A. A deep sodden mass of sky and a permanent fog breathing inside the windshield. The wipers flicking. Back and forth, fack and borth. He drove around, wandering, steering randomly.

He was home. Russ felt returned.

Maybe he would go past the old house. Just for the kick. Tamarind wasn't too far. 1322. The Packard made a left across Beverly, coasting up Fairfax. Right on Sunset. Not even a direct route. Russ was in no hurry to get there. He didn't even bother shifting out of second.

When they'd first moved here, Hollywood had been a small town, a village, the outer limits of L.A. sprawling across the plains of southern California with nothing to stop it but the rim of mountains and encroaching desert. Now it was a film "colony," as if it had been invaded from without and conquered. A coat of arms planted in the sandy soil. *I claim this land in the name of* . . .

He was glad he was among those who had tried to make their way in this new world. He grew up practically in the shadow of the Hollywoodland sign. They had been living over on Court when it was raised up on the hill in 1923. After they'd moved to Tamarind, Russ always liked to come out the front door, violin case in hand, and feel it watching over him to the north.

Some people in this town still looked down on him because he had risen through music rather than movies, but the talkies had them reading their lines out the other side of their asses now. His voice was an asset. Desirable. You could hear the movies, and he was meant for the listening.

His brother had kept the Tamarind house after Russ bought the one up on Outpost Circle. It had proved a good home for the family, and John was welcome to it. Russ was glad to give the folks a place they could be proud of, so his father wouldn't worry about losing all his money again, and Mama could rest the great bulk of her weight, her swollen legs, her overwrought heart. She had raised, and lost, so many children. When Fiore had been killed in the auto accident that July of '29, Russ beheld her grieving, and thought she would never rise from her chair again. Now, whenever she held his hand, he could feel her grip tight, fingers laced, as if unwilling to let him leave her side, holding on for dear life.

HE CAME upon the house quicker than he had expected. It was on the east side of the street, not two blocks from Sunset, with the wide cemetery expanse of Hollywood Memorial framing it on the south, where Valentino found his last rest.

Lansa—Lansing Brown, Jr., Russ's best friend and a Hollywood portrait photographer—had enjoyed dressing him as the Great Lover. One night Brown had been called by ex-Follies danseuse Lina Basquette, who had been married to one of the Warner brothers (Sam) until he'd made her a twenty-year-old widow in 1927 and was attempting to crank-start her movie career. She wanted to change her image from the Baby Pavlova (she had a six-year contract as a ballet prodigy from Universal when scarcely ten) to something more darkly alluring. Lansing photographed the two of them performing an insinuating apache dance, Russ in billowy shirt, two-tone shoes, oily hair flapping in his eyes, the gleam of knife held to her shoulder blade. She was vamping it up, a full-grown flapper, bobbed and waved like a radio kilocycle, sporting a cigarette, putting her fingers in her pouting mouth on the greenish sepia tint of a *Motion Picture* spread. "A girl must suffer if she syncopate" read the lurid copy.

Satin shirt rubs satin dress. He raises the nape of her neck in his right hand, surrounds her waist within his left arm. She lies on the marble floor as if in a swoon; he kisses her by the jaw's hinge, the valley between her back teeth and her cheekbone. Even though she's posing, eyes closed, he can feel her stir beneath him. There are photos Lansa doesn't send to the magazine.

He has known Lansing Brown since high school, when they used to pal around with Sally Blane, all growing up in the threshold excitement of a small town discovering it wants to break into the movies, and realizing they already live there.

The three friends. Each with their own entry point. Russ had the music, Sally could walk in front of a camera and twinkle the lens, and Lansa would step outside the frame of the present and take a picture at its stillest moment, squeezing the shutter.

Brown was known more as a man's photographer. Even Lina thought that when she sought him out. Douglas Fairbanks, Jr. Arthur Lake, who would play "Harold of Hollywood," hands on hips, pressing his groin forward, dress dissolving into shadow. William Bakewell, now starring in *All Quiet on the Western Front*, his *Screenland* portrait emerging from a depth-of-field mist to clarity, head turned sharply left, a blurred object beyond vision's range that snaps into sudden focus. The mating of the eye socket and the camera lens.

VALENTINO'S ALLURE is a mixed blessing for Russ. It types him. A genre of star, but a swordsman who cuts both ways. The Latino lover, machismo and dandyism rolled up in one. Are these cross-purposes? Valentino rose to prominence as an Argentinian tango dancer in *The Four Horsemen of the Apocalypse*. He never played Zorro. Instead, we remember him as The Sheik, an enrobed Bedouin from the other side of the Mediterranean, a Moorish hint of harem. The darker hue.

Not wholesome like Doug Fairbanks, or Ronald Colman, professing virtue, ever gallant: the asexual Robin Hood. The Latin would take advantage, using the opening as gateway. Their motives differ: one to resolve; the other to entangle.

The studio heads are still wary of Valentino, his puffed sleeves, his wristwatch. Worn as a bracelet, it seems a womanly touch, the effeminate symbol of plunder, the fetish of capture. When he stars on screen, he is known to be especially responsive to his female leads, so much so that he allows them to set the pace of performance, mirroring their mood and energy and projection. With Gloria Swanson, he overdramatizes, gestures extravagantly, an "Are the cameras rolling, Mr. DeMille?" that is the most powerful image of silent film acting principles to remain in the common consciousness. Nazimova (*Camille*) hardly allows the camera to cut from her to him, draping the lens in gauze, transfixing the spotlight. Nita Naldi hypnotizes him with an unwavering stare—a man who cannot "care for any *one* woman"—first in the Castilian *Blood and Sand*, then in *Cobra*, where Rudolph plays the Italian Count Torriano, from toreador to *toro*. He steals their scenes. It is his way with women.

They fascinate him, as "that cobra does its victim."

RUDOLPH VALENTINO SERENADES
IN CASTILIAN STYLE.

. . .

TOO LATIN. That didn't stop them from singing his songs. The movies were about disguise, anyway. Russ didn't see what was so different about Gary Cooper opening his mouth in *Wolf Song* and Russ's voice piping out, or singing "How Am I to Know" (lyrics by Dorothy Parker) sitting in a jail cell pretending to be a thin-mustachio'd Mexican prisoner in the 1929 *Dynamite*.

When he first enters cinema, he's literally behind the screen. Uncredited. Only his guitar's chords are heard (playing the "shave-and-a-haircut" riff) when society heiress Kay Johnson comes to arrange marriage with condemned murderer Charles Bickford. As she walks in, the warden pulls a shade down in front of Russ's cage, isolating him from the action.

He accompanies their tomorrow-night marriage from the next cell, which the camera has entered to capture his voice and guitar, while the incessant hammering from the morning's gallows under construction provides a pre-industrial beat. He gazes at his own beloved's picture on the wall. When the dialogue interjects, he moves to the wordless, hum-sings along, oohs to aahs, precursing croon. The guard interrupts him: "Hey, buddy, not so loud with that languid love stuff! The other prisoners are kickin'." Russ licks his lips, shrugs. "Let 'em kick"—even the way he says this is musical, lilting "kick" up, and returns to his threnody.

He plays the Spanish guitar in *Dynamite*. An A^6 chord, four strings covered with one finger. Uses a pick. It's fun to imagine what he might have been like had he lived down the street from the Whisky A Go-Go instead of where the Trocadero would be opening a few years later, in late September of '34, sunrising Sunset.

Cecil B. DeMille is behind the camera, directing his first "talkie," for which he's invented the long-boom microphone. When he looks at Russ's typecasting, he can visualize an epic of Pancho Villa, the war of Mexican revolution, a peasant army flocking down the hills in crossed cartridge belts like serapes, the forces of aristocracy rising to meet them in a great wave of historical inevitability, our war of natures. For *Dynamite*, his more modest class struggle takes place between the polo-pony playboy of Conrad Nagle and Bickford's earthy miner, mimicking "kind-to-kind" concerns of DeMille's as far back as the 1919 *Male and Female*; even Kay Johnson has to choose between the poles of "good girl" (one who apparently doesn't smoke, as Bickford keeps blowing out her match in the climactic love scenes) and "bad girl" (a fleet of flapperettes who drink highballs and cocktails, showing off their high-stepping heels). It's no wonder DeMille is best known for his biblical epics.

But Russ doesn't really like the role of stand-in. There is a sense of stunt double, only in reverse. He's the one doing the serenading, the importuning, and just as she's about to surrender, the director yells "cut" and the hero dollies back in for the kiss.

You can hear him synching Lewis Stone's lips in MGM's *Wonder of Women* in 1929 and catch him around a trailhand campfire with, yup, Gary Cooper, in 1930's *The Texan*, based on O. Henry's "A Double-Dyed Deceiver." He is credited as the Singing Cowboy, too early to be Roy Rogers, though the idea is there. He writes "Is It Love?" for Leo Carrillo's pre-*Ceesco Kid Hell Bound*, released in 1931, still known as Russell Colombo.

He replaces one *o* with a *u*. Now he has but two.

○ ○

*Y*oo *hoo.*
Boo hoo.

The double *o* of crooning. A circle squared. Times two, or should we say *too.*

It is one of the predominant vowel sounds of the twenties, witness Betty Boop, the archetypal cartoon flapper, all rolling saucer eyes. More a thirties role modeling twenties singer Helen Kane's squeaking "Boop-oop-a-doop," she was nostalgic even in her modernity. Animator Max Fleischer scored her to what seems like a perpetual Cab Calloway soundtrack of "Minnie the Moocher." *Boop boop be doop.* Be doop, that's what Betty advises. Whoops!

Where does the croon begin? In early 1914, Billy Murray records "My Croony Melody" for Edison's new Diamond Discs; later that year, he is followed by the prolific (Arthur) Collins and (Byron G.) Harlan, who cut two versions, fairly playing off Columbia and Victor. In June 1916, Edna Brown and James Reed (the pseudonyms of Elsie Baker and Reed Miller) release "Croon Time" on Victor; in 1925, the Honey Boys "Keep On Crooning a Tune" for Perfect, while the International Novelty Orchestra will "Croon a Little Lullaby" for Victor; in 1926, the Crooning Cavaliers buck-and-wing to "Sister Della's Fella." In between is the 1921 "Crooning," performed— oddly—instrumentally by both the Metropolitan Players (a sprightly brass, sax, and violin version on Resona that hearkens back to the oompah of the town square) and the (Edgar A.) Benson Orchestra of Chicago for Victor, a smoother, slower, more expectedly urbane reading with a complex moving tuba line and flamboyant banjo. The lack of vocal speaks to the croon's musical core, its lyricism beyond the lyric. You croon without words; though "Crooning" does have them, written by Al Dubin and Herbert Weise to William F. Caesar's music. They admit: *"All we do is croon a love tune / When you're in love there's never much to say."*

When Vaughn De Leath, one of the first radio singers, was invited into the original Lee De Forest laboratory, where the three-element electron tube had been invented, she was asked to sing "Old Folks at Home." Knowing that the high notes of sopranos often blew out the delicate tubes of the transmitters, she cuddled up to her microphone and apocryphally uttered the first croon.

O plus *o*. It exerts a magnetism over the language of seduction. We woo. Soothe. Swoon. Perhaps with your favorite quadroon, or octoroon. This is a time for the races to cross the musical color line, mix and mongrel, to move back and forth in a dance that will procreate the American popular music of the twentieth century.

The rounding of the lips, preliminary to a kiss. The slight purse. A prime sound, primal: *Ooooo*.

Then the *n*, the tongue at the back of the upper front teeth, preparing to come out of its cave. The tongue lingers in the gap between the buck tooths, unlike the short flick of the *t*. Hey Toots!

In the wordplay of popular song, it mates easily with "moon." "Croon, Croon, Underneat' de Moon" recommends Metropolitan Opera contralto Sophie Braslau in "A Southern Love Song" from 1919. Sam Coslow's "Learn to Croon" (*"If you want to win your heart's desire . . . just murmur 'boo ba boo boo boo'"*) was cut for Oriole by Bob Causer and His Cornellians with "Moonstruck" on the flip side. *"Drowsy waters softly croon"* writes Wendell W. Hall in 1922's "Underneath the Mellow Moon," sung by the Shannon Four, a dappling miragic fantasia repeated in dozens of sheet-music covers. Swim in the liquid reflection of a "Moonlight on the Ganges," Chester Wallace and Sherman Hines's 1926 "Fox-trot Oriental" *"where the wa-ters kiss the si-lent shore"* and *"a Hin-doo maid"* awaits, or bathe under the "fox-trot romance" of "Oriental Moonlight" a year later in 1927, courtesy Marvin Smolev and Bernie Seaman. Even the original "Crooning" begins *"Be-neath the love-moon . . ."*

These are journeyman songwriters, workaday scribes in Tin Pan Alley, newly moved uptown from West Twenty-eighth Street, choosing and churning out the one pure popular image ("Turn On the Popular Moon" advises the William Friedlander–directed musical comedy *Moonlight* in 1924, with music by a pre-managerial Con Conrad) that will capture the public's flighty

THE CROON

imagination and set them singing along to a song's chorus. Their lunar land-scape beams over all manner of nooky; a full or crescent glow (hardly ever half or gibbous, though "Half a Moon Is Better Than None" pragmatically decides Nat Shilkret batoning the Victor Orchestra in 1926) a-lighting the shadowed corners of the earth, a beckoning beacon: "Under a Texas Moon," "Blue Kentucky Moon," "Lazy Louisiana Moon," "Indiana Moon," "Rocky Mountain Moon," "Dixie Moon," "Swanee River Moon," "Cuban Moon," "China Moon," "Japanese Moon," " 'Neath the South Sea Moon," "Moon-light in Mandalay." Rudy Vallée can't make up his mind between cocooning "Underneath the Russian Moon" and gazing up at his beloved "Old New England Moon." Finally he decides it doesn't matter: "I Love the Moon." And the generic: "(Yoo-oo-oo) Under the Moon," the hoot of owls as played by Victor Miller and His Versatile Band in 1927.

"Get Out and Get Under the Moon" prescribe Chas Tobias, William Jerome, and Larry Shay in 1928, and the Yankee Ten Orchestra are quick to oblige, as does Helen Kane, whose perfect mating is "Me and the Man in the Moon." "Give Me a June Night, the Moonlight & You" plead Abel Baer and Cliff Friend singing through the mouth of Joe Darcy, workingman's cap and all, in 1924. Both Sidney Phillips and Bert Williams agree that "The Moon Shines on the Moonshine," while George Olsen couples "Out Where the Moonbeams Are Born" with "The Moonlight March." For Duke Yellman, it's the "Same Old Moon." Freddie Rose is "Serenading the Moon." Kate Smith is "Making Faces at the Man in the Moon" and signals her appearance on radio with "When the Moon Comes Over the Mountain" (or does the moun-tain come over the moon?). Jimmie Grier, leading the Cocoanut Grove Orchestra, finds "Music in the Moonlight." Harry Halstead conveniently translates his "Moonlight and Roses" into the euphonic rolled R's of Spanish: *"Rosas y el Rayos de Luna."*

Shake a tail feather with the night-colored "darkies" in the jazz age "Shimmy Moon" (1920). Light in darkness is the moon's duty, as turning the tides is its privilege. There is an overlap of minstrel here, black mask over white mask over black mask, grace notes tributaried alongside the tonic scale. In 1900, the sheet music for *Two Negro Songs* features "Down de Lover's Lane," subtitled a "Plantation Croon," while its composer, Will Marion Cook, is also credited with the "Negro Love-Song" of "Wid de Moon, Moon, Moon." Ada Jones wonders "If the Man in the Moon Were a Coon." Mack Gordon and Harry Revel, in 1932, shortly after their stint as chief writers for the previous year's Ziegfeld revue, describe life "Underneath the Harlem Moon": *"Cre-ole babies walk a-long with rhy-thm in their thighs,"* and Ethel

Shutta, her velvet headband slanted sloe-eyed over short, lightly bobbed hair, whose radio theme would be "Rock-a-Bye Moon," rakishly agrees: "*Ev-'ry sheik is dressed up like a 'jo-ja' gi-go-lo; You may call it mad-ness but they call it 'hi-de-ho.'* " They, the Other. Crossing the bridge of Moon. To We. Oo-ee, baby!

"Shine On Harvest Moon" was not a new song on January 13, 1930, when Texan Seger Ellis recorded it for Okeh. Originally written for the second edition of the Follies in 1907, it was sung therein by its co-writer, comedienne Nora Bayes, the "Wurzburger Girl." She had penned it with her husband, Jack Norworth (who, with Albert Von Tilzer, homered another slice of Americana in "Take Me Out to the Ballgame"), and watched it become a vaudeville staple. They were billed as "The Happiest Married Couple of the Stage" until their divorce in 1915.

Ellis was a high tenor, light-throated; his voice was held stiffly in the neck, starched, like a collar. Houston-born, twenty-six years old, and a pianist, he often recorded with the Dorsey brothers, James on reed and Thomas on brass.

A keyboard theme paves and ripples into the setting of scene. "*The moon refuses to shine.*" The little maid is afraid of darkness. The boy sighs. The boy tells his "*tale of woe.*" He implores the moon to greet the coming harvest. It is the last days of summer before the frost. He needs to cross the distance between him and her, before it's too late and the moment is lost.

"*To spoon beneath the moon.*" Nestled together, tucked one into the other like silverware, as that huge hanging orb illuminates the night sky. Joe Tarto plucks a bass fiddle string in the middle break so hard you can hear it slap against the neck. Guitarist Eddie Lang comps as Ellis plays with the melody, lofting it so that it grazes his falsetto.

The moon is like a silver spoon in his mouth.

CON

C on Con. Do the Con-ti-nen-tal.

He'd win the first Oscar for Best Song in 1934, Fred Astaire and Ginger Rogers escapading with a dance craze—"*You kiss while you're dancing*"—that he'd practically named for himself. It fit him. He was light on his feet, was Con. Light-fingered. The perfect dance partner.

In Español, *with*. A Con-fidant. On your side, a choreographer helping you pirouette through your paces. The unsilent partner, the co-respondent of the dance; the song itself, keeping the bodies swaying to his own tempo, the rhythm of his melodic words, and the sounds of their follow-the-bouncing-ball syllables.

Con Conrad was a Broadway songwriter, attuned to the tin in Pan's alley. Always on-the-scheme. The bigger the ideas, the easier they seemed to put over. Con liked to think huge; if he didn't ask for the moon, he'd never have a hunk of its pie-in-the-sky green cheesecake. He was a pitchman, sure, but if they listened to him, they could all make a fortune. His hit songs proved he knew how to make people prick up their ears.

There was "Margie," written with J. Russel Robinson—"the white boy with the colored fingers," as the QRS piano roll company referred to him—and words by Benny Davis, named after Eddie Cantor's five-year-old daughter (a sly move, that, guaranteeing Cantor would debut it at the Winter Garden in 1920). Cantor was also responsible for the success of "Ma! (He's Making Eyes at Me)," with lyrics by Sidney Clare, featured in *The Midnight Rounders* revue of 1921. In 1923, Cantor took a Conrad and Billy Rose novelty composition based on a popular comic strip named *Barney Google* and similarly promoted it. It was ready-made for the saucer-shaped double o's of Eddie's "*goo-goo googley eyes.*" Olson and Johnson based a racetrack vaudeville skit around the characters, Georgie Price recorded it for the Victor Talking Machine Company, and Con and Rose immediately went to work on a follow-up, "Come On, Spark Plug!," about Barney's horse.

Yes, he got their attention. Along with his hummable gifts, Con knew the cajolery of the song-plugger, the quick buttonhole in the hall, the backstage magnum, the jeroboam and rehoboam, the courtship of the potential introducer of the song, as important as the mating dance between song and listener, or the song and its inner protagonists. The thrill of fingersnap when the party of the first part says yes to the party of the second part or the party of the first part cuts in the party of the third part to share some of the performance royalties and the party of the fourth part assumes copyrights in foreign markets, and so chimes the quartet harmony of the music business. Joe or Josephine Blow goes on to sing it at the Hotsy Totsy Club where it gets heard by Jolson or Cantor or Tucker and is included in a new variety spectacle on Broadway. The presses move into overtime to churn out the sheet music. Sheet music counters are swamped. It is recorded in twelve different versions. Everybody wants to sing his hit song! It's a hit!

Con was no stranger to the capricious moonlight. "Moonlight" was the name of a song he'd written in 1924, not to be confused with his songs for *The Popular Moonlight* in the same year. He may have fancied himself the ubiquitous man in the moon, but he found himself on the orb's dark side when there was a frenzied knocking on his door at the Claridge Hotel that April, where he was registered under the name of "Mr. and Mrs. Charles Gorman." He opened it pajama-clad to find his brother-in-law Louis, sister-in-law Stella, her sister (his wife), and a lawyer. They uncovered the blonde hiding in a closet. It was the second time he'd been caught within the month.

He had been married to Francine Larrimore, a Broadway comedienne, since December 5, 1922, united in a secret ceremony before a justice of the peace in Port Chester, New York. She was a niece of Jacob Adler, the Yiddish actor, and specialized in portraying a similarly sociologically ethnic type, the up-and-coming flapper. They'd kept it quiet—or rather, Con had wanted it kept quiet for the sake of both their careers, so he said—though when she found him with the girls, once at the Ansonia and again at the Claridge, she said she was sick and tired of being a bit character in one of his songs. Or maybe she just took heart from the Conrad-Rose 1923 Sophie Tucker smash, "You've Got to See Mamma Ev'ry Night (Or You Can't See Mamma at All)."

Francine stormed off to Paris—born in Verdun, she had French blood—

and Con followed her, hat in hand. He knew the European landscape; in 1912, turning twenty-one (he was born Conrad K. Dober on June 18, 1891, in New York City's Lower East Side), he and his partner, Jay Whidden, a boilermaker turned violinist, headed for London with the proceeds of their first published song, "Down in Dear Old New Orleans," which had been added to that year's Ziegfeld Follies. Con had been playing piano since a teenager, accompanying the flickers at the Vanity Fair Theater up on 125th Street, or William Fox's Union Square nickelodeon, making occasional forays into vaudeville on the Keith circuit with Whidden. But he tired of rolling the keys to signal an impending thunderstorm, or climbing the scale in suspense when the villain snuck up on the heroine.

Con, as always, took the long shot. He and Whidden went to London, where he obtained a small part in a musical revue. A benefit performance — "attended by scores of Lords, Dukes, and Ladies" — created a demand for the duo, though Con realized immediately where the money was, stepping off the stage and into the role of producer. The two brought over American plays like *The Honeymoon Express* and *The Million Dollar Girl* and helped introduce Broadway-style revues to London, though the outbreak of the Great War brought a halt to their continental endeavors.

It did give him an enduring song — "Oh, Frenchy!" — that he sang when entertaining the troops in camp. He never thought it a hit until Will Von Tilzer, the publisher, called him. It taught him that "a popular song is a funny thing, for you never can tell when and where a hit will pop out.

"Several of my big hits were rejected a dozen times," he told the *Morning Telegraph* in December 1925. "Half a dozen prominent publishers thought 'Barney Google' was a joke when I submitted it. The song became a sensation, but why it did is more than I can say."

Not more than you can sing. Con had an ear for the insinuating nature of melody. More than once he had demonstrated a song in a publisher's office — "Would you like to hear the world's worst song?" he'd ask, before launching into "Palasteena" or "Don't Be a Fool, You Fool" or "Since Ma Is Playing Mah Jongg" — and get turned down, only to have the publisher run after him a few moments later, unable to get the tune out of his head.

"The composer thinks in melody," he told *The Sun* in June 1926, shortly after the debut of *Kitty's Kisses,* for which he'd penned the score, as he had for *The Greenwich Village Follies, Mercenary Mary,* and *Broadway Brevities.* "Maybe it's the rhythm of the elevated, maybe the rumble of a truck that, readjusted, furnishes the motif for a song." The whole song was in his mind before he even touched a piano.

He had a good imagination and he let it roam free, following the inclina-

tions and instincts of his heart. He was never far from the romantic possibilities of his melodies, or from their buck-making probabilities. Impulsive to a
fault, he bought the Kaiser's yacht for five thousand dollars after the war, according to L. "Wolfie" Gilbert, author of "Waiting for the Robert E. Lee," dis-
mantling it for shipment and failing to put it back together; he purchased a
delicatessen so he could have a slice of salami whenever he desired. And he
married Francine on the same rush of emotion that he felt when he crested
into an indelible refrain.

Only she wasn't having any. She'd had enough of separate addresses, he at
the Friar's Club, she up on Park Avenue, and his relentless *shtupping*. She
wanted six hundred a week alimony, with no chance of reconciliation.
Though they came back on the boat from Paris together, by November 1924
he was lamenting to the *Graphic* that "We certainly are not living on the Fan-
nie Hurst plan," referring to the doyenne of slice-of-life melodrama, whose
"marconigraphic" prose (as one contemporary reviewer put it) and verbless
sentences were a literary equivalent of the lyrics he melodically inscribed.

"I'm hard at work here on my music, and haven't time to think about tri-
fles. A month ago things were a little different. Yep. You're talking about love,
are you? Huh. Why should I talk about love? I'm here to work, not to love."

Already the melody was forming in his head, along with the imminent refrain.

IF FRANCINE had started him "Singing the Blues," the title of his second hit
with J. Russel Robinson, lyrics by Sam Lewis and Joe Young, then it was Beth
Beri who put Con in the red. Bankrupt.

She was a girl with "Million Dollar Legs," a dancer with the Follies and
Kid Boots, just back from Europe in the summer of 1927 with dreams of
Broadway top billing. She agreed to Con's invitation to lunch at the Astor
Hotel, and he pulled out all the stops inventing her bright future. For once,
Con's capital equaled his enthusiasm; as the weeks progressed, they discussed
her theatrical showcase, hearts aflutter. By the time 1928 loomed over the
horizon, Loew's Victoria had been booked, songs written, and scenery
painted, and expenses totaled $30,000. This did not include the cost of the
engagement ring Con had presented to her and she had accepted.

She was taking flying lessons at Mitchell Field—Con could see the front-
page headlines now, as she barrel-rolled into each new city where the act was
booked—but he didn't realize that she could just as easily fly the coop. There
was a quarrel, and Beth departed in a huff for Europe, leaving Con holding a

bag in which magnates like Otto Kahn and gamblers like Arnold Rothstein had invested substantial sums. In July, his lawyer was forced to enter federal court to tell the world that Con Conrad was broke, and the Friar's Club was advising reporters that he was "out of town."

Fortunately for Con, he had somewhere to go. William Fox had called him to Hollywood to work on his studio's new sound musicals, and Conrad saw how much difference this auditory dimension could make when he wrote a theme song for a Louise Dresser silent, Not Quite Decent. She played a "coon-shouter," and Con, accompanying her, even put on the burnt cork himself (kind of like adding an extra o to his first name) to film the scene in which she warbles it. The effect was so rousing—Louise had come up through vaudeville, and surprised everyone with the warmth of her projectile voice—that the director, Irving Cummings, decided to make an additional "Movietone" (Fox's appellation for its sound division) of the scene, as well as the later "denunciation" segment in which our heroine saves a young girl at the risk of her own reputation.

Almost by accident, Con was at a vital crossroads for the movies. Reputations were being won and lost with this volatile come-on-spark-plug combustible added into the movie's moving pictures. Now you didn't only have to look the part; you had to sound it as well. Sing it. It was as if you could hear the film reel and phonograph disc grinding away in the editing studio, each on its own casting couch. Needing the part. Sure they'd get it.

He was merely following the Tin Pan Alley trail. Where once he had made the rounds of the dance halls of Surf Avenue out in Coney Island, hoping his tunes would catch on with those who came to be lapped by the Atlantic, watching as Publisher's Row migrated from his old Union Square haunts through West Twenty-eighth Street and up to Times Square, tracing the trail of song exposure, he had now gone further afield, to a new source.

Sound needed songs. The new media—the radio, the phonograph, the movies—meant you didn't have to be there at all. You could travel like canned goods to where the living audiences were, in their living rooms and the communal living rooms of their local theaters. The listeners didn't have to home-play it themselves, on a piano or a ukulele. They could be pure ear, and now an accompanying eye. Already the sale of uprights was plummeting, the orchestra pit a yawning moat in front of the proscenium in theaters. "Vertical integration," it was called, theaters owned by movie chains; "five acts and a picture was the rule," said publisher Edward B. Marks, and if anyone knew which would prove expendable, push coming to shove, it was he. Marks had plugged songs back in '97 along the Bowery, taking the steam locomotive down the Third Avenue el to Canal Street to see if the ladies' orchestra at the Atlantic Gardens was playing any of his tunes, running a publishing house that kept up with the times: Rudy Vallée had autographed his photo on the 1930 cover of "Chimes of Spring," dressed in a white suit with full megaphone.

Fox Movietone Follies of 1929 was no Flo Ziegfeld bonanza—Fox didn't have the deep pockets of Paramount, which had been working on an adaptation of the Follies for a year—but it was a pleasurable girl-parade that interpolated Con's compositions to good effect, especially a "Walking with Susie" that became a minor hit (at worst, Con figured, there were a lot of girls named Susie in the last year of the twenties).

He took easily to the Hollywood social scene, the sweep of avenue that stretched down Hollywood Boulevard, a parade of limousines chauffeuring from the Roosevelt to the lot near Vine where Alexander Pantages was building his answer to Sid Grauman's *chinoiserie* palace. He liked driving over to Wilshire in a brand-new LaSalle, stopping at the Brown Derby for a meal and then walking—or driving—across the street to listen to Arnheim reprise the hits at the Cocoanut Grove. He knew him—Gus had accompanied Sophie Tucker on piano before he came west. He also was keeping an eye on Arnheim's singer, Bing Crosby, one of the Rhythm Boys trio.

Con had to admit the skinny kid had a great throat, though he was reputed to be a handful . . . or was that a snootful? Crosby could drink, and often did, though the word around town was that his new wife, Dixie, had read him the riot act after his last bender and he'd gone on the wagon. Or at least kept himself on a very tight leash.

Besides, Crosby was far too popular already. Paul Whiteman had given him his avuncular blessing, despite firing him for no-showing, and he'd been the only Rhythm Boy seemingly with the appeal to become a Rhythm Man. He was already bigger than Arnheim. Since last July, when Gus had returned to the Cocoanut Grove, it was Bing who was pulling in the crowds, especially at College Night on Fridays and the Saturday teas. He already had a recording deal on his own with Brunswick; he was in Mack Sennett's two-reelers. Con was looking for someone a little less . . . formed. He wanted the contract written in his favor. A Con-tract.

Crosby wasn't the only one out there. Con saw what was happening with Rudy Vallée and some of the other radio singers. People couldn't buy your song unless they heard it; give it a chance to capture the hearing. You could spend your whole life, nightclub by theater by small hall, trying to convince the paying customers that you were worth the buck of sheet music they hummed on the way out; or you could sell them the performance itself. Hear it before you buy, that was radio. All the bandleaders and theatrical impresarios were worried that it would put them out of work—"It's the equivalent of having the best jokes of a comedy or the dénouement of a mystery given away on the air," grumped George White when he sued to stop the airing of Scandals' songs, not realizing that a song that relies on a punch line will hardly stick in the imagination—and it would, but not in the ways they thought. There was opportunity. Money to be made. And always, for Con, songs to sing.

A singer, that's what was called for. His own instrument, to play his own songs.

RUSS WAS waiting for him under the Pyramid.

Columbo had opened his own club, at 5610 Hollywood. It had been a garage, and would be again, but for now, in early June 1931, it was a few blocks east of the Pantages, a hideaway for some from the film colony who didn't want to make too public a splash. But public enough.

The Pyramid Club ushered some distinguished visitors to its ringside dance floor tables in its first few weeks of existence. Russ had been a popular local musician, and he'd crossed paths with many of the stars in his bit-part work. Tom Mix, Gloria Swanson, Erich von Stroheim, Joan Crawford, Joan Bennett, Jack Oakie, and Ramón Novarro were among those who stopped by for a late-night apéritif.

Still, the club was struggling. Funded by John DiMarco, his brother Albert's best friend who owned a restaurant and grocery store and was in the wine business, Russ was barely breaking even. It was better than working his orchestra at the Silver Slipper downtown, an Italian eatery at 110 Market Street where he felt like a side course to the $1.50 dinner special, but then he wasn't getting their calamari either.

He recognized Con when he came in with a large, boisterous party that included Oakie, Crawford, June Collyer, and bandleader George Olsen. He knew Conrad by his songs and reputation, his round face and high-domed forehead; he had seen him over at the Grove talking at people, not pausing to let them get a word in edgewise. His voice was raspy and hoarse, and he gesticulated almost like an Italian.

Russ went over to the corner table to say hello. Con recognized him as well, the young violinist from Arnheim's band. Hadn't seen him for a while. *Oh, nice place you got here. Russ, is it? Yeah, I remember now. Gus's fiddler.*

Hey, I liked that "Peach of a Pair" number. And don't she now . . . though I'll never figure out why she runs around with that palooka. You want a smoke? Yeah, thanks. "Memory Lane" is one of my favorite songs too. . . .

"Do you know him?" he asked Olsen, when Russ had gone off to the bandstand.

George nodded. "He's a chump. These crooners are a bunch a' hooey, if y'ask me. Vallée . . . he should pipe down with all that row." Olsen had had the collegiate market sewn up with "The Varsity Drag" in 1927, before Rudy came along with his hand in his pocket.

"So what's this I hear about you thinking of offering Columbo a two-year contract?"

"What snake in the grass told you that?"

"Never you mind," said Con, settling back to watch the kid.

RUDY

Russ couldn't figure him out. Actually, he was a little too easy to figure out. He was a cornball, a goofy giraffe of a guy. A tall rube.

Like Goldberg. Full of contraptions, and he was smarter than he looked. First the little mini-megaphone that he invented out of his trombone mute, then the genuine cheerleading thing, which went along with the boola-boola frat-house collegiate fad of raccoon coats and pep rallies and pennants waving overhead on a late Roaring Twenties fall football afternoon deep in the Yale Bowl. Hip flasks. Stutz Bearcats.

Rudy Vallée had the white-and-blue pennant displayed proudly over his bed. Class of '27. And across from that on the other wall, point and counterpoint, were framed pieces of sheet music, his hits. Over the fireplace in the next room there hung five foreign editions of "The Stein Song," the old U. of Maine marching / drinking anthem, placed side by side by side by side by side.

He, and now she, lived on Central Park West, number 55, near Sixty-sixth. His brother resided in the other bedroom. There were six rooms in all, each with its own radio, except the bathroom, where Rudy sang to himself. He'd given some of his finest performances there.

The bedroom was a dark blue. It was supposed to be the most restful color. Rudy liked his sleep.

Much to everyone's surprise, the former Hubert Prior Vallée had gotten hitched to the former Fay Webb that July 6 of 1931. They had snuck across the border to West Orange, New Jersey, and were trothed in holy wedlock by

Judge Herbert Lithplite, a justice of the peace of no known denomination. William—the brother—was along, and so was Rudy's broadcast manager, Ed Scheuing, his secretary, Kenneth Dolan, and his lawyer, Hyman Bushel. Eloped.

Hoping to keep it a secret, especially since he wasn't sure how his fans would take it, he tipped the judge several hundred dollars. Unbeknownst to Rudy, his manager also paid him off. When the story made headlines not two days later, Rudy was as peeved about the double-tipping as he was about the repercussions.

She was a bit actress; "in the movies" was vague enough. He had been filming *The Vagabond Lover* when she first saw him in Hollywood, two years back. Wallace Beery pointed him out across a crowded room at a luncheon given in honor of Winston Churchill. She next caught his glance at the opening of some RKO theater. He was onstage, she in the audience. Her beckoning eyes.

Met. On the dance floor of the Hotel Roosevelt. Introduced by Marie Dressler. She tells him no the next day when he calls; when he calls again the day after, she agrees. "Don't get funny or be persistent. Remember, my father is a policeman." The chief of cops in Santa Monica.

Fay should have known after the first date. He hired them an automobile, drove her to the studio to watch him work. After, they went to his apartment, had dinner, went out dancing. Back to work.

Rudy was a hot-blooded sprout, always on and on, but she liked to kick her shoes off. Go barefoot. She gave him what-for, not a bunch of yeses. She wasn't the vegetable type. When she was a kid, she wanted to be a butcher. She ate only meat, and that was what Rudy liked in her. A carnivore. She finished her meals. Not that she had any illusions about what Rudy would be like when he went back to being everywhere at once the first free moment after their wedding. He did like his screwing around.

Russ saw Vallée's name all over the place when he got to town. Out at the pavilion in Manhattan Beach. 660 WEAF at midnight. At the Paramount for the debut of Sylvia Sidney's *Confessions of a Coed* (*"Today! My flaming story steps from the pages of my Intimate Diary"*). Opening his *Collegiate Rhythm* in the heart of Times Square with the added attractions of Jesse Crawford on the big Wurlitzer organ, and Ethel Merman, whose hit "I Got Rhythm" meant that white America had picked up, however haphazardly, the manifesto of black America, and was going to create . . . what? Russ didn't exactly know. He felt uncomfortable when the jazz turned hot. There was no reserve there. That was the province of the European.

A lot of it was hokum. Bunko. Flashpots and funny hats. Russ couldn't abide that kind of hick behavior. If you wanted to be a hillbilly, call up Ralph Peer and tell him you once knew A. P. Carter's dentist. He didn't want to watch Rudy re-creating those glorious moments at the Heigh-Ho Club—so foxhunt!—tootling his horn and acting the clown. Russ found it unbearable. But every once in a while, Rudy would stop trying to be the college head cheerleader and just sing. Just sing. He'd heard him rehearsing at the Apollo Theater for *George White's Scandals* of 1931, letting the inanities of the show carry him along until his vocal of "The Thrill Is Gone" entered from stage left, a mournful moan of imminent despair. A clairvoyance of sudden realization. It was as if Rudy was looking into his own mortal shell, though he'd outlive them all. He'd make sure of that.

Rudy didn't even stop to take a honeymoon. He and Fay were seen the next weekend waving from the platform of a Penn Station train, heading for Atlantic City to fill an engagement. Vallée had already ducked reporters on his way to the NBC studios to broadcast his radio show, on his way to the Hotel Pennsylvania to play the grill and the upstairs ballroom, four-a-day vaudeville shows, rehearsals, song auditions, recording. He was the "pilot" of the Connecticut Yankees, and the number one singing heartthrob in the city. It was a nineteen-hour-a-day job. When was he to sleep?

And with whom? He was obsessed with Fay, of that there was no doubt. She was his Type. He could even name the moment he realized he had a type. It was like the Irving Berlin song sung by Harry McDonough in 1916: "I Found a Lover on a Magazine Cover." More precisely, the November 1926 *College Humor*. He still had the issue saved.

Heart-shaped mouth. Head tilted. Pupils covered in night and barely peering out. A mass of coal hair; the neck a foot long and endlessly ripe for nibbling and nipping and nuzzling. Now, in southern California, the cover had come to life: "Dark, sultry . . . heavy-lashed eyes and luscious lips which could contrive one of the most enthralling come-hither smiles I had ever witnessed" was how he remembered meeting her. He was as star-struck as one of his fans.

The Man with the Megaphone. Well, it certainly got his voice out there, up close, closer, able to focus in on that one face, upturned, caught in the spotlight. He loved seeing just the right girl, the eyes in the crowd that suddenly dilate until you're playing just to them, she to you. Performance was taking that trick, and having every girl in the audience think it was she you were staring at. And you were.

Really, it was for the girls. The guys came, grumbling and full of piss and vinegar, but that was because the girls were there. He sang to the feminine, and they understood he knew their secret fancies, and fancied secrets, enhanced by the romance rags and the scandal sheets and the on- and off-screen romances that told them how it was supposed to be.

Was it real? He believed in the same myths; he had to. He was a crooner, a grave responsibility where the vulnerable gal-heart was concerned.

Getting married was a risky thing for a man in his position. What would his flappers say when their matinée ideal became unavailable for the ultimate *beau coup*? A bridesmaid, never a bride. Not to walk down the aisle with him. Let them speak now or forever hold their justice of the peace.

Would he be the dreaded . . . *washed up*? Would Morton Downey take his place on the radio dreamwaves? "I'm not fitted for marriage," he'd caddishly winked—as if anyone would take him seriously—shortly after his annulment from the first Mrs. Vallée, Leonie McCoy, the daughter of a wealthy caffeine merchant and older than he. But all the frails loved a challenge. He'd settle down for them; they'd be the ones to cure his wandering ways. He'd want to be with them, all the time, each tender moment. That was what love was about.

It helped that he was rolling in dough. He had taken in over twelve and a half grand a week just last January at the various Paramounts; more from the radio and the Connecticut Yankees' incessant touring. More. Because he knew how to reach out and let them know their aching hearts could find relief in the soothing massage of his croon, the muscular undercurrent of its barely restrained desire, like giving a girl a backrub, slowly sliding down the ladder of her vertebrae, the curve of her lower spine. Skiing the slope.

Fay had a beautiful back, and she loved to drape furs over her shoulder blades. Skins of sable, swaths of ermine. Silver fox collars. A four-carat diamond-and-platinum ring twinkled from the proper finger. She, dressed in ruffled black-and-white satin for the formal press introduction, and he, wearing a double-breasted blue suit, white boxwork shirt, with the glisten of pomade in his hair, stood outside the NBC broadcasting studios at 711 Fifth Avenue.

They had kept the secret for three days, but the truth slipped out, part press agent, part fairy tale. Rudy was sure his manager had told them. "The lone eagle of the air is a lone eagle no longer," the radio announcer intoned.

They made their entrance to the press corps, posing for a formal portrait, Rudy smiling away, assuring his fans that "I don't think they care about me except through music. And anyway, judging from the telegrams I've gotten from the girls who hang around the stage doors and at the Villa Vallée, I think the few who desert us will be few and unimportant." So there.

And, he thought, those weren't the only telegrams and letters and calls he'd been receiving. There was a darker undercurrent, those waving breach-of-promise suits and supposed babies and God-knows-what favors sought and granted during those backstage grapples and wild humpings in the back of a hired car and separate rooms in some beachside hotel.

There was that girl from Hewlett, Long Island, who started sending him crazy letters. He hardly recalled meeting her at the Brooklyn Paramount, and forgot whatever he had to when he got her letter, dated June 23, 1930: "I was six years old," she remembered—that gave him a shock, until he realized she was reliving her past—"which left a scar that I still have on my arm because I couldn't get what I wanted the minute I wanted it and I have been that way ever since.

"But don't tell me you have forgotten me. If I am the girl you have in your heart why didn't you say: 'Sweetheart, I love you,' when we were speaking to each other over the phone, and I would have named the big day when we could be married and you would be my husband. Then I wouldn't belong to anybody else and you wouldn't neither."

Of course, he got more than a thousand letters like that a week.

"Oh, my God, Rudy, please don't go away and leave me. I couldn't bear the thought ever.

"My God, do I have to tell you any more? Don't go away leaving me dreaming dreams again."

The odd thing was that, as he read the letter, he could feel himself seduced, affected, empathizing with this dear girl, feeling her sing to him, whisper her croon to him, conveying her longing, her caring, her need to be near him, and he her.

"Damn it, I belong to you, not even to my mother or father and I know that I have their consent to marry you."

Well, there it was again. Now he'd have to say he'd never even heard of her. She was a crank. Just like that seventy-year-old woman who claimed Vallée had made love to her over the radio with a musical horn which repeated her name. Well, do-you-take-this-woman-to-be-your-lawful-wedded-wife should stop all that. He'd removed himself from the marriage sweepstakes. Fanny, or Ethel, or MaryJeanBarbara would have to wait. Rudy was taken.

For a ride, he later thought. Ruefully. On the Rue de Vallée.

SCHEMES

S*oon.*

That's what Con would tell Russ in the weeks after they arrived in New York. Just be patient. Sit tight. Hold your horses. Don't get your bowels in an uproar. These things take time.

Which was a damn sight different from the way he'd gone on and on and on inside the Pyramid after closing time, Russ thought. By the time Con finished his *spiel* that night, expounding on all the wonders New York had to offer, the nightclubs and radio hookups and Broadway babes and recording opportunities—all Con's *contacts*—and how they were lying in wait for a guy with his stage presence and looks and voice and way with a song, it seemed as if only his signature on a dotted line would be what it would take to set the bump-and-grind of dame fortune into motion.

They'd stayed up until dawn, Russ at first resistant, Con pressing ahead, warming to his importuning, in full twist-o'-the-arm seduction. George Olsen made him an offer—halfheartedly, Columbo thought, especially in light of Con's champagne enthusing, and promptly retired from the battlefield—but after his stint with Arnheim, Russ knew that working for someone else was not a viable option. He could hardly shake Con long enough to consider the offer. After the club closed, Con followed him home, waking his folks, telling them that their boy was destined for greater—the greatest!—things. By nine o'clock the next morning, they were at Con's lawyer's office, drawing up a contract that, in return for Con's assuming the expenses of their trip east, Russ would pay him 25 percent of his future income.

And, he had to admit, Con wasn't doing that badly. Conrad might have had to sell his week-old Ford—to Bing Crosby, of all people—to raise the money for their train fare, but they were ensconced at the Warwick on a free-flowing tab. On Thursday, July 2, they'd gone over to the Victor studios and made a test recording of "Out of Nowhere" with Con accompanying Russ on piano. Victor hadn't made a decision yet (Con thought they were waiting to see what kind of a stir this young singer could provoke on his own), but Con was only warming up. Later that week they had an appointment with Ziegfeld himself. Russ had only to look out his window at the Warwick to see the wedding-cake curves of Flo's theater. He could hardly contain his excitement.

THE INTERVIEW with Ziegfeld was anticlimactic, to say the least. The great man was smaller than he appeared in photographs—there was some resemblance, Russ thought, between him and the glass figurine of the elephant perched by his inkwell—as he sat impassively behind the polished gleam of his desk in the theater's seventh-floor office, an unprepossessing room with a door that led off to a private balcony box, and an upright piano.

Harry Richman was there. The current Follies toastmaster had a reputation for taking a cut of the songs he introduced. Con didn't particularly want to share the wealth, but he was shrewd enough to realize that even getting a couple of tunes into the Follies would be a coup. Or at this point in their fortunes, a recoup. The Big Front was costing big bucks.

Richman wasn't in the best of moods. He'd been out late last night, and he planned to be out late that night as well. Sweet, sweet Virginia. He would pick her up at her dressing room after she did her Indian dance at the Paradise, and then she'd do the routine for him all over again in the master bedroom out at Beechhurst. She was a wild one, all right.

He looked at the singer Conrad had brought with him. Dark-haired. Dark, period. A wop crooooner. He'd heard about these guys. Sang like a sissy. Didn't know how to sell a lyric, act it out. Where was the old song-and-dance? These guys, like that Vallée, or Crosbeee, just stood there, limp-wristed, humming and hawing along.

The songs weren't bad. There was one about a "Prisoner of Love." He could do that one to a turn, break the ladies' hearts, but it needed to bust out at the end. The guy couldn't stay behind bars for long, unless he owned one. And that "You Call It Madness. . . ." Simply simpering. The third was called "Who Am I?" A good question, and Harry figured Russ would be asking it when he was on the train back to California, wondering what happened.

"That's not the kind of singing they want here," he told Russ bluntly when the last notes had hung in the air. Harry knew Con would be grabbing him by the balls if he asked to have his name inserted as one of the authors.

Flo shook his head. "They're not hit tunes," he agreed. To be honest, Ziegfeld had hardly heard them, so softly had the kid Conrad brought along to sing performed them. Oblivious, it didn't occur to him that Con was hoping he'd notice the kid as much as the songs; for him, Russ was just another Tin Pan plugger. Flo could hardly keep his mind on anything but his unraveling fortunes. He'd lost it all in the stock market, and the worst part was that it was over some two-bit piece of shit. For once, he'd gone against his high-rolling instincts, lost his temper and carted the whole office staff down to testify when those ratbag Strauss sign painters took him to court over a bill totaling $1,600. There was no one around to get the frantic call from his broker that the bottom had dropped out of Wall Street. When he got back to the office, he was ruined. Just like fucking that.

He was thinking this Follies would turn his careening ship of fortunes around, let Broadway know that he hadn't lost his Midas touch, the glitz and the gilt and the pan-o-rama he'd created from his own sense of the magically magnificent, his instinct for the right star at the right time.

"Nothing doing," said Flo Ziegfeld.

IT DIDN'T bother Con that Ziegfeld had passed on his discovery. He'd already had enough of Broadway's vagaries—hey, that could be a new revue!—and anyway, he had secured an audition for Russ at NBC's Blue Network.

Their visit to the Fifth Avenue Air Castle, as NBC's headquarters near the soon-to-be site of Rockefeller Center was known, was met with casual interest. John Royal, the president, came to watch. He was very much aware of the appeal of a Vallée, who was on WEAF, and Downey, over at WABC, and even Arthur Tracy, the "Street Singer," as he called himself. Radio stars.

Radio had insinuated itself into American life through the 1920s, growing to be an all-purpose common campground pumping news and commentary and every type of music that could fit into a broadcast studio or be remoted over the airwaves. In New York alone, on any random Wednesday or Thursday night, barbershop quartets (WABC) and Merle Johnston's saxophone quartet (WOR) and the Brox Sisters (WJZ) and the Boswell Sisters (WABC) rubbed up against Winegan's orchestra (WMCA) and Tommy Christian's orchestra (WPAP) and Johnny Lane's orchestra (WEVD) and Will Osborne's orchestra (WABC) and Guy Lombardo's orchestra (WEAF) and Ozzie Nelson's orchestra (WMCA). Bill Butler offered Hawaiian melodies (WLBX), there was an unnamed "Jewish orchestra" (WBBC) as well as a "Colored orchestra" (WPCH), a "blackface minstrel show" (WOR) and a "Polish orchestra" (WNYC), Neapolitan songs (WFOX) and Sicilian music (WHOM) and German *lieder* (WLBX). All on the same dial.

There were only a few "shows" in the traditional sense, though the idea of radio theater that would characterize radio's golden dramatic era was just over the horizon. Rin Tin Tin, Sherlock Holmes, and *Death Valley Days* were attracting regular listeners, and *Amos 'n Andy*—a blackface comedy— was already popular, daily (except Sunday) at 7:00 P.M. over WJZ, the NBC flagship station located at 760 kc. Even the musical offerings, live renditions of the featured performer skipped over the airwaves instead of sliced into a recording master, were becoming more sophisticated, with sponsorships and guest artists and announcer scripts. Still, there were a lot of fifteen-minute slots to fill, from sign-on at 7:30 A.M. to sign-off sometime after 1:00 A.M. An enterprising station could always find room for something potentially new and appealing between *Household Hints, Hollywood Snapshots,* and Robert Ripley's *Believe It or Not.*

NBC took its time mulling over Russ. While they waited, Con visited Earl Carroll, a Ziegfeld competitor whose Vanities hardly pretended to Flo's elegance. He liked the songs and offered $350 a week for Russ to sing them. In addition, he took Con and Russ over to the Hotel Pennsylvania roof, where Vallée held forth nightly in between his own radio broadcasts, and asked Rudy to give Russ a turn on the mike.

The next day, NBC called Con. They'd heard of the Vallée appearance, of Carroll's interest; word had gotten around. A few well-placed ten-spots on Con's part had seen to that. Royal's Air Castle allowed as how they'd put his boy on at midnight, starting Monday, July 27, a four-week tryout to see if he could generate any fan mail. A hundred and fifty dollars a week. Their final offer, take it or leave it.

Con took.

RUDY VALLÉE

VAGABOND LOVER

The shadow play. A popular thirties photo trick. There's one of Russ holding a pipe, his silhouette in sharp outline, his own 2-D cartoon character following him around at a respectful distance, another with a microphone shading him in duet. Here's one of Rudy holding his saxophone as he would a lover, right hand around her bare back, fingering the high keys, left hand on her swivel hip, low-keyed, head bending down, as if in prayer. As if.

"I sing with dick in my mouth," Rudy took delight in saying. Projected on the wall, the neck of the saxophone, with its bulbous mouthpiece, looks like an erect penis. He might be preparing to give it a blow job. His reference was to the sensuality of his delivery; but it also further recognized the blurring borders between masculine and feminine, the mingled genders of the croon.

"Me and My Sha-dow / Stroll-ing down the a-ve-nue." He in a soft white suit and softer focus. The very essence of Colleege.

By 1929, Rudy Vallée (accent on the first *e*) had risen to become a household word, at least in those homes that had a radio along the living room wall. Still regarded as a novelty sensation, somewhere down the totem pole between ethnic comedians and razzmatazz like somersaulting dog acts, he was distinctly a new medium of idol.

He had never been afraid of technology. When he was a kid growing up in the outer barrens of Westbrook, Maine, Rudy had seen his first motion picture projector. He was drawn to watching "the film with fascinated eyes as it went past the aperture plate, with the bright light from the arc lamp shining on it; and the hum of the machine as the operator cranked it by hand, and the smell of film and film cement meant as much to me as the picture itself." He wanted to see how it worked. Years later, when he had the editing table and the movie camera and the developing room in his Central Park West apartment; and still more years later, when he would have the screening parlor and the underground storehouse of memorabilia at Silver Tip, he knew he'd put the pieces together just right. He played the film over and over for visitors.

Rudy had it figured out; a system. He split his orchestra in half, four pieces in the "back row," a rhythm section of piano, banjo, string bass, and drums. In front were his "voices," the two saxophones and two violins, divided again by permitting only one of each to take the lead melody at any one time. There was no brass. To keep the full sound, everyone seamlessly playing, he alerted the band with his own specially devised finger code so he wouldn't have to remove the instrument from his mouth. He was both saxophonist and director of the Connecticut Yankees. "I am really busier than the proverbial one-eyed dog in a sausage shop," he wrote in his first autobiography, *Vagabond Dreams Come True*, which had gone through nine printings by March 1930, its second month of publication.

Somebody had to be the "pilot." "I do the thinking," he told the Yankees, and asked only that they pay close attention to him at all times. Good lines of communication kept everybody on their toes, to make sure the crowd was having a good time, to call the key changes ("Every key has its own tone color . . . versatility and contrast have been two of the cardinal features of my work from the very beginning"), five flats shifting to two sharps, a continual upward modulation, the crowd alternately perked and energized or lulled and soothed, falling into each other's arms as Rudy orchestrated their stirrings, pulled their strings.

His performances were programmed like a pep rally before the big game. On a good night, he made sure that the audience kept their spirits up, believing in their team, that they all could stumble over the goal line at the last second and score the winning touchdown for dear old alma mater. Mother soul.

He welcomed this new-fashioned microphone, much as he'd leaped at the chance to cut down a half-megaphone to carry his voice. He wasn't spooked by it like many performers who rose to prominence in the early years of the century, suspicious, still unsure of how this vibrating metallic device could transmit their vocal to a circumpolar radio speaker, and displeased with its timbre when it got there, anyway. Harsh, squawky. It wasn't acoustical anymore. But then, hardly anything would be.

Early on, Vallée recognized it as another instrument, as important to him as his horn. When he saw the effect his voice had on radio, he cobbled together one of the first in-concert amplification systems, complete with carbon microphone and several radio receivers. It was even more sensuous than the megaphone in its ability to reach out, to throw his voice like a ventriloquist so that it seemed to emanate from right next to the listener, and it left his hands free to hold his instrument. If he needed to gesture, he would sling his saxophone—still an odd sight on the bandstand—under his shoulder, devil-may-care, a musical soldier with his rifle, and lean in.

He could project his voice, but after cheerleading, it was a relief not to have to shout. Even his instrumental delivery was stepped back from the precipice. He played his saxophone in the mellifluous manner of his hero, Rudy Wiedoeft, the author of "Saxophobia" (1921), "Saxarella" (1923), "Saxemia" (1924), and (with Oscar Levant on piano) "Sax-O-Phun" (1926), inventor of the "slap-tongue" technique. He eventually took his first name from him.

The boys at Sigma Alpha Epsilon had started calling him that after he pledged, between paddlings, seeing his fixation with Wiedoeft, the "sax god," but he'd grown to like it. And Rudy Vallée sounded a lot more like Rudolph Valentino. He'd even traveled to New York specially to meet the great man, who tucked his empty liquor bottle in a desk drawer and advised him "that anything is legitimate so long as it produces the goods." He recommended college instead of band school, and Rudy went back to his studies at Yale, a lesson learned. By the fall of 1927, the pupil had surpassed the master. Rudy introduced Rudy at the Keith in Flushing, Queens, and later went back to the Wiedoeft house for dinner, "to sit for pictures taken of the both of us playing together."

VALLÉE WAS a good host. Very convivial. Over the airwaves, because WABC—the then-small station from which he first broadcast—couldn't afford an announcer, he graciously introduced his own numbers, in the manner of a kindly ceremonial master, and kudo'd songwriters and welcomed listeners. He exhibited a "radiophonic" personality that soon made him the medium's top singing personality, debuting on-air in February 1928, though the only thing he'd heard previously was a prize fight. Rudy liked talking into the ether, the imaginary lover that a singer sings to; and his penchant and enthusiasm for hard, relentless work kept him expanding his audience. He would always show up, on time with carefully designed set list in hand, eager to please and take his pleasure from pleasing.

It helped that he loved women. They were his chosen audience. He de-

sired them, adored them, craved them, couldn't keep his eyes off their sashay
when he strolled down the street, into the subway, through the crowds that increasingly mobbed him as '28 passed into '29. Once he walked into a fire hy-
drant, cracking his shin, because he couldn't take his eyes off a passing fancy.
Though he wouldn't be waiting for the subway anymore. His schedule was
too tight. He was due onstage somewhere in five minutes, and somewhere
else a few dozen choruses after that, to count off the downbeat and let the
games begin, and there would be women there. To sing to, to coo to, to pitch
woo to, to smooth-talk in their own accent, a softer and more understanding
bi-lingual than they'd been used to from his kind.

He filled their need, their consuming passion. He was sincere. He admitted to this weakness for the feminine, which he described as "a cross between
a hobby and a complex," and he encouraged his frequent dates to look the
part even if he didn't. Rudy appreciated the false eyelash, the high heel and
painted nail, the tight-fitting dress. "I've always made a fetish of the looks, the
sheen, and the feel of satin on a fair lady," he cheerily admitted in his second
autobiography, *My Time Is Your Time*, written with Gil McKean in 1962.
Like the initial rush that characterizes love itself, the can't-eat-can't-sleep obsession, his success came in a sudden tumble of love-at-first-hearing. The
Heigh-Ho filled; when he moved to a failed speakeasy at 14 East Sixtieth
Street, the owner even named it after him: the Villa Vallée. The vaudeville
circuit called. When he debuted at the Keith on Eighty-first Street, his radio
audience showed up *en masse* to see what he looked like. They loved Rudy's
wavy hair, and that he sang, even live, just to them.

To hum them a tune. That was his chosen occupation, and he was happy
to have one in such a frolicsome era as the twenties' curtain call. Brighten
their day and his night. "Making Whoopee" was a Victor record he cut on
January 10, 1929, and he bounced the Walter Donaldson–Gus Kahn lyrics
off the tip of his tongue. Characteristically, he dispenses with the introductory
verse, drawing out the *o*'s of "whoopee" like a car sliding around a slow curve.
Less than a month before, on December 18, 1928, Eddie Cantor had
recorded it at a slower tempo, also for Victor and under the direction of Nat
Shilkret's house orchestra, his voice just as high as Rudy's but without the
fluttering inflections; his emphasis is on the *p*'s, playing for comic effect.
Both deal with the consequences of the God-given urge; but even with the
quickened pace, Rudy comes off the more personal. The nameless "he"
could be he, and with Fay Webb, soon would be.

Sometimes it seemed everybody was whooping it up, with the stock market
on overload and Prohibition a national joke. All the great mass cultural en-

gines were in place—the movies, the phonograph records, the radio, even the first glimmerings of television—and they were about to change the way entertainment was generated, just as the printing press had led to the celebrity exposé of the fan magazines.

The stays on the bodice were loosened. The skirt raised. The clothes following form following bodily function. There was a lot more room to maneuver, especially in the rumble seat of a Model T. Don't forget to attach your foxtail, like a trophy, to the aerial (the car has a radio!) to show it's hunting season. The call of the wild.

He stalked the flapper: the rolled stocking, cloche hat like a helmet, hair in permanent waves. When she danced the Charleston, those hands with the scarlet-colored nails would flap limply at the ends of her wrists, like tiny bird wings, almost vestigial. It made a man want to have her warmth nestled on his eggs. The lure of the nest. *That's what you get, folks, for Ma-king Whoopee. . . .*

He practiced what he preached, and Rudy had always believed in practice, sometimes five, six hours a day. Nor could he stay away from the ladies. For him, music and women were one and the same, as when he would record Irving Berlin's "A Pretty Girl Is Like a Melody" at the end of 1934, fifteen years after it had first appeared in Ziegfeld's extravaganzas.

Practice makes perfect. Be prepared. He did have something of the Boy Scout in him, gathering his merit badges, rubbing two sticks together to make a fire. "My Time Is Your Time," recorded in early 1929, was his theme, and he realized that your time comes around only once, to grasp fame's outstretched hand and be pulled into the chauffeured limousine. He'd often thought about what he would do when he got his shot at the big time, and he wanted to be ready.

For one, he would play only choruses. That's what people remembered about the song, not all that unnecessary exposition.

CUT TO the meat of the matter; the sweetmeat, closer to the bone. "Simple melodies, played in a simple way."

His medium "of expression" was the dance band; his mode of, or maybe motive. That was Rudy's commercial formula. "Music that would readily sell itself, that would easily reach the heart, that anyone and everyone would like and understand." He wanted to be liked. An inscription on a band business card. *For your listening and dancing pleasure.*

He was proudest of his "very slow fox-trot. The average orchestra leader, fearing that his dancers will not know what to do with such a slow tempo, ruins these numbers by playing them in regular tempo. . . . I have antagonized some people by playing it, especially the middle-aged and elderly couples. . . ." Flaming Youth, as Duke Ellington phrased it, recording in the same January week that Rudy cut "Making Whoopee," strikes again.

Though they might seem from different worlds, and they were (even to the point of differing Victor numerical series), Vallée did come up the same time as Duke Ellington, perhaps walking along upstairs on his way to a booking agency at Roseland while downstairs at the Kentucky Club on Broadway and Forty-ninth Ellington was developing his orchestral approach. Each had to make do with a small band—Ellington's was a six-piece, Rudy's an eight— but the difference in approach was not as great as their differences in impact and aspiration would suggest. Both realized that earlier musics had needed to emphasize volume and a certain bombast to get heard by large groups of listeners, even—since the media were hardly mass—outside their region. Now, with a whole nation ready and able to hear what they were saying, the thing was to make it more personal: softer, inverse, to draw the listener in closer. Dynamics. If they got louder, it would seem twice as loud. They got their breakthroughs in virtually the same month, Duke Ellington preparing to move uptown to the Cotton Club on December 4, 1927; Rudy bandstanding at the Heigh-Ho Club, 35 East Fifty-third, opening on Monday, January 8, 1928. There go the neighborhoods.

Rudy said he appreciated the "hot" style that was jazz, and its desire to "*tap the feet*." Italics his. He simply heard it a lot more directly; no improvisation. There was no time for harmonic complexities. "Though I myself enjoy a finished rendering of this type of music"; and you can imagine Vallée tapping his toe in cadence to King Oliver's "Tin Roof Blues," brow knit, analyzing how the instrumental charts mesh, trying to see the separate links so he might reproduce it, or at least pick from it what might be immediately useful, marveling at a change here but sensing a bit too frantic backbeat that might be unsettling to his listeners, and finally deciding that the music required more attention than most people had inclination for. He understood the difference between music made for musicians, interested in form and intricacy and thought-inducing content, and music for "the great masses of hardworking people who come home at night from a hard day's toil and seek comfort and rest in music of a sweet, smooth and quiet nature, either from records and radios or theater." Unthought.

Music that will "easily reach the heart." But is the heart that easily satisfied? Doesn't it require a bit more derring-do? *Dooo*, as Rudy might sing it.

To engage that pumped artery which beats for more than comfy feet propped up on the couch, tuned in to the radio, wondering what's for dinner and re-hashing the latest on the Starr Faithful murder in the *Graphic*.

Rudy didn't mind being *commercial. Straight.* " 'As is,' with everything round, full, rich and clean." As is.

He wasn't of a mind to challenge preconception. Like Mother Nature, he was more interested in the conceive itself. He had to assure the species' sur-vival. Make a living. Live it up. He knew what they desired, those swaying partners and their courtship rituals. Rudy would grant them their trio (or even octet) of wishes, though no requests, please, at the college mixers, the frater-nity soirées, the country club tea dances and homecoming parties. *Betty Co-ed* education: "Flirtation is an art . . . she's happy with a fellow on each arm," as he reeled off a rainbow of colleges, Harvard red and Navy blue and Prince-ton gold (Betty Boop will star as Betty Coed in a 1931 Purdue-black and Georgia-white Max Fleischer cartoon rendition). He understood what higher education was about. People wanted to cut in, pick their partner, get drunk in the quadrangle, steal a little kiss and frantically rub up against each other. If he could help with their mutual mating, then they might think kindly of him and ask his band back. Sometimes, watching them out on the dance floor, churning and parting and parrying ("I have found that the woman is the first to suggest sitting down . . . when the length of the dance is increased, a man . . . will be well satisfied at the end"), he felt like the third partner in their twirl.

Serenading, he was destined to be the odd man out: "The Lonely Trouba-dour," as he was called in a 1929 song "Dedicated to and featuring Rudy Valleé" (accent mistakenly placed on the final *e*): "*List-en to my song! / And let my mel-o-dy pro-claim for me.*" Words and music by John Klen-ner. Front shadow portrait by Hal Phyfe. With ukulele arrangement (tuning G–C–E–A).

The way they measured hits in those days was by sheet-music sales. Songs were not so much about personality as they were about songs, and because the media for hearing them were so diverse—in vaudeville theaters, in hotel ballrooms, even on the newly chatty silver screen—and live music (for they hadn't gotten around to playing records as entertainment) demanded a con-tinuing turnover of new hits, a popular song of the day was meant to be per-formed by all.

In department stores, there would be a sheet-music counter, often with a piano player "demonstrating" the latest consecrations from Tin Pan Alley. Song-pluggers roamed vaudeville and nightclub floor shows and enticed performers into "introducing" the latest numbers. Once a song caught fire, placed in the repertoire of the nation's collective hum, it was not so much covered as regenerated, coast to coast, broadcast to you in the darkened back room of your local nitery, or at home if you could pick out the notes on the piano and sing-a-long the phrases.

Rudy had an ear for a song. He took from very unlikely sources. "The Stein Song" was a college lift-your-glasses that had begun life as "Opie," a march written by German bassist Emil Fenstad in 1901. It was borrowed ("arranged") by Adelbert Sprague, a University of Maine freshman, for a school song contest three years later. Another frosh, Lincoln Colcord, added the words to Sprague's sample. Maine was a dry state, but the university president allowed for a drinking song with the stipulation that the steins were "containing milk or water." Rudy's re-arrangement made "The Stein Song" a hit when he played it on a Thursday night of his radio show in the fall of 1930. He left the studio to go to the Paramount, and by the time he got to the Villa Vallée for his late-night show, the melody was on everyone's lips. He had to encore it three times that first night alone.

He was the ultimate collegian. His version of "Doin' the Raccoon" opens with a rah-rah cheer; his signature melody is the Yale football rouser "March, March on Down the Field." College was no longer a sobersided preparation for life in the ministry or mathematics; it was a bathtub-gin-soaked fraternity party, a pep-rally bonfire, a singles' mixer-and-mater. The band's oompah grounding served as a bridge between the Sousa march that opened one end of the century and the cheerleading that became a performance style in the closing millennial other, three years into the reign of Britney 'N Sync.

Rudy used up a prodigious number of songs, which made him a favorite with an aggressive breed of song plugger, feeding a procession of radio broadcasts, culminating in the ten-year run of the Fleischmann Yeast Hour, which came along in the wake of *Vagabond Lover* (the moon also rises) and lasted until the eve of World War II, along with continual public engagements and forays into acting. Then there were the songs he required for the hopeful female singers who were lying in waylay for him in the towns to which he traveled, and he'd want to help their getting somewhere in this show-off-and-on business. He finds the female voice enchanting, which is why he's not afraid to sing like one. To earn their trust.

They underestimate Vallée. Dancing past on the arms of their dates, or their successive cut-ins, they're more inclined to look at the dark Jules De Vorzon on the second violin; Rudy senses their disappointment as he is introduced. Girls come up to him on the bandstand and ask "when will Mr. Vallée show up?" His is not the romantic image; he has to earn their love, to make them see his wellspring of soul.

Yet once he tongue-slaps the microphone, who can resist the Vagabond Lover, those downswept eyes and their disarming droop? In the movie *Glorifying the American Girl* (1929), with Yankees drummer Ray Toland whisking his high-hat like a scrupulous Rudy valet, he sings his theme in the midst of a Ziegfeld Follies that also stars Helen Morgan perching on a piano, Eddie Cantor in a Jewish-tailor skit, and a series of breathtaking incandescent tableaux that give some idea just how radiant the Follies were in living, breath-holding two-tone Technicolor. How they celebrated light.

Incandescence, streaming across the stage. In sequins and headdresses. Spilling trains. Vaporous fabrics. The curtain parting to reveal the array of glowing female, sparkles pulsing from each exquisite creature, ravishing and famishing.

The song was in the thrill of the girls, the rays from their stark white forms in the follow spot. Posed just so, a classical painting enacting some mythological scene, it was a diorama that gilded the assembled lilies, Venus on the half shell, a birth of Athena, some (any) tale of Aphrodite. Or in dance, high-stepping as one girl with sixty-four lower limbs, moving in V formation.

He needs their shimmer. They fill him with their sexuality, give him emotion and motivation. On his own, he comes off more like the movie version of *Vagabond Lover*, a 1929 Radio Pictures vehicle that capitalized on his sudden ascendance, a stinker of a picture that he later wishes had been burned in the warehouse fire that miraculously spared his epic shortly after principal photography was completed. Even his name on the marquee at Broadway's Globe Theatre, or the premiere at Portland's Star Theater and the accompanying homecoming celebration for one of Westbrook's "most illustrious sons" on November 30, 1929, couldn't stem his embarrassment at seeing himself on screen. He'd have to work on that. The only good, Rudy thought, to come out of his California trip was his first sight of the "oriental features" of the lovely Miss Webb, and that turned out to be the worst nightmare of all.

HE AND the Connecticut Yankees trained across America early that summer, greeting crowds wherever they whistle-stopped. The radio had spread the word. In Chicago, the press threw him a breakfast. They woke Rudy up at night halts to take his hat off to local photographers. A few miles out of Los Angeles, fifty media representatives climbed aboard the train to ride shotgun into Union Station.

They were waiting for him: the Sheriff of Los Angeles County (over the years, in Rudy's mind, it became the Mayor), with a bevy of chorus girls from the studio. He was "pushed and pulled" among them, and then "presented with a big saxophone of wood and a large gold key." Then he climbed into the waiting motorcade with his mother (the rest of the boys had brought their wives, except the still-single Rudy and the "he's available, girls" bass player, Harry Patent). Riding in a Rolls-Royce surrounded by a phalanx of motorcycle policemen: "This last gave my mother the greatest thrill she ever had, and I can still hear her, hysterically half-laughing, half-crying," wholly proud of her Hubert.

When they got to the Blossom Room of the Hotel Roosevelt, Irving Aaronson and the Commanders greeted them with a chorus of "I'm Just a Vagabond Lover" to signal their arrival in Hollywood. It was an ex-projectionist's dream. Despite his work ethic, and the turnover events of the last year, Rudy was slightly stunned.

It might account for his wooden saxophone personality in *Vagabond Lover*, a what-is-my-motivation that makes him seem hardly suave. Unless you pronounce it *swah-vey*. The directorial choice accentuates the playacting. Marshall Neilan hasn't had to deal with dialogue much before. He hit his high spot as Mary Pickford's most sympathetic director, from the 1917 *Rebecca of Sunnybrook Farm* to her Gold Rush comedy *Stella Maris* (1918) to 1919's *The Hoodlum*, in which the golden-curled Mary goes slumming. He sees his films through a viewfinder. If you turn the sound off, *Vagabond Lover* is surprisingly better-emoted, as if Rudy is watching himself from the projection booth of his hometown Star Theater ten years previously. It's Neilan's next-to-last movie.

As usual, Rudy is overly prepared. He has spent hours choosing the songs for the picture, auditioning them backstage in his dressing room at the Brooklyn Paramount. It's hot in June, and he's just gotten offstage, but he listens to each over and over, between shows. He doesn't believe in first reactions. He's also constricted the story line: no "hackneyed night club, back stage and college campus ideas." This cuts off all interesting possibilities that might show Vallée in his natural environment, and strands his Connecticut Yankees at a mansion owned by a Wiedoeft stand-in, "Ted Grant" (Malcolm Waite), waiting aimlessly for the love interest to show up.

She is Sally Blane, forever to be known, though not then, as Loretta Young's sister. She will die so anonymously in 1997 that the Academy of Motion Picture Arts and Sciences overlooks her in their yearly roll call of departed stars; but for now, she is an actress on the rise. A Neilan favorite (he will also star her in *Tanned Legs* that same year), she is ravishing in close-up, a blond beauty with a huge expanse of eyelid darkly stretching to her drawn-on brows, and a melting smile.

The Yankees are debonair (pronounced *de-boner*) in vests, a glimpse of spats, tight-fitting suits, and shellacked hair. It's to Rudy's credit that he wants his band with him in his screen debut, and they have the best lines. At times, he just sits there while they exchange repartée, like a tossed solo. His generally doleful expression makes it puzzling why he is the leader, to which Rudy might agree. He knows he doesn't give a good first impression. He's a hard worker, but he makes it look easy. He is not a Joe Motion, he admits, as musicians call one whose "showmanship is used as a cloak to prevent the expose of a great weakness. . . . All my life I have believed in conservation of energy," and so he just stands there and sings. He hardly moves at all, saving his concentration for the staring contest that will take place between him and his intentions.

Who will blink first? In the only scene with real chemistry, Rudy sings "If You Were the Only Girl in the World" to Sally, eyes locking across the valley of crowd. She still thinks he's "Ted Grant"—another case of mistaken identity—but he has attracted her attention by slowing the seduction. The song is a dozen years old, and "had failed so miserably as a fox trot that its publishers had soured on it. I tried to convince them that it was a hit song if played as a slow waltz."

Unfortunately, the diminished pacing didn't help the movie's plot, which revolves around Rudy's paying an unscheduled visit to his mentor, "who discovered Ben Bernie" (as Ben's brother Herman gave the young Rudy one of his first New York jobs) and now runs a saxophone correspondence course. He shows off his inspiration's latest model: "a brand-new gold-plated super-toned dee-loox . . . listen to those low notes." Leaving the low notes to the saxophone, Rudy mostly sings at the top of his range. It gives him the demeanor of a choir boy. He holds on to his sax for dear life, in the one-and-seven position, pausing to tuck it under his shoulder, holster-style, when it's time to chat. Sally looks similarly primed for battle. Her hat is like a bathing cap with wings, hugging her scalp; a pelt of dead animal hangs from the crook of her left arm.

"I've always wanted to meet a musician," she says, though she's already met one. Russ might be playing with Gus Arnheim over at the Cocoanut Grove later that evening. If they wrapped early, she could have dinner on Wilshire and watch him.

"I'm not what you think I am," says Rudy, as a steamrolling Marie Dressler, encouraged to flutter her hand on her breast and roll her eyes, crashes in through the door, going over the top with her role as a society dowager, raising the hysteria level.

Blane struggles gamely with Rudy's relative reticence, but the stiff dialogue is weighted down by explanation and exposition. He looks reluctant. She is able to turn on her acting ability only in an "I never want to see you again" scene where she berates the now-revealed Rudy for letting down the children of the orphanage, for whom the charity benefit is scheduled. The radio hookup is in place. The real Ted Grant will be arriving to beam over his "protégé." Four "orphan girls" from the school will come out to soften the crowd, all budding Shirley Temples—in fact, isn't that Shirley herself on the far right?

"Boys, are we going to hide behind a woman's skirts?" Rudy asks his musicians when it becomes clear who's going to provide their salvation. "Sure!" the Connecticut Yankees chorus, like any good cheerleaders, the boys in the band.

A MONTH after the stock market tumble, *Vagabond Lover* is released. Rudy grouses that he doesn't share in any of the profits, not that there should be any, though he did settle for eleven grand a week for five weeks, more money than he ever thought possible, and then was mad because he could've gotten a quarter of a million, easy, and maybe even a piece of the pie, but he had a flat fee and his accountant at NBC's Artists Service had put some money into the stock market against his better judgment, and there you go. He hates himself on screen. He's acting, and he shouldn't be acting. If he's playing himself, he has to *be* himself. And he had to laugh. Because if he really played himself, the brush-by in the hall behind the stage, the pupils grazing each other, the slick sound of satin slithering over silk, a scratch like the nail on the back, the skirt lifting, so slow as to reveal each won millimeter of leg, crossing no-man's-land, the geography of upper thigh merging into buttock rising in the distance.... That would be a true motion picture. Nobody would believe his story.

IN THE last month of the twenties, the Dancing Masters of America, at their annual meeting in Pittsburgh, adopt as their prize step the "Rudy Vallée": "a catchy bending of the knee which makes for grace and was inspired by the smooth, soft music peculiar to its namesake."

He did know how to bend the knee. That slow fox-trot.

DOROTHY

Russ saw her as he entered the room.

She was looking sideways, left elbow on the chair's arm, left hand splaying to cradle her face. Two fingers under her chin, pointer and pinkie supporting, casual yet constructed, like a suspension bridge. Over which her exquisite face rode, a Terraplane aerodynamic.

He took in her legs next, tight skirt well tucked yet a good two inches above the knees, stems crossed and stemming downward. Black velvet pumps. Big hat, some sort of frou-frou around the neck.

Miss New Orleans.

She was in what was to be Ziegfeld's last Follies. She couldn't have known that, since this particular Glorification of the American Girl had seemingly weathered its out-of-town growing pains to open to fairly good reviews, which is what happens when you mix plenty of bootleg hooch with ogleable females and stir with a slice of lemon served chilled to the newspaperman of your choice. Only a week late. They had originally been scheduled to debut on June 24, but the show had stayed longer in Pittsburgh. Business was "so good," Flo told the papers, though they all knew he was giving them the business. The first run-through had run over five hours, and even Ziegfeld—with his reputation for o'er-the-top extravaganza—was running out of patience.

Florenz Ziegfeld had reason to be concerned. Part grand opera, part minstrelsy, part vaudeville, the Follies were what had happened when he let his imagination and pocketbook run wild in 1907. He had kept them going for nearly a quarter of a century, contributing stars and their songs to the gilt panorama of Broadway galas in the teens and twenties. Despite their history (who could not fail to be moved by the sight of Fanny Brice leaning gamine-like against a lamppost singing "My Man" in 1921?), the revues were more like statuary these days, living tableaux of costumery and veiled nudity that had petrified into spectacle. The whole unwieldy construct—dialect parodies and peacock pageantry and papier-mâché elephants—needed to be chipped away, but really, whose act was going to be cut from this year's edition? There was "dissension among principals" as to which moments of grandeur were due for the hammer and chisel.

Dorothy Dell was a principal. Fifth from the end in a cast of twenty-seven, perhaps, but at least she wasn't in the chorus, like Miss Memphis or Miss United States from that Texas beauty contest, where Dorothy's legs had gained her acclaim as the Louisiana export. They had all tried for Miss Universe, but she was the only one still in the running, or was it dancing, or was it musical comedy? Dorothy knew she had a long way to go where it mattered, on Broadway. Even Reri, the Bora-Bora beauty whom Ziegfeld imported at a cost of three thousand dollars from the "South Seas" after he saw her breasts bobbing down waterfalls in the movie *Tabu*, was given higher billing. But at least Dorothy was here, in the Nut Club, in New York's very own bohemian Greenwich Village, in Harry Richman's party. Gladys Glad and her husband Mark Hellinger. Virginia Biddle, Harry's this-week girlfriend. That shy girl, Helen. Talk about *Puttin' on the Ritz. . . .*

It was Paul Yawitz's idea to cook up a romance. *The same old hokum,* Russ thought. Why did they think anyone paid any real attention to it? People paid notice after the fact, when they heard you sing. Otherwise it was all *bubkes.* He smiled when he heard that word coming out of his mouth, echoing in his mind's ear. Been hanging out with too many Yids. That's Tin Pan Alley for you.

A light veil draped over her hat's broad brim shadowed the face and brought the sharp outline of Dorothy's lips into relief. She was a softer blonde, not brassy like Mae West or Harlow. The slashed pencil overline of her eyebrow, the lilting Creole edge of her voice, slinkified her. Her song in the Follies, "Was I Drunk, Was He Handsome, and Did My Ma Give Me Hell," brought her to the notice of what Yawitz liked to call Rue Regret, the Rialto, or at least her manager, Jack Blum, which is how Paul came to hear of the Richman party at the Nut.

Have her meet Russ. Get the photogs out and maybe make the bulldog edition of the *News.*

Russ had been "romantically linked" before. To squire around some lovely who was as hungry for the spotlight as he, in hopes that they might help each other up the ladder of success; or be the dashing young escort for some silent-film dowager who's suddenly—overnight—become yesterday's technology, well, that was hardly one of life's problems.

Con had wanted to celebrate. He was getting ready to pop the cork on the champagne. *He got we got NBC*, Conrad hummed to himself, like a refrain. *He got wheee got NBC*, the needle stuck on a record. That's all he could hear, running around inside him. *Whee got NBC*. Over and over. Hill and dale. It sounded like a hit song. He'd have to write it someday. Hell, he was writing it now, over the radio.

"This calls for a toast," he told Russ, and Paul went to the telephone to call Blum.

YAWITZ TOUCHED her on the arm. She turned slowly, lazily, broke from her reverie. Russ watched awareness return to her gaze, focus, brighten, arrow in on him, even as Paul was saying to her, "Miss Dell, I would like you to meet Russ Columbo, the singer I was telling Jack about. He's just come into town from Hollywood. . . ."

Dorothy Dell raised her veil. The backlit sparkle dazzled Russ's vision. It brought the curve of her jawline into sharp relief; Russ found his stare sliding up the slope of her neck until their eyes compassed. Magnetic north! Just like in the movies. Paul's voice faded, and both of them, used to turning on the charm, tried their skills on the other. Pleasantly surprised.

THE VILLAGE Nut Club, 99 Seventh Avenue between Barrow and Grove, was in full swirl, no dress code; but for all Russ and Dorothy cared, it was like a projection behind them, a scenery unreeling to give them motion, as if they were being filmed in the back of a soundstage cab.

Close-up. Total attention. Keeping their wary distance.

"Is that your real name?" he asked.

"Oh, Mr. Ziegfeld asked me to change it." She lifted her shoulders, shifted her eyes to the side, as if there were a third companion at their table. Russ thought he could ride the sweep of her lashes, all feathery and fanned to match her wrap. "My last name is Goff."

"That's pretty simple. You wouldn't believe me if I told you what I started with." He recited her his fifteen syllables. Then he softly sang them to her, with a smile to show he wasn't completely crazy.

She giggled, glad they had something to laugh about together. He'd been in the movies, and she felt a little tongue-tied.

"How did you get here?" he asked. He rummaged in his pockets for his cigarette case, popped it open, extracted an Old Gold, offered it to her (she waved no), tapped it on his left thumbnail twice, balanced it in his mouth, pulled a match from a book lying on a table. Talking geography.

She told him she had been born in Hattiesburg, Mississippi. Moved to Louisiana. There couldn't have been much more, since she was hardly seventeen. And because she trusted him, she told him about winning the bathing suit competition in Galveston the year before, and how the suit had cost two-ninety-eight and how Miss Memphis had flounced around in front of all those judges, and that she had a sister, Helen, a couple years younger, who wanted to become a showgirl too, and that she loved dogs.

Russ struck the match.

VALLÉE

The plane carrying a grieving Rudy touched down at the airport in East Boston just before dawn. He had left Newark at 3:15 A.M., and took off immediately again for Scarborough Airport in Portland, landing at 6:25, accompanied by his brother William. His brother-in-law, also named William, had a car waiting for the twelve-mile dash to Westbrook. The Maine State Police supplied the motorcycle escort.

His mother was dying. During his honeymoon.

Fay waved goodbye to him from behind the fence at Newark Airport. She would be following by train, trailing five feet of fox fur—head and all—around her shoulders, a veil only enhancing her enormous eyes. Both wondered whether news of their elopement had hastened Margaret Vallée's heart into cardiac arrest. She hadn't approved of Rudy's matrimonial leap.

It would be hard to imagine two more different Mrs. Vallées. Margaret was gray-haired, plain, and practical. She didn't know what to make of this oiled and perfumed creature that Rudy had eloped with, an eye-shadowed specter from the other side of the continent, raising talk among the neighbors. She'd had more in common with Rudy's first wife, the older Leonie, recently divorced, with a two-year-old child, whom he had married in the spring of 1928 after a weeklong courtship. It lasted a day. On their nuptial night, he played at the Heigh-Ho Club until it was time to head over the Fifty-ninth Street Bridge to Forest Hills. Rudy refused to carry her over the threshold, and the marriage was annulled.

He was in Atlantic City with Fay when the news of his mother's illness broke on Sunday, July 12, hardly a week after their wedding. His mother lingered in a coma until Rudy arrived on Monday, briefly recognized him, then expired late on Wednesday morning. He was at her bedside, "hearing the echo of her own lullabies she used to sing to me as a baby," holding her hand.

"I had planned to make her so happy," he told the *Mirror*, which had sent a reporter along on the plane. "She was so proud of my success, and it was all due to her. She gave me everything; my musical talent, my training, my ambitions. She slaved for us all, sacrificing her health and her strength for our future.

"And now it is too late to show her what all her love and toil meant to me." A son's lament.

HIS MOTHER had believed in him. His father, on the other hand, called him a "cheap faker" and hoped he would continue working in the family's Rexall drugstore. Rudy stopped slinging ice-cream sodas in June of '17, when he was sixteen, aiming for any career in show business, happy to be cranking the projector at the neighborhood Star Theater ("To stand there looking out through the square aperture watching the picture come to life on the screen by the magic of *my* right hand"), promoted to head usher at Portland's prestigious DeLuxe Strand Theater, entering the U. of Maine.

But the drugstore sold Victor records, and Rudy liked to crank the demonstrator phonograph as well. "Get your nose out of that gramophone horn," his father yelled. "Can't you see there are people waiting at the fountain?" Rudy didn't care; he was saving his coins for bigger fountains. He remembered, in *My Time Is Your Time*, that he would " 'beam' the sound at these potential customers," thinking megaphonic even then. He must've listened "a hundred times to Al Jolson's 'Sahara.' " He learned to play drums, clarinet, finally an instrument "about which very little was then known and so rare that there probably weren't two performers on it in the entire city," a C-melody saxophone whose brass was beginning to green and tarnish. He joined bands: Harold T. Pease and His Society Orchestra, Welch's Famous Novelty Jazz Orchestra, the Famous Harmonic Orchestra, the Crescent Orchestra, the Vega Orchestra. He appeared as "Saxophone Soloist, Hubert Vallée" at the Strand, and left the paper where his father would see the advertisement. His dad cried.

He was shedding tears now. Rudy walked up the stairs to the family house, putting an arm around his father, who looked a trifle bewildered at the unexpected turns his life had taken in the past few years. It was not how he figured it to be, raising his family in a quiet Maine town, with a good business and New England virtue. Charles Vallée removed his jacket, two-button suspenders supporting a portly demeanor, while the press took pictures of his son.

Rudy was thinking of his mother, of the song he wanted to write for her. "It is just possible that Mother herself had a touch of the entertainer in her. She was bright, attractive, dignified, animated. . . . I often think that any gift I have for 'doing impressions,' as they call it, certainly stems from my mother's delightful personality."

As they call it.

IN BETWEEN matriculations, from enrolling in Maine to his graduation from Yale, Vallée went abroad, to London, for an expansive '24–'25 school year. He played at the Savoy Hotel, bought a Chesterfield coat and a hundred fifty ties, acquired one of the first Dunhill cigarette lighters. He took an English girl to France. He sang "If You Were the Only Girl in the World and I Were the Only Boy" for the first time, which a friend had picked out of an American Doughboy Revue called The Bing Boys when it passed through London near the end of World War I. When he brought home the words to the Pier on Old Orchard Beach, Maine, returning in June 1925, crowds "would congregate in front of the stage . . . I would croon them out in my little nasal, plaintive voice while the spotlight played its varied colors upon me."

Yale was Ivy League, the preserve of Protestantism, a college élite celebrated in the pages of Vanity Fair that gathered in a country-club atmosphere of eating clubs and fraternities, sororities and secret societies. Skull and Bones. Masons. There were words that must not be whispered, clandestine handshakes, and a disconcerting air of exclusion, at least where Rudy was concerned: "I was never so miserable as at the first Yale fraternity dance at which I played. . . . Good-looking, well-groomed and well-dressed young men, feeling very gay, danced by me holding in their arms the most beautiful creatures that my eyes had ever seen."

He determined to win them all. His how-to manual was a romantic novel, The Guarded Heights, written by Wadsworth Camp, whose hero, George, is a menial worker on a great estate owned by the Planter family. After she is thrown from a horse, he declares his love to the fair Sylvia, the daughter, who responds by hitting him with a riding crop. The father throws him off the property. Enrolling in Princeton, George becomes a football hero, and using "the riding crop in the picture of Sylvia Planter" as inspiration, he begins a regimen that alternates study and "physical and mental football practice" for sixteen hours a day, allowing eight hours for sleep. By will and discipline, he overcomes her aloofness, earning the right to be hers.

In *Venus in Furs*, the fifth of six novels in his *Love* miniseries (which in turn is just one subdivision of the massive and penitently unfinished *Heritage of Cain*), Leopold von Sacher-Masoch stands in front of a similar portrait with his friend Severin. "A beautiful woman . . . was resting on an ottoman, supported on her left arm. She was nude in her dark furs. Her right hand played with a lash, while her bare foot rested carelessly on a man, lying before her like a slave, like a dog. . . . " The man is Severin.

" 'That is the way I saw her in my dream,' cries Sacher-Masoch.

" 'I too,' replies Severin, 'only I dreamed my dream with open eyes.' "

On Thursday evening, Fay Webb arrives in Westport. Rudy goes to meet her. When she steps off the train, she is like the cover of *College Humor*. Her raccoon eyes meet his raccoon coat. She tilts her head for him to kiss. He clutches her tight and buries his face in her fur.

AT THE funeral Friday, Rudy spends a few moments alone at the grave as the mourners depart. He kneels, says his prayers, and then heads with Fay for his summer home in Lovell for the weekend. It stands adjacent to the cottage of his friend Don Dickerman, who had given him his first real break by asking him to bring a small group into the Heigh-Ho Club the week after New Year's, 1928.

He'd been kicking around New York since graduation, bouncing from band to band, dragging along his scrapbook and a stack of phonograph records featuring his saxophone to each audition. He even brought a "portable talking-machine" to play them on, eager to demonstrate his eagerness. Vallée had been experimenting with recording as early as 1921, when he used a Dictaphone (or Ediphone) at the University of Maine to study phrasings. On his Easter vacation in 1922, he paid Columbia's Personal Record Department fifty dollars to record "Japanese Sunset" in the same studios as their regular artists, with the option of purchasing a copy of the master at a dollar, in lots of five hundred at fifty cents each. He failed his Edison test later that summer, but gained valuable experience when he was in London with the Savoy Havana Band, even backing Gertrude Lawrence and Beatrice Lillie on one occasion. His Heigh-Ho renown earned him a Victor contract in 1928, and soon he was busily checking "playbacks" to arrange the orchestra around the microphone, and then attempting the master recording.

Bandleader Bert Lown introduced him to Dickerman, who was looking for a band to brighten his new nightspot at 35 East Fifty-third Street, just off Fifth Avenue. There was talk that the orchestra he'd hired for New Year's Eve looked too Jewish, and Don wanted to appeal to an exclusive clientèle. Dress would be "absolutely formal. . . . Herbert Hoover could not get in in a gray suit and Otto Kahn could not get in dressed in tails, if you get my meaning." Rudy had no qualms about Jews — the night before his Heigh-Ho opening he had played tenor saxophone (as opposed to his usual alto) at the annual Jewish Theatrical Guild dinner at the Commodore. But it helped that his Yale Collegians (as he called them) were New English.

It was Dickerman's fourth or fifth club of the twenties, still well under the number of his ongoing marriages. In Greenwich Village, he'd set up the Pirate's Cove, with buccaneer décor and brigs to imprison young ladies; there was the Blue Horse, and the Country Fair. New Yorker cartoonist Peter Arno (himself a Yale man) was frequently along for the ride, chronicling the doings for a new punch line of cartoon. The Heigh-Ho Club was given a Galápagan theme, with underwater sea creatures viewed through a bathysphere portal and a white cockatoo placed behind the bandstand. The band dressed in tuxedo pants and billowy Russian-style satin blouses, high-buttoned and sashed. Rudy fit right in.

Lown had moved into band management after coming up as a violinist with Fred Hamm, who himself was affiliated with the Benson Orchestra of Chicago. Bert wrote the classic "Bye Bye Blues" in 1925 with three other members of Hamm's band (and Hamm himself on vocals), and they recorded it for Victor starting April 21. Thirteen takes later, on May 1, they achieved their master. Lown was as much promoter as musician (he would go on to lead the Hotel Biltmore Orchestra, taking over from Roger Wolfe Kahn, Otto's son), and a month after Rudy looked like he was a hit at the Heigh-Ho, suggested a radio wire. Rudy obliged by coming up with his catchphrase, "Heigh-ho, everybody!" It was a pity that the radio audience couldn't see the sailor hats, the props, the synchronized hand gestures.

The lack of brass — an economy on Dickerman's part — mellowed the tone of the newly renamed Connecticut Yankees (an emissary from Yale had complained, and Vallée had just seen the Rodgers and Hart musical of the same name at the Vanderbilt Theater), and the smoother texture suited Rudy's lovelorn demeanor. When Don was offered the chance to design a club in Cuba with a King Arthur theme, moat and drawbridge included, Vallée moved to a supper club called the Versailles, at 14 East Sixtieth. The owner, a Hungarian named Charles Morton Bellak, had decorated it with murals of French garden idylls; the site would later be home to the Copacabana. For now, it was an empty room that Vallée was sure could be filled with the help of radio, and his own growing popularity. He had seen the mounted patrol-men controlling the crowds at his vaudeville opening at Keith's Eighty-first Street, the jostling flappers and "the crush of eager radio fans" all testifying to the drawing power of the broadcast announcements he'd made about the ap-pearances, and his lubricious voice over the air. Rather than give him more money, Bellak suggested renaming the Versailles the Villa Vallée. How could Rudy refuse?

In April 1929, he played the vaunted Palace. In May he began a ten-week stand at the Paramounts. Hollywood was calling. There were tea dances at the Lombardy, the Victor recordings, and his picture on a billboard at the northwest corner of Seventh Avenue and Twenty-third Street advertising Old Gold cigarettes ("Not a cough in a carload"). His brandished megaphone is the last gasp of acoustic before the voice turns electric. It will be Rudy's con-tribution to twenties stereotype; a monotype.

NOTHING LASTS forever. Rudy could feel them nipping at his heels.

"Is Rudy Vallée Slipping?" they couldn't wait to ask in *Radio Guide*. Has marriage "dimmed his popularity? Public opinion is a fickle thing, and Pop-ularity, one of her glad children, is a snare and a delusion," like one of Ray Toland's rim-punctuations.

"Now that I'm on top, I expect my troubles to begin," Rudy declared. Get-ting there was one thing; staying there, and there, and there, was another. He had hired Will Osborne to lead a relief band for him at the Villa Vallée when the Connecticut Yankees were out on the Keith circuit, and now Will was suing him, claiming Rudy was imitating *him*! Osborne, to the delight of the newspapers, challenged Rudy to a ten-round boxing match, and introduced a song called "I'd Like to Break the Neck of the Man Who Wrote the Stein Song." He was only one of many competitors. Even before his mother was laid to rest, Ozzie Nelson looked to overtake him in the *Mirror* radio poll of the best broadcasters. And if the rumors were true, Bing Crosby was on his way to New York for CBS. That's all he needed. He'd heard the Rhythm Boys with Whiteman; here was a guy who could sing and looked even less impos-ing than Rudy. Better watch out.

It was Vallée's town, and he meant to keep it that way. Stay one step ahead of these birds. He had conquered the Paramounts; it was time for something new. Agreeing to a spot in George White's eleventh Scandals, he hoped to step up in the hierarchy of the theater district. A formal revue was just the ticket, and Rudy had his first bought for him by a wealthy college-mate for the 1926 Scandals, with Harry Richman and DeSylva-Brown-Henderson songs like "Birth of the Blues" and "Black Bottom." He had been duly impressed. Now he was discussing songs with Lew Brown and Ray Henderson in White's office. It was their first show without DeSylva.

They treated him like a "fledgling." Rudy responded in kind. He wanted to do his Maurice Chevalier impression in the show. White turned him down — "This is Broadway," George told him, "not a goddam five-a-day grind at some lousy theater," before giving the Chevalier impersonation to Willie Howard, who added it to his Jessel, Jolson, and Cantor. Willie, along with his brother Eugene, was the show's comic turn, as they'd been in 1928 and 1929. Rudy was hired to stand there and sing. He wanted to do more than just sing. He wanted to make an impression.

To White, Vallée was a mere radio personality, hardly legitimate theater. Rudy couldn't see the show but for his own place in it. He fumed as he sat through endless rehearsals, waiting in the dark of the Apollo Theater for his turn onstage, grinding his schedule to a halt. He wasn't used to such enforced idleness, "without being asked to say 'boo' or sing a chorus or do anything for the four weeks of the performer's time that the Actors Equity [gives] the producer at no cost whatsoever to him."

Ethel Merman came aboard the show in Newark, hoping to stir ticket sales as the Scandals approached its New York opening on September 14, joining other acts like dancer Ray Bolger, the operatic Everett Marshall, and the Gale Quadruplets. Ethel Barrymore Colt, going by her married name, was making her musical comedy debut. And though Vallée never got over feeling that his Chevalier imitation had been unfairly lifted from him, that "I had nothing in the show that would in any way distinguish me or bring any huzzahs from the audience or the critics," he was granted four songs by Brown-Henderson that gave his gift for emotional mimicry a personal tinge, when he finally attained the Broadway pantheon he hoped for.

"Life Is Just a Bowl of Cherries," "My Song," "This Is the Missus," and "The Thrill Is Gone" were recorded over two days, August 7 and 8. They run a gamut from optimism to depression, which described the mood swing of a country whose sense of destination had violently retracted and left it with only the hope of enduring.

Rudy is cheery; his life is a bowl of cheeries. *"Why are we here? Where are we going?"* How can you lose what you never owned? The song's sing-along rhyme scheme—from *mysterious* to *serious*—scales down life's theologies to a happy-go-lucky present. *"You can't take it all when you go-go-go."* Rudy imitates Willie Howard's chorus in the show, a caricature of a caricature. White insisted all the performers know all the songs of every other performer, and often switched them around in the programme.

In the Scandals, Ethel Merman got first crack at "Life Is Just a Bowl of Cherries," especially after her manager complained that she wasn't featured on enough songs. In the ensuing argument, the agent was knocked out by Brown; he and Henderson would spend much of the pre-production complaining about the presentation of their work. By first night, they were in court trying to halt the opening and prevent the use of their songs in the show. They said White had agreed to pay them 6 percent, when, in fact, they were getting only 4. Winchell dismissed it as "nerves," and said the pair were worried that people would think they couldn't make it without Bud DeSylva.

Merman and Marshall were teamed with Rudy on "My Song." The familiar melody is one of Henderson's most pan-American compositions, tailor-made for the muted trumpet in the second chorus, the hint of rhumba that Rudy does his best to square. A song about *yoooo.* The lyrics are the songwriters' simple tribute to their tuneful calling, a prestidigitator's art that can "change your *no* to *yes."* Brown's wordplay singles out Franz Schubert and Irving Berlin, as much for the sound of their syllables as a measure of popular song, like any good Broadway songsmith.

Rudy showcased "This Is the Missus" with the ensemble, though he felt ill at ease putting it over. The song predated his elopement, but the newspaper headlines gave it a topical touch. And where *was* his Missus? Rudy wasn't sure. She didn't want to meet him at the Hotel Pennsylvania Grill after he got off rehearsal; he wasn't even sure that she was tuned in to his radio program. Fay was talking about going back to California for a visit with her family. She was going to be away for a month! What was he supposed to do in the meantime? He had needs.

He smiled gamely, trying to maintain his air of rascality while singing of domesticity. His marryin' kind is proprietary and rooted in insecurity—"I own those lips! I own those eyes!" His fear is that he'll lose all those other girls, the ones who believe in him, now that he's introduced them to his wife. The word still sounded strange in his mouth. "This is my wife." He hadn't gotten used to it yet. He knew he felt different, like he had been joined at the hip, though he noticed he hadn't stopped wanting and desiring the random female. He had his eye on Alice Faye, a young chorine, and sometimes caught himself watching her raptly while she went through her prancings.

The show's spiritual, "That's Why Darkies Were Born," is performed by Everett in full "cork," beginning in silhouette on a plantation and finally showing black folk—this is folk as Charley Patton's blues—ascending as white-haired angels to heaven. At this point in minstrelsy, blacking-up is regarded as a way to infuse spirituality into a white secular presentation, presented as the form itself is about to pass on to its greater reward. The sinner gets religion in the end.

No one seemed right for another Brown-Henderson song, "If I Thought I Could Live Without You, I'd Die." Ethel Barrymore Colt had first sung it to a baby in a cradle. Sister of Lionel and John in the famous theatrical family, she would join them in Hollywood the next year for a shot at the screen in *Rasputin and the Empress*. She proved too much of a Broadway icon to make the switch, even if she believed movies could finally and adequately represent her actor's craft. The song was handed to Willie Howard in a black wig, on his knees to a woman with gray hair, ostensibly his mother, though Howard was over sixty at this point. When the stage manager brought White's instructions for Rudy to take a turn, the implication was unavoidable.

He knew it would generate resentment among his female fans, an "apparent attempt to capitalize on the death of my mother," and George belatedly apologized. Vallée much preferred "The Thrill Is Gone," which was given to the solemn Marshall for opening night, though Vallée recorded it on August 8, at Victor's Studio 1.

The piano sounds as if it's echoing in an empty house, the chords ringing mournful and lost as Rudy wanders his now-deserted halls of memory. He waits until the orchestra has rounded the choruses twice over and settled down. It's just him and the piano for the verse; there is missing in her kissing. *"The nights are cold, our love is old. Now I don't appeal to you. This is the end. Why pretend?"*

It's over.

THE RADIO microphones are out in full array on the City Hall steps: WMCA, WOR, Columbia, and NBC, going live this July 22 at 1:00 P.M. sharp. The sixty-piece Department of Sanitation strikes up a cadenza. Mayor Jimmy Walker leans over to Kate Smith, presenting her with a loving cup that acknowledges she is Queen of the Air, according to the more than quarter-million votes cast by *Mirror* readers. Ozzie Nelson, despite a strong finish, is only able to secure Most Popular Orchestra Leader (he has not yet met Harriet). Morton Downey is Leading Singer; veterans Weber and Fields have garnered Most Popular Skit; A. L. Alexander is Best Announcer. That leaves Rudy. The Favorite Broadcaster. With a fifth of the tallied vote, he is number one. King.

George White relents and gives him his damned Chevalier imitation.

HELEN AND VIRGINIA

It was horrible the way the girl had been burnt.

All summer they had been going out to yachts, making the rounds of the boat clubs and rolling estates overlooking the harbor and the eligible young heirs who liked nothing more than to partake of their gold-digger glamour. That was part of their job description. Follies showgirls, the toast-esses of Broadway.

There was even talk that some of the girls had been seen lounging on Earl Carroll's sloop. When Mr. Ziegfeld found out about that, boy, was he steamed. Carroll's Vanities ("Through these portals pass the most beautiful girls in the world") had been his slightly more risqué imitator for the last nine seasons. He even fired a couple of the chorines for "getting sunburned." It was all the talk over at the drugstore on Seventh and Fifty-fifth where they gathered between rehearsals and sat at the fountain and ordered lemon phosphates and lime rickeys and talked about who had sent whom a dozen dressing-room roses and what little bejeweled trinket might be entwined around the thorns and which lucky Johnny would be waiting at the stage door.

Helen Walsh couldn't believe her luck. Her friend Gladys Glad was one of the stars of the revue; some said she was the most beautiful. She was The Ziegfeld Girl of 1931, the Rialto's royalty. Gladys was married to that oh-so-dashing columnist of the Great White Way, Mark Hellinger. After Saturday's matinee on July 25, she had taken Helen aside and said that a bunch of them were going out to Long Island on Harry Richman's boat after the night's performance, and would she like to come along? And she just a Bronx girl, accustomed to gazing at Broadway from the last stop on the number 1 line. . . .

Would she? Even though she'd been a Follies showgirl for nearly four years now, she knew she wasn't moving from the chorus. She wasn't even a dancer, and though her role as living diorama was higher in the pecking hierarchy of the Ziegfeld backstage than the hoofers, they at least had a skill to fall back on, and some of them did fall back, thank you. Helen was pleased with her looks, but you needed more than a wiggle in your walk to become a principal. There were a lot of beautiful girls working on Wall Street, typing away, hoping to increase their wpm so they could get the work done faster. Only then there'd just be more of it, and some potbellied lug to go along with it. She'd had her fill of carbon copies.

Going out after the show with the gang was one thing. Harry liked to head over to one of the speaks along Fifty-second Street (like Leon & Eddie's, where the sign over the door read "Through these portals the most beautiful girls in the world pass out!"), or down to the Nut Club with a bunch of swells after the Follies strutted their stuff; but this was different. High class.

And she respected Mark. He always steered her right. Hellinger had written a good chunk of the current Follies book, as well as his "All in a Day" parables of life in the *Daily Mirror*, rye-highball tales of bathtub-gin mills filled with happy-go-lucky proprietors who ordered a bottle of the "good stuff" delivered to his table and despite his nay-saying pressed on him a stiff one, but then he realized that he had been given "the bad stuff" meant for the tourists and when the proprietor asked the waiter, the reply was "Oh, I thought that's what you told me to always give to Hellinger." Even his English bulldog Charlie had heard that one before.

Highballs and lowbrows. Prohibition just gave a clandestine air to the usual carryings-on. The secret knocks and name-droppings were all faithlessly recorded by the entertainment beat columnists—Walter Winchell, Sidney Skolsky, Louis Sobol, Ed Sullivan—who created their own cachet by overhearing the whispered goings-on, or made it up as they went along. Follow the dotted lines. The demand for on-the-q.t. gossip, supplied in no small number by a battalion of press agents whose sole job was to match names to places, couple to uncouple, was insatiable.

Competition could be fierce. Hellinger and Walter Winchell delighted in mock-sparring over the *Mirror*'s entertainment beat. Referring to Hellinger as "dear old 'pallor,' " Winchell joshed that "I look better now than Hellinger . . . who has been dead five years." Replied Mark, "I would advise Mr. Winchell to do more writing and less wishing." There was a more genuine animosity between Winchell and Sullivan. Still, they were becoming as much the stars as those they wrote about, fame by proxy.

After the curtain call, the Follies party headed out toward Long Island. The plan was to pick up Harry Richman's cabin cruiser, the *Chevalmar II*, at his home in Beechhurst, and sail from there to Greenport out on the far eastern tip of the Island to spend the Sunday deep-sea fishing and escaping the city heat. Along for the ride were Gladys and Mark, Helen and another member of the ensemble, dancer Virginia Biddle, and Harry's chauffeur, Robert Levy. Harry and Mark had originally asked Dorothy to come along, but she'd declined. Some of the chicken à la king they'd had the night before at George LaMaze's supposedly swank spot in the east Fifties off Park had unsettled her stomach, not to mention the five bottles of White Rock and its "mixer." No wonder the tab had come to $94.70!

Richman sang the lead in the Follies. He was the resident star, a onetime "It"em with Clara Bow ("*To my Napoleon—From his Waterloo*" she'd autographed her picture), a theatrical veteran who had risen to fame accompanying Mae West and the Dolly Sisters on piano; after arriving in New York from Cincinnati sporting some vaudeville experience with the Jewel City Trio and Those Three Boys; before graduating to *George White's Scandals* in 1926. Born on August 10, 1895, he still had some of the old century within him. He took to the stage in a style reminiscent of Al Jolson; florid, staunch, extravagantly gestured, with a slight air of the bulldog himself in his selling of a song. He pumped the underlined words from the back of his chest, mid-sternum.

His specialty was the hat-and-stick. He'd practice in front of a mirror for hours—"cock the hat, twirl the stick." He said he never heard of Maurice Chevalier, over in France with the same shtick.

Richman gained the most notoriety from his self-named nightspot, the Club Richman, located at 157 West Fifty-sixth Street backed against the rear of Carnegie Hall. It had been an old stable when he opened it in 1925, but he designed the club to look like a Floridian patio, complete with fake windows and painted palm trees behind them and a sky-ceiling with tiny winking lights representing stars. It was almost like his back deck at Beechhurst. A brick hideaway with a lawn that rolled down to the bay, a stone's throw from Flushing Airport, where Harry stored his airplanes, including his favorite Sikorsky amphibian, the enclosed sunporch looked out over Long Island Sound. He installed a steam cabinet in the master bedroom, made up a bar curtain of two thousand champagne corks, and fitted the top floor out like a cabin cruiser, tapered at both ends. It slept several; Harry liked company.

The Club Richman was even more like home once Harry finished installing a secret door between the ladies' room and his office. By an elaborate series of hand signals, Harry could arrange a liaison with a particularly beautiful patron of his club, and often have her back blushing in her seat with her escort before the floor show began. Harry loved the ladies. "Girls, girls, girls, girls. . . . No minute with a girl is wasted," he would fondly remember in his autobiography, A *Hell of a Life,* and then he would be off down Broadway from Columbus Circle to Forty-second Street in his Rolls, giving away ten-dollar gold pieces to the cops on the corner, a fifty-dollar Charvet tie around his neck, a thirty-five-dollar Sulka shirt on his back, chuckling over the memories of his private train ride to Pittsburgh that Ziegfeld had arranged for the out-of-town tryouts of the '31 Follies: ninety cases of liquor, ninety beautiful girls. A hell of a life.

He was cresting as a result of his appearance in *Puttin' on the Ritz* in 1930, for which he'd written "Singing a Vagabond Song." Richman exuded a genuine sincerity. *Bonhomie.* On "Thank Your Father," recorded in New York in May of 1930 for Brunswick, one of the only discs of his that is probably still in any kind of print, Harry gallantly shows off his love for his gal by appreciating her moment of conception. He is especially effusive to the father, who was "a bit tight" when he asked for her hand. The band oompahs brassily. Gratitude inflates his bosom; he has proposed to her in an old-fashioned horse and buggy. *"Though your fa-ther's name was Stan-ley / Thank good-ness he was man-ly."* Who's marrying whom here, anyway? On croon tag-words like "moon" and "June," Harry brings out their *u*-ness. *Me-yuun.* Like a sliding pond.

Somewhat illingually, he doesn't rhyme the expected "marriage" and "carriage" in the chorus. *"Thank goodness for their marry / And for that baby carry."* He drops the *g*'s, an action-present verb where once stood passive nouns. Gladys Glad, resplendent in G's, had more than her share.

She was a girl who brought a whole new meaning to the pencil silhouette. Even walking next to the dead girl's mother less than a week later, supporting her in the unbelieving caisson march from the family home on Riverdale Avenue to the Catholic church across the street, her drape was stunning.

THEY WERE on the boat by 2:00 A.M., leaving Harry's private dock in Queens. The chauffeur packed picnic baskets with smoked turkey and cold cuts and chilled champagne.

The vessel was a beauty. They all oohed and aahed and admired its thirty-six feet. Harry had bought it two weeks ago from the Broadway producer Alexander Aaron for $4,500; it had gone for fifteen g's new. A twin-screw cruiser, with a pair of hundred-horsepower engines, broad in the beam.

Greenport is just north of Shelter Island on a sliver of land that separates Gardiners Bay from the Sound. Hellinger, Richman, and Levy took their turns at the wheel while the women slept in the cabin. Mark watched the dawn rise, a light breeze moving in from the southwest, pushing the boat along toward the ocean. He felt nautical, or at least relaxed. The show looked like it had staying power. The reviews were good; but he was of the Guild, and his friends at the drama desk were expected to be forgiving. Still, leaving the hustle of Mad-hattan behind, he felt New York recede in the distance, and took a deep breath.

Harry shut down the motor and the boat shifted lazily on the water.

Off Broadway.

THEY REACHED their docking at about nine-thirty on Sunday morning, intending to take on more fuel and some tackle, as well as a sea captain to pilot them to a fishing point near Green Hill.

By 11:30, 140 gallons of high-test gasoline had been fed into the tanks, and Captain Samuel L. White had come aboard. Mark and Gladys were on the rear deck, arranging the fishing tackle. Then they moved to the bow for launch.

Inside the cabin were Virginia Biddle, Helen, Harry, and the captain. Virginia was Harry's girlfriend; the press described her as "Junoesque." Her flowing brunette hair and headscarf gave her a biblical air. Ziegfeld had forbidden her to cut her hair, which made her exotic enough to be one of the Polynesian dancers astride the elephant's tusks in the "Legend of the Islands" skit that opened Act Two. Her "stage mother" had brought her out of Kansas ("That's a state that God forgot") through Chicago where she'd met William Anthony McGuire, a playwright who wrote for Ziegfeld. He put her under contract and stage mother and stage daughter decamped to New York. She had opened at the Ziegfeld Theater with *Rio Rita* and had moved through *Show Boat* and *Smiles*.

Like most of the girls, she doubled at a nightclub after the show. At the Paradise Restaurant, in a display called "Goddesses of the Ages," Virginia assumed the role of Pocahontas, wearing a rhinestone harness with her braided hair roping down over her nipples, a G-string unconcealing a long stretch of leg. While Alfred Cheyney Johnson took her formal Ziegfeld portrait, her roseate areola peeking through a shawl, her mother sat just out of camera range. He posed her in profile.

Harry had stared at her head-on, sitting in the front row with Ziegfeld as the girls took their places to start the run-through. She could feel his eyes zero in, and Virginia felt flattered, especially when he asked her to Gallagher's for a steak between shows. Her mother approved; so long as Virginia turned her paycheck over to her at the end of the week, she could go anywhere she pleased.

Helen also was her mother's sole support, her dark-eyed piercing stare unsmiling and unsentimental in her portraits. She knew life wasn't the bowl of cherries Rudy Vallée kept sticking his spoon in. She had her mother's mortgage to worry about. Her father, a police lieutenant, had died several years earlier, and she and her sister Marion were the only thing keeping their family together. She tried her hand at business, but she didn't like stenography. Instead, she parlayed her looks into modeling for a Fifth Avenue department store. Marilyn Miller—the danseuse of the company—introduced her to Mr. Ziegfeld, and she'd been in the chorus almost four years now.

She was still unmarried, but she knew enough about the way things worked to figure that if a big magnate from the pictures wanted to take you out, it wasn't to talk about the pictures. They might all claim to be good eggs, but she wasn't about to sell herself short for a ring and a wristwatch. And she couldn't stay out late, because there was that hour trip back to Riverdale. She had bills to pay.

And a doctor to marry her. She was engaged. To a Dr. Michael Tettleman. A good Jewish boy, just like that Olive McLay in the chorus and her Mr. Lipschitz. What would her mother say when she heard about that! And Father Doyle across the street!

Gladys liked Helen, didn't feel she would upstage her or use her to get to the next social group, and began inviting her around. Mark was preoccupied, as were most writers, mentally taking notes and thinking up witty catchphrases; inscribing his life as he went along. She needed someone to talk to, and Helen was a good listener.

They were about to cast off. Virginia and Helen sat together, across the stern, over the motor. Virginia was doing her imitations, of Marilyn Miller holding her arms up in the air before she went on so the blood would rush out and they would appear whiter, or Old Man Ziegfeld, talking through his nose. Helen was laughing, still in her pajamas. Hellinger reached down to free the ropes. Harry checked the fuel gauge, punched the starter button.

Ignition. The spark of electrode as the plugs fire. Before the gas from the fuel tank has a chance to flare, the very vapor in the air explodes.

The cabin blows outward. The sudden blast of light creates a vacuum of incomprehension.

Virginia rises on a hand of hot air. She sees flames around her legs, smells singeing hair. No pain. Then the decking collapses from above.

Harry Richman is felled, momentarily stunned by the hatch cover falling on him. The captain is knocked over by a hurtling body; a woman. He feels a sharp pain in his left hand.

There are flames everywhere.

Hellinger rushes toward the cabin. A mattress blazes on the floor; he can hear muffled cries from under it. As he struggles to pull it off, still dazed, Richman comes lurching through the smoke. They pull the mattress off and see Helen Walsh lying there, her hair and torso on fire.

Richman, his suit smoking and smoldering, gathers her in his arms, bursts from the rear hatch and into the water. Levy leads Gladys Glad through a rear hatch and to the dock. Behind him limps Virginia Biddle, Hellinger helping her.

The captain, in shock, wanders toward his home, a fishhook protruding from between two knuckles. "Please take this out for me," he asks bystanders, who stare at him like some ghost who walks the seabed. Finally, he reaches over and extracts it himself, working out its barb as he would from the mouth of a bass.

Helen Walsh lies on the shore, cradled in the arms of a spectator, waiting for the ambulance and the last rites. "My face is my living," she moans, shudders, sobs.

"I hope it isn't burned."

A DAY later, only a few minutes before the curtain rises on the regular Monday night performance of the Follies, Helen Walsh succumbs to her injuries. She has gotten her wish—her face isn't burned—but she is in deep shock, and can hardly retain fluids. Though the doctors have tried to assure her that her wounds might not result in scarring, she hears the reassurance in their voices, as if they felt they had to skip mere assurance. And though she's no longer on fire, she can still feel the flames' inexorable crackle as her skin continues to scald, blister, infect from the inferno she's been through.

Nobody dares tell Harry.

Even without the *If-not-for-me*'s, he is feeling terrible. His arms and legs are bandaged under his tuxedo, and it hurts like hell when he fills his chest to reach the rear balconies. There are no microphones on Ziegfeld's stage.

At 8:30, the orchestra strikes up the fanfare, "Bring On the Follies Girls!" They prance out, dressed in pink organdy. If they were crying backstage, they hit the lights with brave smiles, at last the actresses they all aspired to be.

It's Harry's turn. His song is "Help Yourself to Happiness (and Happiness

Will See You Through)," a spirit-reviver if there ever was one. He bears up, well, manly. He doesn't know, and it's agreed in a hurried backstage huddle by Hellinger, Winchell, Ziegfeld assistant Gene Buck, and Ziegfeld himself that he mustn't, not yet. Every sweep of his arm brings the torrid scrape of burn to the surface; every deep breath he takes to rise to his tenor feels like a hammer to his ribs.

"How is Helen?" he keeps asking between his turns onstage, so often that it becomes like a chorus. *Hope she's feeling well-en-uf nooowww. . . .* He'd have to sing it to her when she got out of the hospital. He knew he hadn't turned on the fans to clear out the bilge, the gas of the gas from the tank displaced as they'd poured fresh fuel into the on-deck intakes slowly gathering in the lowest part of the boat, where Virginia and Helen sat on their ill-fated bench.

During the intermission, the audience pauses in its lobby stroll for an orangeade and a cigarette to listen to a newsboy shout out the blackened headline. The news goes no farther than the stage door. The entire cast comes out for a heartfelt reprise of "Happiness Will See You Through." Everyone sings along, wanting to believe in the power of homily.

Then, as they leave the stage, their smiles wink off, like the lights of Times Square on closing night.

IT WAS near dawn in the hospital room. Virginia Biddle lay awake, the residual simmer of her burns penetrating her dreams. She had been awakened two nights ago when Harry had shut down the engine and started the bilge pump; she could hear his voice talking to the chauffeur, and the boat gently swaying on the water.

Helen had slept next to her that night, and now she still slept, only she'd never wake up. The doctors had come in as the sun had flickered its last rays and the curtain came down around her bed. There was no final curtsy. Virginia knew she was still inside there, and wondered if it would be her turn next.

They'd tried to pump fluids into her and Helen, anything wet from water to iced champagne. Gladys even spooned it into Helen's dry lips, sip by painful sip, and was happy when she managed to keep it down. There was no intravenous, and Helen's kidneys couldn't handle the strain. It was just a country hospital, good for tonsillectomies and childbirth. Virginia had waited what seemed like hours on a gurney while they summoned a doctor to look at her.

Helen's doctor fiancé had come out to supervise, but by the time they realized her kidneys were failing, she was gone.

Virginia was badly burned, perhaps worse than Helen. Her lower torso was done to a turn, the muscles exposed on her rounded bottom, the Achilles tendon of her right foot seared raw. She had posed semi-nude, and now she'd gone one step further. Skinless. Third degree.

It could have been me, she thought. That was fate. The change of a place, left instead of right, and it would be her lying behind the closed curtain, in the ultimate wings. She'd never go on to Hollywood, where she would dub her tap rhythms to the stars on-screen and have a walk-on in the credits of a Cecil B. DeMille film, only to return to New York and the Paradise, where she'd be fired after a girl snitched that she was newly married to Bob, and move to Long Island, get divorced, relocate up along the Atlantic shore of Connecticut where she and her second husband, Bill, would raise horses and go boating and sell real estate and her son would die of alcoholism and her daughter would be a nurse and she would turn on the television Tuesday nights at 8:30 for Dr. Jim and Rexella Van Impe's interpretations of the Book of Daniel, reading his prophecies on Belshazzar's wall and his vision of the four beasts and the raptured believers and the furnace of Nebuchadnezzar. It gave her faith.

VIRGINIA BIDDLE-BULKLEY,
2000

She lay there until Gene Buck came to see her in the late morning. She called him Ziegfeld's "girl Friday." "What's over there?" he asked.

"That's Helen," answered Virginia. "Helen's body is still here."

"Overnight!" sputtered Buck. "They've left her body in here with you overnight?"

He had a fit. Then he stormed out of the room, determined to raise Hell-en.

BING

He has beaten Bing to the radio. Bingo.

Russ hears the hubbub from the Ziegfeld across the street as he gets into his cab at the hotel with Con. They're on their way to the WJZ studio, where he makes his debut tonight at midnight, 760 on the dial. The cusp. It's hard to tell whether he'll be the last thing you hear on Monday, July 27, or the first when Tuesday the 28th kicks off. Poised between yesterday and tomorrow; foot on the running board, he grips the handle and nervously pulls at the door. It opens suicide-style, counterclockwise.

Russ is no stranger to the radio. Arnheim had broadcast a few times a week from the Cocoanut Grove, and Columbo even duetted with Crosby over the airwaves; but this is his own show. "Songs," it says simply after his name in the *News*. And Orchestra. Also, the Blue Rhythm Boys. The same edition had been plastered with news of Richman's yacht fire. As he leaves the Warwick lobby, he glimpses the updated one-star headline of next morning's paper. FOLLIES GIRL DIES. He feels a sharp pang. He wondered how Dorothy was taking the news, now that the worst had come to pass. He'd called as soon as he'd heard about the explosion, and she'd said she didn't know how the Follies could go on tonight, but they were all troupers and that's the way Helen and Virginia would've wanted it and could you believe that Mark was such a hero he's usually so reserved even though he must have something for that Gladys Glad to see in him and poor Helen. . . .

Relieved she was safe, Russ disengaged from her pleasant enough twitter and, amid thoughts of her nesting bosom, returned to his own immediate upcoming concerns. He wondered if everybody would be so grief-stricken that they couldn't bear to tune the dial before they went to sleep, or maybe it would work the other way, they'd need a return to life's eternal medley as he sang them toward slumber. They'd fall asleep to the radio, and he would merge with their dreams. Perhaps some bon vivant would turn the radio on for an after-hours soirée along the Upper East Side, or a restless construction worker would get up for a late snack in a Jackson Heights railroad flat. A first-generation immigrant family from the Bronx could eavesdrop at the radio as it crossed the air shaft, amazed that they were really living in America, a short hop to the Grand Concourse. Russ could imagine the signal skipping along its assigned frequency out into New Jersey and up to Connecticut, and who knows where else if the cloud cover parted his way.

Bing was on *his* way. But Bing wouldn't be able to get on the air till the end of the month. Maybe a bit later, given his troubles with the Musician's Union in California. That would allow Russ the full four weeks to prove himself to NBC's Blue Network, a radio star in the newfound firmament.

He knew Bing. All too well. "Binge," they used to call him when he didn't show up. Russ had observed him from a violin chair at the Cocoanut Grove, and heard about him years before, when he was just a gawky kid from Washington State; Spokane, queen city of the Inland Empire.

There was a dryness to him; maybe it was why he liked to drink. Spokane was practically desert anyway, a spud's throw from Idaho.

He was clever, Russ gave Bing that. There was a tensile determination behind his glide. He made it look effortless, casual, a downshifting into character. But you couldn't let it fool you. As Bing unwound, his unsprung delivery spiraled like a reverse phonograph horn, homing in on the note's flow as it moved one interval to another, lyric enunciated low in the chest, then high up behind the nose, voice spouting into the microphone's vibrating diaphragm. Lung to lung. He kept the melody in perfect flight, an aviator moving through slipstreams of wind, like a golf ball slicing the air currents, and pretty soon he would find that his affable way with his public allowed him more time with his not-so-secret passion, the wood and the nine iron.

In 1931, Bing was still a long pilgrimage from the universal Father Chuck O'Malley of *Going My Way*. "*Would you like to swing on a star*," he'd ask then, the swing era already peaking in World War II's midst. Bing would be ready for anything. He could sing the "Ave Maria" with eyes arched and the submissed gaze of a crooner, and still knock the dimpled ball out of the sand trap for a double eagle in a match with his Fatherly Superior. Rebuild the holy church. Restore love and honor to a needy world. He'd re-create that

role in *The Bells of St. Mary's,* where Ingrid Bergman played Mary Magdalene to his White Christmas.

Sometimes, Russ wondered, the real miracle was that he was able to put
that twaddle over on people.

He'd seen flashes of the hidden Bing, the steel gates that shut down over
his eyes when his anger flashed. Crosby could be comforting, but he liked
things just so. Though the studio regarded it a stretch for a musical star to play
a priest, the role fit him well, as if he was born to the moral strictures of the
tight white collar. He could take your confession, prescribe penance, lay the
wafer lightly on the tongue.

But that was later, when his iconic stature in American song was con-
firmed. In 1931, Bing was a heartthrob, a sensual being, pale water-blue eyes
and bedroom lashes. A crooner.

WHAT IS this thing called Bing?

He's genteel. Gentle. Gentile. There is a fragility to him, as if a shout
would suddenly crack and shatter his body. But he doesn't have to holler. He
knows the air waves, how to swim them.

He bobs with the riptides, beats the sea at its own game. He can float on top
of the melody, hear the instruments in back of him and choose which notes
and phrasing he'll borrow from the bassoon, the chording guitar, the tenor in
the backing quartet. Which note on the piano. Which drum accent. He has
them all stashed in the back of his neck.

Bing doesn't really play an instrument, nor does he read music. There are
pictures of him holding a ukulele and whisking a single cymbal with a fly-
swatter in the Rhythm Boys, accenting and punctuating between the twin
white upright pianos of Harry Barris and Al Rinker. He'd been a drummer in
Spokane, cutting up at the Gonzaga U. dances; but when he and Rinker set
out in a "beat-up jalopy" (a folk-lyric totem) for Los Angeles and Rinker's sister, Mildred Bailey, who would introduce them around, he'd placed the
rhythm in his vocal cords the way you'd pack a suitcase, filling in the nooks
and corners with socks, or an extra undershirt. He didn't want to provide the
rhythm; he wanted to wear it.

He had jazz to inspire and point him. Washed out of New Orleans like a
Mississippi flood in the early 1920s, spreading over the alluvial plains of pop
music, "Dixieland" whitened almost immediately, even as it cast a mahogany
stain. Edmond Souchon, M.D., remembered seeing King Oliver at Tulane
University in the years between 1913 and 1917 and being disappointed that

his style was already "much more smooth, and that his band was adapting it-self to the white dancers. . . . At 'Big 25' [a brothel in the Storyville district], it was hard-hitting, rough and ready, full of fire and drive . . . he subdued this to please the different patrons of the gym. . . . It was still very great music, but something in the inner feeling of the band was shaking itself loose from the roots from which it had sprung." Transmittal was inevitable, with technology shortening all distances, making things instantaneous. It worked both ways, changing those on the receiving end, and then converting the very things transmitted. The barter system.

Harry Lillis Crosby set out to make his fortune on October 15, 1925, when he was twenty-two, accompanied (one might say arranged) by Alton Rinker. He acquired the nickname "Bing" after a cartoon character, and the sound-effect moniker suited him. Al, five years his junior, had played with Crosby in a collegiate dance band called the Musicaladers, and when that dissolved, they crossed the Cascades to Seattle, where they tried out their act at the But-ler Hotel. Wandering southward along the coast until their flivver finally overheated and ran out of gas on a ridge overlooking the promised land, Los Angeles, they hiked the last mile and a half into town, or so Bing embroidered the tale in later years. Mildred got them an audition with a booker for Fan-chon and Marco. He hired them for a vaudeville variety show called *The Syncopated Idea*, touring California, a harmonic comedic duo.

"Two Boys and a Piano" was how they were billed. After thirteen weeks on the road, they returned to Los Angeles and spent most of 1926 honing their act. Will Morrisey's Music Hall Revue gave them $150 a week and sent them to San Diego and San Francisco, as well as featuring them at the popular Or-ange Grove in downtown Los Angeles. Joe Partington of Publix-Paramount caught them at the Grove and booked them into the Metropolitan, a large-scale vaudeville theater where their growing reputation caused Paul White-man to send a couple of band members over to see what the fuss was about. He offered to double their salary and give them a spot in his orchestra, at that time as immense a presence in American music as the avuncular violinist himself.

Bing went to work for Whiteman, the so-called King of Jazz, as part of what would become the Rhythm Boys. Was there ever a cartoon caricature as per-fect a mythos as this? Paul is hardly recalled today except as a savvy em-ployer—yet he had a sense of commercial adventurism, and being the King, he didn't have to do much but sit on his throne anyway. He had the luxury of being able to choose the best of a new breed. Anyone who would put Bix Bei-derbecke and George Gershwin (premiering *Rhapsody in Blue* in 1924, eventually Whiteman's theme) and Ferde Grofé and Eddie Lang and the Dorsey Brothers and Red Nichols on his ample payroll—has to be a good judge of musical character. The Whiteman Orchestra was large enough to encompass all types of music. More, all it took was a Bix to step to the front with a solo and the sound took on the permeation of Bix; the tinge could seem more jazz than Whiteman really was, guilt by association.

Musicians—inquisitive creatures that they are—were extremely intrigued by the challenge of a suddenly absorbing new approach. Once, musics had stayed within their regions for a long time, incubating, inbreeding; now they could travel easily and quickly, causing sudden brush fires. Everywhere the musicians of the 1920s listened to themselves in flux. New Orleans came to Chicago and moved to New York and headed for the Coast, with stops in Milwaukee and Des Moines along the way. When the Whiteman band caravaned through city after city, Bing in tow, the musicians went out and listened to the best in town; and as the rhythms they heard got slipperier and slicker, the harmonies more subtle, it broke apart the conventions of turn-of-the-century phrasing.

Nowhere was this more apparent than in the style of scat, which vocally slid away from lyrics themselves to approximate the attack and motivations of instruments. From talking drum to singing drum set, Dixieland's endless embellishments on themes opened the way to the primacy of the soloist and the hierarchy of the singer.

Louis Armstrong, and the long shadow of his Hot Five and Hot Seven of 1925–28, is usually sited as ground zero, his "Heebie Jeebies," cut on February 16, 1926, as the first popularly recorded scat. Louis claimed to have dropped his lyric sheet on the floor during the take, improvising his voice as he would a horn solo. But used to framing his solos with his expansive embouchure ("Satchelmouth," they hail him, on the way to "Satchmo"), singing lines to the band in rehearsal, playing air horn as he walks down the street, he is no stranger to pouring himself through the twisting passageways of hammered brass. The casual spontaneity of "Heebie Jeebies" itself—the lyrics are hardly more than guttural growl with a few catchphrases thrown in, while the music is fairly well developed, lending credence to the surmise that it was probably an unfinished title concept—sparked improvisation. Armstrong doesn't mind. The band is having a ball, and he's enjoying his run as leader.

All he has to do is say "Heebie Jeebies" every so often and then his voice be *heebeegeebeed*, the scat so natural that it grows upon the second verse unawares. Part of the section's success, the one who makes it seem as if it's surely a planned part of the song, is banjoist Johnny St. Cyr, who unrolls the bass movement of his chords like a red carpet under Armstrong's strutting feet. The rest of the band discreetly drops away. Armstrong and St. Cyr kick up their heels, Heebie and Jeebie, like a pair of "spasm" youngsters on the tattered street corner of Perdido and Liberty. On this second song of a session (they would yield six sides that day) that would reverberate throughout popular music, you can hear just how loose these Hot Five are, savoring their moment in time's flow when future history passes through their musicality on its way to incalculable influence. They don't notice because they're too busy goosing themselves on the ending. Lil Hardin hits a piano chord twice. Kid Ory leaps in with "I got the heebie-jeebies." Lil hits it again. Louis gravels "Well, *I* got to have the heebie jeebies." Hey, they're catching!

THE WORDLESS song, the confined definitions of scant language as it gives way to music. Why should the voice be held back when there is so much more to say?

Cliff Edwards, known theatrically as Ukulele Ike, was *"eefin"* (as he called his wordless singing in 1923, when it shows up on his first record for Pathé, "Old Fashioned Love"). He refines it through a 1924 version of Gershwin's "Fascinating Rhythm," though there's always the feeling that he's using the scat for comic effect rather than emotion that can't be semantically described. Edwards learned his riffage accompanying the silent movies, adding vocals to his stock of sound effects; when he sings a chase chorus, trading licks with Red Nichols's cornet ("Dinah") and Adrian Rollini's bass saxophone ("I Don't Want Nobody But You"), it's one step removed from the Keystone Kops careening through a busy intersection.

Bing, as a kid, is incessantly humming and whistling as he goes about his errands on the streets of Spokane. It's only likely he would add instrumental breaks. When he performed with Rinker, Crosby aimed a kazoo into a coffee can, using it for a "wah" effect, much as a trumpeter might employ a mute. He was ready to take a solo.

The scat enjoyed quite a vogue as the twenties ended. Even the relatively straitlaced Ruth Etting got in on the act in 1928, humming answering phrases to a Hawaiian guitarist in "Happy Days, Lonely Nights." It would reach rococo heights within the work of Leo Watson, a late-thirties eccentric whose vocal streams approximated Joycean free association and mood swings (swinging mood?), quoting nursery rhymes and completely different songs in his solos with an errant logic. Before he found a temporary home with Slim

Gaillard, another who bent language to his will ("*Vout*" in flat-foot-floogie di-alect), Leo was known for marathon drum solos, which might be why Gene Krupa took him on for eight months, before Watson was involved in a train brawl and tossed off the road. He was scat's farthest orbit; from there the good-humored bounce of Ella Fitzgerald and Mel Tormé's more composed scat seem almost comfortingly familiar modes of musical vocabulary.

The Mills Brothers went all the way. They wore the mask of instrument so well that a casual listener would not suspect anything out of the ordinary in their musical backing. A disclaimer—"No musical instruments or mechani-cal devices used on this recording other than one guitar"—invited skepti-cism, but the Mills Brothers always approached their impersonations without showy effect. Actually, as a band, they might've been a little dull. No matter. On their October 1931 recordings of "Nobody's Sweetheart" and "Tiger Rag," the tongue-twisting scat is displaced by a trumpet solo played on the mouth alone. They were like a well-tuned horn section: John on tuba, Harry and Herbert on trumpets, Donald on trombone; and they could add saxes, clarinets, and oboes as needed. Their essentially barbershop harmony (the boys' father, John Senior, even owned a barbershop), with bass and tenor par-alleling the lead, baritone crisscrossing the melody, would find its measure in the rhythmic nonsensical syllables of doo-wop background vocals.

There will be time enough to go solo. Under Whiteman's wing, Bing is part of a harmony group, where the dictates of precision require musical clockwork. You are the part next to you. To really float free, there has to be a greater separation between accompaniment and soloist; right now the em-phasis is still on ensemble.

Whiteman hires Crosby and Rinker more to supplement his chorus than as entertainers on their own. His vision is symphonic. Since there's no such thing as a singer who doesn't do anything else, Whiteman fixes Bing and Al up with fake instruments to hold while they're waiting their turn. Bing gets a Peck horn with the mouthpiece removed, and a violin with rubber strings. No wonder he craves a drink.

AL AND Bing stopped in Spokane before joining Whiteman at Chicago's Tivoli Theater on December 15, 1926. While their hometown received them as conquering heroes during their Liberty Theater engagement over Thanks-giving, they were less certain of their place in Whiteman's grand circus. Whiteman put them at ease by introducing them as two sprouts he'd met in an ice cream parlor in Walla Walla, a town whose name was a horn lick itself, and gave them a showcase spot. Rinker and Crosby passed the test of their first Midwest shows with distinction, and saw their breadth of jazz enlightened when they caught Armstrong at the Sunset Cafe, playing with Carroll Dickerson's Orchestra. Then it was on to St. Louis, Cleveland, Youngstown, Indianapolis.

Their dreams of instant gravy train derailed when they opened at New York's Paramount Theater in January (itself a relative newcomer, a venue only since the previous April). Audiences used to the *bonhomie* of a Jolson, who "delivered" a song instead of intimating it, hardly reacted to Al and Bing's vocal one-upmanship, and their comedy was corny to Broadway audiences who had heard every joke yet invented. Chastened, they slid down the ladder of Whiteman's regard, reduced to playing intermissions in the lobby of the block-long nightclub he hosted on Broadway and Forty-eighth Street, in what was once the Cinderella Ballroom. Two boys and a pumpkin. Midnight tolled, their fairy tale over, Rinker and Crosby found themselves exiled to the backstage crew, reduced to hauling the stage curtain up and down, having come so far so quickly and now in danger of being sent home with their tale between their legs.

Luckily, George Barris was also waiting on the fringes of the Whiteman organization. He'd studied music at East Denver High School with Whiteman's father, Wilberforce, and had been in a dance band with Whiteman violinist Matty Melneck (as well as Glenn Miller and Ted "Amateur Hour" Mack). On the road as a professional musician since he was seventeen, he had toured as far afield as Japan and China, inspiring his first penned song, "Hong Kong Dream Girl."

He stuck to the geographic with "Mississippi Mud." Its rollicking Dixie cakewalk, auditioned for Bing and Al in the lobby of the Belvedere, became the clay of the Rhythm Boys. Barris was brash, energetic, a snappy dresser. If Rinker was the bones and Bing the flesh and muscle, Barris was the lifeblood. And he could write a helluva song.

"Mississippi Mud"—and by extension the Rhythm Boys—was such a hit with audiences that it was cut three times by Bing and Co. On January 20, 1928, for Okeh, Crosby exchanged minstrel repartée with Frankie Trumbauer and His Orchestra, a Whiteman subgrouping that included Bix Beiderbecke on cornet, guitarist Carl Kress, and Frankie on the C melody saxophone, one of the few jazz musicians to use this daredevil tuning. He would later give up music to become a test pilot. Bing sounds a bit hoarse, but his loose-limbed performance far outstrips the Whiteman official version for Victor, cut on February 18, where, except for a few scattered scats, the

Rhythm Boys and Bix are relegated to second-class status. The instrumental solo goes to clarinetist Irving "Izzy" Friedman, while the lead vocal is taken over by thrush Irene Taylor, who sounds as if she's trying to fit a square peg into the song's round voice box.

On their own version, recorded six months earlier and released the previous fall, "Paul Whiteman's Rhythm Boys" couldn't be starker. Their three voices and Barris's barrelhouse piano incorporate the song into a medley that approximates their live show. "Mississippi Mud" is coupled with "I Left My Sugar in the Rain," while the flip segues "Sweet Li'l" into "Ain't She Sweet." They try it three times on that third Monday in June (Whiteman likes to record every couple of weeks while he's in New York, usually using Liederkranz Hall in Manhattan instead of the Victor studios; his orchestra needs room to breathe). The first take is destroyed, the second is a professional, not-quite-there rendition marked "Hold conditional." Three's the charm, as it should be for a trio.

When the darkies beat their feet on the Mississippi Mud. Whiteman saw in Bing the black innuendo, the vocal jazz. One of the first numbers he recorded with Rinker and Barris on the 29th of April, 1927, even before they are officially dubbed Rhythm Boys, is "I'm Coming, Virginia," with its minstrel slang (*"Virginny"* rhymed with *"agin' me"*), and bright *"southern moon, once more I'll croon, that dear ole mammy tune . . . my Dixieland home."* Whiteman gave Crosby a lead chorus on a surprisingly jaunty "Ol' Man River" on January 11, 1928, as if to take advantage of Bing's southern-simmered phrasing, allowing a sepia tinge to enter a twenty-two-piece band that had to remain segregated in order to work. It would be another ten years before the border between black and white musicians would become a two-way street (a thoroughfare still routed through rough neighborhoods), but now it's just a matter of when. There's too much cross-reference in and on the air. When the Broadway shows finish up, the Rhythm Boys head uptown to Harlem and the Cotton Club, stomping grounds of Duke Ellington, Cab Calloway, Ethel Waters. Bing has insinuated the melismata of jazz in his voice; it unsettles him enough that he is prone to sudden fits of lost control, when the alcohol suddenly takes on a life of its own, when he wonders why he has been chosen the messenger of this new way of speaking in tongues.

Bing is color-blind, both in actual fact and in musicality. Whiteman solos him early with a March 7, 1927, recording of "Muddy Water," and the rich brown sediment rises to the surface. By 1931, Bing will join voices with the Mills Brothers in a rendition of "Dinah," then the 1932 racially entendre'd "Shine," which takes "curly hair" and bootblack shading into the realm of syllable-tumbling scat, Bing easily infiltrating and integrating the Millses' horn lineup.

Crosby will participate in more than a hundred sides under Whiteman's supervision in his first three and a half years of recording. Some are with the Rhythm Boys, but at other times he's part of a male chorus, or on his own. His and Rinker's first record for Whiteman, recorded in Chicago a mere week after they arrive near Christmas, 1926, is "Wistful and Blue," which Bing calls "a vocal without words." By the time he makes his last record for White-man on May 23, 1930 (a Rhythm Boys take of "A Bench in the Park"), the recording studio is no stranger to him. He is one of the first singers not to have to rely on projecting his voice as did the artists of the acoustic era. He always has the microphone, and he uses it to develop "a sound which resembled the human voice with a bubble in it." *Boo-boo-boo* to you.

ON NOVEMBER 10, 1928, Paul Whiteman's Rhythm Boys cut a scat-ridden "My Suppressed Desire" for Okeh. When they break into actual lyrics, it takes a while to decipher the rapid-fire syllables, so used is the ear to hearing them as sound particles, lapsed into a foreign accent.

Bing knew of suppressed desire, and the causal urge to cut loose. He respected those who wielded authority, whether it was the Jesuits' Father Sharp ("a stern disciplinarian but a fair Joe," notes Bing in his autobiography, *Call Me Lucky*), or Father Kennelly ("the prefect of discipline . . . his discipliner . . . a key chain ten or twelve feet long, with a bunch of keys on it. He kept this weapon coiled up under his cassock"), or Mother ("our family disciplinarian. The small Crosbys got a healthy amount of corporal punishment. . . ."). Even the principal at Webster, his grade school, bends him over a chair and lets him "have a few" with a yardstick. Bing shrugs it off; he's irrepressible, no stranger to stricture.

"Youthful indiscretion" is how it's usually described, but for Bing it's more self-discovery. He's got a wild streak, no doubt about that, and likes—needs—to let loose, to "have a few." It hardly matters that this is Prohibition. But he doesn't want to streak like a meteor across the sky and be gone, flaming the Roman candle at both ends. He can already see Bix doing that during the time they spend together with Whiteman, never sleeping, hitting the bottle until it knocks him unconscious.

He becomes more-than-friendly with promising starlet Dixie Lee when the Rhythm Boys are resident at the Montmartre, a second floor dining-and-dancing café that overlooks Hollywood Boulevard, in 1930. The winner of a

Ruth Etting sound-alike contest in Chicago when she was seventeen after having been raised in New Orleans (she shared the same migrations as jazz), Dixie (once Wilma Winifred Wyatt) had been signed to Fox and was working her way up through the studio system. She had parts in several movies as the twenties ended, starting with Fox's *Movietone Follies of 1929* and proceeding through such paeans to optimism as *Happy Days* (Con Conrad wrote the music), *Cheer Up and Smile, Let's Go Places,* and *Why Leave Home?* At this point, she was probably better known than Bing, at least in movie circles, and his unpredictable reputation caused consternation in both William Fox and her father. Dixie Lee's womanly wile recognized Bing's awaiting possibilities; her overwhelming stage fright stood in the way of her own. She was willing to give up her career for his.

But she wasn't about to stand for his drinking. He was married to her, not to alcohol. He had sung "I Surrender, Dear" by way of proposal, the song written by Barris and lyricist Gordon Clifford: *"To you my love, my life, my all . . ."* She answered, cryptically, "Darling, I'm lost." They kept their wedding plans secret until the end of September 1930, then showed up practically unannounced (her mom was kept in the dark till the morning of the wedding) at the Church of the Blessed Sacrament in Hollywood. Six months into the marriage, she'd had to lay down the law—her or the booze—and to prove she meant business, packed up and left him at their Cromwell Avenue home in Los Feliz, surfacing in Agua Caliente, Mexico, a gambling town across the border from San Diego where Bing had passed many an overlong weekend. Good for the goose. He pleaded with her by phone. She reminded him of the time he'd passed out speaking to her long-distance from New York, the receiver still clutched to his ear in the Belvedere Hotel room he shared with Frank Trumbauer, asleep to the tune of $130. This memory from early in their courtship made her love him even more, forgiving to his entreaties, and she finally relented. He promised to put a lid on his drinking, and he did. For a while.

What was unusual was that he never forgot the lessons inebriation taught him about a lyric, to stretch the angle of lean, teetering the way a drunk might walking down a street, a rush of steps and a lurch, balancing precariously, miraculously reaching his destination. Still upright. His voice took liberties, had a boldness that came with Dutch courage. Still, Bing was anxious to avoid the next-morning hangover. He had to be on a film set by half past six. The Ambassador nightly. Recording sessions. He couldn't fuck up now.

So he tightened himself, padlocked his gnawing demons inside his gut, hid the key up his ass; but since his singing conveyed an insouciance, an ease and flutter that was his short-stroke vibrato, he had to catch himself somewhere. Keep a tight grip while maintaining intensive relaxation. The body pulling in two ways at once; lacing the fingers and interlocking thumbs, axis of the spine straight, the swing and follow-through. The pinpoint concentration of striking the orb just so, on the concentric, propelled in the half-circle of flight, the verse of the fairway and the chorus of the green.

Bing's fore play.

THE RHYTHM BOYS performed in the shadow of "Pops" Whiteman. Even when he sent them on their own tour to upper Midwest and eastern vaudeville houses during the remainder of 1928, they were introduced by a life-size cardboard cutout of his egg-shape, along with a recorded announcement welcoming the audience to see "my Rhythm Boys." My, my.

Like young'uns, they misbehaved, stopping songs to walk into the audience for a comic mind-reading act, spoofing tap dancing, at times letting Whiteman know they were too good to be let go because of a tale of drunken revelry reported by an irate theater manager. Whiteman understood what he had, and by 1928–29 he had a first-class dance band, if not hot then slightly warmer than luke, especially when guitarist Eddie Lang and violinist Joe Venuti joined his string section. He knew hijinks, and he knew musicians needed to blow off steam. Lang had his pool playing; Crosby liked to golf and get loaded. Usually, he kept his band working so hard that no one had time for drinking to get out of hand. He'd have to watch these Rhythm Boys, but right now he kept them well booked and in the studio, and out of trouble.

The frequent recordings of the Rhythm Boys not only gained them nationwide exposure, but, added to the radio show that Old Gold cigarettes had finally enticed Whiteman to do, were about to reach untold numbers of potential record buyers. He had initially resisted the wireless, having had a million-selling record in 1920 ("Whispering") before radio had gotten out of the crystal-set stage. Whiteman worried that it would cut into his personal appearances and record sales, but radio seemed to have the opposite effect, and it sure hadn't hurt that squirt Vallée and his Connecticut Yank-Its over at the Heigh-Ho Club.

You can't mess with the modern. Recorded in Chicago on November 11, 1927, "That's Grandma" plunks the Rhythm Boys' elder generation into a world of flappers, Peggy Joyce, and rapid-fire "celebrity" impressions of Eddie Cantor and the two Black Crows, Moran and Mack: "*She does a Lindbergh in the sky.*" It's more a showcase for Rinker and Barris's fancy repartéeing than

Bing's vocal and cymbal interjections, Crosby hardly getting a word in edge-wise. This is not his specialty, though he has a wry flair for the comic. Yet when the trio join their own band, for a wah'd and scatted final chorus, you can hear the Rhythm Boys going over with a bang as they embark on their RKO circuit travels through Ohio, Michigan, Wisconsin, Minnesota, Illinois, and Iowa.

On March 14, 1929, Bing records the first tunes that will be issued under his own name by Columbia. Backed by a small trio to save on recording costs (Rube Bloom on piano, violinist Venuti, and either Kress or Lang on guitar), "My Kinda Love" captures Bing at his most tremulous, fluttering the words while Venuti matches him vibrato for vibrato, lunging forward into a jazzed-up second chorus before settling into the outstretched arms of the finale. The flip, "Till We Meet," is similarly casual, and though neither side is a hit, the two songs give an indication of Bing's bag o' tricks, the rush and retard, the easy movement between tenor and baritone vocalese, how well his voice mingles with his accompanying instruments.

If he seems to be pushing his vocal to its outré limit, it's because he's used to Whiteman's full orchestra backing him, or maybe he's just eager to prove himself on his own. The next day, March 15, he's called back to the studio for an orchestral version of Leo Robin's "Louise," and back in his accustomed role, he sees to his chorus and gets out of the way. Whiteman's crisp tempo makes Bing's spot more like an elocution contest, the diction of the debating society, one of those epic poems like E. Kellogg's "Spartacus to the Gladiators at Capua" — "Ay! Thou hast given to that poor, gentle, timid shepherd lad, who never knew a harsher tone than a flute-note, muscles of iron and a heart of flint; taught him to drive the sword through plaited mail and links of rugged brass, and warm it in the marrow of his foe; — to gaze into the glaring eyeballs of the fierce Numidian lion, even as a boy upon a laughing girl!" — that the young Bing memorized and recited in grammar school. (The microphone will even change oratory; gone are the flamboyant politicians of Bryan's "Cross of Gold" era, speech-givers grandly gesturing to massive throngs. They will be replaced by the radiated intimacy of FDR's Fireside Chats, and the self-conscious reaction shots of close-up television.)

A month later, on April 10, the Rhythm Boys cut their own version, which begins virtually a cappella, amid some novelty dialogue. Cue ringing phone: "You want to speak to Bing? Oh, we're making a record. . . . " "Wonder who would be calling me when I'm recording? Hello, hello. . . . Oh, it's Louise. Oh, well, that's different." It certainly is. Bing introduces the verse, and then the trio "help him out" with the chorus, impeccably stacked, in blended bemoan, until "the boys" get "awfully hot" and break into a couple of energetic scatting bars. "Hold the wire, Louise," Bing says to his caller. "I don't think the song should be sung like this." Bing reins it in, wandering off on his own with Rinker's piano trailing him, but even he can't resist joining a high-energy scat as the chorus comes flying around. She hangs up. "Don't worry, Bing," Al and Harry advise him. "There's girls everywhere." By making him the romantic star of the skit, calling him by name, the Rhythm Boys acknowledge their internal hierarchy, the pack order that is their three's-a-crowd camaraderie. Bing is the odd man out.

Things started to break apart when Whiteman took his band out to Los Angeles in June 1929. Carl Laemmle of Universal had signed him to make *The King of Jazz*, but the original plot put "Pops" in the role of romantic lead, which Whiteman—never one to overestimate his sex appeal—found preposterous. Though the studio footed the salaries for the musicians, there was nothing to do until a new script was delivered, and only so many sound tests they could run through for the Hollywood technicians, who seemed to be learning on the job and took it far too seriously for Whiteman, who knew full well how to balance his band. The Old Gold show was once a week, and that was a Tuesday. Most of the musicians immediately bought Model A's (the Af-*Ford*able car) and set about exploring Hollywood nightlife. Actually, the stag-party atmosphere had begun on the chartered train ride to L.A., twelve days and sixteen cities, an Old Gold special hired to transport the Whiteman band, Paul's auto, eight coaches of musicians, a dining car, and a club car. Transcontinental!

With days of golf and nights of hooch, the Rhythm Boys were in full swing. Filming had hardly begun in November 1929 when Bing was involved in an auto accident in front of the Hotel Roosevelt, arrested for HBD (Having Been Drinking) and tossed in the Lincoln Heights jail for forty days. Whiteman was so peeved that he took Crosby's solo in the film away and gave it to John Boles. Bing was relegated to sharing "A Bench in the Park" with the Rhythm Boys and the Brox Sisters, and a short run-through of "Mississippi Mud" with the Boys seen in silhouette behind a screen.

Bing felt he deserved better. They were already beginning to single him from the Rhythm Boys. When they appeared at the Montmartre, hired by Eddie Brandstatter while waiting for the movie's script to be finalized, he could see the excitement he created in the collegians who swarmed up from UCLA and USC. Crosby made the rounds of the studios, testing, but his jug ears and wiry disposition were not conducive to a winning first impression. The responses weren't encouraging.

BING CROSBY

This didn't mean he was out of options. He could sing, and after seeing Jolson's triumph in *The Jazz Singer* in October 1927—again, hardly jazz, but an important racial signifier of aspiration, as well as the first cinematic musical—Bing knew he could be next in line. He would always claim Al as his greatest influence, and recount a time when Jolson came to Spokane to appear at the Auditorium in *Bombo* (Bing mostly remembered Jolson rushing offstage to count the take in the box office). Crosby may have tried to sing like Jolson, but his influence on Bing is as much reactive as emulative; Crosby is like a child who moves against the grain of his parent. Where Jolson employs the sweeping gesture, the broad stroke, Bing plays it down, close to the vest, making his listeners draw closer, to concentrate on the slippage of the melody, its slur and slide.

He is the next step in minstrel tradition, the first singer who can absorb characteristics of the opposing race and not have to wear blackface, as important a bridge from his starting point as jazz, which, in the persona of Louis Armstrong, meets white pop halfway in its journey from The District. Even as Armstrong emerges as a solo voice from the Hot Five, not willing to be hemmed in by the conventions of Dixieland, so Crosby moves beyond the Rhythm Boys, with a certainty of destiny. He will transfigure popular song; but first he has to get out of his contract with Whiteman.

IN THE end, it's not as hard as it would seem. Whiteman, having returned to New York while Universal tinkered with their script, is on his way back to Hollywood in October 1929 when the stock market goes into convulsions. They arrive at L.A.'s Central Station the day after the crash.

Though *The King of Jazz* is considered a success, taking in more than $100,000 in its first week at the Roxy in May 1930, the second week slips to $62,000, even with George Gershwin appearing onstage with the Whiteman Orchestra, playing the piano part of his *Rhapsody in Blue*. Times are already getting tough. The Old Gold sponsorship is canceled, and Whiteman band manager Jimmy Gillespie gives notice to ten members, offering a salary decrease of 15 percent to those remaining. Remembering their success at the Montmartre, the Rhythm Boys are convinced they have better opportunities on the Coast, and are starting to feel the pinch of Pops's paternalism. In March, a few days after what would be the group's final recording session released under the Whiteman Orchestra banner, reprising some of the tunes from *The King of Jazz* (including "A Bench in the Park" and Bing backing up Boles on "Song of the Dawn," which still rankled), insult was added to injury when Crosby was offered a singing part in a Paramount film, *Honey,* recommended by songwriter Sam Coslow. Whiteman refused to release him from his touring duties. The matter was taken up with Whiteman on a northwest tour in April (Bing would later claim Whiteman had fired him and the Rhythm Boys in Seattle over a dispute about bootleg liquor), but the trio accompanied the orchestra to New York for the premiere. The pay cut was the breaking point, and Bing was broke anyway.

By June, the Rhythm Boys knew they had made the right decision. Back in L.A., they filmed a two-reeler for Pathé, *Two Plus Fours,* and on the 27th, at 8:30 P.M., debuted over KFI radio in a show sponsored by the Union Oil Company. On July 15, they made a grand entrance at the Hotel Ambassador's Cocoanut Grove with Gus Arnheim's Orchestra, broadcast each evening over KNX in the hand-holding hours between 10:00 P.M. and midnight. The Rhythm Boys had come into their own.

Or had they? It's Bing who's drawing the crowds, stealing the show, even getting a speaking part (well, a line — "*Hi, gang!*") in *Reaching for the Moon,* with Douglas Fairbanks, Sr., and Bebe Daniels.

Harry Barris is also on the rise. Always as much songwriter as performer, after three years Barris is attuned to the sway of Bing's phrasing. He composes some of his best melodies with Crosby's developing "cry" in mind, including "It Must Be True," which is Arnheim's first recorded featuring of Bing on October 29. The Rhythm Boys are given a lightweight "Them There Eyes" in November (it sounds retrospective, an old-fashioned two-step that will be their last disc together), and then it's all Crosby. Barris's "I Surrender, Dear," written with Gordon Clifford and recorded on January 19, 1931, dramatically arranged by Jimmie Grier in willful tempo changes and dramatic upsurges, gives Bing his showcase, as Dixie's acquiescence demonstrates. It is his most requested number at the Grove, and the more whispery and husky he gets as the night wears on, the more the crowds cluster around the bandstand, listening to his voice weave and transverse emotions.

He is being noticed. Mack Sennett signs him for a series of two-reelers, mostly grouped around a song and some broad comedy. Like a modern music video, they take a couple of days to film and chop together, hanging a flimsy plot and a cute femme on the dubbed performance. The first is "I Surrender, Dear," and of the other songs he sings in the film, "Out of Nowhere" will become his first solo recording for Brunswick, contracted by Jack Kapp and cut near noon on March 30. Anyone can see he's leaving the Rhythm Boys behind.

Especially Russ. He's in the violin section with Sterling Young and Harry

Haworski when Bing records with Arnheim, from the "It Must Be True" session through "I Surrender, Dear." He's sitting behind him as Crosby puts his arms around the audience at the Grove, admires his nonchalance and diffidence, all eyes follow-spotting him, a glazed glow that films over the crowd's collective stare, Bing's movie projected onto a blank corneal screen, unreeling on the sprocket of the socket.

Watching Bing through their eyes. Accompanying him in the upstairs studio whenever Abe Frank wants a weeper to go out on the airwaves. Taking a smoke break during intermission, Bing in the corner playing cards while Carlos Molina's Orchestra has a turn, bringing out the Latin rhythms of the other indigenous culture of southern California. Chuckling while he waits along with the other members of the Ambassadors, enjoying Gus's and Abe's mounting discomfort as it's obvious Crosby isn't about to show for the Tuesday show, wondering whether he'll stagger back from Mexico three sheets to the windward. There are bets made, last straws drawn.

Abe Frank is caught in a bind. Crosby is making him look foolish, but he doesn't want to lose him. He tries docking his pay, but that only makes Bing more contrary, petulant, harder to control. Even Dixie is starting to get disgusted with Bing's continual returning at dawn after a night of blackjack and drinking with "the boys," preparing to draw the marital line.

Only a single violin is called for on March 2, and Columbo isn't present. Arnheim splits his session for Victor in half, a pair of songs for Gus ("Thanks to You" and "One More Time," acknowledgment and encore), and then two under Bing's own name, "Wrap Your Troubles in Dreams" and "Just a Gigolo." Bing has found a new place in his chest to seat his voice. He's always transferred easily between his upper and lower ranges; now his baritone seems to expand in sonority, catching the resonance and warmth of the microphone's condenser. His intonation is impeccable.

"Wrap Your Troubles in Dreams" has the surety of confidence. On a line like "king for a day," Bing acknowledges his link to Jolson (or rather, since Harry Richman introduced the hit, his lineage) by broadening the delivery; the second time the phrase comes around he accepts his knighthood, in service when he might well opt for the royal, flourishing even then a commoner's touch. The song's sense of lightened burden suits a year when financial woe is everywhere, when it's becoming apparent this isn't just an economic shortfall, that the hard times are not going away. Barris, the principal writer, has wrapped his troubles—he's not far removed from the bottle himself—in what looks like Crosby's dream, and it's about to move from dream to vision.

Jack Kapp of Brunswick signs Bing at just the right time; now, here. "Out of Nowhere," Crosby's first solo for his new label on March 30, is a spooky affair, like wind whistling through a crack in the wall of a deserted house. There is a supernatural air to his highly fluttered vibrato, and the close-microphone vocal presence gives him license to sing softer and softer, stepping back to rear his voice or hold it in abeyance, releasing his note on the far side of the beat. He slips sideways around the song. The music pulses unassuming beneath him, hardly noticeable. He's emerged from the orchestra's shadow. "Out of Nowhere," a Johnny Green ("Body and Soul") and Edward Heyman song, is an instant success, and its vocal style distills Bing, the moonshine of his mannerisms. It's not by coincidence Russ will sing "Out of Nowhere" at his Victor audition on July 6, doing Crosby with Con reprising the role of Barris on piano.

Bing's last session with Arnheim is more a favor to Loyce Whiteman, the female singer Gus has brought into the Grove, and to whom all the boys have taken a liking. Harry especially. Bing duets with her on "Ho Hum," and does "I'm Gonna Get You" on his own. He goes back to Brunswick for a session on May 4. Victor Young's Orchestra has added Bunny Berigan on the trumpet, the Dorsey Brothers, Lang, and Venuti. But it's Bing who takes the instrumental solos in "Just One More Chance," a line of *buh-buh-boo-boo* and two of whistling, repeating the title. The theme is repentance, *jury* and *trial* and *sentence*. He pleads his case. It's the way he says "more," breaking it up into two or three or four pieces and as many notes, that invites forgiveness, expiation.

ABOUT THE time he closed a deal with Brunswick, Bing hired Roger Marchetti to oversee his legal affairs. Roger's brother Mario owned a popular after-hours Hollywood hangout for musicians, and Roger was connected in town; his specialty ran more to behind-the-scenes executives than out-front talent. Bing knew he had a lot of extricating to do. He needed someone who was an insider. Whiteman may have let the Rhythm Boys go with two years remaining on their contract, but Abe Frank had a nine-month option and was not about to relinquish his greatest attraction without a fight. On May 16, the Rhythm Boys failed to show up at the Grove, effectively walking out on their agreement. By June 1, Frank filed a complaint with Local 47 of the Musicians Union, which gave the Rhythm Boys another night to return to Frank's stage. When they didn't, they were placed on suspension, unable to sing with a union orchestra.

No matter; Bing is already on record. Despite the ban, he can be heard by the head of the Columbia Broadcasting System, William Paley, on board the S.S. *Europa* while sailing the Atlantic. It's a matter of some dispute how "I Surrender, Dear" came to Paley's attention, whether Crosby's brother Everett or Marchetti sent Paley the record, or whether Bill overheard it from an adjacent stateroom and was captivated by Bing's sound. Either way, Paley set in motion plans for Bing's migration to New York to star in his own radio show, despite Crosby's erratic reputation and penchant for contract breaking. Paley could see that Bing was on the verge.

Rinker is less surprised than Barris when it's clear that the Rhythm Boys are over. His role in the trio had long been taking a back seat to Harry's and Bing's collaboration (Harry even played solo piano when Crosby recorded "At Your Command" at the end of June, a bravura performance that gave his keyboard flourishes as much space as Crosby, and an inkling as to how much Bing absorbed from Harry's leadings and teasings and colorings). It's Harry who thought he and Bing would stay a team, and is devastated when Bing decides to go on without him. He returns to the Cocoanut Grove two weeks before Crosby departs for the East Coast, taking solace with Loyce, becoming her piano player and songwriter. They will be married on November 22, 1931, virtually on the rebound.

For the moment, Bing is still stuck in Los Angeles, unable to work. There's some untangling that needs to be done, but he'll be heading to New York next month, and he'll find Russ waiting for him, already on a rival network with his own show.

Seeing him play the crowds at the Grove, Russ thought *I can do that.* Con told him he could do that. That made two thats. That's that.

The taxi pulls up at the Fifth Avenue "Air Castle." Up the elevator to the studio where the orchestra is waiting. The Blue Rhythm Boys are warming up their voices; they've jumped up on a bandwagon. Up, up, up.

Con passes around the hand-copied sheet music for "You Call It Madness." No one has heard it yet. The clock crosses midnight, strikes the graveyard shift, two hands merging. The red "on air" light glows. Russ looks through the microphone at his unseen listeners and sings them each their song.

ZIEGFELD

All the Follies stars came up to Riverdale Avenue for the funeral. The neighborhood had never seen the like before. Harry. Mark and Gladys. Ziegfeld himself, and Bobby Connolly, who taught Helen how to dance. Jack Pearl, the comedian, and his wife. Songstresses Helen Morgan and Ruth Etting.

Ruth had recorded "Back in Your Own Backyard" in New York on January 3, 1928, for Columbia, the same year Russ gave it a go. Her pace was more leisurely, decorative, and she was in from the intro, her voice flute-like, capable of a good trill, an oval-faced angular-bodied girl with something of the ibis to her. "*As we live we learn / That we left our happ-i-ness be-hi-hi-hind,*" she warbled, accompanied solely by Phil Schwartz's art deco-rative piano. They break into a canter in the middle chorus—*hot-cha,* baby—before settling back for the final flourishes. Three bouncing descending notes for the last *ya-ha-hard.*

It was what Helen Walsh had moved to Riverdale for, the backyard, the second-floor porch not far from the Hudson, the sense of the natural landscape. Manhattan seemed a valley away, this part of the western Bronx rising on a bluff overlooking the towers of the city, high on the cliffs opposite the Palisades. She had bought the house for her mother when she started at the Follies four years ago, when she was twenty, the '27 edition in which Claire Luce had ridden across the stage astride a live ostrich with a rhinestone collar and Helen had tootled along on kazoo to Irving Berlin's "It's Up to the Band" with half the girls while the rest plinked white grand pianos.

The frame house was number 6005, on the west side of the Avenue; six rooms. It was in a good neighborhood, right across the street from St. Margaret's R.C. church, and the parochial school, built in 1911. Apocryphally, Saint Margaret had been condemned by the governor of Antioch to be eaten by a dragon, whereupon she cut herself out of the beast's belly with a crucifix in her right hand, only to emerge and be beheaded. She was the patron saint of childbirth. Helen's mother's name was Margaret.

Now her oldest daughter lay in repose in the front room. White roses and orchids—a gift from Mr. Ziegfeld, who hated red flowers—adorned the casket, setting off her white gown with its high lace around the neck, to conceal her burns. There had been a suggestion that Helen be buried in the pink dress that she wore in the Follies opening scene, but it was thought a bit too suggestive for someone about to meet God, or at least his Son. Not to mention His blessed Mother. The whole family.

Her mother sat in the dining room, rocking silently, her lips and fingers telling the Rosary beads. Across Helen's bier was a crimson velvet banner, IN HOC SIGNO embroidered on the edge. In this sign, I conquer.

She'd hadn't done too badly for herself. She'd been in *Show Boat, Rio Rita, Smiles,* and *Whoopee.* A glorifyin' showgirl. A Ziegfeld official told a reporter she was "a credit to the organization."

They'd all come to pay their respects; the stagehands, the electricians, the musicians and dancers. Newspaper photographers. The curious. They filed past her, until at ten o'clock in the morning, the Thursday after the tragedy, the casket was closed, and they began her final chorus line.

The procession had only just come down the steps and begun to cross Riverdale Avenue when Harry, James Moore, and composer Vincent Youmans ("*No, No, Nanette*") took the place of the professional pallbearers. Harry assumed the lead on the left, Hellinger right behind, his coat still tucked over his arm. Jack Pearl followed the cortège, hat in hand, bringing up the rear.

The cluster of mourners proceeded across the street to hear Father Thomas Doyle read the requiem high mass. An aunt sang "Hark, I Hear the Angels Calling." Three tall candles stood guard around her casket in the center aisle of the church. Three flower cars followed the white hearse to the Woodlawn cemetery.

Mrs. Walsh clung to Gladys Glad at the grave site while her brother-in-law James struggled to hold her upright. A tombstone inscribed MOTHER rested in front of her disconsolate form; she was as good as gone already.

She had lost her firstborn. A wail of anguish like no other.

. . .

FLO ZIEGFELD watched the crowds stream into the theater that William Randolph Hearst had built for him in 1930, across from the Warwick, perhaps in thanks for introducing him to Marion Davies in '16. The Follies that year featured a Shakespearean motif, with Bert Williams as Othello and takeoffs on great lovers like Romeo and Juliet and Antony and Cleopatra. Hearst played his own Othellian role, coming to the show for eight weeks straight to watch his Desdemona onstage (*"It is the very error of the moon; She comes more nearer earth than she was wont, And makes men mad."* Act Five, Scene II). The new theater bore Flo's name.

The poor girl, he thought. *She was a sweetheart.*

He had sent a three-hundred-fifty-dollar wreath to Helen's funeral, and a huge grapevine in a big tub—almost a tree, with orchids on it and actual hanging grapes—over to Virginia Biddle's hospital room. His bill at the House of Flowers on West Fifty-sixth Street was getting out of hand, as, now that he'd reminded himself, were all his other bills. He was *schvitzing* money like night sweats, and he was having enough of those, dawn after dawn, waking with a start, awareness flooding in with awakeness, his troubles pressing cold and clammy upon him. Migraines. Sciatica. He was beginning to feel worse and worse.

Flo was losing his grip on Broadway, though he would be the last to admit it. Once he had owned the Main Stem, had them watching his every move, imitating him. Now it was all going to hell. People wanted their spectacle at the movies these days. They didn't give two kosher craps about real live glamour. They wanted it up on a screen, flat, harshly lit, all shadows and out of focus and squashed perspective.

"One hundred and fifty girls in the flesh, not in the can," he'd trumpeted in the ads. "You can't fool the public!" But he was caught between the great unwashed's contradictory desires. On the one hand, they came for the flesh, admittedly higher-class flesh than the likes of Mlle. Lapisch from Vichy at the Republic Burlesque on Forty-second just across the street from the New Amsterdam; but the glisten of female nonetheless. The only difference was his copious adornment of the undraped form, and their lack thereof. At least he didn't stoop to wrapping his nudes in cellophane like Earl Carroll.

And on the other, musical hand, they could turn on the radio to hear the popular songs. Play them over and over on the phonograph. They didn't need to come to Broadway to bring some music into their lives. He was left in the

middle. That was no place for the likes of Flo Ziegfeld. He never did anything halfway.

Vaudeville was almost a goner. Even the vaunted Palace was struggling.
Alexander Pantages, Loew, Ben Keith's circuit: they were all getting into
screening movies themselves. Why keep a bunch of temperamental and half-
crazy performers in motion, like some dog-act juggler, when you could
freeze-frame the moment and send it around the country by proxy, on eight
or ten film reels, and still own the theaters—excuse me, movie palaces—and
rake in even more profits. A film-can wouldn't show up drunk, or get pregnant, or threaten to quit if it didn't get more money.

He'd given the movies a shot. As soon as he saw Jolson in *The Jazz Singer*,
he had called up Jesse Lasky and Walter Wanger at Paramount and said he
could do it better. But they dicked him around for eighteen months, and by
then everyone was making squawkies. He was just one of the crowd, and that
wasn't Flo Ziegfeld. He'd even gone to the point of staging his own premiere
at the Astoria Studios in Queens, lavishing on *Glorifying the American Girl*
the proper photoplay cachet. Mayor Jimmy Walker showed up, as did Adolph
Zukor, Otto Kahn, Irving Berlin, and he'd filmed them alighting from their
limousines and strolling into the lobby as if it were a real opening night. But
even in two-strip Technicolor, the finale that was supposed to represent his
spectacle resembled it as much as his papier-mâché elephants could be mistaken for the real thing.

He had loved elephants ever since one of the Ringling brothers had shown
him and Anna around after they visited the circus. When they met Lockhart,
the animal trainer, he gave a prearranged signal and the great beast lifted
Anna in his trunk. "I am the Queen of India!" she joyfully chortled after she'd
gotten over her fear; and Flo looked at her outstretched arms and infused delight and embrace of life and loved her even more. From then on, he'd always
regarded the elephant as his own symbol, a colossus of gargantua.

But you had to worry which way their trunks were pointed. Up for luck;
down for misfortune. When someone sent him three white jade elephants on
the eve of *Hot-Cha!*'s opening, their trunks curled under, he nearly went
apoplectic. "Do you want to ruin me?" He wasn't satisfied until his secretary,
Goldie, had taken them to the alley and smashed them.

He didn't need more bad luck. His own trunk seemed to be pointing down
these days, no matter how many chorus girls he was auditioning. The revues
were on their last legs, a throwback to a time when most all of the performing
arts could be contained on one stage. Now singers could make records, actors
could go into the movies, comics could be on the radio. The revusicals tried

to cram too much into their glitteration—song, dance, comedy, pathos—and it was hard to keep topping yourself. The format was like his papier-mâché elephants, ponderous, slow-moving, collapsing under their own weight. Off to the pachyderm graveyard, even though those ivory tusks were still beautiful to look at, especially with a Follies girl perched thereon. He could feel his hand running down their ivory burnished curves, the slim line of thigh and calf.

And the public, in their own myopic way, knew. Even this early in the run, only the second month, attendance was off. He couldn't afford to close the show so quickly; not with his reputation. He couldn't afford to keep it open. "Couldn't" was not a word that sat well with Flo Ziegfeld.

Still, he had no compunction about staging this Tuesday afternoon benefit to help Helen Walsh's family. He'd always liked her; the way she cuddled up to him as he placed his hand on her rump, then quickly batted her long black eyelashes and scooted away. "The quiet untouchable," Hellinger called her, as Flo wrote out the $17,800 check for Mark to give Helen's mother. And him Mr. Gladys Glad. Marrying her! You couldn't ask for a better story. With Harry as unlikely hero (it was a wonder he didn't cause his own explosion, what with all the champagne and Scotch inside him waiting for a stray spark), Helen was front-page news. It was a better publicity coup than the time he'd had a satchel of Anna's gems "stolen" from a train in Harrisburg, Pa., or when a dozen burly men unhooked the Held horses from her hansom carriage and hand-carted her down the Great Light Way. She had certainly created more stir than that birdbrain Reri, who inanely answered any reporter's questions with "I like a chocolate soda."

He had a duty to his girls. Glorification came with responsibilities. They didn't call him "Daddy" for nothing. He always carried in his pocket a few scraps of crêpe de chine scarf or silk stockings to hand out to a favored girl; though he could snap any errant chorine back into line with a quick command. He had gotten fanatical about fastidiousness; he could spot a mark on a girl's dress from his balcony perch, and she'd hear about it in a sudden directive to Bobby, or Gene. The old man was watching. And he hated straight chorus lines. Hated them. A woman was meant to have curves, even if there were twenty-four of them lined up in a row.

This wasn't the goddam army, marching in lockstep. Even though he was as patriotic as the next man. His 1918 show had proved that, with its "Forward Allies" tableau of trench warfare, complete with doughboys in battle and sylphs of liberty urging them forward. It was the first time Eddie Cantor had appeared sans blackface; Will Rogers emceed; and Frank Carter sang Irving Berlin's "I'm Gonna Pin a Medal on the Girl I Left Behind." He had spent three hundred dollars apiece on a dozen satin pillows for the show, and Marilyn Miller's ballet was enhanced by a fresh costume nightly at a cost of $175. The New Amsterdam had never looked brighter, at least until the next year's extravaganza, when John Steel tenored Irving's "A Pretty Girl Is Like a Melody" and the Prince of Wales clapped along to Gene Buck and Dave Stamper's "Tulip Time," or 1921, when he'd spent more than a quarter of a million dollars on the production and he'd had to move to the Globe because the New Amsterdam was booked with his *Sally*, or '22 when "It's Getting Dark on Broadway" sepia-tinted the influence of Harlem rhythms and Evelyn Law danced across the stage with one leg lifted over her head and Gilda Gray shimmied " 'Neath the South Sea Moon": *"By the love la-goon. . . ."*

He shook his head, breaking his reverie. The theater named after him was rapidly filling up. It outdid the New Amsterdam, he thought; though the old place had a certain charm. He'd staged his Follies there after 1913, when he'd moved his productions from the Jardin de Paris (actually, the tin roof of the New York Theatre at Broadway and Forty-fifth). He remembered the *Midnight Frolics* atop the roof of the New Amsterdam, the girls garbed as light itself: northern lights, lightning bugs, evening stars. He could feel the warm glow. Enough time had passed now that he was feeling nostalgic.

Not a good sign. When you dwell on the old glories, chuckling at the follies of your young self and how they remain your follies, his persona walking out onstage as naked as any of his girls each time a show opened, it meant that better days were passing you by. With too much past to remember, you spend less time on your future memoirs. And it wasn't as if it was getting any easier. Especially since he felt so sick lately. *Show Boat* had closed in less than a year. He'd had three flops in a row: *Show Girl, Simple Simon,* and *Smiles.* He had lost over a million dollars in the stock crash. He was being tracked by process servers and bill collectors and the sense that the sumptuousness that had long been his calling card had gotten too dear even for him. Past due, and he didn't have the cash to pay up.

It won't be long now. He'd banished clocks from his sight. He couldn't bear to see them ticking his life away. He had always followed his impulse, gambling without a system. The hunch, and then bet it all. Big shot. Make sure they can't match you. Gambling as an Olympic sport.

He wouldn't go down without a fight, especially to show that imbecile George White with his Scandals that he wasn't just a girlie show like that other nitwit Earl Carroll. He'd gotten new songwriters—Mack Gordon and Harry Revel—and rehired Joseph Urban to provide his sets. The Viennese-born Urban had come to America when he designed the Austrian pavilion at the 1904 St. Louis World's Fair and had stayed on as a freelance stage director. Ziegfeld first commissioned him to design the 1915 Follies. The theme was underwater, all blues and aquamarines, and as Ziegfeld painted with light, so Urban did with color. He was a born decorator; his settings always seemed to draw the eye into motion, a frame that often—in an optical illusion—became the primary. He was the contexture of the Follies, and later the artistic director of the Metropolitan Opera beginning in 1917. Flo had Urban design the preliminary sketches for the Ziegfeld Theater, its bowed front and Romanesque mass, its sense of breathing through the long oblong windows of the second-floor lobby; and he was responsible for the elliptic shape of the auditorium and the medieval murals, all castles and knights and jousters, that gilded the walls of the gold-draped theater. Alberto Vargas painted the program cover of a composite Ziegfeld girl, her hand cupping her left breast. He was paying Gladys Glad $500 a week. Gene Buck, his faithful jack-of-all-trades, had returned to the fold. The old gang was assembled.

He'd be sending a telegram tonight. Flo liked the staccato rhythms of the wire, only necessary words, language boiled down to its essence. He couldn't wait for the mail and he disliked talking on the trio of gold telephones that sat on his desk. He didn't want any answering back, anyway. This is how it should be done, period. That was the Flo Ziegfeld way.

Up by the door of his balcony office, the man who showed Broadway how it was done for the first third of the twentieth century gave a hand signal to Bobby to let the show begin. The orchestra struck up the fanfare. The gold Celanese curtain rose, like a harvestigial moon over the 1931 Follies.

THE THEME was Old vs. New. Then and Now, which in New York time meant looking back about twenty-odd years. A fifth of century, please. Vintage.

It was, not coincidentally, Ziegfeld's look back at his own Old and Then, his beginnings in the showbiz frontier of the 1890s, and his ascendance to Broadway impresario. He had caught the fever pitch of the '98 Klondike gold rush (he'd just seen that re-created on the screen, *The Trail of '98*, with Dolores Del Rio slogging through the arctic blizzard), only Ziegfeld had gone prospecting on the frontier of Times Square.

Flo was still a carny, in many ways. When he'd started, a teenage boy thrilled at the pageantry of Buffalo Bill's Wild West Show, he went for the strong man; The Great Sandow, lion-rassling. It gave him a sense of the colosseum; and a taste for rippling flesh.

The women loved to watch Sandow. Flo had found him at the Casino Theater on Broadway and Thirty-ninth in 1893, an arabesque edifice that framed its variety show in oriental splendor. Sandow had bested "Samson" at the London Aquarium to claim the title of "the most powerful man on earth," but his act was yawn-provoking. He held people in the palm of his hand; he bent iron pokers with his teeth, dressed in animal skin. Standard big bozo stuff.

Ziegfeld framed him. Stripped him. Covered his member with a thin membrane of silk. Darkened the theater. Reached out a spotlight to touch his arm. Shine on his chest. Another targeted his muscular calf. Forearm. Rippling stomach, each ridge defined. His triceps were especially fine-chiseled, a coil of cable encircling each upper arm. He assumed his place, like an artist's model. Rodin's Thinker. An Olympian, thrower of discus, tosser of javelin. "The Modern Hercules." "The Perfect Man."

It wouldn't take a Thomas Edison to figure that such an electric-light principle applied to the female form could significantly broaden box-office appeal. Ziegfeld needed a leading lady, and on a trip to London, between brothels, he discovered her. His match.

Anna Held, she of the milk baths and the eighteen-inch waist and the blue-and-gold thirteen-room suite at the Hotel Ansonia, with whom he had originated the idea of the Follies from Paris; the word itself was French, from *folies*. Naughty, naughty, those Parisiennes, or so everyone in America thought. But the sequinage proved irresistible.

Anna had been in the Folies-Bergère, in fact was under contract to Edouard Marchand of that very organization when Ziegfeld discovered her. She remembered she'd fallen in love with him when she told him that she couldn't sign his contract, and the disappointment staggered him, as if, in the act of proposing to her, he'd just found out she had a husband. And she was married, well, estranged, to a Maximo Carerra, who was about to lose his own fortune, precipitating her flight to America under Ziegfeld's wing. Flo, at the age of twenty-nine, had lost his heart. He brought her to America in the fall of 1896 to have a small role in *A Parlor Match*, a revival of comics Charles Evan Evans and Bill Hoey's well-beloved farce. Cast as a phantasm in the final act, she came out and sang "Come and Play with Me," though in her appealingly French accent, it came out as *wiz me*, and audiences were delighted.

Soon she and Flo were common-law wed, since her Catholic marriage remained in rather distant effect. Anna danced, sang, and *ooh-la-la'd* as Flo presented her, stage-managing her ebullience. It was very much catch-as-can-can entertainment; at Koster and Bial's Music Hall, she shared the bill with a xylophone team, Adelman and Lowe; a contortionist; a high-wire act; and a trapezist. The circus had much in common with the music hall.

Flo indulged Anna, acquiring from Lillie Langtry a private railroad car for her, installing her in a suite at the Savoy that duplicated the boudoir of Marie-Antoinette. In 1899 Paris, he celebrated the Festival of the Flowers by having four horses pull their carriage down the rue de Longchamp, with a white silk canopy and three thousand orchids entwined. In the first month of the new century, she was cast in pure gold by the sculptor W. H. Millins.

Anna was starring in *The Parisian Model*, a 1906 Harry B. Smith play, when Flo began to hit his stride of sumptuous staging and diaphanously clad women. In one scene, Anna vanishes behind a screen of chorus girls and reappears dressed only in stockings, corset, and see-through nightgown. For each verse she changes costume. As the Held Girls undress around her, baring shoulders, legs, ankles, Flo reclothes them in light, prompting not modesty, but an accessorizing of beauty. In silhouette, the stage projects and protects their virtue. "I Can't Make My Eyes Behave," she sings, with the delight that Flo loves, the drawling *I'se* of cakewalk giving it a little minstrel lilt, and the loosening mores of the twentieth century that will result in riot grrlls is begun.

The Held Girls were the first Follies show beauties, and when Abe Erlanger and Mark Klaw salaried Ziegfeld two hundred dollars a week for a show sans plot like *The Parisian Model*, Flo remembered the variety extravaganzas he had seen in Paris, and their elevation from common vaudeville; their wonderment. The performers—singers, dancers, dialect jokesters— were the same. It was the show people came to see. They wanted to be infused with light. Be dazzled.

He wasn't just indulging the audience's fantasies; his own sense of skimp came into play, his instinct for the right moment to provoke undress. One of his accountants suggested saving money by giving his girls *cotton* underwear, but Flo never cut corners on lingerie. He knew the difference in how it made his girls feel, that they were as liquid as the fabrics they held close, as languid as their stage slouch, mouths open, a tinge of smile, ever the limpid *coquette*. His sensibility was neoclassical; his scenic re-creations were art, meant to be hung on the wall next to Botticelli's *Birth of Venus* and David's *Rape of the Sabine Women*. Only they moved. Ever so slightly.

Elaboration was Ziegfeld's mode. His revues surpassed vaudeville in their quest for the divine, *Gloria*-fying the American Girl. Passion plays, their *Magnificat* set pieces interleaved with songs and comedies, dance troupes and razzle-dazzle, it was truly a night on the town. By the time he reached 1907 and the first actual Follies, his sense of the grand was in the ascendant.

The premier Follies was a hodgepodge of Held Girls dressed as little drummer boys, as bathing beauties, as Salomes dancing each of the seven veils, and Flo was surprised at its success. He had saved his energies for Anna's starring vehicle, *Miss Innocence*, in 1908, for which he constructed the then-largest electric sign in America, with eleven miles of wire and a design of flashing lightning bolts. Framing her name were more than two thousand gas globes; it cost more to flick the switch than to illuminate the Brooklyn Bridge.

During the previews of *Miss Innocence*, Anna discovered she was pregnant. He forced Anna to get an abortion. It seemed to poison their marriage, and they drifted apart. Flo, meanwhile, had taken up with Lillian Lorraine, "The Most Beautiful Girl in the World," a street urchin compared to the aristocratic Anna; she seemed to personify the new century's coarse ardor to Ziegfeld. In some ways, she was his truest love, though she tormented him, marrying another right as the 1911 Follies opened. (That year, the Follies girls were garbed as the seven deadly sins and other vices.) Finally, at a New Year's party welcoming 1914, they argued and she left in a huff. That was the midnight he met Billie Burke, a sweet, angelic creature, whose blond shine was very much like his own lighting effects. She radiated, simply. Movie star (she was the Gloria of *Gloria's Romance*, a twenty-part 1916 serial) and Broadway doyenne (she was the *Mind-the-Paint Girl* as well as *Mrs. Dot*), she was one of America's sweethearts (the practical purity of a Mary Pickford and the passion of a Jean Harlow). Billie would become his guiding rock, and amidst the dalliances, his last wife. They shared a daughter and a home along the Hudson.

Ziegfeld moved through the teens and into the twenties as the undisputed king impresario of Broadway, his shows providing a forum for many of the greatest names in show business, and in his wake spawned the revue: Scandals, Vanities, *Greenwich Village Follies*, *Lew Leslie's Blackbirds*. He was not merely a ringmaster. As the producer of *Show Boat*, he also displayed his flair at more dramatic themes; *Show Boat* remains a genuine classic of the Broadway musical stage, one of the first book-musicals to attempt to integrate its plot, song, and dance into a unified theatrical presentation. Despite Ziegfeld's reputation, it was not especially showy in its use of color (Ziegfeld favored grays, blues, and pinks for the production); and the 1932 revival contained one of the landmark performances of the Broadway century with Paul Robeson's "Ol' Man River."

Just keep rolling along. Flo had cut his own channel down to the sea. He knew his riverbed well, and the canyon it had carved through his life. After years of overflowing banks, it was getting harder and harder to reach flood tide.

Years passed. His face became rounder, his figure permanently portly, rotund. He hardly ever smiled, oozing a placid serenity that could nonetheless be quick to sudden currents and eddies of pique, until it came time to dispense the fertile silt of his largesse. Then, sitting behind his desk, handing over a $17,800 check to Mark while outside the eponymous theater taxis and cars zigzagged up in a jumble to discharge theatergoers to Helen Walsh's benefit, he resembled nothing so much as a somnolent Buddha, with his faithful Ganesh grazing off to the side. The Man in the Moon.

And they called *him* crazy.

THE AIM is to restore the glory of the-*fying*. A defiant return to form, especially the feminine one.

"Bring On the Follies Girls," and they saunter on from left to right, shoulders a-slope, led by Gladys Glad. The embodiment.

Harry is toastmaster, a spot that cannot help being measured against past great emceremonials like Eddie Cantor and Will Rogers. He faces the inevitable comparisons unflinchingly, with the same aviator bravado that will cause him to fill up a Vultee monoplane in 1936 with fifty thousand Ping-Pong balls stashed in the wings (for buoyancy, should he make an unscheduled ocean splash) and take off for Europe with a co-pilot and single 1,000-horsepower engine. He'll get as far as Wales before careening into a cow pasture—not the first (actually he's the twenty-ninth to make it across the Atlantic), but there, by God. And back, only to topple into the Newfoundland mud.

As host of the Follies, he's a little more reserved than was his stock-in-trade at the Club Richman. With prices at two dollars a ginger ale, a dollar for a tray of ice, and a six-dollar cover charge for the privilege of bringing your own flask to the party, he could afford to be a tad racier. This, however, is the Ziegfeld. It wouldn't do to introduce a Helen Morgan as he used to bring out his newest femme thrush each floor show at the Club, pretending to calm her nerves, patting her on the back, running his hand down to her ass, fondling her to the chortling delight of the audience, leering and winking. Still, he could always fall back on the congeniality he had acquired at the Richman. The glad hand. Making the rounds of the tables. The sly sidle of paying off the revenuers. Strutting the songs he'd made famous: "Sunny Side of the Street," "Walkin' My Baby Back Home," "There's Danger in Your Eyes, Cherie."

He was beginning to miss the old joint, destroyed by a fire in the early morning hours of September 22, 1929, leaving its revel room open to the sky. Now there were real stars winking over the dance floor. Harry had to appreciate that. And he'd gotten out just before the stock market went up in smoke. He was glad he wasn't around to see how his former customers fared.

The thought of flames yanked him back to the moment. Helen Walsh's benefit. Damnation. He could not fucking believe he had pushed the starter. Virginia had said something about smelling gas, and then Helen had said something about all the corned beef and cabbage at Dinty Moore's and then he'd said something and his hand in motion toward the button had forgotten why it should stop and then everything went white heat. As much of a shock to the retinas as the incandescent opening number of these '31 Follies.

"Help Yourself to Happiness and Happiness Will See You Through." Harry was living 120 proof, the power of positive living. He dressed the part. Double-breasted. The high silk hat. The straw boater. The lights catching the pierce of his blue eyes, his twinkle burnished by the deep tan of his skin. A slight lisp that only endeared him more to his fans. Twirl the stick.

He was being especially nice to Virginia. And her steel trap of a mother, Lutie. She still wasn't out of the hospital, though he'd gotten her moved from the quackery out on Long Island into the city. Before the show, he'd brought over a platinum chain bracelet to her room, with an octagon drop that had an engraved M and a Y and then DEAREST spelled out in square-cut stones: D for diamond, E for emerald, A for amethyst, R for ruby, another emerald, a sapphire, a topaz. He didn't trust the mother; there was already talk of suing in the air. And he missed Virginia, the pearls draped down her bare back and around her throat, the askance glance. He couldn't believe those beautiful haunches had been burned.

Harry takes his bows, and the show settles into its set pieces. Hellinger has written a takeoff on *Grand Hotel*, only this time the lobby is filled with such character-tures as "Polly Adlervitch, Queen of the Russian Ballet" (Helen Morgan), "Alphonso Smith, late King of Gibraltar" (Milton LeRoy), "Cecil B. Goldwarner of Hollywood" (Jack Pearl), and "Baron Al Capone" (Harry Richman). Richman had met the real Capone several times—the first time quaking in his shoes when he played Chicago with the Scandals in 1926. One of Harry's ex-wives had married a Capone lieutenant, and when Scarface Al invited him to an aftershow soirée at the Hotel Lexington, Richman thought it was curtains. He needn't have worried. Prohibition made strange drinking buddies and odder bedfellows, and blood was hardly thicker than bootleg Scotch.

The scene switches to a re-creation of Rector's nitery, a "Broadway

THE PRINCIPALS OF THE 1931 *FOLLIES:*(*left to right*)
GLADYS GLAD, JACK PEARL, RUTH ETTING,
HELEN MORGAN, HARRY RICHMAN, DOROTHY DELL,
HAL LEROY, MITZI MAYFAIR

Reverie" of the years before Prohibition dried out the land: *"It's not the way it used to be."* There are more impressions—Harry does an Al Jolson turn on "You Made Me Love You," Jack Pearl mimics Sam Bernard's "Who Paid the Rent for Mrs. Rip Van Winkle When Rip Van Winkle Was Away," and Gladys becomes the Queen of the 1915 Follies. The most intriguing juxtaposition is Ruth Etting as Nora Bayes, singing "Shine On Harvest Moon."

Harry had known Nora from a show they shared in 1922 called *Queen of Hearts,* which had a short run at the George M. Cohan Theater before folding its cards. She told him that she derived her vocal charisma from jaunting up to Harlem where she went to clubs where no whites had ever been, and listening. She took Harry with her, and Harry resolved to cultivate a male version of her bosomy voice, which paid off when DeSylva, Brown, and Henderson gave him "The Birth of the Blues" for George White's revue. "If Jolson was my god, she was my goddess," he liked to say.

Fittingly, George Rector's cabaret on pre-Times Longacre Square had been Mount Olympus for such Broadway entertainment society in the early years of the century. Ziegfeld had courted Anna Held there, and the *nouvelle royale* lobsters and champagne eleganza of the restaurant, with its Louis XIV furnishings and chandeliered shimmer, seemed to suit this new tuxedoed class. With dining *and* dancing *and* drinking, in the same room! under the same roof! places like Rector's and Shanley's and Reisenweber's were not above attracting in 1915 the reform ire of a Mrs. Henry Moskowitz who headed a municipal committee to ensure that such suspect goings-on were morally separated, to what end nobody could figure until Prohibition in 1920 onsetted the Noble Experiment. Not that anyone stopped drinking or fucking.

Or spooning, 'neath the mooning. Ruth Etting knew a lot about the lunacy of love, the pain and insanity and unreason, for she was married to Martin Moe "Colonel Gimp" Snyder, a small-time racketeer who never let her out of his sight. He was a horror, everyone agreed, taking credit for Ruth's success, barging into Ziegfeld's office to demand more money and sketch time, complaining that she was billed equally with Helen Morgan, beating up anyone who looked at Ruth sideways and slapping her in the lobby of the Hotel Piccadilly and then getting all remorseful and tearful and calling her "Pookey." The girls referred to him as "The Watchdog." Ruth knew he was generally making a complete ass of himself, and yet she couldn't tear herself away. There was the fear of what he would do, that he might kill her, and that was part of the attraction—that he was so dangerous because of her, because he loved her so, because he was not in control of his senses when he was in her presence, and that he wanted the best for her, and if he couldn't get it, then who knew what love could make him capable of? And there was the general affection. He was such a big baby.

She stayed with him, and in a way it helped her to sing. Song was the only place where her dreams worked out the way she hoped they would. Her popularity is such in 1931 that she duels with Kate Smith ("When the Moon Comes Over the Mountain") for the title of radio's most popular singer, and at the moment of these Follies, even Ziegfeld refers to her as "the greatest singer of songs" he's worked with in forty years. Her voice hearkens back as much as it moves forward, still brassy, more trombony than trumpet (like Sophie Tucker), or even cornet (like Fanny Brice). There is a touch of Mae West delivery that comes with her sassy projection of a song, rather than the breathing of it into a microphone. Yet her singing has been touched by the bent notes of jazz, the movement away from the chord's major resolve, melisma-ing the blue tinge, and she incorporates it into her delivery.

For "Shine On Harvest Moon," it is a rediscovery, and Ruth's version makes it a hit all over again, bookending Ziegfeld's span of Follies. She records it twice in July 1931. The first attempt occurs on the eighth, barely a week after the Follies opens; there are three takes, as well as her companion song in this edition of the Follies, "Cigarettes, Cigars!" They are ARC (American Record Company) rejected, and you can imagine Colonel Gimp in the control room, gun dangling from his hand (as he once did at a radio station), telling the engineer where to move the microphone to catch Ruth's belt, her theatrical filling of the theater; and the technicians knowing it's not necessary, they'd like to consider the more natural sonorities of her voice. There is the placement of the band to take into account, their spatial relationship to Ruth and the room, the red line of the recorder. If he lets them, they can surround her; the listener can be within the performance, best seat in the house. Front row. We have entered the age of the electrical recording. No longer merely capturing the physical acoustics of the sound wave, it is the moment the phonograph—no longer gramophone—begins to develop its own voice and manner of speaking. But Moe's just making sure his "Little Lady" is taken care of. Paid protection.

Ruth was aware of filling her space. She could sing measuredly, giving up dynamic contrast for an eventide of clarity, losing perhaps some mystery as a result. She sang songs from the lyrics out, learning the words and fitting the melodies after she knew the story. This added to a literal style that lent well to the stage; a performance with song accompaniment, though ironically, the movies eluded her. Even though she made more than a dozen *Vitaphone Varieties* and *Broadway Brevities*, short one- and two-reelers in the early thirties, and was enough of a marquee presence to heighten the box office of any film, like *Roman Scandals*, she never seemed at ease with pure dialogue. It came out of her mouth stilted, seeking background music, or attention-diverting trick photography, like the time she performed with a piano duo, one of her next to each piano, superimposed, her own duet. With Moe around, directors or early co-stars like Humphrey Bogart couldn't work with her, because they would have to go through the Gimp first. And he was a bad actor.

She returned to the studio on the 28th, and cut both songs again. It was the day after Helen had died. They are the released versions. When she climbs up to the chorus, she pleads with the moon to keep the night alive a bit longer; she remembers the almost desperate hope they'd felt last afternoon, when Helen was supposedly improving. "*Ain't had no lovin' since January, February, June or July....* " Never to have love again. What would that be like? And when she sang out "*For me and my gal,*" she sent Helen a sisterly Godspeed.

Dance duo Earl Oxford and Hal LeRoy, the Caucasus version of the second act's Buck and Bubbles, who do "In Harlem" in their slot, as if anyone mistook where the border was drawn, perform their synchronized two-steps, four legs. It gives everybody a chance to change costuming. Show folks. Even the stagehands rushing back and forth with props and scenery don't spare a look at the undress backstage.

Ruth has to make a quick transformation to a Cigarette Girl in the Club Piccadilly (no relation to the hotel) during Prohibition. Her breakthrough hit "Ten Cents a Dance" was the highlight of the 1930 Ed Wynn vehicle *Simple Simon*; in that song, written by Rodgers and Hart, she's a girl of the streets. Chaste and chased. What raises the pathos from Dickensian is its humor about her customers, and the sense that it could just as well be called "Ten Cents a Song." Ever the dutiful hostess, she tried to take good care of her audience, and Moe as well. *"Tough guys that tear my gown." C'mon, big boy. You can step on my feet anytime.* She was woman enough to take it.

This time around, Gordon and Revel cast her as a tobacco salesgirl, proffering "Cigarettes, Cigars!" with the same mixture of winsome lose-some. The abbreviated costume shows off her legs for the first time. She is not so much sexy as coy; there's none of the hellzapoppin' in her. The tobacco tray that hangs from her shoulders cuts her in half at the waist, bisects her, as if the legs belonged to another girl.

She's come from the sticks. She's one of the fools. Now she can't get a break. Broadway's a fake. She goes home at dawn and throws herself across her bed and weeps. There is no hint at humor, even in the middle crescendo. Along with Camels and Chesterfields, Luckies are namechecked; Flo had done a magazine ad for them—"It protects the voice . . . my voice remains unirritated after a strenuous time directing rehearsals"—and was probably experimenting with in-show commercials. If only he'd known.

The skit employs a host of gangster types and speak patrons, caught in the crossfire of a shoot-out between rival mobsters. A stray shot kills the effeminate emcee, played by Hal LeRoy. He collapses into Ruth's arms. There were dancers (Virginia was one of the dozen girls, with names like Pearl and Vera and Bernice and Iris), Ethel Borden playing club hostess Texas Guinan—even then a sin-onym for New York nightlife with her "butter and egg man" and "Hello Sucker" references (though Harry always swore he'd invented that one for her); and Dorothy Dell as Miss Universe. Ziegfeld liked beauty-pageant winners, though she had leaped over the ranks of showgirls to start as a starring principal, which meant there was something simmering there, and she proved it in her song, "Was I," penned by Chick Endor and Charles Farrell.

It's time to clear the stage. Jack Pearl and Cliff Hall keep the audience entertained while the most ambitious Urban scenery of the production is rolled into cityscape place for "Doing the New York," Ziegfeld's hymn to the metropolis that gave him Times Square as his personal playground, and he'd returned the favor by igniting the grandeur that helped make it a city on a par with the capitals of the past: Constantinople, Alexandria, London and Paris and Moscow and Berlin and Rome, another City of Lights. He was used to tooting the hometown horn. "The Broadway Glide" was a dance step A. Seymour Brown and Bert Grant crafted for his 1912 *Moulin Rouge.* Flo knew how to do its rag.

Even though Harry's "Doing the New York" struts and strolls to the *"beat of people walking on the street,"* contrasting *"old / new . . . hot / blue,"* and other somethings for everyones, the recently opened Empire Building, as it's called in the program, is the true star. Its skyline jut is sensurrounded by the clamor of elevated subways, crowds thronging, the nonstop chug of the great electrical substations of the city, and like a ziggurat, the jackhammer energy of the world's tallest building being risen in one year and ten months on the site of the old Waldorf-Astoria torn down and reopened sixteen blocks north and a couple east, ribbon cut on May 1, 1931, the sundial shadow of its spire able to reach across the Ziegfeld Theater a mile away at approximately one o'clock on the afternoon of this benefit performance, letting the audience of street insiders and friends of the Ziegfeld family and press agents and hustlers, and aspiring no-counts and accountants and lovers of a good time and girls or guys on the make or break, know that they are at the crossroads—it's not just some dark Mississippi midnight went-down-to-the-x-roads that you make your bargain with the devil-may-care—of Broadway and the New York Times Square. World central.

The first act finales.

IT'S ELEPHANTINE time. Flo has waited all night for this. Five giant papier-mâché pachyderms, lunging headfirst out over the orchestra pit, stagehands inside manipulating limbs while outside they carry on their trunks beautiful Tarzana creatures, Gladys Glad in the middle as, yes, The Queen. Virginia is usually perched to the left of Gladys, chosen for her long dark hair, which matched the jungle setting in *Legend of the Islands;* but she won't be able to return to the show until September.

This had been Reri's big scene, where she sang "Mailu" and bouncy-bounced around the stage, but it was clear by now that she was lost in the urban underbrush of New York. On the verge of letting her escape to the Brooklyn flatlands and be done with her, Ziegfeld would reorient the "Tom Tom" number using the more balletic Albertina Rasch Dancers and leave the audience gasps to the elephants and the pulchritude.

A perfect moment for the entrance of Helen Morgan. Just her, her pianist, and the piano. Her trademark, enshrined in the torch hall of fame, is sitting upon the horizontal, lounging upon it as if it were a bed. She's been doing it since she was a young girl, when as a twelve-year-old she'd been hoisted over the crowd and perched on the lid of a battered piano in a Montreal cellar saloon. And there she'd remained.

Except, in this Follies, she seems out of place. There is little for her to do that she hasn't already done, and she's not challenged in the show. She had originally been given a Noël Coward number called "Half Caste Woman," an all-too-obvious reference to her own most triumphant moment in 1927 as Julie Dozier, the octoroon in *Show Boat*. Jerome Kern had discovered her himself, a bit player in *George White's Scandals*, a singer whose emotional turbulence seemed ready to spill out of her eyes, like the blinked glisten of held-back tears.

She had made classics out of her two numbers in that show, "My Bill" and "Can't Help Lovin' That Man," throbbing declarations of fealty to her "ordinary" man. Where Etting had control, Helen lost hers. She tried to steady her nerves with drink, and the federal agents who battered down the door of the speakeasy she ran on West Fifty-second Street did nothing to help when they raided her on December 29, 1927, two days after *Show Boat*'s New York opening, creating huge headlines (she was never sure that Ziegfeld hadn't tipped them off).

When "Half Caste Woman" garnered a disappointing response, they teamed her with Harry to sing Walter Donaldson's "I'm with You." Harry, for his own part, had found a distinct lack of chemistry with Ruth in their pairing, "Here We Are in Love," and found audiences hard to convince of their mutual ardor. Harry was on more familiar ground with Helen's sex appeal. Compact and curvaceous, she reminded him of Clara Bow, whom he'd tried desperately to marry in July 1930, giving her a $10,000 ring only to have her bid adieu to his bed, return home, and leave twenty minutes later for another's. He knew. He'd followed her. It was quite a letdown from when she had come to New York to see him five months earlier and he had met her at the train with dozens of newspapermen in tow. A $15,000 1928 electric-blue Isetta was sitting outside Grand Central as a gift. The steam from a nearby engine swirled around his feet, his raccoon coat was recklessly flung open.

He raced from window to window, searching for her. When the photographers caught up with their tripods and dangling cameras, the embracing pair seemed almost surprised by their presence, posing again and again. She too wore fur, and carried a doll in the crook of her right elbow.

Helen got to sing her own song with the mordant "Here Lies Love"; even here, the timing was off. Ruth always thought the number should have ended with a pinspot dissolving, instead of a blackout. "A blackout is for a joke," she told a reporter. Helen didn't care. Under the arch of the proscenium, leaning on a table covered in gold cloth when the drink got too much, she held her love letters in hand and got mournful. Nobody could do it better.

Ruth didn't even try. Her dialect sketch with Jack Pearl was the picture of innocence, playing a couple exchanging other people's pictures through a lonely hearts club. They sat on a humpbacked trunk on a buggy; he wore high-button shoes, she blond curls and a kerchief. It was a different era.

Flo had lived through it once. The show continued its unfold: the Albertina Rasch Dancers against a white cyclorama in Dmitri Tiomkin's "Illusion in White"; Mitzi Mayfair's waltz, "Dance Away the Night"; Mark Hellinger's "The Africans Had a Word for It" with Jack Pearl playing Judge Crater Horn (though the original Judge Crater's disappearance had long since faded into bad jokes such as these, it was reported that he had last been seen at the Club Abbey, run by Harry's old partner Lou Schwartz, in the Hotel Harding), Bubbles playing Rumba, "a Servant," Harry as Ravioli, and Gladys Glad cast as, yes, the "Beautiful White Goddess"; "The Changing of the Guard" with marching bagpipes and Buckingham Palace as a backdrop; "Clinching the Sale" with Harry singing and Dorothy Dell as his Customer, while the showgirls dressed up as Finger Brush, Scrubbing Brush, Floor Mop, Whisk Broom, and various dusters; and "Victim of the Talkies," Flo's snub at the Hollywood that seemed to be rising as he was falling.

They were right, he thought, taking his watch out of his vest pocket. *The show is too long. The second half slows to a crawl.* He couldn't figure out what to do about it. That was what scared him.

It wasn't just him. It was the whole damn country. People out of work. Banks busted. Strikes. Fear and hunger in the air. This was America. It was only supposed to get better. Bigger. More.

Not the way it used to be. He wondered if knowing how it used to be took away the thrill of how it is. *This is what it's like*, Flo mused as the entire company came on for the grand finale, walking to the elephant boneyard, ponderous, surprisingly agile but feeling the weight of behemoth. His kind of entertainment was giving way to ones that were at once more grand and more

intimate, able to span dynamics he could hardly have dreamed with his enclosed stage and pit orchestra and arrayed Follies girls.

"Happiness Will See You Through." Ziegfeld was through, and he wasn't
happy. A year later, on July 22, he would be gone.

IN THE orchestra, Russ sat beside Con, who sat beside Paul, who sat beside
Harry. They were about fifteen rows back, off the left aisle.

The seats were filled with "theater habitués," as Klaw called them. Among
the ticketbuyers were George Gershwin, Gary Cooper, Guy and Carmen
Lombardo, Billy Rose, Irving Caesar, Fred and Adele Astaire. Not all could
make it.

He couldn't take his eyes off Dorothy. Whenever she bobbed into view, he
could feel the show become background music. He watched her perform in
isolate; hanging on her reactions to the swirl around her, studying her subtleties, seeing her personality peek through her stage mask.

She was nervous, but appealingly so. Russ could sense her thrill at being on
Broadway. She was over her opening night jitters; but she'd yet to get jaded,
or even professional. Her twirl on the stage couldn't disguise the feeling that
she was overjoyed to be in her own skin, and it was a lovely skin, half-draped
in the Ziegfeld manner. She did have incredible legs.

Con leaned over to him. "That dame is sure some sweet patootie," he said.
"But you better watch your step. The last thing you need is some dummy jane
hanging around your every move.

"Take it from me, these girls are murder. That Beth Beri took me for everything I had. I was busted. Flat on my ass. Thirty fuckin' g's."

Russ shifted in his red velvet seat. He was humming along with the music,
but so low that it was more like a thrum in his chest, his internal motor running, revving.

"Don't fuck it up. Remember, you've only just got on the radio." It was
true, he had a broadcast set for that evening at twelve. "We don't even have
the contract finalized with Victor yet. They're not going to like hearing you
have a girlfriend. Look at all the trouble Vallée got himself in when he married that dizzy Mexi-looking broad. His fans are deserting him in droves."

Let Con talk. Russ knew that you have to sing to someone. Not anyone. Or
even everyone. Some one.

Onstage, the Ziegfeld company moved into the reprise. Flo had originally
wanted to have all the chorus girls line up in their accustomed manner, with
a vacant place where Helen would have stood. A single spotlight would fill

her missing position, the rest of the stage in semidarkness. The girls had protested, fearing they would break down and weep at such a heartrending scene, and Ziegfeld acquiesced. Everyone was feeling bad enough already.

Instead, the "ladies of the ensemble" poured out from the wings in an unending stream. It was as crowded onstage as a Manhattan rush hour.

Russ could only look at Dorothy. Delicious.

RECORDING 1

It was Con's idea to have a signature tune. The all-important introduction. The announcement of arrival.

He found a youthful Gladys Dubois at a Hollywood party. She wanted to be a songwriter, she shyly told Con, and gave him the lyrics on a scrap of paper. Yawitz spread to the press that Conrad and Russ finished it on the train as they crossed the country, but Paul Gregory, a Broadway second-stringer who had appeared in both movie and play versions of *Whoopee*, polished the lyrics when they got to New York, and the writer's credit was split four ways. Conrad got the publishing.

The song is "You Call It Madness but I Call It Love." Columbo's calling card.

Russ's four-week trial run for NBC had been left dangling after his final show on Saturday, August 22. Jack Royal was still sitting on the fence, and Con wasn't helping, storming into his office loudly demanding renegotiation and respect and God knows what else. Royal was about to pass when he took notice of CBS's interest in Bing, to the tune of a healthy $1,500 a week. On August 25, CBS announced its deal, sustaining Crosby until he found a sponsor, and much as Royal couldn't abide Conrad, he needed to compete. Russ was back on the air by August 28. With the radio deal in Con's hand, Victor fell into line, and on Thursday, September 3, 1931, Russ Columbo entered Studio 1 to make his recording debut as a solo artist.

.   .   .

THEY WERE talking about Bing when Columbo walked in about 1:45 in the afternoon: Fred Erdman, who today would be known as a head of A&R (Artists & Repertoire, though repertoire then took precedence over artists); some guy named Weatherald, Russ couldn't quite catch his name. He was too excited to take much notice. Nat Shilkret, the orchestra director, came up and shook his hand, introducing him to his brother Jack on piano and the rest of the small band. There was a violin player, a clarinet and trumpet, a guitar and a string bass. Cozy.

Nat had dismissed a few of the musicians from the larger morning session. He had cut "I Idolize My Baby's Eyes" and a couple of other forgettable tunes with an aggregation that Victor was going to call the Troubadours Orchestra, though it was a simple house contract session with Chick Bullock out front like he was with everyone from the High Hatters ("Singing the Blues") to Duke Ellington ("Sam and Delilah"), and that was just for Victor. A singer who would record prolifically in the thirties (he was a special favorite of Bunny Berrigan's), Chick woke on the morning of his departure for Hollywood to discover the white of one eye had turned black. He never made it to the movies.

Erdman was saying that he thought Crosby's delay was a publicity gag. Keep up the suspense. Bing wouldn't dare show up drunk to CBS for his first show, would he? Not after all that money had been shelled out, and his speakeasy predilection well known. Two nights running? It had to be throat trouble. He'd heard it was because of this new icebox air-conditioning they had over at CBS.

Weatherald shook his head. He'd gotten wind of Bing and Roger Marchetti going up to Jack Kapp at Brunswick headquarters, shortly after Crosby had arrived in New York in mid-August. He recorded "Dancing in the Dark" and "Stardust" with Victor Young, and then Roger told Jack their contract was about to expire. That was when they learned Brunswick held an ironclad option.

None of it mattered now. Bing had caught the public imagination, and if he had been celebrating his radio show a bit prematurely, what of it? He hadn't said a word last night, leaving the announcing to Harry Von Zell, who apologized for "the delayed appearance of that sensational baritone . . . favorite of California." Blame was laid on a "severe case of laryngitis" brought on by golfing in the rain with a Danny Walker who makes no further appearances in history.

But here, at last, was "fifteen minutes with Bing Crosby . . . his inimitable song interpretation . . . the moment you have been waiting for. . . . " Bing might have missed Monday and Tuesday, but on Wednesday at 11:00 P.M., he didn't disappoint, noticeably husky but smoothing as he gained confidence, opening with "Just One More Chance"—was he singing to Paley?—and closing with "I'm Through with Love."

Venuti and Lang underpin him, the violin taking flight in "I'm Through with Love." Crosby had specifically requested Eddie's presence. There was something about his brush of the strings that framed Bing's voice, gave him a solid footing to manipulate the rhythm, Lang's chord voicings suggesting melodic phrases and leading tones. In "Just One More Chance," his voice slides when he heads uphill, and shying, he lays out from the first scat section, the orchestra caught suddenly unawares. The second time around he takes his chance, going for it. Eddie lunges forward with him. "I'm Through with Love" is Bing at the first moment of his movement into legend. As the last notes fade, Von Zell reminds his listeners to tune in "each night at this time, except Sundays. Bing Crosby wishes you a very good evening."

Bing never took his gray slouch hat off during the show.

RUSS DIDN'T participate in the conversation. He was saving his voice.

Shilkret flipped through the music, distributing the lead sheets to the musicians, explaining the procedure to Russ. They'd do two takes, using the second in case anything went wrong with the first. He showed him the lathe in the control room, the *gematria* dial settings—A6, .9, Int. 14, −2, 0, 3—that determined the size and angle of the needle, the wow and flutter, the curve that carved and chiseled the canyons of the wax master disk.

Like many zoologists, engineers were still better at capturing than reproducing sound. Playback equipment couldn't handle as much information as the grooves could retain; a boon to listeners half a century in the future, along with the newly astonishing concept that there would be listeners in the future, this ability to bottle sound. A movie could be thought of as a painting come to action. But to replay sound, that was something unexpected. Even Edison was surprised when he came upon the principle, having been looking for a way to transcribe the dots-and-dashes of Samuel Morse's telegraph code.

Nathaniel Shilkret was an old hand at overseeing recording. Born on Christmas Day, 1889, the first year that commercial recordings were sold in America, he was a classically trained clarinetist and pianist who became associated with Victor at the age of twenty-four. A musical director for the company as it straddled the acoustic and electric eras, he first managed the

Foreign Department, conducting an average of seventy selections per month, absorbing Russian, German, Pan-American, and even hillbilly stylings, as he showed when he accompanied A. C. "Eck" Robertson on July 1, 1922, in what are considered some of the first "country" recordings. As a bandleader, he had his hits (the 1927 "Flapperette" is most associated with him), and a group of all-occasions configurations: the Victor Salon Orchestra, the Victor Concert Orchestra, the Victor Symphony Orchestra, the International Novelty Orchestra, the Hilo Hawaiian Orchestra, Shilkret's Rhyth-Melodists, the Eveready Radio Group, and the Victor Schrammel (Viennese) Orchestra, as well as countless sessions he produced and supervised.

It was just another day in the studio for him. He liked the familiarity of the laboratory atmosphere, the challenge of getting three good takes in as many hours. Nat had little taste for the road—he left that to a showboat like Whiteman. He also was getting first pick of the available songs. In fact, Shilkret's insider position was one of the reasons Paul Whiteman left Victor in 1928, or so studio scuttlebutt had it (and the fact that Columbia was offering him considerably more money).

The trouble between them had really started on April 21, 1927, when Whiteman went in to electrically re-record *Rhapsody in Blue*. Gershwin, present at the session, thought Paul was speeding the performance unnecessarily to give it a more "jazzy" effect; the disagreement led to Whiteman's storming out of the studio. When he returned, Shilkret was waving the baton, conducting Whiteman's own orchestra. "Pops" slammed the door on his way out for a second time.

All this practical experience served Shilkret well in his afternoon session with Russ. Nat had paid close attention to Crosby the evening before (NBC even made test recordings of Bing on the radio, to study what their CBS competition was up to), and decided a smaller scale would benefit Columbo. In particular, Shilkret brought the guitar closer in to the recording balance, the instrument's strummed texture burnishing the voice, as it would increasingly within popular music, reaching a height in the second half of the century.

THE CLARINET steps closer to the microphone to deliver the hummable phrase, the trumpet hangs back by the far wall in paraphrase, slightly delayed. Columbo's voice is full, thicker than Bing's, darker in hue; Shilkret finds baritones easier to record than tenors, which might be why Russ sounds unforced, casual, even as he begins singing the verse in his highest register.

"I Don't Know Why (I Love You Like I Do)" never leaves its indelible chorus from there. The song, an Ahlert-Turk composition, goes three successions in its deliberate turn of phrase, tempo variations keeping the textural interest as Russ barely varies the pace of his delivery. The first chorus is slow, the second double-times for the first half and then settles back, the third—the band instrumental—trit-trots for eight bars, even as Russ comes in for the dénouement, a languorous tease.

He sways like a pendulum amid this underplay of releasing build, a trapeze artist who nears the end of his arc and slows before plunging again. He lingers over the *ooo* of "but I do." The last notes clamber up his backbone, transiting the regional registers of his body, the bass clef under the sternum, the treble located somewhere behind the bridge of his nose. He crosses from one to another with no break in posture, no sense of in-line shift. If the musicians seem to be dragging him along when they accelerate the second verse, Columbo's angle of backward lean makes his reentry all the more plausible. He has not broken the mood.

The same rhymes—"do" and "you"—provide the basis for the next song. In "Guilty," written by Gus Kahn, Richard Whiting, and Harry ("Am I Blue?") Akst, Columbo sings of love's transgression, an original sin, culpable in his confession. *"Maybe I'm right, maybe I'm wrong,"* he admits, his ambivalence entering a realm where morality loses its power to influence behavior. *"But I'm Guil-ty for loving you."* His unnamed flame has made up her mind: their "love is so wrong," compounding his complicity. Yet he seems unconcerned; love for him is its own justification. A crime of passion. He isn't responsible for his actions; he pleads insanity.

Love as madness.

THE CROON makes its first formal appearance for Russ in "Guilty." On the borderline of self-awareness, it's still too early to be used as a signifier, like a wedding ring, or a key chain worn on the right. Soon it will gather enough cliché to define type, as in "a crooner."

For Russ, it is a useful musical accessory, an adornment, his plumage displayed. After the third chorus, when the band has taken its turnaround and he's provided the framework of the verse, he lets fly with the *ba-ba-bahs*, his voice at its upper altitude and attitude until it rolls down the incline of the song's tagline. He does this twice. *"Is it a sin?"* Is this a crime? He asks the question and answers it, toying with the vocal as if he's playing with himself. Is this art or masturbation?

No wonder he's guilty. His brain could flow out his ears. He could go blind. But he can't hold himself back.

He spills his seed into the microphone.

AH.

A sighing, separating two ways of experiencing the same emotion.

It splits the infinitive of "You Call It Madness . . . but I Call It Love," unspoken in the title.

Love and madness are not really mutually exclusive. In its unsettling, love sidesteps our best intentions. Sanity assumes there's a reason why we do what we do (and we *dooo*); a why things happen. Of course there's a reason for love. You think you know what you want.

That is the maddest thought of all.

Ah . . . It's the dawning realization, mingled with an exclamation of pleasure. Sinking into a warm bath; sliding within; the moment here at last.

You think I'm nuts. And I am. I'm nuts about you.

BY FOUR in the afternoon, they're ready to record "You Call It Madness."

A single piano note bells the beguiling. The arrangement couldn't be more simple, violin and clarinet surreptitiously padding, silhouetting the melody as the guitar and piano play four-strokes-to-the-bar rhythm.

The refrain, with its piano hooks (a high chordal figure to set the title line, and a seven-note lick tying the second section chorus lines), is obviously Con-derived. In fact, it might be Con, taking over the keyboard on a song he knows will make or break Russ. But even if he's not there, he's written his parts into the sheet music, so whoever performs it will be quoting his score.

Love expects reciprocation. *"You made a prom-ise to be faith-ful / By all the stars a-bove. . . . "* But you've left me, *"made a plaything out of romance."* And the final curt dismissal: *"What do you know of love?"*

Don't start something you can't finish. Russ knew he was stirring emotions and expectations. He would be performing at one of the events Con was dragging him to, guesting at a nightclub or coming out of the radio studio, and he would meet one of his fans, and she would be looking at him in a state of disbelief, trying to connect his voice with his features, his sung *onliness*.

There is the possibility of threat.

That's part of the attraction. Love thrives on uncontrol. It needs madness. Just like I need you.

Everybody but the piano sits out for the verse, a reminder of Harry Barris's duet with Bing on "At Your Command." Russ pauses to consider his consequences. How have things gotten to this sorry state of affair? A slight suggestion has grown to *"haunt my mind."* He once needed only himself. Now that he has *"found you,"* how much of himself shall he give away? How much can he expect in return? " *'Twas that e-ter-nal ques-tion . . . my love I had to share."* The self-interest of a child becomes the wish-fulfillment of a man: *"I built my dreams a-round you, / Some-how you made me care."*

Then you left. But I still love you. How crazy is that?

THE MUTED trumpet overtakes the main melody, granting Russ the instrumental solo. Madness is contagious. The croon is now heard as a language of the subconscious, escaped from self-restraints, free to roam and choose its own mnemonics, grammar, and vocabulary. This is dialect not bound by geography or tribe. Emotion only hints at translation. Like the Eskimos with their fifty words for snow, or the Chinese, for whom the register of a voice can change the gist of a word, there are shades of meaning that only those who live in its lingual world will understand.

He's nearing the end. The session has gone well. You can hear the thrill in his voice, the exult, as his croon gives way to the triumph of the final chorus, orbiting the song as planets do the sun, or the moon runs centrifugal rings around the earth, a satellite under the gravitational pull of another.

"By all the stars above." Infinity's number.

THE SESSION breaks up around five. The next morning, Bert Lown and His Hotel Biltmore Orchestra will enter Studio 1 to cut another version of "You Call It Madness" with Elmer Feldkamp on vocals, though they fail to get an acceptable take and will have to return on September 16 to wax the released version. A day earlier, on September 15, Kate Smith records her interpretation in a session that includes "I Don't Know Why (I Just Do)" and "Shine On Harvest Moon," the same day that Mildred Bailey takes her vocal turn with the Casa Loma Orchestra. Phil Spitalny, soon to lead the Hour of Charm All-Girl Orchestra, records his cover for Perfect on the 18th. On October 21, Ben Selvin and the Hotel Commodore Dance Orchestra (with Tommy Dorsey, Joe Venuti, and Benny Goodman) cut "You Call It Madness" with Orlando Roberson on vocals. Helen Rowland will sing it with Freddie Rich's Radio Orchestra in November for the aptly named Hit-of-the-

Week label, a flexible record made of durium, while Smith Ballew releases his rendition for Crown in December. In future years, it will be covered by the bandleader and amateur magician Richard Himber, who comes out of Rudy Vallée's Yankees with his concept of rhythmically pyramiding horns, and by tenor saxist Don Byas, with a rhythm section of Cozy Cole on drums and Billy Taylor on bass. A standard.

Con knows there's a difference between the singer and the song. He wants both. Love's madness.

SWEET AND LOVELY

Six days later, on September 9, 1931, Russ records "Sweet and Lovely." Five days after, Bing puts his version to wax. The Battle of the Baritones is joined.

The rivalry makes for good copy. Both profit by the attention. The newspapers love a conflict, and Con and Yawitz are happy to stoke the fires. They have Bing snubbing Russ at a social event, Russ sniping at Bing in the Broadway columns. At the CBS dinner for radio "scribes," Bing visits a table of journalists. "How's your pal Russ Columbo?" he's asked.

"Pal," huffs Bing. "Say, listen, the first time I meet that guy Columbo, and it won't be too soon either, I'm just going to give him something to remember me by . . . and it won't be grapefruit." Jerry Wald, the "Not on the Air" reporter from the *New York Evening Graphic*, rubs his editorial hands together. "Tickets for that fight would be at a premium." Rudy is soon added to the mix as reigning male vocalist, especially with *George White's Scandals* opening at the Apollo Theater on Broadway the next week, on the fourteenth, with Ethel Merman, Ray Bolger, and the Gale Quadruplets. His role is to look askance at these pretenders to his radio throne (he still takes the *Mirror* poll in 1931), recalling his well-publicized feud with Will Osborne. There is no end to the sides they can take against each other, like a game of rock, scissors, paper.

Actually, Rudy didn't mind Bing. It was Russ that unnerved him, or was it that Columbo was also on an NBC outlet, starting to look like the new boy on the block? He had caught Fay listening to him on the radio one night when he had a rare evening off, dancing with her eyes closed in the living room with its sprawling park view. When he walked into the room, she didn't even look up, or notice him.

RUSS AND Bing shared the song's lineage. "Sweet and Lovely" was from Gus Arnheim's book, written with Harry Tobias and Jules Lemaire. Any resemblance to "Lovable and Sweet," composed by Oscar Levant with lyrics by Sidney Clare, which Gus performed in the 1929 movie *Street Girl* starring Betty Compson and Jack Oakie, was purely coincidental. Arnheim must not have thought the tune had hit potential. When tenor saxophonist–arranger Jimmie Grier asked Gus for his usual $25 to orchestrate the song, Arnheim haggled with him, settling instead on 5 percent of the writer's royalties, a decision he would come to rue with each new cover. By the time "Sweet and Lovely" was featured in 1938's *Two Girls and a Sailor*, Grier had made his fee many times over.

Gus recorded his version, spotlighting tenor Donald Novis, on July 19, 1931. If he wanted to distance himself from Crosby's shenanigans, he couldn't have done more to square off the rhythm, and Novis's reading is perched high and dry, sounding closer to Kate Smith's soprano than Bing's dusky overtones, each word enunciated floridly, as if it were smoothed and pomaded with brilliantine. The song becomes a staple with Arnheim, however, and by 1933, it functions as his calling card. Gus uses it as both opening and closing theme in a 1933 broadcast from the Cocoanut Grove, giving the chorus a bump-and-grind swing of the hips before the announcer billboards "the star of entertainers and the entertainer of stars . . . enchanting music to guide their dancing feet in gay fantasy," and Arnheim waves the orchestra into "You Don't Need Glasses (to See I'm in Love)."

VICTOR WANTS to release two records by Russ on September 25. His contract calls for four songs the first month, and to get the final side, Shilkret slots him at the end of an afternoon session with Gene Austin. The passing of the microphone is symbolic, for Austin, whose 1927 "My Blue Heaven" has been among the largest sellers of the twenties, is about to be supplanted by a new breed of singer.

Gene was one of the first to use his voice orthophonically, as Victor called their electrical process, to the microphone's advantage, though his performing roots were so wedded to the acoustic era that he hardly knew what to do with his newfound vocal freedom. He was able to lower the volume, but couldn't shake the derring-do of his delivery. Even the *doo-doo-doo*'s on "My Blue Heaven" fall unerringly on the beat, with minimal instrumentation, a piano and a single violin and a sine-wave-like whistling solo. Everything is high-pitched.

Austin was born June 24, 1900, in Gainesville, Texas (just across the state from Palestine, where Seger Ellis got his start, and Houston, where Smith Ballew hailed from), as Eugene Lucas. Gene viewed the circus and the army as much the same escape route, and ran away from home to join first one and then the other, winding up in war-torn France as a bugler. He teamed with Roy Bergère for a vaudeville act, and then went solo in 1924 when the pair scored with "How Come You Do Me Like You Do." Austin began recording for Victor in the spring of that same year, working early on with Nat Shilkret, or his brother Jack. It was Jack who would supervise the first electrical recording session issued on Victor a year later, a regional release by the Mask & Wig Club of the University of Pennsylvania, from their production of *Joan of Arkansas*. Nat collaborated on another well-remembered Austin composition, "Lonesome Road." Gene's Rio Grande roots were further revealed in his April 1928 hit recording of "Ramona." In some ways, its south-of-the-border flair heralds the singing cowboys of the thirties, a music more suited for the camaraderie of the campfire than the intimacy of the fireplace.

Whispering. It was all the rage, like Whispering Jack Smith over in England. But a tenor could only sound foolish when the voice drew close, the squeak of falsetto hardly the stuff of manly persuasion, at least until the Four Seasons came along. The age of the *castrati* was in decline, though not before Alessandro Moreschi recorded "Ave Maria" in April 1904, suspended nether-gender between the sacrificial and sacramental, sung in the doo-wop language of Italian.

Gene finishes shortly after four, a "Love Letters in the Sand" and a "Blue Kentucky Moon" with a small six-piece band. Shilkret introduces the two as Russ comes into Studio 1. Their handshake is like the palmed passing of a discreet message. A tip. It's Columbo's turn now.

RUSS IS dragging his tail. He went out to the speaks with Con after last night's radio show. Though he sang only four songs in fifteen minutes at his usual lullaby hour of 11:30 P.M.—last night's batch was "It's the Girl," "With You on My Mind," "Now That I Need You," and "Memory Lane," which Con especially liked, since it was his melody—he's often too wound up to go home to sleep.

He's had to match New York's rpm, like the way a phonograph once had to be hand-cranked to speed. Con had him on the run, singing "You Call It Madness" at a radio plant dedication (where he appears with other up-and-comers like Jessica Dragonette and Cab Calloway), odd nightclubs, making the round of booking agents and potential sponsors. "This is the big one," Conrad kept telling him. Con could recognize the signs; he had seen first-hand once or twice when it had all come together; the brass ring in hand. That was the easy part. It was a tougher sell not to get flung off the carousel when someone sped the turntable. Keep the balls juggling in motion. Make a fortune. Go bust. That was Broadway and Wall Street, both.

Shilkret handed around the lead sheets. The musicians—a saxophone and trumpet, a string bass and guitar, a violin and piano—could hum the tune already. It didn't take long for a hit to get around.

Though the rhythm's pulsing metronome is underscored by the guitar's four downstrokes, the effect is lilted, lightened by the violin's swirl. It's a delicate entrance for Russ, floating in and swelling on the double *ee* of *sweet*; the cascading double *uu* of *lovely*. His voice rides its tenor, throat and note at the same height, until he dives under the waves to where the baritone lies immersed, alveoli like coral in the aquarium of the lungs, the broad pool of chest, the vowels causing ripples of current around the heart.

THEY MIRROR the same song. Bing starts with the verse; Russ takes the chorus. They will converge in the croon.

The verse is a tricky navigation of stop-and-start melody; it's almost a recitation. You can imagine it in a musical, a prelude to a production number, a framing device. Bing has a conversational tone to his voice that lends itself to narration, patiently explaining his situation, setting up the woodland images of doves and roses and summer breezes. All paling next to *"The one and only one I love."*

Two ones. Which must be why he needs two words to describe her. He's telling the world, letting them in on his secret. Making them party to his romance.

Russ doesn't need the outdoor scenery. He knows it doesn't matter when you're so close that her face fills the screen. He doesn't want to distance himself from the song. He's there. For you. He lets the band take the verse on its own, giving it the hymnal strains of a Victorian sentimental ballad, biding time.

They're feeling each other out. Bing has the fancier footwork, Russ the more concentrated stance. He's waiting for Bing to let down his guard, to have his adversary come to him.

They clinch on the second chorus. Bing takes a swing. Russ awaits in abeyance, readying.

Then the croon is upon them.

It circles their separate duet as they circumnavigate each other. Their feud, like their phrasing, carefully gives each his own space, room to maneuver. Russ answers the violin's solo lines, ever the courteous gentleman. At one point he stretches the suspense until the last possible moment before adding his curlicue, a responding that is the playful empathy of a partner.

Bing steps out on the choruses as a horn might. He is halfway in spiral as he nears the croon, and at one point gets so enamored with his improverbal spin that he turns a dizzying *yheeee* like a somersault. He lands on his feet and keeps the vocal on the rebound. He should feel good. His radio show is a hit, and Publix has called about the Paramount. There's still the union ban in California, which looks like it's going to cost him a bundle. It's worth it. He can't lose now.

DIME-A-DANCE. Who's leading? Croons combined. Evenly matched.

Sweet and lovely, lovable and sweet.

THEY'RE CALLING him names. Dorothea Kardel of the *News* hails the Tender-Toned Lochinvar of the Air who sings Song Sermons. Jack Foster of the *World-Telegram* dubs him Baron of the Baritones. Even Con can't resist an appellation, telling A. J. Liebling of the same paper that Russ is "just a slob ballad singer." The word doesn't refer to Russ's dress sense so much as it combines "slow" and "sob." A NBC public relations handout says that the baritone crooner is "something like Vallée, but lower."

On September 25, Victor takes an ad out in the dailies heralding Columbo's first two releases. In it, Russ is a "lonely lover," an apparent oxymoron in more ways than one. "A couple of flowery young men rushed up to the manly Columbo," Foster relates after one appearance, "and attempting to embrace him, cried ecstatically, 'It was so beautiful we almost cried.' " A repetition of cries. Cry upon cry; two different cries.

Victor has coupled "Guilty" with "I Don't Know Why"; "You Call It Madness but I Call It Love" with "Sweet and Lovely." The company is adjusting to the idea that they are owned by the Radio Corporation of America, the

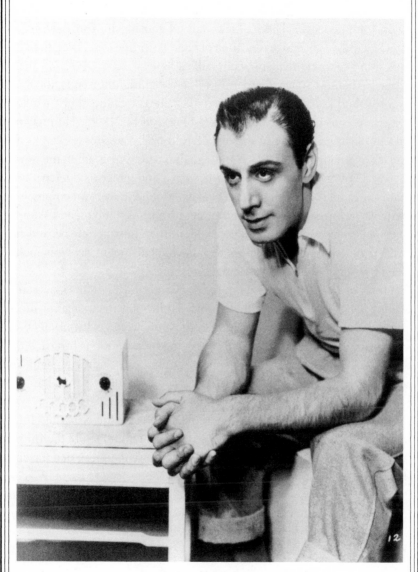

RUSS AND RADIO

media conjoined. They offer "the music you want when you want it," these "New Records by The New Radio Sensation." Two wants, two news; one for each disc. 22801/2, for the discographically inclined.

On the air at midnight this evening, backed by Leon Rosebrook's Orchestra, he'll sing "Guilty," "Whispering," "Little Mama Doll," and "My Happiness Is Your Success." There's NBC talk of moving him to 8:00 P.M. to compete with Crosby's new start time of 7:00. It's prime time, even then, the family sitting around the living room radio as one.

Over at Madison Square Garden, at Fiftieth and Eighth Avenue, the Radio Electrical World's Fair is taking place. Nikola Tesla had tuned his "wireless" as precisely as a musical scale in the last years of the 1800s. He imagined sparks of electrical energy in the air, derived from the sun, resonating frequencies originating in one place and signals received in another, the way he once saw a vision of his dying mother from afar and understood telepathy.

Now the radio is everywhere, the trade fair proclaims, with an emphasis on novelty items. Among the Fadas, Stromberg-Carlsons, Philcos, and Westinghouses are radios tucked in pillows, hidden in grandfather clocks and fireplaces, reduced to midget sets. A bedside hookup might account for the sudden blossom of romantic baritones.

Yet most of the excitement seems to revolve around a ten-foot glass screen weighing 350 pounds, on which are projected live moving images by means of a photoelectric scanning disc. It takes three nights to get it working properly. Already there are small stations operating for an hour or two each day, like W2XCR, from 655 Fifth Avenue, beaming out flashes of light and shadow that are received and translated as motion pictures, silhouettes, animated cartoons.

NBC has built an experimental studio (W2XBS) atop the New Amsterdam Theater. In July, shortly before moving to the eighty-fifth floor of the Empire State Building to use its tower for an antenna, they'd demonstrated traveling light-rays by focusing on figurines of Mickey Mouse and Felix the Cat, revolving on a platform, reconstituting them as contrasting shades of black and white with clearly defined features that can be seen as far away as Kansas City. Cat and mouse. It's down to distance and size now.

Sight broadcasting. Television.

OBBLIGATO

Like a cat.

He tells people, "One of the things they seem to like best is the voice obbligato on repeat choruses. Very much as I used to do them on violin."

Obbligato. An obligation. His honor is at stake. He has made a promise.

Kept. He seals a pact with his violin, the call and response of obbligato's witness. He is now able to think in the instrument's language. It isn't hard to translate song into the vowels of nonverbal singing; his voice just becomes a different creator of sound. No more the vocal cord. The string and bow emanate from his throat.

The music remains the same, the melody's beating frequency, its arrangement of intervals. Higher. Lower. Held. Let go.

Repeated.

Voice and violin. The vowels traded: I and o, me and you. Exchanging places; -ce and -in becoming sin.

Russ mostly writes his songs late at night. "I get some of my best ideas after I've gone to bed."

Oooo, saucy.

He nudges closer to her.

Whaddya think a girl is, some kind of floozy? I'm not fly like you'd like to think, Mr. Smartie. You can't put one over on me.

She squeals, squirming away from him on the banquette. Not really. Just enough to wriggle. Giggle. Pleased with her prettiness.

. . .

HE TURNS to catch the eye of a waiter. The Argonaut Club is crowded tonight.

Onstage, Jean Malin is finishing his star turn. Her star turn. Whichever.

S/he is the mistress of ceremonies, dressed in tie and tails. They are the same man and woman.

New York is caught up in a pansy parade, as tabloids like the *Broadway Brevities* alternately decry and exploit, tickling the fancy of "horticulturally" inclined readers and sensation-seekers. What better to have a delicious thrill than at the expense of you—the other—winking at I?

This may be gay minstrelsy on Times Square, but it is not a straight man imitating a gay man imitating a woman. It's the real thing. Jean—once Victor Eugene James—Malin, up from Greenwich Village, where the genders flirt, the races and nationalities melt. America has found its twentieth-century recipe: immigrants and marginals rife with inequalities working various shell games.

Malin was born the same year as Columbo, in Brooklyn. His earliest drag role was of a Ziegfeld showgirl, Imogene Wilson, known for public fisticuffs with her lover, another Follies star, the blackface comedian Frank Tinney. He never told her he was married—"I have a mortgage and an appendix as well . . . why bring these things up and spoil a pleasant time?" he breezily said—and the resultant assault and battery wound its way into court. Malin enjoyed re-creating the moment when Imogene took the witness stand in a blue suit, pink stockings, and cloche hat. His costumes only elaborated from there.

When he moved uptown, booked by Louis Schwartz of the Club Abbey in the summer of 1930, he switch-hit to the more sedate tuxedo of a ceremonial host. The impressionism was broad. *Ooooh la-la. . . .* He lisped, limped his wrist, pranced and tossed his head like a sulky colt, poked his pinkie in the air. The effect was sassy, especially when backed up (and you didn't want to back too far up to Madame Malin) by six feet, two hundred pounds of heavyweight sissy. Jean didn't mind a good fight. He knew how to defend himself.

At the Abbey, he took on catcalls and hoo-hahs, and started a craze on Broadway for effeminate men—"male impersonators," wrote one paper—that was in full handbag-swing by the end of 1930. In December, when the Pansy Club opened on Forty-eighth Street just west of Broadway, the secret sex was out in the open, at least within the gilded frame of the Times Square floor show.

Manhattan's crossroads was no stranger to cross-dressing. Most celebrated was the actor Julian Eltinge, born William Dalton in 1883, who had been playing female roles since he was ten. He had changed his name to the softened syllables of a racier French, *parley vooooh la la*, and after appearing in the title role of *The Fascinating Widow* at the Liberty on Forty-second Street, was renowned enough to have an entire theater christened for him a few doors down in 1912. He was best known for starring in *The Crinoline Girl*, and his portrait was incorporated among the painted female deities of the theater's arched cupola ceiling, where it can still—within the confines of a multiplex—be seen today.

Schwartz found Jean downtown at the Rubaiyat in full feathers, but when Malin came to work at the Abbey, he reversed his portrayal. It was more *betrayal*; he became what he was, a gay man essentially playing himself. This was different from an out-and-out female impersonator like Ray Bourbon, who had a vaudeville act with Bert Sherry under his *nom de femme* Rae (Bourbon and Sherry: Bert was the straight man), and would later open his *Boys Will Be Girls* revue at Tait's Café in San Francisco.

Like other exotic outsiders—the Yiddish melodrama of Second Avenue or the Harlem "chocolate" Renaissance as it spilled over to Broadway—the actual purveyors of individual genre had taken a while to present their calling cards at the front door of entertainment, after years of using the back servants' entrance. Part of the appeal was novelty value: at this stage, on these stages, the stereotypes ran inarguably crude. There is a hint of zoo in Malin's stroll through the Abbey, exchanging repartée and hand-on-hip humor with the ogling, semi-sophisticated swells that fill the club. Come see the fairy! "I'll lay you out in ten dozen shades of lavender!" "I'd rather be Spanish than mannish," which said much for the hothouse-flower appeal of the Latin Lover. His favorite book, he told Sidney Skolsky, was *Grimm's Fairy Tales*. The stereotype worked in his favor, just as it did for Paul Robeson, typecast as a savage jungle king in *The Emperor Jones*. When Robeson sang "Ol' Man River" in the 1932 revival of *Show Boat*, his performance moved toward archetype. Type: first impressions are superficial, though telling. You can't deny attraction. Even arranged marriages are awkward at first.

Malin's betrothal to and subsequent sundering from a GIRL!—the dancer Lucille Fay Heiman, whom he'd met when he sang Richman's "There's Danger in Your Eyes, Cherie" to her—made headlines in January 1931, the same month that Dutch Schultz came into the Abbey and demanded to know from manager Charlie (Chink) Sherman why his Bronx beer money wasn't good enough. Chink pulled a gun and started shooting wildly at

Schultz, at which point he was rewarded with three bullets and twelve stab wounds from Dutch's enforcers. Coupled with hints of a Sodom-and-Gomorric retribution engendered by the Depression's salted pillar, the Abbey—a favored after-hours spot that opened at 4:00 A.M.—was permanently shuttered. Malin would ply his trade around New York for a time, then decamp to Boston, and finally follow the golden road to Hollywood, where he would open a club named after himself and have a bit part in MGM's *Dancing Lady*, with Joan Crawford, Clark Gable, and the Three Stooges.

His car plunged off a Santa Monica pier on August 9, 1933. It was as if he had nowhere left to go.

RUSS WATCHES the shifting sexuality with interest. *It's not so far from what I do*, he thinks. The croon is made for the feminine. He is the torch singer, the male alight. You looking pretty-pretty and gladys-glad and yet watching you from behind this pool of eyes is a stranger waiting to greet you over a great divide. It's time we bridged the gap.

He has to absorb the feminine. To see love as would the opposing sex, studying him in the mirror of her fan-shaped compact. He's transforming. He must convince her that he understands yearning, the depths of his own sincerity if he is to sing to her. That he has permission to enter her.

He turns to look at Dorothy, cheeks slightly flushed from drink, knowing she'd never seen the transgendered like in Louisiana. Helen Morgan, Jr., enters to wolf whistles and applause. The ruffles of his southern-belle gown trail the floor in *Show Boat* fashion. Dorothy—who has lived by the Mississippi—knows the real Helen; or does she? This Helen assumes Morgan's mannerisms, distills her essence, sees her from without, as others would. There is the shock of recognition. Lying atop the piano, unsteady glass in hand; the caricature is too close for comfort.

The sexes change partners. Dorothy presses her thigh against Russ's leg. She slips her hand under his jacket, trailing her fingers along his rib cage. Her hand snakes around his chest. She cups his breast below its curve, flicks at his nipple under the starched shirt with the pointed nail of her finger.

He hesitates, enjoying his reticence. Uncertain. He doesn't want to hurry it along. Be considered too willing. Easy. Yet he feels a tingling in his nethers, where his tailbone comes to a point, his body responding. He feels turned upon.

A five-piece orchestra takes the stand, wearing red fezzes. Hal's Sultan Syncopators: the leader is a pencil-mustached Russian Jew of about Russ's age who has learned his pianist's trade up in the Catskills and in the dance halls of the lower Bronx, a member of Local 802. They open with a sprightly novelty number made popular in 1926 by both the Yacht Club Boys and Tommy Christian's Orchestra: "*How Could Red Riding Hood / Be so very good / And still keep the wolf from her door?*"

The wolf understood. Dressed up as Granny.

Dorothy suddenly clutches at him. He can feel her sudden capitulation, letting herself go limp, moving past the coy to the caught. Couples stream past their table on the way to the dance floor, but they are too involved in each other to notice. It is the moment of dawning love in which anything can happen. Come what may. In no sense.

"*The modern child is running wild. . . .* " His hand slides up her leg, touching the top of her rolled stocking. The material has a slick feel; she has rolled them low, so he might brush the slippery skin above her knees, silk to silken.

"*Please let me ask it? Who filled her basket? . . . Why was she dressed up in bright flaming red? Unless she expected to knock someone dead?*"

"Russ," she breathes, and the *sss*'s trail into a sigh.

"*I've heard of a lot of strange things in New York / But who ever heard of a wolf that could talk?*"

They leave the table, retrieve her wrap, drop a sawbuck into the palm of the *maître d'* who whistles them a cab, and exit the club. As they settle into the backseat of the taxi—Dorothy with a slightly giddy bounce—Russ tells the driver his address.

She cuddles up next to him, insinuating her head between his chest and arm. "My wolf in sheep's clothing," she says, flicking her tongue in his direction. "Let's see how you howl." She huffs her *h*'s at him.

Russ purrs. A mewl of deep heat.

Oh, Granny, what big teeth you have.

PRISONER OF LOVE

His is is the skill of the nocturne. The fingers singing, the singing fingered with the touch-sensitive pressure of tips on strings, bow swooping and skimming and sliding and skidding. Finging. That's what it is for Russ.

He knows the bent knee of an instrument. Its genuflect to the player. He plays himself, imprinting his own emotive even as his audience plays upon him, each rapt listener overlaying their own expression and expectation. A prisoner of his reflection. *I'm just a Prisoner of Love. . . .*

Whisper to whisper. The nocturnal croon. Moon overhead. In your can*oooo*. The warm exhale, up close, inside the maze of the ear, oars arcing over the water in cadence. The gentle lap of the waves. Just you and I here, in this moment in time. In this lifetime. Just You. You, I. We can't escape the fate that has brought us together. Destiny is paddling our silver boat, bringing you to me. Moving our chesslike pieces.

We know the nocturne from Chopin. The most vocal of his slender canon, twenty-one selections in all. Songs in their brevity, a continuo of mood. The young Frédéric-François had first learned his scales from a violinist and pianist, Adalbert Zywny, a Bohemian. He gave his debut performance at the age of nine and was immediately an object of fascination for women, who became his greatest admirers.

Chopin utilized many old-fashioned—for their time—fingerings on the piano. He would place his thumb under the little finger, little finger under thumb. He would slip from key to key with one finger, not merely from the black to the white, but white to white. He liked scales beginning with the black keys, and when practicing, played the C major last.

He divided his hands, keeping time with his left while his right wavered in the breeze of the melody, the singing hand accompanied by the rhythmic, as he wrote: "Fancy a tree with its branches swayed by the wind—the stem is the steady time, the moving leaves are the melodic inflection."

And on another occasion: "Everything is to be read *cantabile . . .* : everything must be made to sing."

The blurring of the edges between self and instrument. The music coursing through the body, like a river or a lake overflowing its banks. The canoe travels over flooded terrain, oars dipping into the water, left-right, then a succession of lefts, and a succession of rights as the water parts to let it skiff through. The surrender.

Russ responds as the winding string, sensing the friction of the bow hairs rubbed against his stretched surface. Taut, tuned to a *twonk.* His note resonates in its amplifying chamber of wood, fingers pressing on the strings to give embellishment, just as the piano's pedals follow trails of sound as they head toward inaudibility and become air again.

While he's singing, he holds the violin along his left leg. His arm is extended, the right holds the bow. It would be awkward to use his hands to gesture, so he stands somewhat stiffly, loosely erect, jacket buttoned once, cummerbund peeking out, nipping his waist. Eyes downcast, centering his attention on the gathering vibrato in his throat and the shape of his moan.

The tuning pegs of the violin silhouette against his dusk jacket. Satin cuffs, face painted to stark the light, eyelids steeped in shadow. He is listening to the song deeply now, and as he concentrates on nuance and note, he forgets the band around him, New York pros waiting for the next cue, music stands shaped like harps and a look of askance.

He's not singing to them. He is transforming himself into the listener, reaching out along the microphones of radio and the cameras of motion pictures and the styli of phonograph recordings so that he can be there, even if he's not there. To entertain from afar, and be so very near. *As near as I am to you, here in the deep of night.*

I like the way you sing in my ear. With each word, I can feel your breath heated by the inside of your body, passing into me. We should write our song together sometime. Might I partake in your dance? A slow romantic valse on the verandah.

You have captured me. Truly. To feel that rush of feeling—you couldn't put a name to it—it's all I can do to break away from your embrace, here in the moonlight, shimmering like a silken camisole off the water in a New England summer (Rudy had seen to that), *and take my position in front of this square box of microphone, and tell you how you have captivated me, your prisoner yours.*

HE RECORDS "Prisoner of Love" at his second full session for Victor. Nat Shilkret again directs the ensemble: piano, violin, guitar, cello, string bass, two saxes, and a trumpet. Inside the control room, Con Conrad and a Victor representative, Fred Erdman, watch over the proceedings.

It's a Friday afternoon at the Twenty-fourth Street studios, October 9. By a quarter to two, everybody's in place. The three-hour session has already been invented. "Time on My Hands": a good descriptive of the recording process, historicizing for all time these few minutes, drawing sound on the master disc as it's caught by the microphone, sliced into wax, soon to be stamped negative to positive and become a disc for the ages.

He knows his voice now, tremulous. He lets it bounce on the notes of the melody, the accents, soaring ever higher in slowing motion like a trampoliner, a trailing legato, then floating back to catch the melody's tail and reel it in, until with one mighty loft he enters the realm of the croon, the *ba-ba-ba* solo taken with the violin, the mesmerizing.

Wordless. Mouthing the basic shape of sound. *Ba;* like *do, re, mi.* A new alphabet of the notes. *Ba*-sharp, *da*-flat.

"Time on My Hands," the first song undertaken, is written by Harold Adamson, Mack Gordon, and Vincent Youmans. There are rhymes practically every third word; the piano sprinkles arpeggios. The violin underlines the melody under his voice until it's croontime, and then as he breaks into his vocal violin solo, the true violin steps back in register to let him take the lead. Back and forth, they move in parallel, exchanging tenor and baritone, like the tocking tick of a clock.

"Goodnight Sweetheart" is next, a serenade slowed to a drowse, the effect more somnambulistic than soporific. The verse is used as a bridge, surrounded by repeat choruses; it seems almost sprightly when it enters with quickening steps. English bandleader Ray Noble had written it, and Vallée had given it an "American arrangement," which probably had more to do with publishing and royalties than musical restructuring. It's a standard showcloser; Russ makes its time elastic, the fast-forward and rewind of a dream, the walking-in-place of half speed.

Like any lullaby, it lulls you into sleep's overtaking. The head nodding, caught between the chest's swells, a sudden jerk upright, the body in involuntary twitch. Falling back. The head lolls free on the neck. The pillow's cupped palms cradle the head. The rhythm section prances on all fours during the verses, skittering them along, and then abruptly lays out during the chorus, leaving Russ to do the importuning.

And yet it's not quite sleep. It's more nap, suspension, the awareness of bridging twilight, between two worlds. Neither; as the pianist sits between his right and left hands, moving them through their black-and-white dance. Up and down the scale, fingers rippling over the spinal vertebrae. For Chopin, the right hand is often cheerful, a bright melody sprinkling ripostes and sudden, implied syncopations. The left exposes *zal*—the Pole melancholy, and for Chopin, the nostalgic loss of his homeland. The seventh nocturne (op. 27, no. 1 in C-sharp minor) places a dissonant E-sharp against the dominant C-sharp. Not even an F will do to still his seething temperament. He dedicates the dischord to Madame la Comtesse d' Apponyi, the wife of the Austrian ambassador, his song willfully clashing at the site where their ardor and attraction meet and checkmate. Its unsettling character is a far cry from the chromatic modulations of op. 9, in E-flat major, the second of his published nocturnes, written for Mme. Camille Pleyel, who jilted Berlioz, and on January 26, 1832, arranged for Chopin to have his Paris debut in her rooms at 9 rue Cadet.

"PRISONER OF LOVE" begins abruptly. There is no instrumental introduction, merely the breathless *ahhhhaahh* of *a-lone* and then he and the violin are on the dance floor, the bow flourishing when the voice stops its phrasing.

Chopin wrote for the dance, the polonaises and mazurkas of his homeland, and imagined the intricate steps that provided courtship ritual amongst the common folk and aristocracy of Europe. In the fall of 1831, with Warsaw fallen to the Russians, he made his way to Paris, beginning his exile. That same year, his great love, George Sand, came to live in the city, and published her first novel, *Rose et Blanche*, in collaboration with her first husband.

A centennial later, Russ could tell of his own captivation. The song, copyrighted January 19, 1931, was originally titled "Beggar of Love." Written with Leo Robin, a Hollywood for-hire wordsmith who juggled syllables ("My Cutie's Due at Two to Two Today"; later to win a 1938 Oscar for "Thanks for the Memory"), the song had been performed by Russ earlier in the year over KMPL in Los Angeles. But he was no beggar, not now, not with a newly hired chauffeur and butler and a hit radio show. There were too many beggars in these days of economic ruin. No one saw any glamour in asking for a handout, be it money or love. Besides, he no longer belonged to himself. He was theirs, his listeners', and the image of one so held against his will, jailed much as in his Zendaesque *Dynamite,* seemed a more enticing role. What woman would not wish to put him under such exquisite power, and who might resist the dramatic prospect of setting him free, only to imprison him again in her own heart?

There was Dorothy. She of the long waist, the neck hollow. She made Robin's words come alive for Russ, even the unsung ones that never graduated to record. *"Why can't I own my own soul?"* he pleads in an intro that was cut from Shilkret's arrangement, before the refrain places him at his most submissive: *"For one command I stand and wait now / From one who's mas-ter of my Fate now."* Though later in the lyrics, the performer is given a *she / he* choice, there is no question who becomes the feminine in Russ's reading, master and mistress. They have changed partners. He opens himself to her whim. She blindfolds his closed eyes. He can only hear, and in listening, hear his song. She calls the tune, he will sing it.

Within the refrain, a short middlebreak, moving first between the G minor and the D^7, voice clambering the scale—*"What's the good of my car-ing, if some-one is shar-ing / Those arms with me?"*—and then the flick to G major, set against the D^7, a hanging resolve even as the submitting is acquiesced—*"Al-though she has an-oth-er, I can't have an-oth-er / For I'm not free."* It is the same effect Chopin utilizes in op. 27, no. 1, teasing with glimpses of the C-sharp major even as the piano lies at the bottom of a dark minor-key whirlpool. There is a flurry that sucks down all who come close to its spiraling spout, and then the eerie silence of water as it closes over its victim, a liquid calm that tries to appear nonchalant—just us lapping waves here!—even as it feels drowning transpiring beneath its eddies.

A music of mood swings. The underlying. If op. 27, no. 1, is Chopin's nocturne as aria, op. 9, no. 2, is his pop song. The leap from the I chord to the V always signifies a climatic change; entire pop empires have been built upon its global warming. The E-flat Nocturne homes in on the B-flat many a time, melodic lines implying syllable, repeating its four-bar theme in ever more variations, returning to it in the manner of a riff, accessorized with all of the riposting techniques at a virtuoso's command.

Chopin's chops: Frédéric as performer. Sure, he was just another guy off the Vienna scene. A child prodigy, but who wasn't those days? No, the young, wan Frédéric had to have something in hand to move him from estate to estate, giving his piano lessons and taking sustenance in the drawing rooms of the rich. Frail, weighing less than a hundred pounds, his fortissimo moved toward the diminutive. He relied on the intimation. His pedaling technique alone could create faint in his bodiced listeners; lingering notes held by the toes, tapping, letting the piano's undamped strings continue their overtoning shudder, vibrato on the ivory keys.

He preferred Graf and Pleyel pianos for their lighter acoustics, and a pianoforte style modeled on bel canto singing. He would take in the operas of Rossini and Bellini at the Théâtre-Italien in Paris, and try within his notated embellishments—the simple shake, the transient shake, the shake from below, the turn, the inverted turn, the acciaccatura and appoggiatura and double appoggiatura—to ornament his nuanced expression, blurring harmonies, masking the entry of notes, rippling wide-ranging trills that breathed through the wrists, thinning sonorities, moving between octaves as if in a glide.

His *tempo rubato*, literally "stolen time," the slight push-and-pull of the meter, reacts against the clockwork mathematics of music. He stretches time-on-his-hands—counting the seconds of his en-duration, moments left to serve, how many bars before the song is ended. Elongating, discovering the metronomic clock is further along, and rushing to catch up. A surrender to time's relativity.

Caprice does not come without price. The body is punished, providing an altar for romantic sacrifice. Perhaps Mendelssohn, stricter, was stauncher. He disliked such vulgar displays of "passion and despair." His *Songs Without Words* adhered to the meter, no quarter given. Perhaps this lack of deviation gave them what appeared to be a life-sustaining quality. In a *Record Collector* magazine from June 1984, John Sam Lewis describes the near-death experience of his music teacher, who wakes to the strains of Ania Dorfmann interpreting the *Songs Without Words* on an RCA album. "He cried tears of joy, perceiving that he had been near death and was still alive to hear Mendelssohn played again."

The pianoforte was an improvement in expression over the harpsichord, but it was no match for the grasp of hand on violin neck, the strings in direct contact with the fingers, the bow capable of endless sustain, touching enough notes to make a chord, on its way to becoming an electric guitar. Chopin—a pianist writing for his own instrument as opposed to the grand symphonic scale—wove his way into the Victorian parlor as pianos migrated from the aristocratic salon into the homes of the middle class in the late nineteenth century, foreshadowing the radio. Women were most often the players. Chopin's music lent itself to the drawing room, the damask curtains and velvet couches, the grippe and the consumption.

At the same time, Niccolò Paganini leaped the transverse between the pianistic and violinistic, the occult-spelled magic of willful technique. Among his heirs, Jan Kubelik toured America in 1911 and '12. From Prague when it was part of Austria (born July 5, 1880), he had made his reputation with the flashy Paganini D Major Concerto, and initially came to the United States in December 1900, one of the first violin stars of the new century. Kubelik's virtuosity, a virtue implied by his selfless devotion to his instrument (which, in Paganini's case, was ascribed to a bond with the devil; à la Robert Johnson, "Crossroads Blues"), was augmented by a piercing stare and a shock of unruly dark hair. His 1913 Witmark music book, *The Artistic Violinist,* shows a dreamier side: one can imagine the young Russ opening to page 28 and sawing away at Donizetti's "Sextet" from *Lucia di Lammermoor,* or Tchaikovsky's *Song Without Words* (op. 2, no. 3), or the assorted "Reveries" and "Romances" and "Melodies" alongside Frédéric's Nocturne op. 9, no. 2, which by now is reduced to a sing-along replete with *poco ritards* and *dolcises.* When Kubelik performs, he throws out his arms—bow in one hand, violin in the other—to accept the crowd's plaudits, the calls for encore. Chopin the miniaturist would have been amused.

Victor Red Seal violinists like Mischa Elman and Jascha Heifetz repertoirically record the E-flat Nocturne, though not Fritz Kreisler, who does, however, take cowriter credit with Chopin on the A Minor Mazurka (op. 67, no. 4). The dance floor beckons. Ambrose, a uni-named London bandleader who holds sway at the Hotel Mayfair, catches wind of the J. H. Squire Celeste Octet's "Nocturne in E Flat" for English Columbia ("Magic Notes" is their trademark) in exaggerated waltz time, and slyly arranges it for his Orchestra in the four-leggeds of a fox to trot. (Bert) Ambrose has been remote-broadcasting on the BBC since August 1929. His signature song is "When Day Is Done"; the flip side of his Decca recording of (simply) "Nocturne" is "Midnight in Mayfair." We are deep in the tolling twelve of night, divided by four, which equals three, and brings us back to Chopin.

There are other matters.

The nocturnes transgress gender. Like the croon, they confuse, play with stereoarchetype. Chopin loves a woman who wears the outer trappings of a man; Sand loves a man with the trapped innards of a woman. Everything about the nocturne—whether as invented by John Field (who nonetheless referred to Chopin as "a sickroom talent") or impressionistically smeared by Debussy or painted in gradations of gray by Whistler or Albert Pinkham Ryder—points to the female, their intended cantabile receptor; the inherent dreaminess, the freedom of modulation, their sentimental brevity and ornate decoration, or at least how feminine music was regarded in the early nineteenth century, the encoded signals of genre and social placement. To nine-teenth-century mores, the nocturne was "A love poem sung by a man to a woman," as Jeffrey Kallberg puts it in a study of our evolving response to Chopin's repertory, *Chopin at the Boundaries*. "On the one hand, a nocturne found its embodiment in the actions of a man; on the other hand, it expressed the soul of a woman," a pianist ambidextrous, the twilight between androg-yny's sunset and herm-aphrodite's rising moon.

It is a short step to the supernatural, the sylphic. He was said to be touched by faeries, an Ariel of the piano. He didn't play for the gallery. He was hardly meant for the concert stage. If he rose to fury, it was only briefly; instead, he allowed his fingers to take the measure of his inner rile, to spin his five-limbed dance partners into ever more complicated and swooning curlicues, arabesques, each hand seeking to swirl around the other, stepping forward, back, racing up the board in tandem, then backpedaling away from each other; one slowing, the other speeding up; finding their registers and res-olutely pounding in place, individual digits dancing within a dance. The con-centration of coordination.

"Fragile Chopin," Sand calls him. Made to be taken under a wing, looked after and mothered, hand cupping a flickering candelabrum in a damp hall-way. He begged to be bled, leeched. His health declined, his lost affair with Sand took its toll. At one of his final performances, he played for Queen Vic-toria in 1848. Even then, he retained his gift for intimacy. "As he gazed upon the groupings of the brilliant crowd flowing past him," wrote Franz Liszt of Frédéric live, "he became enamoured of some isolated figure . . . and sang for her alone."

Now Russ imagined his alone, and the many alones. He drops the key of "Prisoner" a twelfth tone from the written version, beginning on an E minor seventh, relatively minor to G; the resolve moves to D. The verdict of his fate leaves him no choice. He yields control, and finds that he remains true to his self-imprisoning. He cannot unlock the door by himself.

He needs her. In the realization of his needing, he accepts the justice of the sentence meted, rendered.

IT WILL prove his most enduring song. In the spring of 1946, Billy Eckstine and Perry Como share it as a chart-topping hit. Les Paul and Mary Ford record it ten years later during a single all-night session that also covers "Sweet and Lovely" and "You Call It Madness," in unconscious homage to Russ's first months of recording as a solo artist. And in early 1963, a rhythm-

and-blues shouter from Georgia named James Brown will get down on one knee and Famous Flame it into the Top Twenty.

This is farther in the future than Russ can conceive. He has other things on his mind. He can think only as far as tomorrow, when he will open at the RKO Albee in Brooklyn, proceeding from there to make a circuit of the boroughs, a different theater each week: the Kenmore out at Church and Flatbush in Brooklyn, the Fordham up in the Bronx, the Coliseum along Broadway in Washington Heights, the Chester God knows where.

He can feel the crest. It's going to happen. Over the top.

As he leaves the recording studio at five, the Lincoln awaits. He and Con stand outside the studio, dazzled by the late-afternoon light, the sun spearing its rays through the buildings as it sets over New Jersey. They've been inside, locked in a dark cell. Confined. Released. The sense of space is sudden; walking out the front door into the open city is like standing on the jailhouse steps, manacles unlocked, newly free. He's paid his debt to society, a felon serving time on his hands and knees, seconds counting down as surely as sleep turns to wakefulness; the nocturnal day.

He's a little winded from the last notes of "Prisoner," still keyed up from the session. His heart pounds with the excitement of his impending future. He squints against the glare, its pin-lit dazzle, hears a roaring noise in his ears, as if a train was rushing atop the Third Avenue elevated down the street to his left.

"You okay, kid?" Con asks him from what seems a long distance. He feels the older man's hand grabbing his elbow, supporting him, giving him a point of return. Aligning his tilt. He feels like he's reappearing from somewhere, the street a dreamscape backdrop, even he himself not corporeal.

"Sorry," Russ shrugs, tugging at his jacket, adjusting the brim of his hat, reaching for the cigarette case in his inside pocket. "Must've got up too quick."

MAID OF ORLEANS

They are on the phone. Receiver in one hand, cupped next to the ear, the thin licorice rod of mouthpiece in the other. It takes two hands to make a phone call in November 1931. With the other person at the other end of the line, it's almost like dancing.

Russ reclines. He is in full dress shirt, white, pleats and tucks, studs for buttons, starched sleeves folded back once at the wrist, cuff and link. To show his relaxation, he wears a wine-red brocade smoking jacket. Overlooking Manhattan.

Wire to wire, their two rooms connecting in different parts of the city, Dorothy lounges backward on a fringed and tufted divan. Her legs are elevated, calf running parallel to the floor, foot kicked up, mule dangling. She is dressed in layers of gauze. She wiggles her right foot, juggling the white puff, making it dance on her toes as she speaks, ever the on-point dancer.

It was a whole new way to talk with your loved one, as new a mode of seduction in its own way as the microphone. Like the recording medium, it had evolved from squawks to actual representations of the human voice, in all its subtleties.

You could speak from afar. Before, you were confined to letters, the epistolary arts. Handwriting had its own revelations, much more elaborate and extravagant than the typing that passed for passion these days. A word typed didn't have the same intimated innuendoes as the curl of script, the swirl and swoop of letter after letter, then space. The song of penmanship.

And why write when you could call? It was better than special delivery, that mouthpiece, cradled in the arm. You could have flowers dropped at the door. Send a telegram. Leave a calling card when there was no one home. Drop a postcard into the mailbox when you were away. Nothing compared to the touch of voice.

A letter can be composed, the way you would a song. Dear so-and-so, and so. You make up a phone conversation as you go along. Departing from the script, each a part that must not be omitted. "Sweetheart We Need Each Other," sings Scrappy Lambert for Ben Pollack with Jack Teagarden playing his partner on clipped cornet in August 1929. Obbligato's cause-and-effect.

Over the phone you could sing your letter. That whisper of want, inches away in the dark, lying next to you on the pillow, heads slightly touching, eyes darting shyly, circling the corneal edge, straining to find meaning in inflected flecks. And you're not even here. You're blocks away. Next to me.

SHE WAS a maiden of Orleans.

On a steamy Sunday in August 1930, Dorothy rode into the city in triumph, much like Jeanne d'Arc at the gates of the conquered fortress, the hallowed symbol of France's struggle against the coarse English. New Orleans was still waging the same Hundred Years' War, a hearkening back to the Battle of 1812. Even though the red-light district of Storyville had been shuttered after the onset of Greater War, folded into the more drunken, less libidinous revelry of the French Quarter, it remained the most Continental of America's cities. Every time Dorothy came into town with her family, she felt washed and moisturized by the damp air. Her skin glowed even more than usual. She was un-usual. That's what people said about her.

They saw it right off. Her mother had taught her to stand tall when the judges came by, to look them in the eye and say "Pin that blue ribbon right here," and tap her chest, point to her beating heart. She remembered the gesture later, recognizing it when she met Shirley Temple for the first time. That willing winning spunk.

It had started early for Dot. She was the most Beautiful Baby in Hattiesburg at thirteen months; the May Queen in grade school; Miss Biloxi and Miss Eagle in 1929; Miss American Legion in 1930 on her way to the Miss New Orleans title at the "Pageant of Progress" held in the Spanish Fort along Pontchartrain Beach. She would have won it a year before, in 1929, five hundred years after Joan entered Orléans, but the judges knew she was under sixteen. They made her a runner-up, though she never got along with the Queen.

DOROTHY DELL

Later it would be said that her father owned a plantation in Mississippi, but really all he did was sell lumber. Elbert L. Goff was a good-looking, strong-willed man who butted heads with her equally unflinching mother, Lillian. Dorothy Dell Goff (named after Lilly's favorite doll) was born on January 30, 1914. By the time she was ready to enter beauty contests, her mother had moved her and younger sister Helen to a home at 4120 Perrier Street in the Garden District of New Orleans. Her best friend, Dorothy Lambour, lived on nearby LePage Street. They went to Sophie B. Wright High School together, and Dorothy was able to have Dorothy—or "Dowie," as they called her— become her alternate.

The International Beauty Contest in Galveston, Texas, was intent on celebrating "Beautiful Girlhood." Dorothy wore her bright blond hair in old-fashioned curls, with a pale pink net dress trimmed in black, and a bathing suit in light blue, a living cornsilk. Among the judges was King Vidor. There were thirty-one American entrants and another seven from foreign countries. When they announced her as Miss Universe and handed her a check for two thousand dollars, she said "I'm so happy I could cry," an intersection of emotion.

Now it was time for her triumphal procession. The fleurs-de-lis were in place. The acting mayor met her at Union Station, and they paraded down Howard Avenue to Dryades Street to the Roosevelt Hotel. Wearing her sash like a battle standard, she carried herself with the corona'd demeanor of a homecoming queen.

The bells ring *Te Deum Laudamus*. Dorothy moves through the gates of the city on her white horse, the Bastard of Orléans on her left, wind shifting to ripple in her direction. As she passes through the clamoring, jubilant townspeople, her pennant catches fire. She reaches back with a wave of her hand and snuffs the flame, much to the delight of the crowd.

SHE GOT the standard offers for a beauty queen; there was more than one Miss Universe circulating in the United States. Earl Carroll asked her to step into the Vanities; Ziegfeld sent a telegram from the Follies. But Fanchon and Marco said they would also find room for her mother, sister, and best friend. They would become an "F&M idea," the "American Beauty." Helen was appointed Miss Mississippi, and Dorothy Lambour was Miss Louisiana. Lilly was not given a place onstage, though she fancied a turn.

The tour opened the first day of fall 1930 at the Pantages in Hollywood. Hoot Gibson's wife, Sally Eilers, joined them onstage. They dipped over to Long Beach and came back for two days off in Hollywood, where Dot got her first taste of wining and dining. One evening, while she went out, Helen and Dowie and Mother went to Grauman's Chinese Theatre to see the Marx Brothers in *Animal Crackers*. Sometimes they felt like the Goff Sisters.

By October they had left the bright lights behind and were into the grind of touring, Fresno and San Jose and up through San Francisco on the Fox circuit, taking time out to wave in oil company parades and at store openings. "This week," Dorothy L. writes in her diary for October 10 through 16, "we're having a beautiful prologue of Joan of Arc. I'm supposed to be a French maiden. What a costume!" Dorothy, of course, is lit at the stake.

A week in Oakland, and then up to logging country. They stop over in Salem, and in Portland are taken through Jantzen Swimming Mills, each given a new bathing suit. One day they get away to the mountains around Mount Hood along the Columbia. There the three sisters run in the forest as if they were ten again, a world of bygone baby carriages and chase games. They are photographed standing atop a tree stump, their sexuality dropped like an overcoat that's taken off to play, the once-little girls they are.

The weather turns colder, drier. The box office is held up one night in Tacoma; in Seattle they open at a theater along Fifth Avenue, and Dorothy drinks in the wet air, the seaport shanty of Puget Sound. An Episcopalian group holds a church social and invites the boys and girls from the cast of *New Moon*, playing down the street. November moves them deeper into Washington. They spend Thanksgiving between Yakima and Butte, Montana. The Dorothys wonder if they'll ever see home again.

Still, when the news comes in Joplin, Missouri, that the show is closing after the St. Louis engagement, December 10–24, Dot is shocked by how much she doesn't want this life to end. She even gets mad at Dowie for writing to her mother; she didn't want anyone back home to know.

They'll part soon. After a tearful cast party on Christmas Eve, Dorothy Lambour heads back down the Mississippi to New Orleans, where she will wear an 1890s bathing suit at the Manger's Beach and Style Show at Loew's State to win Miss Way Back When. A couple of years later, she'll decide to try her luck in Hollywood, where her old friend Dorothy Dell has prospered. She'll have dropped the *b* from her last name by then, a sultry image to enhance the foreign exoticism of her screen type, a native girl from the French Quarter, saronged and on the road, where she will provide the love interest for Bob Hope and Bing Crosby.

RATHER THAN settle down to the slow, humid pace of New Orleans, moment of glory over, the Goffs decide to keep up their road momentum and head to New York. Dorothy had no illusions of her eventual worth as a pretty girl. Sightly objects, no matter how fascinating, always blend away to wallpaper. "You're just another beauty queen," Billy Rose told her when she walked into his office. You had to keep their attention. She could sing. And dance. *Pin that blue ribbon right here.*

Dorothy never thought that Ziegfeld would go for her in such a big way. He thought she could be Ruth Etting's understudy, sing "Cigarettes, Cigars!" for the matinée crowd if Mo was a bit too hard on her the night before. Then he thought to find her something more to do in the show, and found the Chick Endor and Charlie Farrell song that seemed to give her just the right touch of innocence and sashay. She had the Maw to prove it. Who gave Flo hell regularly if she thought Ziegfeld wasn't treating her right, and made sure to let Harry Richman know that Dorothy was still technically a minor.

Russ was a different story.

Between Con and her mother, she thought she would go crazy. They were both whispering in each of her ears, a stream of advice she wished would just *shut up* and *go away* and *Don't they trust me enough to know I know what's best for me* and her waiting for Russ to call.

They were trying to break them up. Her mother had been a teenager when Dorothy was born, and she didn't want Dorothy to have to re-live out her dreams of stardom through *her* child. It was time to tie the apron strings, tell the baby the facts of life. It wasn't the stork that brought her. Her mother liked Russ, but didn't think they should wed. The managers were a different story. They wanted nothing less than severance; her own, Martin Starr, who had run the Galveston beauty contest and was not about to let his star attraction become someone else's housekeeper, and Mr. Conrad, who kept going on about Rudy and this horrible witch Fay and Russ needing to be seen as every girl's dream, and he was too young and she was too young. . . .

And they're too old, she pouted. They didn't remember what true love was like. Russ knew. She could hear him humming over the receiver. She shut her eyes, so it would be only the two of them speaking in a void of black space.

Hearing voices.

BLUE AND GOLD

I t is the moment when birds begin their song, expecting the sun. Night catches a gleam from beyond the horizon. It's time to sleep or wake, depending on who shares your bed.

This is dawn, not dusk, light's time-lapse as important as its shading. The gradual addition of day's color is contracted by the slow, leaking removal of twilight in the evening, the air thinned, drained. The lingerie of atmosphere is removed from the night sky. Disrobed, the universe is unveiled in all its wonder and terror.

Someone waits for me is the reassurance that the sun will rise anew. "Where the Blue of the Night (Meets the Gold of the Day)" is not only a song of love, but an expression of religious faith. By the end of October, Bing has chosen it as his hymnal theme, his name inscribed as one of the writers alongside Roy Turk and Fred Ahlert.

RUSS WAS being impudent. There is no other way of looking at it. By recording the song on November 18, five days before Bing, he was even insulting. It violated their gentleman's agreement, a direct challenge, a gauntlet toss. Everyone knew that Crosby had been testing two songs during his radio show as possible themes, alternating them weekly. "Love Came into My Heart" by Harold Adamson and Berton Lane was looking like a distant runner-up at this point. Bing had also considered Harry Barris's "I Surrender, Dear," or rather, Barris hoped he'd consider it, but Crosby obviously wanted a break with the past, and besides, the only one Bing surrendered to was Dixie. She was here in New York because they were still living at his brother Everett's out in California, and she wanted a place of her own. They were fighting over turf, working out the territorials of their marriage, who was to give in to whom, though it would all be rendered moot when the kids started arriving.

The air of resignation of "I Surrender" was not what Crosby had in mind, even if the Mack Sennett short featuring the song had been released to theaters in mid-September. The radio sponsorship and the Paramount contract were locked up. He was "The Cremo Singer," huffing and puffing smoke rings on a big cigar courtesy of the American Tobacco Company, broadcasting twice nightly from WABC at 7:00 and 11:00, six nights a week. Though he wasn't posting the ratings numbers of Vallée (who had nearly a quarter of the available listeners for his show) or even Whiteman's one fifth, his 6.9 percent of the audience was a very vocal demographic.

There were still injunctionary problems to deal with back in Los Angeles, but a settlement was in the works with the Ambassador Hotel. It shouldn't (and didn't) interfere with his November 6 opening at the New York Paramount: four appearances a day, taking in $2,500 a week. At that rate, with three weeks' work, he could pay off the Cocoanut Grove, though they were demanding more than he'd made there during his entire stay, and still stay afloat on his radio salary alone.

Bing was savvy enough to see he'd gotten out of California just in time. "The thing that decided me to go to New York," he told *Screenland*'s Samuel R. Mook, "was hearing a chap who had substituted for me at the Grove on my numerous nights off, singing my stuff over the air in a brazen imitation of me." There was no doubt to whom he was referring.

Russ and Bing were neck and neck. Adam's apples bobbing, hoping to be the first in Eve's garden, they curled around each other like braided snakes, entangled and entwined. Both recorded "Goodnight Sweetheart" in October. If Russ's version turned down the covers, fluffed the pillows, a cozy comforter, Bing's was more like a bedtime story. Upbeat and cheery, he instilled well-being. "*Sleep will banish sorrow. A dreamy dreamland beckons you and me.*" He whistled, like a small boy walking past a graveyard at night. "*With the dawn a new day is born.*" Sleep didn't have to mean it was over.

Bing even spoke, haltingly, to show he meant it. "*Even though I'm not, I'm not always right beside you . . . want you to know that my love, my love will always guide you.*" The hesitations remind me, on the other side of a lifetime, of Elvis, another one-named wonder. They will pass into history within the same year.

· · ·

THE RKO chain had turned Bing down in October, "on the theory," opined *Variety*, "he isn't yet well enough known around this area to draw sufficiently to offset the salary he's asking." They were able to get Columbo considerably cheaper. Publix, on the other hand, was more than willing to flash its bankroll and open the Paramount doors to a steadily ascending radio star.

"Another stage scoop!" Bing's opening week was heralded, "the voice that thrills millions nightly." Crosby was given full star treatment, headlining a stage show that—combined with Ruth Chatteron's melodramatic *Once a Lady* ("One hour of indiscretion, a lifetime of disgrace")—seemed to satisfy the Paramount's box-office expectations. His first Saturday afternoon wasn't capacity, but pleasantly filled.

Crosby sang five songs, mostly his better-known numbers like "At Your Command," "I Apologize," and "Wrap Your Troubles in Dreams." He entered center stage, appearing within a silhouetted set, singing to a girl. He told the audience how glad he was to be here before perching on Mrs. Jesse Crawford's rising Wurlitzer for another vocal. He went offstage for his third selection, accompanying a ballet performed by the Danny Dare Dancers in oriental costumes, complete with Chinese silver fingernails, and a scantily clad terpsichorean named Vanessi, who shimmied her way through a rhumba. The piano-comedy team of Jimmy Conlin and Myrtle Glass tried to generate some guffaws, and then Bing was back in a café setting for another pair of songs. The microphone followed him wherever he went, like a faithful terrier.

On the same Friday Bing opened at the Paramount, Russ was uptown at the Peacock Charity Ball. Held in a suite of ballrooms at the Waldorf-Astoria, the gala society event, hosted by Miss Ruth Vanderbilt Twombly and benefiting the Association for Improving the Condition of the Poor, was being broadcast live over WJZ. Rudy Vallée was present, as were Nick Lucas, Marion Harris, and a good portion of the Follies trucked over after the show by Richman, including Ruth Etting and Helen Morgan. In one room, a "Russian Gypsy Music Box" was outfitted with Isa Kramer singing Muscovite songs; down the hall, a "Tavern Apache" celebrated the nightlife of the Parisian underworld.

Not to be outdone, on November 15 Bing showed his charitable streak by marching in a nationwide Parade of Stars broadcast over both NBC and CBS, in support of the Unemployment Relief Program. With feeds from Los Angeles, Chicago, and New York, Bing was joined on the East Coast by Eddie Cantor, Douglas Fairbanks, and Morton Downey. He was keeping good company.

By the end of November, when the New York Paramount celebrated its fifth anniversary, it was clear the theater had thrown in its lot with radio. Kate Smith came over from a stand at the Brooklyn Paramount and brought down the house with her "St. Louis Blues." The four Mills Brothers chordaled. Bing was looking less like a novelty act than an assured and genial host, though his hectic schedule sometimes frayed his voice. There were times when he hardly had time to learn a song before he sang it over the radio. His uncertainty showed. He needed time to figure out how to riff it, to song-and-dance the melody. He was learning about staying power.

IT WASN'T as if they never sang each other's songs. Con assured him he had personally been asked by Crosby's publishers, DeSylva, Brown, and Henderson, to have Russ record "Where the Blue of the Night." He was sitting watchfully in the control room around 1:30 P.M. when the session was scheduled to begin. Conrad knew they were opening against Crosby in eight days at the Brooklyn Paramount, on Thanksgiving Day, and he wanted to make sure they were evenly matched.

The song was the important thing. A look at what passed for charts in those days—monthly listings in *Variety* that recapped New York, Chicago, and Los Angeles sales by the "3 leading Phonograph Companies"—Brunswick, Columbia, and Victor—showed that record buyers liked having a variety of interpretive choices. September saw "Sweet and Lovely" a hit for Guy Lombardo on Columbia (number one in New York and Chicago), Ben Bernie on Brunswick (number two in Chicago, though Bing had nailed half the six spots on either coast), and Russ for Victor, with Gus Arnheim topping Columbo in Chicago. Bing's version of "Sweet and Lovely" had taken over October's listings, while Ben Bernie had the hit on "You Call It Madness" for Brunswick and Kate Smith shared the honors with Smith Ballew on Columbia. No wonder Con kept one foot in publishing. By November, it was "Goodnight Sweetheart"'s turn, though Guy Lombardo seemed to be the hands-down winner on Columbia versus Wayne King's version on Victor. Russ was runner-up.

Shilkret has organized a slightly larger than usual ensemble, with a shift to the strings: three violins, a cello, and a string bass alongside the piano, guitar, saxophone, and trumpet. For Russ, the songs represent some of his most assured work, a product of his growing confidence and experience, a flip insouciance in the delivery, on and yet off-the-cuff. In "You Try Somebody Else," a clever DeSylva, Brown, and Henderson (there they are again!) song that opens the afternoon session, he broaches an "understanding" to see if love holds up to the litmus of temptation.

It's a trial separation. The double-dare of *"We're both acting strange, we both need a change. . . ."* And double meanings: *"If I was meant for you if you were meant for me, / Nothing can keep us apart."*

"Let's take our fun where we find it." Out on the town, painting it red. A bird's mating dance, fringed to catch the glance, satins to sparkle, setting the eye sliding down the slippery strut and ruffling feathers of plumage. The Russling.

He leans in close, warming the air next to her ear. In the intervening selection, he offers her a cast of characters: "Call Me Sweetheart, Call Me Darling, Call Me Dear." He can be all of them, but some he'll only intimate, unspoken, in the pre–Hays Code anything-goes before the movies are called to confession.

"Call Me Sweetheart" has German origins, derived from *"Sag Mir Darling,"* written by Bert Reisfeld, Mart Fryberg, and Rolf Marbot, who would all arrive in the United States one step ahead of World War II, and adapted by Philadelphian Dorothy Dick. The violins are given the weight of melodic narrative, the tempo slowing the heartbeat to a waltz. The music has enough room for each partner to grip the other tighter, to find a more responsive part of the back for the hand to brush, for the breath to settle in a fine mist upon the neck. It's a song that sounds older than it is, with something of the sentimental Victorian in its bridge, the baritonalities offset by the violin's solo.

He has crooned in the first song, and on the third, "Where the Blue of the Night," he becomes wordless again. The croon is at its height, halfway between invention and cliché, new enough to be surprising, old enough not to be self-conscious.

He sings only the chorus. As he finishes his second go-round, he begins to step on the rungs of the melody, gliding it ever upward, as if he's ascending a staircase to a bedroom on the second floor. It's still dark outside his window. If there's any doubt, he'll pull the shades down. He'd like the night to last a little longer.

BING'S RECORDING takes place November 23, 1931, accompanied by Bennie Krueger and his orchestra.

It is not the first time he has committed the song to collective memory. In *Blue of the Night,* the last of the six Mack Sennett short comedies filmed between May and August 1931, he undercuts and disarms his celebrity, holding it at arm's length, a trait he will enhance even as that celebrity explodes between the filming and the two-reelers' eventual release in January 1933. Meeting Babe Kane on a train, he plays along when she tells him boastfully she is engaged to marry . . . Bing Crosby! The girl's real fiancé, Franklin Pangborn, bets his Model A against Bing's five dollars to expose the impostor's ruse. After two choruses and a "That's him, all right!" Bing has modulated the car's keys and is driving off in triumph. Heading for New York.

They take it twice, the only song attempted that day. The first is the generally released version, though Crosby will record "Where the Blue of the Night" at least once each decade from now on. Sometimes more than once. This version is the only one that will be enhanced by Eddie Lang, whose lilting guitar arpeggios bring out the pronounced waltz, a pendulum to the melody.

He sings the first verse, not surprising since he has contributed it to the finished version. It gives the song less an abstract air of waiting; instead the mood turns nostalgic, even melancholy. *"Why do I live in dreams / Of the days I used to know. . . ."*

You can picture him observing light he has traveled years to watch, like a spool of film unreeling, knowing what's already happened. The vantage radiates from heaven, a universe within the universe of a beloved's eyes, leading to the unichorus, *"the gold of her hair crowns the blue of her eyes,"* night sun like a halo around the moon. It is simply one of the most beautiful songs ever written.

The melody is derived in some unconscious measure from Gilbert and Sullivan's "Titwillow" in *The Mikado,* especially the answering phrase of the chorus's call and response. It is not surprising, then, as the glimmer of first light crests the curved earth, Bing bursts into birdsong.

BING WHISTLES, the whistling croon, a high-pitched sound that points the ears, like a canine.

He is one of the more accomplished whistlers of his day, a day that appreciates a good whistle, the aerodynamic breath as instrument. His closest competitor is Morton Downey, at least in radio time, because Bing directly follows him. Much ado is made over this showdown of the WABC tweeters, though Mort has the edge since his finale whistle is said (by the *News*) to send a message in secret code to his wife Barbara Bennett, sister of Constance, the movie actress.

Whistling is an achievement at once commonplace and highly unusual. We can all whistle—"just put your lips together and blow," Lauren Bacall pauses at the doorway and winks at Humphrey Bogart in *To Have and Have Not*, the most elemental whistling instructions ever proffered—though there are different methods: pinkie and pointer bracing the oblong mouth, soft breath through a round sound-hole of lip, spit through the front teeth. Bing can *really* whistle, passing tones and slurs and trills. It's the nearest he comes to the pierce of Louis Armstrong's trumpet.

"Whistle a happy tune," *The King and I* commands. You hardly ever hear a sad song whistled. Slight melancholy is about as bad as it gets. In fact, whistling usually engenders a simple, happy-go-lucky air. Everything is gonna be okay.

Gene Austin's purse of the lips in "My Blue Heaven" sounds so split in two it could be doubled digitally. It's barely electrical. Jolson whistled on "When the Little Red Roses (Get the Blues for You)," and followed it with "Toot Toot Tootsie" in *The Jazz Singer*. There's no doubt Bing heard Al's tweet and twoot.

Birdcalls. If nothing answers the call of nature like the real thing—Karl Reich's Aviary in Bremen, Germany, supplied Victor with 1914's "Actual Song of the Canary Bird," backed with "Popular Melodies Accompanied by Nightingales and Canaries," in which two singing groups, in the manner of the later Orioles and Ravens, chirp blithely along with chimed snippets of nursery rhymes like "Twinkle, Twinkle, Little Star"—Mary Margaret McKee's mimic of birdsong comes close enough for her to pass as a member of the flock.

She runs through "Our Favorite Song-Birds" in 1921, covering such intricate tweeters (an interesting etymology) as the "Cardinal Red Bird" and "Wood Peewee," the "Catbird" and the "California Quail," a medley of seventeen different samples of birdsong, each its own hook. All she needs is a quarter-note beat. At her most chirpy, she can approach the velocity of a cricket. Margaret begins her songbird empathy as early as 1908 with "In Venice" for Victor, waxing rhapsodic with "Bird Rapture" on Pathé Actuelle in 1919. She guests with Paul Whiteman in 1921, accompanying Frank Ferera on lap steel guitar in "Honolulu Eyes." There is a plethora of *mmm*'s when she teams with the Merry Melody Men on "Pucker Up and Whistle" for Gennett in 1921. In 1929 she predicts "Bird and That Saxophone" for Brunswick.

A daughter of dance orchestra leader Frank McKee, Mary Margaret made the ornithological transition from acoustic to electric recording in late 1925, when she re-recorded a pair of whistling mainstays with Pryor's Orchestra, "The Warbler's Serenade" and "The Whistler and His Dog." She had been called into the session with Billy Murray after the original whistler, Joseph

Belmont, was forced to cancel as a result of having a tooth pulled. "I have no birds," he exclaimed upon arriving at the studio.

Belmont, born in Shamokin, Pennsylvania, on July 22, 1876, wouldn't make it into the electric era, but he had been there from the beginning. He learned to imitate birds while growing up in Charleston, West Virginia. By the time he came to Washington, D.C., to make records for Columbia, the 1890s were ending. In the dawn of the new century, on November 12, 1901, he would twitter his first record for Victor, "The Whippoorwill Song," and his whistling could soon be heard behind any love ballad that made feathered reference. In 1916 he was strolling along Broadway listening to Billy Murray whistle when he composed "Whistle While You Walk," the blown *w*'s molding the mouth to make their sound, a technique the Seven Dwarfs successfully borrowed for "Whistle While You Work."

Joseph would go into retail after the stock market crash, opening a bird store in Radio City and leading Belmont's Chorus of Feathered Songsters, his own flock of canaries. By the late forties he had a record label with discs designed to teach canaries how to sing, a missionary spreading the word to a heathen tribe only to be abducted by their ancestral spirits. Belmont had gone native.

It was a tradition that stretched back to 1886, when Alice Shaw, America's first professional whistler, made her debut at Chickering Hall in New York (she later recorded with her twin daughters for Edison in 1907). "The Whistling Coon," George W. Johnson, gave minstrel expression to one of the first versions of "The Mocking Bird" (1895), crafting his cylinders as if he were back on the plantation, trilling into two and five recording horns at a time, before "master" reproduction was invented, to satisfy demand. Whistling reached a height with Elmo Tanner in his swingtime with the Ted Weems band, setting a spell on Otis Redding's "Dock of the Bay" and wandering off into the sunset as a staple of movie themes signifying cineramic landscapes and nature's random cruelties: *The High and the Mighty*, as whistled by Fred Lowery, from Palestine, Texas; or the Whistler with No Name featured on Ennio Morricone's epic score for *The Good, the Bad, and the Ugly*.

Lowery was blind. His autobiography was called *Whistling in the Dark*.

WAITING FOR the light you may never see. *"The World Is Waiting for the Sunrise"* wrote lyricist E. Lockhart with E. Seitz's melody in mind. *"The thrush on high is calling . . . and my heart is calling you. . . ."*

Bing is a bird that greets the dawn. Russ stays the night, a nightingale serenading only darkness. In the charming 1923 Parisian silent film *La Voix du Rossignol*, director Wladyslaw Starewicz tells the fable of how a nightingale lends a child her voice during the day, and so can sing only when the world is asleep.

The recorder, from the Latin *recordare*—to remember—was invented by monks in the fourteenth century to reproduce the calls of birds. It is no coincidence that we use the word "recording" to capture our modern songs.

Classical composers often tried to cage birdsong. In Salzburg a hundred years before Mozart, Heinrich Ignaz Franz von Biber wrote a *Sonata violino solo representativa* that transcribed the *Nachtigal*. Wolfgang Amadeus himself was so inspired by a melody he heard a pet starling sing (he bought it on the spot for 34 kreuzer) that he made it the fluttering theme of his 1784 Piano Concerto no. 17 in G Major. "It was written by a bird," he said, no mean admission for such a prodigal composer. Perhaps Mozart fancied himself a half-bird like Papageno in *The Magic Flute*, who enters carrying a birdcage on his back, soon to join forces against the Queen of the Night. His crisp pianoforte tones lent themselves well to the whistle, and even Chopin took note, echoing the canyon wren's chromatic trill down the musical scale in the opening of the Revolutionary Etude.

By the twentieth century, Olivier Messiaen in his *Chronochromie* had replicated the clamor of birdsong, the infernal cheep and caw-cophony of a flock on the fly. Anticipating Hitchcock in *The Birds*, Messiaen could hear retribution flapping in the wind. He was a religious man, a Catholic; his birds were as avenging angels. Their flight could bring annunciation, the discipline of sanctity, the promise of breaking free from earthly desire.

The religious is never far from the glide of birds. In eighteenth-century Venice, Antonio Vivaldi taught the prayerful intervals of resolve and uplift, but he was moving in the opposite direction, toward the secular, and the natural world that happens outside the cloistered walls of the church. He had to get away. The Red Priest—as Vivaldi was known, like a rare species of bird himself—left the saying of mass behind to take over the position of *maestro di violino* at the Ospedale della Pietà, a quasi-nunnery and home for unclaimed girls on the Riva degli Schiavoni in Venice. Hidden from gaze, as they sang his music from behind latticelike grill-work, they reminded him of songbirds in a cage. If it had been two hundred years later, he might have imagined the radio.

Vivaldi's bird-derived *Cuckoo Concerto* and *Il Cardellino (The Goldfinch)* have the flute darting from branch to branch, much as Antonio managed to stay on the road for most of his later life, touring with his singer, Anna Giro, scribbling staves and semiquavers and never reciting mass again.

"It was the warbling of the birds that first gave man the thought of making music," said Debussy. Original sin.

IN FRANK SWINNERTON'S 1917 *Nocturne*, the "stunt" of the novel, as Frank self-effacingly called it, is that the action takes place within the course of a single night. Two sisters on one-night stands. Love and future mates hang in the balance, their moral force bound to a Christlike invalid father who seems as helpless as a child. Being both daughters and mothers, opposed siblings bound together as if they were siamesed, they represent spirit and flesh, expressed in all the elements. Jenny is fire, Emmy earth. Jenny meets her Keith on the water, a yacht moored on the Thames. Emmy breathes the liberating air of theatrical art when she and Alf take in a play and wind up exchanging vows. Daddy's girls; Mama's boys.

The narrative unfolds in South London near where William Blake went about his business of poetics and revolution a century before. His contraries were also those of antithesis, the blurred edge of opposites interacting. "Without contraries is no progression," he declaimed in the aptly named *The Marriage of Heaven and Hell* (1793). "Attraction and Repulsion, Reason and Energy, Love and Hate, are necessary to Human existence. . . . Good is the passive that obeys Reason. Evil is the active springing from Energy.

"Good is Heaven. Evil is hell."

He hailed the goddess of dawn, Athena, as light's cleanse: "O holy virgin," he wrote as a teenager, "clad in purest white / unlock heaven's golden gates and issue forth."

The irony of Swinnerton's *Nocturne* is that he never reaches morning. The night never ends for his couples; they don't have to get on with it, eyes opening to see who's lying next to them, the surprise and shock of returning from the solitude of slumber and finding someone not yourself. Then the sheets are thrown back and thoughts turn to coffee.

Love's invention is to put uncertainty into the lives of rational people who otherwise would merely multiply. An abacus can do that. The bio-illogic goal is to stay awake, for the survival of the species.

It's still night. Anything can happen under its camera obscura. Day's absolution is yet to come.

Sleep. Soul keep, soul take.

Pray the Lord, or are you prey of the Lord?

Hopen your eyes.

TOP OF THE WORLD

Those crooning vagabonds are stealing all our blondes
Now I know what's become of Sally
And ev'rytime you kiss your girl, who is she thinking of?
Crosby, Columbo, and Vallée!

"**Y**our boyfriend is on!" Her mother was calling her.

Celia, in her Red Hook brownstone, got up from bed, where she'd been lying looking distractedly at the barren branches of the backyard trees, and walked downstairs to the living room. The ornate cathedral of the radio took up the inner wall opposite the fireplace. She didn't want to listen to Russ when her parents were around. Especially Papa. He could be as strict as any Catholic father, and for what? She hardly ever got to leave the neighborhood, except sometimes to take the streetcar to Jahn's, the ice cream parlor on Church near Erasmus where Will teased her and James, whom she secretly liked, always seemed to turn on the charm for her best friend, Eleanor.

But Russ, he was all hers. And terrific-looking to boot. When she went to the Paramount to hear him sing, waiting on line the day after Thanksgiving, she couldn't believe how his songs matched her eyes. She wanted to lose herself in his music. That's why she didn't want her father in the room. Or her mother. She wanted to be alone with him.

They'd laugh, and call Russ her "boyfriend," and the thing was, it could very well be. She wished it so with all her heart. She imagined herself across from the Paramount at Junior's, idly twirling a straw in her cream soda, sitting at the counter just kicking her feet in their brown suede one-strap pumps ($5.85 at Lord & Taylor) between shows. He'd come in for a pack of cigarettes. He'd notice her new rough silk frock ($15.00 at Oppenheim, Collins & Co.), catch her profile as it was buried in the French beaver-fur collar of her coat ($17.74 at Gimbel's), her black curls peeking from under her tam beret with the lacquered quill ($3.67 at Macy's), ask if she worked around here. She'd reply, why no, she was a secretary for an important Broadway producer. It was almost true. She knew she was meant for something more glamorous than ringing up the cash register at her father's butcher shop on Court Street. He'd wonder if she'd like to be a guest in his private box, and when she got there all these terribly important people would be making room for her and maybe someone would say, "Miss Trovato, we really love those eyes of yours. . . . " and she could be a principal in the Follies too. Like *blahblahblah*ndie Dorothy Dell, who she knew was only going out with Russ for his money. She couldn't love him like Celia. Nobody could.

If things didn't work out, there was always Vince Calendo, a local boy from Bay Ridge who had just appeared in the *Brooklyn on Parade* vaudeville show sponsored by the Paramount Theater's Neighborhood Frolic Club. She was sweet on him. He was the club president, and had sung "When the Moon Comes Over the Mountain" to everyone's delight. The *Brooklyn Union-Times* called it "an eye-catching number" when they reviewed the show last month. She had the clipping wedged into the corner of her mirror. Maybe if she bought one of those transparent velvet after-five dresses they were advertising at Stern's, he'd turn her way. She couldn't afford the $29.50, not on her salary. Still, she knew he'd sweep her off her feet if he could. She could hear the promise in his voice. Anything was possible if you were in the right place at the right time.

Thirty-nine years later, in the middle of another December, Celia was living in Park Slope. She had just walked past a candy store on Sterling Place and Seventh Avenue when a United Airlines DC-8 fell out of the sky into the middle of the intersection. She always remembered the haunted eyes of the sole survivor, an eleven-year-old boy named Stephen, who lived only a few hours after the crash. She couldn't sleep for a week.

VINCE WAS meeting his idol.

Russ Columbo had come downstairs to the basement of the Brooklyn Paramount, where radio station WLTH was located, and was shaking *his* hand, congratulating *him* for winning the talent show. Vince was thrilled. Columbo and Calendo, together in the same room.

A senior at St. John's College, he'd had a band called the Rajahs of Rhythm with his good friend Axel Stordahl on trumpet. Vince didn't know whether he wanted to pursue music — he definitely wanted to finish college — but he was starting to get a reputation as the "neighborhood crooner," asked to appear at weddings, church parties, school dances. WOV, the Italian-American station in Manhattan, had given him fifteen minutes on Thursday afternoons at 2:15. Maybe he could do this for a living.

He looked at Russ, only a year or two older than he, surrounded by two so-licitous companions, his tuxedo spotless, the white of his shirt blinding to the eye, cuff links adding sparkle to his wrists. The carnation in the lapel.

Oh, yeah. Maybe.

THE KID kept shaking his hand, and Russ had to give him a quick pat on the back and a compliment to break the grip. Good-looking boy. Reminded him of Fiore.

Or himself. The movie he'd seen with Con last week came to mind. James Whale's *Frankenstein* had just opened at the RKO Mayfair. Was he creating a Monster, a crooner in his own image?

He was on top. This was his second week at the Brooklyn Paramount. The Lambert Pharmaceutical Company of St. Louis, maker of Listerine, was sponsoring his radio show. He was opening at the Empire Ballroom of the Waldorf-Astoria on Monday, December 7. The front-page story in *Radio Guide*, with a photo of him in his now-trademark top hat, proclaimed him "Radio's Valentino," adding that he was "Now First In [The] Hearts of Women Fans."

There was even a song, "Crosby, Columbo & Vallée," written by Al Dubin and Joe Burke, warning *bach'lors* and *mar-ried men* to watch out for the *"too ma-ny croo-ners, too ma-ny sax-o-phones / Break-ing up our hap-py homes."*

The croon is tempting. *"They've made a mil-lion married women wish that they were free. . . . "* Radio was sneaking these Lotharios through the back door. *"Who comes into your home and you can't say a word."*

And finally, his own phrase spun back at him: *"Though I call it non-sense they insist it is love."*

It made for a great play on words. "You call it Crosby, but I call it Russ," quipped English comedian Little Jack Little on a recent visit to New York. Bing had his hands full at the Paramount. Feeling left out, Rudy made no ef-fort to hide his hostility to Columbo, especially after Russ opened at the Para-mount on November 26. First he tried to stop the sale of the sheet music, asking that Downey's name be placed between his and Bing's. Then he only responded in pig Latin when asked his opinion of Russ. "Ousylay."

It could explain why Russ was the odd man out when Merrie Melodies — an offshoot of Looney Tunes, founded by ex-Disney animators Hugh Harman and Rudolf Ising on the idea of Silly Symphonies, with their partner, Leon

Fleischer, who would make it home to Porky Pig and Bugs Bunny and the fractured scoring of Carl Stallings—set the song to animation. An "Injun" maiden is serenaded by her eager brave who brings her a radio. Amid sylvan waterfalls and jolly forest creatures, it's tom-tommed that *"Every troubadour needs his loving squaw,"* despite the *"pale-faced enemies"* of our three crooners. Bing is heard offscreen, a snatch of "Many Happy Returns" followed by a signature whistle, while Rudy gets the full cartoon treatment, changing from a woodland dog to his trademark curly hair, *"Heigh-ho, everybody,"* and droopy eyes, singing "This Is My Love Song" through a tree-trunk megaphone. By the time it's Russ's turn, a campfire has spread to a nearby tree, baby birds have to be rescued, the forest animals are in full stampede, and the song is forgotten.

Not Columbo. This was real life, and his name was smack in the middle. No one else had the required three syllables, the repetition of the hard C.

Russ had to hand it to Con. This was beyond Conrad's wildest ballyhoo. Half a year after they arrived in New York, all of the bluster and blown smoke had materialized.

They took an office at 119 West Fifty-seventh Street, down the block from Carnegie Hall, and named their partnership Russco, where song pluggers might stop by and Yawitz could direct the press traffic and Con would have a desk and a checkbook behind the frosted glass door with its gold lettering. There was always someone around to say *terrific!* and *colossal!* and *great!* Yes men. Con had his own stooge, a gray-haired gentleman referred to as Mr. Bloom, whose sole function was to book their social engagements. He would enter a nightclub and request a table for "Mr. Con." The headwaiter, sure it was Otto Kahn, the shipping magnate (or perhaps his son, the bandleader Roger Wolfe Kahn), would direct him to a choice spot, whereupon Con and Russ would enter, entourage in tow.

Publix, who had hoped to transfer Bing to the Brooklyn Paramount after a few weeks, kept Crosby in Manhattan when the rivalry seemed to gather momentum in the public's imagination. They then hired Russ for the city that lay sprawled across the East River, or so it had been only thirty years ago, before Brooklyn became part of a greater New York.

Together, they formed a metropolis. The sum of their parts looked symmetrical in the papers: Crosby and Columbo, boxed side by side, a big round C and a one-syllable first name, the "Romantic singer of songs you love" up against "the Romeo of Song." The warbler over on WMCA, Jerry Baker, was threatening to sue, saying he'd used "The Romeo of the Radio" two years before.

Sponsorship was a hurdle; the network could be expected to sustain you only so long without reaping what they sowed. Bing had Cremo cigars, a masculine touch. Russ had been given a three-show tryout by Maxwell House Coffee the previous September. Wags said Russ sang so soporifically that you needed a cup of coffee to wake up, and since he was already broadcasting close enough to people's bedtime, the company decided against it. That was back before he became a hot property. Human real estate. Listerine, his new sponsor, was a mouthwash.

It was a thirteen-week contract, $2,500 per, and NBC had finally responded by giving him a better time. Beginning on December 7, he was on Mondays, Thursdays, and Fridays at 5:45 P.M.; Tuesdays, Wednesdays, and Saturdays at 10:00 P.M., adjusted to accommodate his schedule at the Paramount. He could do a remote, if need be, from the radio studio in the basement. Also beginning on Monday the seventh was his residency at the Waldorf-Astoria. The hotel had been moved uptown to make room for the Empire State Building, and the thus-named Empire Room was the most elegant ballroom in New York. He felt at the pinnacle.

All this activity would require some precise scheduling.

But let Paul Yawitz read his own press release:

Up at nine for a ride on his roan through Central Park. Back to his penthouse apartment overlooking Manhattan. A shower and a rub-down and then a swift drive through traffic to the theatre where he is appearing. There are four to five shows every day that last until ten thirty in the evening and these are interspersed with rehearsals for the following week, rehearsals of his commercial broadcasts and the broadcasts themselves, the mad dashes between shows across the East River to make recordings of his songs on the discs, and the numerous motion picture shorts and personal appearances.

At eleven each night he leaves the theatre and speeds frantically in his limousine to the Waldorf-Astoria on Park Avenue to conduct his Orchestra while the Mayfair of Gotham dances after the theatre. At two thirty in the morning he is in bed again.

It was the horse bit that got him.

A WEEK later, Louis Sobol, Harry's brother, came to visit backstage at the Paramount. Louis wrote for the *Evening Journal*. He found Russ stretched on a couch, "almost nude," being given a rubdown by his "sepian valet," Gordon

K. Reid. The press liked Gordon, especially the part about his waking Russ in the morning with a bit of Shakespeare, followed by a splash of cold water if he doesn't stir. He mixed drinks the same way.

He's also quoted as saying things like "Lawdy, massa, dat suah am fine singin." The minstrel show has made the radio columns on the heels (or is it the toes?) of *Amos 'n Andy.*

Through the door, the harmonies of the onstage Mills Brothers filter up the stairwell to the dressing room. Their imitation of instruments is spontaneously erupting the crowd. A muted trumpet solo elicits cheers and whistles, and the bass voice of John Junior, the oldest, carries its vibration through the walls.

The Mills Brothers had been in New York for more than a year, arriving in 1930 from their home base of Cincinnati, where they had appeared on WLW radio. CBS picked them up, and on October 12, 1931, for Jack Kapp's Brunswick label, the Brothers made the first of their many recordings. The crowd knows "Tiger Rag," its trombone swoops and flatfoot staggers, and urges them along.

Brunswick puts them within Bing's recording world. Two weeks later, on the twenty-fifth, they participate in a medley from *George White's Scandals,* appearing with the Boswell Sisters, Connee alongside Crosby, singing "Life Is Just a Bowl of Cherries." The contrast between the Boswells' New Orleans white gutbucket complements the compromise of the Millses' carefully scripted black arrangements, siblings learning to share.

In the middle is Bing. He's having a ball. Why not? It's cherries jubilee for him. In a couple of weeks he'll be headlining the Paramount, the *New York* Paramount, where he'd flopped the first time out in Times Square.

The Boswells entwine for "That's Love" to open the Scandals medley, and then Frank Munn answers another eternal question in "That's Why Darkies Were Born." The plantation implication is offset—some might say put in its place—by the emancipation of song—"Sing when you're weary and sing when you're blue." The voice is a double-edged sword, given music's uncanny knack of slipping through the cracks of preconception.

As a process, it takes time. The interracial has its own complicated cakewalk, a get-acquainting built on insecurity and fear, genuine curiosity and sexual attraction. Dating. These two strangers are so shy, each has to put on a mask to confront the other. They can't bear to look each other in the eye directly, plying an elaborate ritual of hide-and-seek.

Bing and the Mills Brothers have little trouble finding their common ground. The Millses have been on the bill with Bing at the Paramount through most of November, until December 3. They join the Columbo show a week later. On December 16, a Wednesday morning before they head over to their respective Paramounts, Bing slips into a Mills Brothers recording session. They try an off-the-cuff "Dinah," an old standard for both of them; its softened last syllable alludes to a southern feel, "Dixie eyes blazing . . . the eyes of Dinah Lee." Bing thinks of his wife as he sings it.

The first take is more relaxed than the second, casual in Bing's up-front delivery, as if he's winking as he's singing. His delivery gets broader until he hands off to the Brothers; the tempo scoots up and the orchestra disappears. Bing takes the first scat, all sixteenth notes, and the Millses romp in back of him. They race to the finish. There is a lightness to Bing's reentry, his playful urgings to the Millses, their *boop-bops* until the final high-hat choke.

They try it again. The second version is deliberate, paced, not as fresh in its self-discovery. They're pushing it; Bing's quick croon in the second scat provides a propulsive energy (he knows they haven't caught the spontaneity of the first version, and he's going to make it happen, because these days it seems like all he has to do is will it so and it happens and keeps on happening), and they catch a ride on the momentum of the rhythm. Everything is up front; Jack Kapp likes that version better.

"Shine" is more problematic. "Dinah" proves a massive hit, and so two months later, to the day, Bing meets the Mills Brothers in the studio to record a song about "chocolate drops," "curly hair," "always wear a smile," "my color is shady baby," "shine away your blueses," rhyming it with "shining shoeses." Caricature: but here is one of the first moments when minstrelsy removes its blackface and white mask, harmonizing together.

Gordon digs his fingers between Russ's shoulder blades. He's listening to the Mills Brothers' voices echo up the stairs, only instead of words, he's hearing cadences, and quick rhymes, intermingling with the snatches of Shakespeare he's been reading. He knows the dignity of the black man, and that Paul Robeson had played Othello in London during the past year, characterizing the Moor as a "great Negro warrior" (though it would take him until 1943 to star in the role on Broadway). Robeson is returning to America next month, opening a recital tour at New York's Town Hall on January 18. Gordon is looking forward to going.

RUSS'S BOOKING is scheduled for ten weeks. He only has to sing now, four songs in nine minutes at the finale, the pit band onstage to surround him. There are plans for a dance routine, a violin showcase. The abundant females in the audience don't seem to care. When he turns on the croon, he feels the warm glow of their iridescence, a moonbeam in reverse.

Gordon's hands continued their ministrations down his spine. Columbo is a "cinch bet," says *Variety*. "A draw bet." Better and better. A betting man.

"Betting on yourself is like fixing your own fight," Russ mused aloud to Sobol, whose owlish presence prompted such small talk, which he scribbled in bite-sized tidbits on his pad. Columbo remembered when he wanted to be a boxer. There were twelve rounds to a bout. Yawitz always claimed twelve was his lucky number, though Paul tended to seize on any available digit as grist for his theory, a promiscuous numerology. It was Russ's place in the birth order, but only seven children had made it out of infancy, and then there was Fiore.

He was glad to have his parents coming to New York. He hadn't seen them since he'd arrived east. His mother needed to witness the excitement first-hand, though she told him by telephone that she hated the winters. She still remembered the chill winds that swept off the Delaware. The family had heard him on Los Angeles radio, over NBC hookup KECA, with Don Voorhees' Orchestra. They had no idea just how crazy it had gotten. They had *no* idea.

His "cook," or "butler," or whatever the press called Gordon this week, went off to scramble some eggs. Russ sat up, stretched, reached for a towel, draped it across his neck. He flexed his fingers, tightened them into a pair of fists, threw a quick one-two combination in the air.

"Gee, Louie," Sobol attributed, first-personally. "Can you imagine this? Remember when I came into town five or six months ago, broke? I can't believe it and now my mother and father are coming Sunday from the Coast and wait'll they see the house I've leased for them. And I wanted to be a prize-fighter once."

Everyone bets on a championship bout. The Battle of the Paramounts. Columbo vs. Crosby. Black trunks, white trunks. Catching a breath in their corners between rounds, kneading fingers rubbing their backs, mopping their brows. You need both combatants to enter a ring. The bell sounds.

Two C's form a circle, each C meeting as in a mirror, divided by the river.

NEW YEAR'S EVE

Before and After.

New Year's Eve at the Paramounts. One into two.

It has been their year, Russ and Bing, and now they're each going to pop the cork on 1931, give it the royal send-off, one upping the other, the annual in which they've come into their own, and then toot the horn for the new, with its circumstance and happenstance and onrushing distance.

The luck of the draw. Time's ricochet.

A *FLING*. She flailed at the air. She didn't mind being a flapper or a floozy in a flivver . . . but a *fling*!

Dorothy was beside herself.

That . . . that . . . *flucker*!

She stamped her heels on the floor.

Con had come to see her this morning. Russ couldn't be bothered. Oh, no, Mr. Flush and Flashy had to send Froggy over. Dorothy had been counting the moments waiting for Con to show up ever since Russ had broken their after-show date twice in a row, and then called to tell her he was busy again, but needed time on his own to think about what they were both getting into, and how young she was, and how he really didn't have a minute to breathe what with everything happening, and maybe next week when things settled down . . .

She'd heard it all before. Nonstop. It was what boys said when they were more interested in themselves than in her. And she knew what it meant. They had other interests. And they weren't settling down.

Giving her the air. The *idea*! She did her best to ignore Con as he began his sales pitch. What did he think, that she was some song-plugger who needed a pep talk? It had been a year since vaudeville had dumped her on the doorstep in St. Louis. She could have turned tail and gone home then; instead, Mr. Ziegfeld called her. She arrived on Broadway and headed straight to the Follies. The show was due to close in New York and go on the road any week now, and though poor Mr. Ziegfeld was planning bigger and better things for next season, with the revival of *Show Boat* and a Lupe Velez vehicle called *Hot-Cha!*, it was no backstage secret that he wasn't looking well. He rushed past the girls hardly glancing at them, head down and preoccupied, and some were trying their chest-out best to catch his attention.

She didn't need to. Dorothy had the attention, and the featured song to prove it. Russ could've been the blue ribbon, pinned right 'cheer. She knew he had a career to come first; so did she. It was Russ who started playfully talking about a home life, the *bambinos*, and teaching her how to cook with olive oil instead of lard. She went along with the joke, making light of it, though the joke was on her. She remembered her own mother, always in the next room, and her father, who was never around, and she had a twinge for a family where all symmetries were fulfilled, the vicarious balance where there are no missing pieces in the jigsaw puzzle of personality. Maybe then she wouldn't miss a man in her life so much that she longed for Russ to sit smoking his cigarette in the next chair while the radio unfolded a dreamy melody, he gliding over in his brocade jacket and glazing his eyes for her in that teasing way . . .

She stopped herself mid-muse. She wasn't going to think another thought about him, not *ever*, even if Winchell was predicting wedding bells: "Dorothy Dell, the Follies dolly, and Russ Columbo, NBC's Romeo of Song, plan to middle aisle it shortly." She had to admit it did look good as a nuptial announcement.

The rumors didn't help calm Con, who was pressing ahead with his case: "You stand between the boy and his success. Can't you see that? How can he be every woman's dream when he's yours! Only you can assure his success, by letting him go."

He'd sung the same tune to Russ—"You are the sweetheart of every girl in the land. If it gets into the papers that you are in love with one girl, the others will become discouraged and you will lose popularity." This was getting to be a whole musical; it's too bad Broadway was in such doldrums.

Dorothy understood all too well, but who did he think he was, throwing her over? Russ was going high hat, getting *too* big for his britches. A big shot.

Dot the *i*, and she was still Dot. He wasn't the shy young crooner who was as excited about being in New York as she. Dorothy knew he wasn't *really* serious about marriage. Her mother would have conniptions if she mentioned getting hitched, and what would Helen do without her big sister? Besides, Bing was married. Rudy was married. Even Morton Downey was married. It didn't seem to hurt their radio broadcasts, or their stage shows. And for Russ to send his sneaky Con-man, who she was sure was in cahoots with her mother, instead of being a real man and bringing her flowers and taking her out to dinner and a carriage ride home through Central Park before breaking her heart, that was too much to bear. To bare.

He was now officially an old flame. She extinguished him, and the darkness closed in around her.

TWO DAYS before the new year, on the twenty-ninth, Russ goes over to Studio 1 to record. There's time for only two songs. He's a busy man these days.

The orchestra has been rehearsing for two hours when Columbo arrives at eleven in the morning. They go right to work. Shilkret has added another instrument, backing him with ten pieces now. There are three violins, a cello and a string bass, two saxophones and one trombone, a guitar and a piano. The musicians are putting their instruments back in their cases by 11:50 A.M.

"Save the Last Dance for Me" is the first song, a Walter Hirsch and Frank Magine copyright, with a sway that arcs before falling back into the arm around the waist, the slight whirl of a waltz. There is some question as to what constitutes a last dance. Is it the one that happens on the dance floor, at evening's end, or the one that goes on after the ball is over?

The lasting; and how long will it last? There were so many dancers in this world. Russ was finding out just how willing partners they could be. He's twenty-three. He'd always been good-looking, and done well with the ladies, but nothing could prepare him for this cornucopulata. His dance card runneth over. "*Let's make this a ladies' choice. . . .*"

Just the other Thursday he had been leaving the dressing room and a girl suddenly appeared by his side. She had blond bobbed hair and eyes like saucers and a coat that fit her like a dress. He could only imagine what the dress looked like. She pulled her hands from her muff, brown sable. The gloves were black velvet.

Turn off the light. Call it a night. Side-step inside the one-on-one.

One or ones. He didn't want to make a choice, because then he would have to give up everything for love, even if that's what he promised, night after night, over the radio, on record, onstage. He wasn't ready. Seymour Simons and Gerald Marks's "All of Me," the second song, addresses that compromised question, framed in the negative: *"Why not take all of me?"* He could think of reasons. He'd taken a detour on that ride back to Manhattan, telling Gordon to park the Lincoln at a small restaurant at Spring and Mulberry, where he knew the owners, and they had a back room with good wine and some hot buttered rum to go with the blond Christmas spirit.

He'd been working hard, and he wanted to reward himself. Con was right. There was plenty of time to think about girls. And plenty of pre-dawns to enjoy their splendored companies. It was the holidays. He was making Mary.

He doesn't want a *"one-sided love affair."* He's a ladies' man. There's nothing left for him to say, and so he *la-da-dees* and *la-dee-dahs*, and afterward she squeezes his hand and kisses him, to let him know he can stay the night.

AT THE New York Paramount, Bing Crosby is riding out over the audience on a giant mechanical crane, theirs on a silver platter. The crowd howls and clutches at him. A sailor comes away with his shoe. Another grabs his socks. The crane gets stuck once, and he has to clamber back to the stage on his own. He doesn't lose his sense of aplomb. He's just a regular guy, even if he is the Master of Ceremonies. Paramount manager Bot Weitman keeps him exiting from stage left, entering from stage right, telling jokes, bantering with the audience, a part of the show's theme even if it calls for a ridiculous costume.

Russ doesn't have that luxury. He never takes off his tuxedo, a Dunhill. For him, seduction is serious business. He could never look foolish. It might break the spell. It's at this moment that they begin their diverge as entertainers. Bing takes the jazz; Russ keeps the jism.

Jack Kapp, the head of Crosby's record label, doesn't want the jazz, though he tolerates it. At this point, it's Bing's version of getting drunk through the music, and hopefully if he hits some good notes he won't be tempted to take a drink. It was the *buh-buh-buh-buhs* that got Kapp's goat. He didn't want Bing to sing to women alone; he understood, possibly before anyone else, that Bing could be everyone, the great conduit of emotion, the blank screen that lit you up with its own light, the moment before and after the movie, when the screen glows with its residual images. He was the perfect foil; a luminium.

Jack knew hits. Early on in his career at Brunswick (he'd started as a delivery boy), Kapp had supervised one of Al Jolson's last great records. The 1928 "Sonny Boy" (theme song of *The Singing Fool*) turned "Mammy" inside out and sold two million copies, with Jolson in a paternal mode and a recitation toward the end that Al delivers in the kind of oratory which W. C. Fields would pick up and broaden in the thirties for his screen persona. It's an electrical recording, and hearing it on an old Victor Orthophonic, changing the needle every play or two, Al nearly blows the speaker out when he rears back and launches into the final heartrending chorus.

Kapp was looking for someone who could do for the electric era what Jolson had accomplished for the acoustic, even if Al had forever signaled the changeover. Someone who could be everyone. Bing, amiable but driven, walking the fine line between his hair-trigger mood swings and his thinning hair, even grinning at himself because he realizes he is the anti-croon, knows he'll listen to Jack Kapp, and cut out the *buh-buh-boo*s. He even hides the microphone in the orchestra pit.

During the traditional singing of "Auld Lang Syne" at midnight on New Year's Eve, Bing looks over to his own *auld acquaintance*, Eddie Lang on guitar, his pick flicking across the flared chest of his Gibson L-5, and settles his snapping fingers on Lang's burnished chords and rhythmic hustle. Eddie is the first coaxial guitar player of the twentieth century. He didn't care that the guitar pickup hadn't been invented yet. Bing heard him moving alongside him, wherever he chose to go, and came to depend on it. He always wanted Eddie playing with him.

Cab Calloway comes down to pay a "surprise" visit to Bing in Times Square. The crowds are already starting to gather in the streets, waving bottles and blowing horns, a welcoming of the calendar's turn that hasn't changed since hunter-gatherer days. It's still Prohibition, but the police don't have the heart to tell people to stop drinking. It's a tough world out there. Many have come to mingle with the crowds in Times Square just to keep warm, or maybe hail a quick nip from a fellow reveler who probably doesn't need any more to drink. It's New Year's Eve in Manhattan, kicking the gong around.

Russ has left Brooklyn for Manhattan himself, limousining to the Empire Room to toast the crowd, waving a champagne bottle in one hand and his top hat in the other, counting down to midnight. 10—9—8. . . . He's not looking forward to zero. The sands of the year are running out and he feels them slipping through his fingers, harder to grasp, like dry water, each grain starting its final tumble into the bottom of the hourglass. There is no one waiting to kiss him in the way that Dorothy could, no sweet southern giggle and a nudge and a promise that next year will be the one, baby, I swear it to you no matter what we do I'll always be true and I'm doing it for you, and you and you and you and you.

1932.

GARBO

$\mathbf{A}$t the beginning of 1932, Greta Garbo was the most enigmatic woman on-screen. She played hard to get, because you didn't know what you were getting.

She confused the sexes. Wearing trousers and other masculine garb, referring to herself as a "boy" or an "*ooold* man," she remained an unrealizable object of feminine desire. "Her Most Intimate Friend" writes in an early (1933) *Film Pictorial* that he, Sven-Hugo Borg, was hired as an interpreter, but "It was I who, in fact, performed every duty of a lady's maid, except, of course, to dress her." Even then, Garbo had at last "found the complete solitude for which she sought all her life . . . cut off from the outside world, forgetting, but not forgotten." A desiring recluse in the popular imagination that will trail her through the century, she wants to be left alone.

Naturally Con thinks she and Russ would be perfect together.

SHE WOULDN'T even have to notice, that's how alone she could be. The only ones paying attention would be the press, and he'd be paying them. Not outright. He didn't have to. Con could only concoct. They wrote the column inches, collecting their paychecks. Tit for tat.

Con had his own contrarian cross to bear. Cardinal O'Connell, of the Boston diocese, had delivered an old-fashioned tongue-lashing against crooning. "A base art," he called it at the Cathedral of the Holy Cross on January 10. "Whiners and bleaters . . . a degenerate form of singing," he calumniated

GARBO

to the three-thousand-strong all-male body of the Holy Name Society. "You will discern the basest appeal to sex emotion in the young. They are not true love songs. They profane the name. They are ribald and revolting to true men.

"No true American man would practice this base art. Of course, they aren't men."

The Cardinal's wrath spared no one. The theater had become a "low down, disreputable misrepresentation of the human race," and as for the fox-trot, "Why, some of them couldn't sit through dinner without stopping to cavort upon the dance floor." Next stop: the confessional and a dozen Hail Marys to go.

Vallée, a lapsed Catholic, tried to sidestep the question when Nick Kenny "asked him if his face was red" about the Cardinal's statement, as if he somehow reflected the prelate's robes. It was all a matter of volume, Rudy avowed. "Speaking for the softer types of voices which some people think I typify, I have found that most of the so-called crooners like myself are able to sing with considerable volume when the occasion demands it." He rose to the occasion, his manhood asserting.

But his thoughts always revolved back to women. "However, we realize that the mechanism of the microphone is such that the voice must be brought down to an extreme softness or pianissimo. This is quite an art, as most persons are unable to stay in pitch when singing extremely softly." Rudy knew the closer you get, the harder it is to maintain your distance, to keep from falling into those blackpooled eyes, the shoulder with its thin satin strap, the wing of blade hillocking the back.

Bing was a Catholic who played golf on Sundays. "I am not a crooner. A crooner is a person who sings with a half voice and takes the top notes with a falsetto. I always sing in full voice."

Man to man.

RUSS IS different. His croon doesn't separate male from female. He sings from her port of embarkation.

He needs a strong woman. Con tells him so, trying to explain away why Dorothy hasn't called him. She was too *dee*-pend-ent, he wasn't getting just her but a whole *fa*-mily, and what girl in her right mind would want to fantasize about some *married* crooner? Yes, Morton Downey is married. Yes, Bing is married and Rudy is somewhat married (if you listened to the whispers), and everybody might be married, but this is *Russ Columbo* and if he's going to have a ro-*mance*, then he might as well *take a chance* and rhyme it with *glance, enhance,* or *askance.* Probably the last.

Con knew his melodies, and that options for Russ's radio show and Paramount engagement were upcoming. There were contracts to be negotiated. This scheme was a sure hit for page one. The press would be told that Greta had sent Russ a telegram, wondering *Why did you not call me as you promised you would?* Lyrics by Paul Yawitz and Harry Sobol.

I had made arrangements for you to be connected directly with my suite. My sweet. It was signed "G.G."

The newspapers had their headlines at the ready: the mating *o*'s of *Columbo Woos Garbo,* the even more seductive *Crooner Warms To Cold Swede.*

Yawitz later re-created Con's instructions. "Sobol," he said to Harry right after New Year's when Paul was out at Leon and Eddie's, "you and Yawitz have got to do some thinking. Columbo's contracts on the air, at the hotel, and at the theater all come up for discussion again in two short weeks. The managements are going to give us a lot of trouble because the price they're paying us now is so exorbitant. But we're going to make it even more exorbitant."

Four syllables. Like a person unfamiliar with a foreign language translating in his head before answering, Con could hear four notes ring out, the second highest before the descent, B-flat, G, F, Ex-*or*-*bi*-*tant* . . .

"Even if they have to take a loss, they've got to be made to realize it is for their own benefit—institutional prestige. Get it?"

"*It*"—"Get Columbo all over the Front Pages, understand? . . . Not even Page 3 will do . . . we want top space!"—got Harry out the door heading for Leon Euken and Eddie Davis's joint on West Fifty-second, where he found Paul perpendicular to the bar, a ginger-ale highball at the ready, hardly even bothering to hide the flask jutting from his suit pocket. His mustache was wet on the ends.

Sobol was agitated. "It's a hell of a job we've got in front us," he said in a voice that sounded unnaturally loud, even with the room's clamor and clink. "What'll we do?"

"Come right over and have a drink." Yawitz waved to the adjacent stool. "I'll stir."

They toasted the music and newspaper and radio and movie businesses thirty-two times. "The thirty second drink was the one we were waiting for!" Yawitz remembered later (or was that in 1932?), and finally resorted to what most journalists do and picked up the latest edition of the *Mirror* to see what was in the headlines. They read that Garbo was in town "pulling an incognito."

It was raining when they got back to the offices. Every newspaper in town had reporters camped out at the lobby of the St. Moritz to glimpse "The Frigid Heir of the Norselands." She wouldn't even talk to Winchell, and he had supposedly chased her down the corridor.

THE UNATTAINABLE, a Swede from the cold climate, the land of the midnight sun, her home an iceberg's wander from the Arctic Circle. Compared to her, Russ was equatorial. If they'd wanted, they could've shared a whole continent between them, meeting somewhere near the Vienna of the Hapsburgs. But it was a preposterous idea. Garbo—to call her by her first name seemed impolite, a breach of etiquette—already had a mate. Herself. Forever monogamous.

Her eyelashes were more than an inch long, or so they seemed. Garbo was seemly. The sculptor Julian Bowes once described Garbo's body as existing in "dynamic symmetry," an exquisite balance, which she kept mindfully in place by immersion in work. "I have no time for anything else," she said, aware that cinematic life was her art, and her greatest love. She refused to marry the actor John Gilbert (described by Florabel Muir of the News Syndicate as "her devoted slave at one time") because she couldn't be unfaithful to herself. "I am very happy to play in pictures with Mr. Gilbert." Then, the fatal flaw: "He inspires me—with him I do not act, I live. But that is not love."

She had crossed the line between the created self and the one she was born with as Greta Lovisa Gustafsson in Stockholm on September 18, 1905. Her first director, Mauritz Stiller, plucked her from the background of a 1923 Royal Dramatic School production of *The Green Dress Suit*; she was already larger than the roles she played, the audience in on her secret life. Even Stiller sought her out, after a chance and forgotten meeting in a Stockholm tobacco shop where he'd gone to purchase cigarettes, her memory staying with him after he left, as elusive as if he'd dreamed it.

Garbo preferred to exist in other's fantasies. Stiller christened her Garbo—a name he had invented and was looking for a female to fulfill, and she kept her first name, which could be misread as Great. Her debut film with Stiller, *The Saga of Gosta Berling*, in which she played a countess who helps an alcoholic priest gain redemption, brought her to the attention of Louis B. Mayer at Metro. He didn't have much faith in Mauritz's understanding of the American market, but he recognized Garbo's laconic sultriness. Even in the silents, you could hear an accent.

There was great interest in how she would bridge the chasm between the silents and sound. It wasn't just the use of dialogue; whole mannerisms that once signified the language of silence were rendered superfluous. Though she had only begun learning English after she arrived in Hollywood, her vocal tones, like her appearance, found favor with the new reproductive devices. Her smoky baritone enhanced her character in the same way she would appear more beautiful when viewed through a camera's eye, her words reinforced by her own expressive eyes and the curling diacritical marks of her forehead. When she orders the long-awaited *viskey* in *Anna Christie* (1930), slumping at a table, she achieves a naturalism that belies the printed film stock and the audience's expectations of what she might sound like. She vanishes into character, a Garbo, her own typecasting. Once the lighting rigs and microphones have been removed, she goes home to an existence prosaically similar to that of every other inhabitant of the moviegoing public.

Nobody believes this, of course, which is why the public retains an endless fascination with her solitude. She would attend no premieres, and refused interviews. There is only one known instance of Garbo signing an autograph. It was not even premeditated withdrawal. Her sense of self ends on-screen; if the actress has given her all, there should be none left over.

She tried men, but in the end they couldn't live with her self-reliance. When she made her first American success without Stiller, he kept coming to the set with suggestions, until he realized she no longer needed to listen. John Gilbert was another matter. She moved into his mansion after making *Flesh and the Devil* in 1927. He pleaded with her to marry him, over and over, spilling into scandal and gossip columns. It wasn't just a press agent's dream; he truly meant it, and to prove he could live without her, he married the actress Ina Claire on a vicious rebound in May 1929, separating by the end of the year. Garbo couldn't understand why he needed her constant reassurance, or even needed, period. He was John Gilbert, the most attractive romantic male star of the 1920s. Wasn't that enough? Why did he need drama offstage as well?

Her severe self-consciousness gave her an aloof air, and a distance that allowed the public to imagine her private life however they chose. The films played into it. In *Mata Hari*, she declares "I'm . . . my own master!" In *Queen Christina* (she would have had only to make *Jesus Christ Superstar* to cover all Christs) she kisses a woman full on the lips. In *Grand Hotel*, she utters the reflexive "I want to be alone" and indulges the world-weariness that would become her trademark. By the time she reaches *Ninotchka*, shortly before her retirement in 1941, the public lines up to see if the dour Swede can actually be funny. *Garbo Laughs!* And so she does.

She is curiously asexual offstage, dressed to conceal, nonetheless a woman about whom sexual rumor whirls. Her relationship with Stiller is described as Svengali-like, an image enhanced not only by the silent-era villain who moves the noun from proper to improper, but by Mauritz's directorial instincts which grew embittered over the distance Mayer kept him from Garbo. He understood her sexually through the prism of his homosexuality; she learned from him how a man values the duty of his work. She was the one who stayed in Hollywood.

Garbo gravitated toward the company of others in the sexual shadowland, especially the photographer Cecil Beaton. His extrovert flamboyance and reflective androgyny delighted in self-portraits in which he was made up and outfitted as a woman, and he combined a talent for social climbing with a gift for lighting that flattered and courted, like a courtier. He approached his subjects—reversing the usual monarchist traditions—with a reverence to their royalty, from society *mädchens* like Eddy Duchin's wife, Marjorie Oelrichs (with Eddy in silhouette behind her, both smoking cigarettes), to the Queen herself, Elizabeth II. He eventually became the official photographer of Buckingham Palace. Garbo had already refused his many offers of marriage, and he had to settle for second best.

There was no chance of sharing lives, given their dispositions. Beaton believed he was who he photographed; Garbo loved to pose, but left her mirror image behind when she left the camera's range finder. She divided the public and private self absolutely, guarding her privacy like a jealous lover. When Cecil published his diaries detailing their interactions, he proved himself unworthy of her confidence.

Garbo's second comedic turn, the aptly named *Two-Faced Woman* in which she plays herself and her "twin sister," was released three weeks after Pearl Harbor, and was lost in the hysteria of the coming conflict. There was never any postwar for her. No one wants to know what happened to Penelope and Ulysses after he returned from Circe; how Sleeping Beauty and her Prince decorated the west wing of the castle. Romance is all seduction and conquest. Having done both with her public, she abdicated, leaving governing to the bureaucrats; Garbo would rather sail off alone, like Queen Christina, gazing at "nothing" as Rouben Mamoulian (later to direct the color-drenched *Blood and Sand*; Garbo never made a color film) advised her, emulating the blank self-fulfilling stare of the movie screen, a vessel on a vessel, with the dead body of her lover in the back of the sloop.

She preferred the photograph of memory, the reclamation of cinematic experience. In *Queen Christina*, she moves about the room in which she has first made love to Gilbert (they have exchanged places: the billing reads

Greta Garbo "with John Gilbert" instead of *Flesh and the Devil's* other way around), fingers memorizing the furniture, running her hands over the wall planks and measuring the spaces between bed and spinning wheel. "What are you doing?" he asks, with the amused indulgence of an old lover. "In the future, in my memory, I shall live a great deal in this room."

They meet in a wayward inn, far from sovereign duties. When she's in her cloak and breeches, he doesn't recognize her monarchy, or even her gender. He calls her "sir," a not-so-mistaken identity, and playing an envoy from "the hot countries," elaborates that love is all "a matter of climate . . . you can't serenade a woman in a snowstorm." Christina washes her face in snow. She believes in love's possibility, but not its existence; "great love . . . perfect love . . . is an illusion. It is the golden fable of which we all dream . . . but in ordinary life we must be content with less." He wants to take her to the "islands of the moon." She removes her crown and leaves public life behind. They are playing to character.

Falling in love changes her mind, though she sees it through the prism of an artist: "This great joy I feel now . . . Antonio, this is how the Lord must have felt when he first beheld the finished world, with all his creatures breathing, living. . . . " Mamoulian agreed, and hoped Mayer would stay out of the editing room.

Garbo's men tended to be father figures, effeminate, or in the case of the art dealer Bill Green, her Warholesque telephone confidant, ready to speak of mundanities. They could be counted on not to go over the romantic top like Gilbert had. Whatever the state of John's recorded voice (Louis B. Mayer made sure its treble pitch would hardly enhance his career in the talkies), there was no question of his wanting a platonic relationship. The press felt nostalgic for the mutual heat generated when she and he were seen at this remote justice of the peace or over that connubial border, the only man who could tame her in the wish-fulfillment of the press release. It was not implausible to imagine Columbo taking Gilbert's place in the same blind item. Just impossible.

No one actually saw Garbo at the St. Moritz. There is a good chance that she was staying at another hotel in early January, the MGM *Grand Hotel*, which began filming on December 30, 1931, finishing on the nineteenth of February, in Hollywood.

IT'S A two-step process to deliver the goods. Verse and chorus.

The reporters weren't buying anything this outlandish unless it had enough innuendo to convince the city editor.

Con throws a party at his apartment right after New Year's, raising a glass to Russ's twin triumphs at the Paramount and Waldorf-Astoria. The *Graphic's* Jerry Wald attends the soirée and watches Con let the phone ring until it seems everyone is waiting in suspense for him to pick it up.

"Hello," he fairly shouts into the receiver, cocking his head. "No, this is his manager. Call what room? Suite 2231 at the St. Moritz. Whom should he ask for?"

He puts the phone down with a quizzical look rippling his brow. He speaks to the air, knowing everybody's listening, answering the unspoken question, aware he's being quoted.

"That's a funny one. When I ask who's calling, they hang up." He calls to a stooge across the room. "Hey, Sammy, you live at the St. Moritz. Do you know who's in room 2231?"

Sure enough, Sammy—the songwriter Sam Coslow—pipes in his background vocal. "Room 2231?" A staccato, finger-snapping rhythm. "Why, that's Garbo's room. I live on the same floor. I know."

Amid the rolling eyes and the slosh of glasses, Con hollers out, "Get me the St. Moritz." Sure enough, the room in question is occupied by a Miss Gustafsson.

Con knows a solo bridge is needed, perhaps a restatement of the theme with a hint of harmony. The next morning, while reporters camped in the lobby of the St. Moritz chew on their pencils and the Speed Graphic cameramen juggle flashbulbs in their pockets, an ostentatious flower arrangement is wheeled through the lobby. A fleet-fingered reporter snags the attached card as it is carried past by two bellhops. It is signed with Russ's formal signature, complete with his standard flourish. The fountain pen had been running out of ink; each letter is two parallel lines swirling like a child's ice skates, with an underline darting from the final *o* and spinning itself like a top in ever decreasing circles.

The chorus telegram is released anonymously, in the key of G.

EVEN WINCHELL was caught up in the excitement. After Con showed him the telegram from "G.G.," he coupled them on the town one night, as if Garbo would leave her hideaway only for Russ. When he found out he'd been had, he was livid. In a particularly stream-of-consciousness column during the first week of January, he rambles from Judge Dunn of Maryland considering "ladies of the stage 'women of more or less easy virtue' " to wondering what ever happened to Judge Crater, anyway, to his definition of horse sense ("you never hear of a horse betting on a human being") to how you "rib a guy" (of special interest to any potential Eves), and then:

> Now poor Russ Columbo is the bait. . . . His pals promoted a gal with a Swedish dialect to keep phoning him. . . . She told Russ: "I luff you so motch, I Garbo. Don't told nobody—I vuss by you place vare you sink and vuss so thrilled.' . . . And spurious pash notes were sent to Russ signed "Greta." . . . He spent a young fortune on posies for her. . . . And some papers went for it, too: so Columbo lost nothing but his dignity.

Dignity! Russ felt goddam em-bare-assed. Greta wouldn't care about him. She'd be livid at Winchell's rendering of her accent; it was still a sore subject. How could Con do this to him? Had he really lost his mind?

The phone rang. It was Nick Kenny, over at Winchell's paper. "I hear Columbus has discovered Garbo," he said before Russ even had time to say hello.

Russ fumbled for words. "What do you mean?"

Oh, that was a great start. "She sent you a telegram bawling you out for not calling her as you had promised. What about it?"

Columbo's breath was harshened by the telephone's sibilance. "Who told you about it?" Hold him off at any cost.

"One of my spies," said Kenny, in his best insinuation. "Did you know Greta in Hollywood?"

Did anybody? "Yes, I did," said Russ, since he had once seen her sitting sulkily at a table with a sloshed Gilbert trying to induce her to dance. "But I made a solemn vow not to discuss her in New York."

"To whom did you make the solemn vow? To Greta?" Nick was desperate for a quote of entrapment.

"Use your imagination," replied Russ, which gave Kenny the excuse to feature the item in his column, whether it was true or not.

Russ prepared to get off the phone, but Kenny wasn't finished.

"What about that fervid affair with Dorothy Dell of the Follies?"

Well, what about it? Russ felt his stomach drop away. He decided to tough it out, humming a snatch from "The Thrill Is Gone," Vallée's song from the Scandals. "I haven't seen Dorothy since the Follies left town."

Then Kenny was back to Garbo, trying for an end-around quote. "Have you been in touch with Greta since she came to New York? Isn't it true that she made her secret trip here just to see you?" Russ held firm. "I have always been a devoted fan," and changing the subject, promptly hung up.

The thrill is gone, he thought, only he saw another meaning in the song now. Dorothy had left town, and taken the thrill with her.

THERE ARE two songs recorded on January 12. The ten-piece orchestra comes in at nine in the morning to rehearse: piano, three violins, string bass, guitar, three saxophones, and a trombone, a syrupy blend. Shilkret is again in charge and Con is along for the ride. Russ shows up at 10:30 and is done in two hours.

"Just Friends" comes from the pen of Sam Lewis and John Klenner; "You're My Everything" is from a slight musical called *The Laugh Parade,* composed by Mort Dixon, Joe Young, and Harry Warren. The sentiments of the songs are at odds. "Just Friends" implies this is all they can be. "You're My Everything" offers limitless possibility. He sings at cross-purposes, a two-faced man, the A and B sides of Victor 22909.

The continual stage and radio work has done his voice good. Though these are not the best songs he will attempt, his singing, usually dark-hued, seems lithe and nimble, a touch of Crosby-casual, though he exaggerates its dip into the bottom registers. His voice uplifts the arrangements, rising like a swing at the far end of its arc before falling backward on the crooning choruses. Live concert performance has given him a sense of dramatic build. He finishes each song as if applause will overtake his final notes.

PUBLIX WAS starting to wonder if Russ hadn't been at the Paramount too long. Despite Con's machinations, business was off. Bing had Times Square and its tourist trade to gather customers. Flatbush Avenue, unless you were on your way to Ebbets Field, was for Brooklynites. It was no time to ask for a raise.

In the first week of January, Russ shared the Paramount bill with musical comedians Williams and Delaney, singer Frances Faye, and the tap-dancing duo of Dick and Edith Barstow. Bing had the Boswell Sisters. *Ladies of the Big House* was the film presentation, with Sylvia Sidney. Russ debuted two new songs, "Too Late" and "Why Did It Have to Be Me?" neither of which he would record. The Boswells moved over to Brooklyn the following week, along with Adler and Bradford, a dance team, and "musical comedy stars" the Rio Brothers. In return, Bing got Frances Faye, the ballet of Ruth St. Denis, and two comedy combinations, Wilton and Weber and the Michon Brothers. The movie was *This Reckless Age,* soon to give way to *Two Kinds of Women* and Ruth Chatterton's *Tomorrow and Tomorrow*, while Burns and Allen, then Lilyan Tashman supported Bing. Russ got Paul Lukas (drumming up advance publicity for his role opposite Chatterton) and the Slate Brothers, dancers from Earl Carroll's Vanities.

Russ could see the way things were going. He was more like "Bing Lipshitz from Columbo," the running gag over at Minsky's Republic Burlesque. Con would be lucky to keep his option intact, not to suffer a cut in pay even as Bing was raised and raised again. To hear Conrad tell it, Russ wouldn't take no for an answer. Introducing two songs in the last week of January, "Cinderella Blues" and "Prince Charming," Russ felt his fairy tale turning Grimm.

IT'S HIS birthday. Twenty-four. Instead of everybody singing to him, he's singing to everybody. The birthday boy.

Blow out the candles.

MARCH

H e is his own vanishing point.

I go to visit the site of the Victor Studio on East Twenty-fourth Street. I have recently learned its address, 153, between Lexington and Third. I have passed the block dozens of times, but never noticed its site-ness. Just another street on the way somewhere. Very anywhere.

Where Jimmie Rodgers cut his last sides, lying on a cot in a rehearsal room between takes. Where Duke Ellington recorded "Mood Indigo." Where King Oliver and Eubie Blake and Carson Robison passed through. Where Russ recorded his entire New York *oeuvre* in his year and a quarter of being a Victor artist. Twenty-seven sides. My lucky number.

The block is empty when I get there. The entire square has been torn down, demolished, excavated for a Baruch college building not even framed in girders at this moment in time. Nothing remains but a hole in the earth around the corner from the George Washington Hotel, a molar pulled out of the island's bedrock jawbone, only the golden glint of the New York Life Insurance pyramid and the Empire State Building stabbing its own shadow some sixty-six winters after Russ hit his Manhattan moment of glory.

It was a good solstice for him, that 1931 into 1932. In town for just half a year, he had taken the Hardened Artery of Broadway and remade it in his image. Depending on which columnist you read, he was making between four and six grand, the same as Crosby, or ten grand a week, which Morton Downey claimed. Downey had the all-important sponsor's contract, a link with Camel, and was appearing nightly at the Central Park Casino. He had the penthouse aerie on East Eighty-sixth Street overlooking the East River to prove it, though Russ thought that the reason he sang all those songs about the moon—"Wabash Moon," "Carolina Moon"—was because Mort was part cow.

Vallée was also on a roll, or was that a role, mooted to be up for the title turn of *Crooner* from a yet-to-be-written original novel by Rian James of the Brooklyn *Eagle* just optioned by Warner Bros. (and Russ wondered who he'd watched at the corner of DeKalb and Flatbush to come up with his characterization), buying a palace in the Hills of Beverly for more than $100,000 to make California his home. Paramount had purchased a theatrical play called *Wild Waves*, retitling it *The Big Broadcast*, hoping to land Bing. The sides would see each other in court.

I try to imagine Russ getting out of the Lincoln on the north side of the street, looking up at the Empire State spire newly spearing the skyline, marveling at it for a moment before going in to make his recording. With so much sudden air in the block's silhouette, I find even that hard, but it's all I have left. I'm too late.

The missed opportunity. The lost chance. The overplay of the hand. Sometimes you win, and sometimes you lose your dress shirt.

Nothing had seemed to go right in the new year. By March, Russ had five thousand dollars in the bank. That was it. He was off the air, dropped by Listerine and the NBC network, given the heave-ho by Publix, tangled up in lawsuits involving that Con-artist *schmuck*. Instead of the Waldorf-Astoria Empire Ballroom, couples swaying to his every emote on the remote, or the prestige of the Paramount, he was going to be spending the summer traveling with a pickup band to the Woodmansten Inn, up by the Pelham Parkway! In Westchester, practically out of town.

Con fucked people, and they fucked up Russ, simple as that. Con wasn't around to take the heat. He was off in Miami, spieling for some other sucker-bait. And he, the Valentino of Song, was as dead as The Sheik himself.

The Waldorf had brought in an off-the-boat pianist to succeed him as conductor of the dance orchestra, twenty-two-year-old Nat Brandywynne, who had even played keyboards for Russ on occasion. Eddy Duchin recommended him. They just loved those society whining-and-deignings over on Park Avenue. *All octaves,* Russ sneered, though if truth be told, he had more in common with Duchin's heavy-breathing piano ripples than he cared to admit. Eddy's theme song was Chopin's E-flat Nocturne. Even his son, Peter, would adopt it.

Columbo had tried to get NBC to broadcast his radio show from the Empire Room, kill two birds with one stone, like Con said, who then proceeded to play both sides against the other to get more money for Russ, from both Listerine and the Waldorf, which was really more scam for Con, because here he was—the great Columboob—subtracting dollars and cents from his personal savings while all the moolah that went to fund Con's management companies and various side interests and cut-ins and cronies and a bar tab in every speak in town had vanished like it was never there.

They were giving him the business in *Radio Guide*—"Russ Columbo is worried. . . . He recently purchased a car which holds only four people, and he has six stooges." *The New York Sun* referred to his "army of chiselers." He was beginning to feel like the goose that laid a golden egg. A big zero.

AT LEAST he was working. Russ sat backstage at the Palace and waited his turn, idly leafing through the *Daily News*, paging backward from the sports section (the Golden Gloves intercity competition had opened between New York and Chicago, the Babe cracked four hits in the Yanks' spring training rout of the Boston Braves), glancing at the headlines about possible leads in the Lindy baby kidnapping and an irate hubby who had the Street Singer, Arthur Tracy, arrested. Reading the comics.

He had to chuckle at *Winnie Winkle*. Winnie was going to help her bosses' lodge entertainment by booking Mr. Ving Columballee, the "famous radio crooner," who is cartooned singing "Time on My Hands" through a megaphone. The boss is wondering how long he'll perform. "When I walk on the stage," the dapper Columballee replies in the strip of Monday, March 21, "my reception sometimes lasts from thirty to forty minutes—and after my act I sometimes bow for a half an hour or more." Foreplay and afterglow. In the middle he presumably sings. No wonder the gals love him.

Winnie, subtitled "The Breadwinner" in those days, and others of her syndicated ilk, such as *Tillie the Toiler*, comprise crooning's core audience: working office girls able to type, take shorthand, and mix dizzy and savvy in one adorable package. Their creators, *Winnie*'s Martin Branner or *Tillie*'s Russ Westover, played upon this fantasy of white-collar women's work, fine-lining determined lassies who were often powers behind the throne, always dressed in up-to-the-moment fashion: heels high, seams straight, hobble skirts flared, a hat with a bow and a feather, the back bared for formal occasions. A fresh outfit every day, regardless of the strip's internal clock.

This was a new female, an independent contractor (with, however, limited opportunities for promotion or boardroom membership), a step up for the lucky some from Triangle sweatshops and domesticity. Work was still viewed as a stepping-stone to marriage (below Winnie was a column called "How He Proposed" — "You the He, may tell it, as well as you, the girl proposed to," and the *News* would pay five dollars for every letter printed), but for once there was a small window where every girl might dream of being on her own, of life's endless possibilities, of an affection pure, beyond the hardscrabble of survival and unemployment lines. The world of romance.

THERE IS a knock at the door. "Five minutes, Mr. Columbo!"

Time to go on.

He is in the second week of the engagement. The Palace is one of the grand old rooms of vaudeville, and tonight is an all-star revue, with funny-bone-ticklers like Al Trahan, Buster Shaver (who is accompanied by two midgets from the *Tinytown Revue* — he gets his biggest laugh when he dances with the female one), and Joe Weber and Lew Fields, a comedy duo celebrating their golden anniversary who haven't worked on Broadway for seven years. The microphone is everywhere, though Weber and Fields prefer not to use it. Last month, at the Newark Paramount, they had poked a good deal of fun at radio; it was a matter of principle. Besides, everyone loved the pool-table bit, and the audience had heard it so many times that they knew all the words anyway.

The Paul Whiteman Orchestra plays two numbers, and amplification is brought out for Jack Fulton, Jr., billed as the Croon Prince of Jazz; and Mildred Bailey. The *News* notes "she is of the same displacement as Kate Smith, but not so tall."

Microphones add a new parameter to a performance. Now you not only have to react to audience mood and your own sense of confidence and interpretation; you have to listen to your voice seized, colored, enhanced, distorted. Static sparks fly.

In mid-February Russ had tried a split run, half a week at the Academy of Music on Fourteenth Street and the other up above Harlem at the Audubon Ballroom a hundred fifty-one blocks north, subdividing Manhattan.

The Academy had a reputation for faulty equipment. The loudspeaker crackled as he sang, and even with the distraction of a dozen girls highstepping behind him and Yorke and King doing splits and Wan Wan San, an eight-person Chinese acrobatic act opening the show, and a coed dance team, an accordionist, and assorted other duos (Roy and Romero, Birnes and Kaye, Rose and Chick), he was hardly stellar. He did three songs and went back to his dressing room at the top of the winding stairs at the right of the stage feeling like the air had whooshed out of his balloon. And it had. Con's hot air. That was what had been keeping them afloat, his ex-manager's sense of zeppelin.

He'd done five songs the week before, including two encores. It started out exciting. The Skourases, who ran both theaters, called NBC on a Thursday, and by Friday morning's opening show, at 11:30 A.M., the Academy had sold more than four thousand tickets. Matinée prices. There was a Jean Harlow picture, *Three Wise Girls*, which would attract the boys; the girls would park their fannies in the seats for Columbo. It was a young crowd.

They are patient but unresponsive to the English juggling act, Davey and Rosemarie, the troupe of six teeterboard workers, and a couple of dance teams. It's Russ's show.

They cast him in a deep blue spot, with a pin on his face, singing into the mike. Russ doesn't move much. He holds one hand on the microphone stand, and puts the other in his pocket. It looks curiously as if he is dancing with himself, using the microphone as a partner.

It takes a couple of songs for the sound to come into focus, to catch his low notes. Everyone's learning microphone technique, even those in the audience. They listen to him differently.

It was four weeks and an option. No guarantee; he was supposed to split any gross above the overheads. Columbo had been pulling down $3,500 at the Paramount, but they'd wanted to cut him down to two grand. He figured he could keep more of his profits here, and by Friday evening on opening night, Russ was pleased to see he had filled the Academy's downstairs and mezzanines. But only a week later there was a smattering of empty seats in the orchestra. That meant empty pockets. Less and less; the only more he was getting was discouraged.

Ed Scheuing of the NBC artists booking bureau connected him with the Palace. At least the Palace was on Times Square. It had opened nineteen years before, on March 24, 1913, its gilded proscenium bas-relief signifying opulence, like a shiny jewel in Manhattan's belly button, the refracted catch-the-light of Great White Way entertainment.

Underemployed performers congregated in front of the Palace. "Panic Beach," they called it, and there were a lot more of them out there these depressed days, wandering from Whelan's drugstore to the St. Regis café on either side of the rippled marquee with B. F. Keith's possessive emblazoned proudly, to the Somerset coffeehouse around the southeast corner of Forty-seventh Street. Russ wondered if he might wind up one of them.

Would he end? Was he, as *Variety* opined, "a freak radio singer, who is not a performer . . . of the Bing Crosby flash-in-the-pan style of ether exhaler"?

Things were shifting all too quickly. Pan-flashing or no, there were more radio stars than jugglers on the first week of his engagement, and the vaude-villians, like the hosts, (Benny) Rubin and (Jack) Haley, were finding it rough going. No wonder; in a spoof of each giving the other the shirt off his back, they strip down to their BVDs. Not something the young ladies who come to see Russ particularly care to witness.

The Palace is trying to cut their losses, shorten Rubin and Haley's engage-ment. There are to be no more long runs. The theater has been losing five thousand dollars a week since the beginning of the year, and the rumor mill has it that the RKO chain is about to drop live shows at the Coliseum, the 86th Street, the Kenmore and Flushing. Only films will be shown from now on. Even the vaunted Hippodrome was said to be in trouble.

"They've seen 'em too often" was a common complaint. But a vaudevillian needed to keep on the circuit constantly to earn a living wage; must never be the dreaded "at liberty." It made for a harried existence, on the run, and Weber and Fields were in the wings to replace Rubin and Haley.

It's the radio stars that are drawing, because they can cast their net every-where at once. At the Palace this week, Gus Edwards's "Radio Revue" even has children mimicking Bing Crosby and Kate Smith; Will Osborne is a Rudy Vallée sound-alike. And then there's Roy Smeck, who's on WOR giving music lessons five times a week, a different instrument each day.

He is as much carny as vaudeville, a technique-colored "Wizard of the Strings" whose way with a strung instrument is preternatural. He can make a tenor banjo sound like three banjos. He plays the ukulele upside down and backward, twangs a jew's harp, blows harmonica, and grass-skirts on the Hawaiian guitar. He concocts uncanny duets with himself, and closes his Palace performance with an impression of Bill Robinson's stair taps on the uke. He knows how to put on a show. In fact, if there is one caveat about his music, it's that Roy is all show and can't play that jazz.

He has different traditions, though; the medicine carnival, *Ripley's Believe It or Not*, *Bring 'Em Back Alive*. He displays the licks he's trapped from the outer imaginations, the Hebrides of hours of practice and self-hypnotic ma-nipulation of the instrument, until it moves from the musical into the sound effect. You can shut off your digital delay and flanged chorus now; Roy Smeck predated effects pedals; and presaged them.

He even climbed aboard the biggest sound effect of all, making the first musical talkie for Harry Warner in 1926 entitled *Roy Smeck in His Pastime*.

The twelve-minute short was filmed at the Manhattan Opera House on Thirty-fourth Street, and featured Roy playing his numerous instruments. It boosted Smeck to headlining status on the vaudeville circuit, and gave him a name for his sometimes accompanying group, the Vita Trio, after Vitaphone. In 1930, he practically invented cinematic overdubbing when he appeared in a split-screen spectacular that showed him playing five instruments simultaneously.

He's not all hokum. He's too sly for that. At heart a sentimentalist, his Hawaii is the sun dipping over the water, the coming of twilight (he records "Twilight Echoes" with Carson Robison for Victor years before Russ gets there, playing something called an "octo-chorda," an eight-string hybrid Hawaiian guitar in E^{13} tuning), the imminence of night and moonrise. "Shimmering Moon," which Smeck cuts for Jewel in the fall of 1929, has his steel guitar backed by a chording standard guitar; the other musician is lost to history. I wonder if it's not Roy himself, a trickster playing his own duet.

He will survive long and merry, unlike the Palace, which will fold its vaudeville tent and end live performance in November, 1932. In the nineteen-eighties, some half a century later, Roy will be living along West End Avenue just above Eighty-sixth giving banjo and lap steel lessons to anyone who happens by. He'll show you his gold-plated 1927 Bacon & Day banjo with engraved pearloid back and a carved lion's head in the heel of the neck, a No. 6 Ne Plus Ultra presented by Mr. Day himself in the company's Groton, Connecticut, headquarters; or the guitars and ukuleles the Harmony company of Chicago named for him. His Hawaiian tuning is A^7—G–A–E–A–C#–E— with the sixth string up an octave, making it easier to roll like a banjo.

He's still there when I go to visit him. I get there on time.

OH, YES. Con is back.

He'd stuck his head in the dressing-room door last week, while Russ was still fuming about having to share top billing with Norma Terris. An impersonator, f'cryin' out loud. F'crissake. As if Ed Wynn telling the story of *Mourning Becomes Electra*, or yet another Ethel Barrymore, was something to bust a gut over, though even he had grinned at her *agoniste* torch singer of thirty years ago keening over "A Bird in a Gilded Cage."

"Anyone home?" Con wiggled his eyebrows, Groucho Marx–style.

Somehow Russ wasn't surprised to see him. He tried to remain calm, impassive, to underplay Con's frontal assault. Plus he was still peeved at the Palace; they had told him he could walk if he wanted, that this was vaudeville, and Madame Terris had long been a favorite with the vaudeville audiences at the Palace, and, yes, they shared the bill. Con would never have stood for it.

"Look, I know things are a little topsy-turvy now," the words were hardly out of his mouth as he edged into the room, starting to gather momentum, "but I do need to talk to you about this Gordean matter. Yes yes, I never should have gone into partnership with him. He was always a slimy sonofabitch but what could I do I needed to get us under way and out of California and here to New York where I could show you what I could do for you annndd. . . . " The phrasing slowed, trailed into suspense, waiting for a punch line. Con pivoted slowly, dragging his glance along the floral arrangements sent by the Russ Columbo Fan Club run by Mrs. Madeline Graw and her friend Genevieve Fitzpatrick of Ozone Park, Queens, the telegrams of congratulations and careless envelopes sealed with lipsticked kisses piled indiscriminately on the table, the champagne in the ice bucket, the clothes rack of silk shirts and tuxedoes, the signed photo of boxer Georges Carpentier tucked into a corner of the mirror.

"Don't look like we done too bad." Con shrugged.

We. *Wheee . . .*

Russ didn't reply. He knew the Gordean matter was not why Con was here. That was just another example of the Gordian knots Con's business dealings represented. Conrad had founded the Jack Gordean Agency back in California "for purposes of his own," as the court papers described (probably, Russ thought, so he could gyp himself), and put it in the name of an employee. Finding himself the titular owner, Jack proceeded to incorporate it and retain 51 percent of the stock for himself and his father. When Con and Columbo decided to draw up a different contract from the one that paid Russ fifty dollars a week, Gordean claimed he was owed 10 percent of Columbo's present earnings, which were estimated at between six and seven thousand a week. That he'd put up three thousand dollars to get Columbo and Conrad to New York. That he and Con were partners. Con had offered him "nuisance" value, but the matter was in the hands of federal judge Henry W. Goddard.

The suit involved everyone, including NBC, the Skouras brothers, and the Lambert Pharmaceutical Company, which marketed Listerine, all having been employers of said Mr. Columbo, who really didn't give a shit because he was making the front money and let the crooks and shysters divvy up the leftover table scraps, and because he wasn't seeing any fucking money anyway. Thanks to Con.

But seeing him scramble around the dressing room, flapping his arms, pointing and gesticulating, still talking a blue streak—"You don't understand what this man has been doing to my state of health and for what? so I can pay for him and his father to go *shtup* their doxies"—made Russ realize how much he missed Con's unflagging boosterism, his sense of mission.

"All right, all right," Russ sighed, waving his hand in the general direction of a seat. The intermission was going to come to an end soon; he was first on after the break. He'd be singing three numbers: "The Song Is Ended," "River Stay Away from My Door," and the aptly titled "How Long Will It Last?" Maybe he would get Con up with him for the encore to do a medley of his hits. They could end with "You Call It Madness."

By the next week, Con's guest spot has worked its way into the middle of Russ's show. Just like he belonged.

PARADISE

R uss still treasured the ring Pola Negri had given him. He brought it to the session on April 6.

Columbo wore it on the fourth finger of his bowing hand, so he could watch it catch the light as he played. Bowing. He inclined his head toward the violin, paying his respects. The ring winked at him.

It had once belonged to Valentino, and Russ remembered when the Countess had passed its opalescent dome into his possession.

She was Mona in *Barbed Wire*, or Anna in *Hotel Imperial*, or *The Woman from Moscow*, or Rachel in *Loves of an Actress*, among the characters she enacted in and around 1927, staring down the looming barrel of the talkies. She photoplayed herself.

"My *Rooss*," she would say in the thickly inflected accent she had brought with her from central Poland, though she had an affinity for the Italian. She had named herself after the poetess Ada Negri. "Please play 'Mattinata' for me. I love that one *ssooo*."

He was not yet twenty, hardly out of the high school orchestra, drifting around the hotel ballrooms that were springing up to serve the Hollywood screen community. Not only the stars, the hierarchy of idols; but the managers, the producers, the costumers, the scene painters, the camera operators, the darkroom techies, the star-struck and star-begotten. They were all accompanists, like the ones who sat in the pit and played along as the nitrate action unfolded on the silver-sanded flecks of screen.

If you thought about it, Russ was the original score. Only he played as the cameras were rolling, providing a soundtrack that would never be heard, reflected in the actor's movements, their swells and retreats and pas de deux. He blended in with the *mise en scènery*.

His part was to get her in the mood. The all-important third in the ménage à trois unfolding as the cameras cranked. She is leaning forward to Rod La Rocque, Conrad Nagel, Ben Lyon, Paul Lukas, Ian Hansen, Antonio Moreno, ready to embrace, kiss, slap, turn away; and he watches over their coupling, letting their passion ripple through him as he expresses staged desire. To help her feel a silent emotion, in a world of the mute. Mouths move, but the arms are more expressive, as are the backs of the hands.

The silents are a movie of pose. The framed tableaux are as close to Ziegfeld's as they are portraiture of movement and moment. A mime, condensing the mmm's; mmmmm . . .

He could make his violin moan, and he could see Pola reclining on the note, leaning up against it, rubbing back and forth against its tremolo as a cat along a leg. Her slink was definitely feline. His violin yowled.

But she wasn't having any, not really. Not in the mood. Even if she did allow him to play Dvořák's "Humoresque" for her in the dressing room, between scenes, as the hot California air was shut out by the cool dark of the movie set. She still loved Rudolph.

And always would. In her autobiography, *Memoirs of a Star*, the ever camera-angled Negri would recall their joining. He brought her an armload of red roses. "*After we had dined he stripped the petals from each blossom, strewing them over my bed. The petals were as soft as a velvet coverlet beneath our bodies . . . and together on this floral bower we rejoiced until dawn broke.*" Then the unearthly sudden parting, a tragedienne's love worthy of any historical epic with a cast of thousands. "*I could feel the ground beginning to give way beneath me. . . .*" The Quake, and its aftershocks.

She temperamentally thrived on upheaval. "I am a Slav," she told Hedda Hopper. "We Slavs *loff* to suffer . . . when I didn't have anything to feel bad about, I invented something so I could suffer." An actress life.

The bereaved role dressed her in a severe grieving black that defined her chiaroscuro, contrasting her alabaster skin and midnight pools of eye and hair that sharpened her outline. She had pride of place at the funeral, which drew throngs to St. Malachy's church on West Forty-ninth Street. Valentino's first wife, Jean Acker, followed her in the procession. His second, Natacha Rambova, was nowhere to be seen. Dr. Harold Meeker, Rudy's attending physician, reported his last words were of Pola: "tell her I think of her." A moment before, he had spoken of fishing tackle.

Valentino had left her side to travel east to promote *Son of the Sheik*. He was disturbed by allegations about his sexuality—the dreaded "pink powder puff" that a *Chicago Tribune* editorialist had daubed him with. "Better a rule by masculine women rather than by effeminate men," crowed the writer. "Hell's bells. Oh, sugar!"

Though he challenged the anonymous name-caller to a duel, a "test of honor" in the boxing or wrestling arena (with its own homoerotic intimations), Rudy might have agreed with the masculine-woman part. Pola may have been sumptuously swathed in filmy and flimsy fabric, but she was harder than she looked, a survivor who had bounced around the great eastern European capitals—a stint with the Imperial Ballet School in St. Petersburg, a Warsaw stage actress, and enough of a starlet within the hierarchy of the Berlin film industry as it came out of the Great War to form a collaboration with director Ernst Lubitsch. She and Ernst were impulsive together; he highlighted those moments when her sweetness, even delicate innocence, was seized by a sudden rash lunge for the libido. Pola enjoyed her sensuality, provoking spontaneous desire at a moment where the dividing lines between good girl and bad were defined by Mary Pickford's child-madonna curls and Theda Bara's vampyric carnal hunger. She felt no need to apologize for having it both ways. There was nothing simplistic about her, though the women she played were consortly. Even when Emil Jannings as King Louis XV kneels to kiss away her toe-jam in *Passion*, she is only doing what she does best, which is to receive homage.

This was royalty Hollywood style: the matched set of white Russian wolfhounds, the bowl of iced champagne with whole peaches dropped in it. She lived like a noblewoman; her role model was Josephine with her Napoleon. She even conceived of a film where Chaplin would play Napoleon and she Josephine; but the project only reached the stage of off-screen romance. "Love is a competition," Charlie told her. "There's always a victor and victim."

Pola knew "The Art of Luring," described in the September 30, 1922, issue of *Movie Weekly* as "one desiring to influence another." Only she liked to control the flow, her own force of nature. She dispensed favor, refusing to emote on cue, ever the aristocrat.

They met in costume at a party. Rudolph wore his *Blood and Sand* toreador outfit; Pola was garbed in the white-and-gold regimental uniform of Catherine the Great's *uhlans* from *Forbidden Passion*, a full riding skirt and a high guardsman's hat festooned with an osprey cockade. Even their respective movie titles looked good double-billed on a marquee.

510/3   Phot. Ernst Sandau Berlin W 8

POLA NEGRI

They played their swords to the hilt, the opposing foils of a climactic *en garde*: up and down the battlements, kicking over tables, midair leaps and lunges, blades crossed. They had both learned the apache dance in the after-hours Paris dives of the teens, a tango that moved from sensuality to brutality. Out of control, and infinitely controlling, they skirted the rapier edge of their dancer's art.

Though the mating might have come about because of its good copy, the two seemed beneficial for each other. Rudolph responded to a strong woman, and he was still confused about his relationship with Natacha, the second Mrs. Valentino, who had brought him to his knees. He had married his first wife, Jean Acker, on the rebound from his mother's death. She—his mother, Gabriella—had always comforted and protected him from his father's harsh discipline. Jean's presence, when he met her at a regular Sunday party hostessed by Pauline Frederick of Sunset Boulevard—or, according to less favorable gossip, the dinner party for Nazimova's *Stronger Than Death* where the actress snubbed him as a gigolo—seemed to shield him from the pain of his mother's passing. The marriage was never consummated; it was rife with sexual asymmetries, and only lasted a single November in 1918.

Acker had been a protégée of Alla Nazimova, the regal Russian actress who maintained a coterie of aspiring young ladies. Nazimova took a more active role in the pairing of Rudolph to his second wife, introducing him to Natacha, her couture consultant, as his prelude to landing the part of Armand in *Camille*. Valentino's career was about to skyrocket as word got around about his appearance in *The Four Horsemen of the Apocalypse*. Still, he shifted nervously before Natacha's measuring gaze; she let him wait a beat too long, then nodded her approval. Nazimova then suggested that Rambova escort Rudolph to the Hollywood premiere of *The Four Horsemen*. Agreed.

Natacha believed in the spirit world, and told Rudolph as much. Their union was to be spiritual, unsullied by earthly passions, the séance their only marital bower. But there were more mundane legalisms to consider. In his attempt to render unto Caesar *et tu*, Valentino was arrested for bigamy when he and Natacha returned from a Mexicali marriage ceremony in May 1922. Before the judge dismissed the case on legal grounds, Rudolph had been forced to plead nonconsummation as his defense; two marriages and no score. Some Great Lover.

But that wasn't the only squeeze Rambova had on his privates. She wanted his fief. To call his shots. She claimed she knew what was best for him—and perhaps she did, wanting to steer Valentino toward the artier films of Europe, where elements of her curvilinear high-deco design might find more appreciation than in low-caste Hollywood. This despite the incongruity of a 1923 Oscar Wildean version of *Salome* she fashioned for Nazimova, designing costumes and sets, writing the screenplay under the male pseudonym of Peter N. Winters. It had a chilling effect on Nazimova's career. By then, Natacha had shifted her attention to Valentino, the bigger star. He had more potential.

Rambova, a defrocked heiress to the Hudnut cosmetics fortune whose real name was the more prosaic Winifred Shaughnessy, was a costume designer who saw Rudolph as her mannequin. It suited Valentino. He worked especially well in costume; specifically, he had a belief in reincarnation, feeling that by putting on the clothes of a bygone era, he would link up with his soul's sojourn in that moment. His billowing sleeves, oiled grooming, foreign formalities, and dancer's grace, along with the slave bracelet he proudly wore (Natacha presented him with one in platinum, but he would always treasure Jean's silver encirclement, and in fact would be buried in it) drew femme-fantasia. At a time when sexual emancipation was in the air, women cherished having it both ways; the way it had been, evoking a more elegant, primitive time when emotions weren't covered with layers of irony; dangerous, to relish that moment when an object of desire moves just short of obsessive; and free to explore their own attraction. They sensed that Valentino enjoyed the sexual preen, the strut, the display. As *The Sheik* strides back and forth, regarding his captive, he acknowledges his own capture. He tosses Lady Diana Mayo (Agnes Ayres) on the divan. She is lily-white; he swarthy, a stand-in for all other colors (though it will be handily revealed that Rudolph's fierce quasi-Bedouin Ahmed Ben Hassan is really the Scottish Earl of Glencarryl). Virtue restored, disguise gives him the license to woo her and rough her, to disrobe her will and dance the deflowering innuendo. He will make her a proper Lady, taming her from the tomboy she was at the beginning of the film, asserting her independence from marriage and skirts.

Though in stills the chalked eyes and formalized gestures of Rudolph's seduction seem archaic, it is his fluid sense of motion that carves his place as romantic figure. He is made for the forward motion of film. Like a piece of music, he needs movement, unfolding; he had made his living as a dancer. Rambova enhances and flatters his image, garbing him as the faun Nijinsky, complete with panpipes, forelock, cloven hooves. Later, Mr. and Mrs. Valentino will go on tour for the Mineralerva soap company, dancing their tango in theaters across America while Rudolph waits out contract negotiations. They dance so well together, it is a wonder they remain sexually opaque offstage.

The Sheik draws out the moment of surrender, as seen through feminine desire. She is helpless in the face of his total attention. She feels strangely alone with him, as if his intense concentration has removed her from the rest of society. She is surprised she wants this. She cannot take her eyes away from his. He stalks her, convincing by adoration and command. "Are you not woman enough to know?" he asks her, as if his secret will be hers solely and soulfully to share. They are as close as two could be. He will know when to stop persuading, and await her assent.

It is Natacha that bends him over backward. She always wants more; it conflicts with his screen image, denying him the character he has created, getting him in fights with heads of studios as she interferes with scripts, lighting, and camera placement, masterminding expensive projects (*The Hooded Falcon*) that will never come to fruition. Who's wearing the pants here? He has built a grandiose estate, Falcon Lair, for Rambova, their own castle in the sky, but she never moves in, even after he furnishes it with rare antiques from the Continent, a stable of Thoroughbreds, a kennel of canines, a garage of Duesenbergs. It is like another movie set to her. Natacha has no interest in acting once the decorative archway that surrounds the love scene is sketched and constructed. She wants real power, like Jesse Lasky at Famous Players. She wants to direct.

It is Pola's surprising down-to-earth demeanor amid grand opulence that gives Valentino new confidence. They know how to play their parts *en tandem*; their arc has been very similar, with a necessary Old World flair still counting for something in this upstart movie capital of an uncouth America. And according to Negri, they've already bedded. For Rudolph, three might yet be the charm. She lets down his guard, allows him to conquer her heart, and trusts him. But his blood is already poisoning, his internal ambivalence tearing him from his insides out, a self-fulfilling hemorrhage.

SHE HAD her film makeup on; it carved her features in sharp contrasts, colors more designed to catch the camera's eye than a subtle human iris.

As she slid behind a painted screen to shrug off her costume, he continued to play, a version of the "Celeste Aida" theme. Caruso. *Il Grande*. Pola liked Columbo's southern *Yoo-rupeaness*, as Winchell would hyphenate, the salt of the Mediterranean washing up on his shores. The swash of his buckle. There was a smolder that reminded her of times she'd been with *Rooodolph*, when the Great Lover looked at her with those eyes that were used to revealing so much burn in their close-ups, as if a flashlight were shining out from behind his corneas, and she was the deer caught in their lamplights. Frozen. On the spot.

Russ didn't have the eyes, but his medium was the ears. The violin stroked her, soothed her, rubbed her temples, and she allowed herself the delicious warmth of sinking into the dark wood tonal embrace of his Caligari's cabinet. He did play beautifully, for one so young, and every so often he would come out of his shyness and sing her a song of the day, or hum it along in his chest, so it would be like two violins, a duet.

She liked to tease him, and yes, she flirted a couple of times, telling him to hand her this or that piece of clothing as her hand fluttered from behind the screen, or once asking him somewhat imperiously to zip her dress, letting him glimpse the ripple of her spine in its silk shift of bandeau. Pola could sense his breathing shallow.

Mostly, though, she forgot he was in the room, letting the music slide into the background as the movie of her life unreeled. She lost herself in the dull void that was her heart. She didn't like the radio; the scratchy disc. She wanted to hear the sound in person, and Rudolph, who could whisper it to her as no other man could, as he could to no other woman in his vast world of admirers, was gone. *Never to retoorn.* Out of body. Snatched from her, and she still couldn't believe it.

"PARADISE" IS an old-fashioned song of seduction. It is the theme of *A Woman Commands*, a starring vehicle for Pola in 1932. Her figure, cloaked in orange-toned sepia on the sheet music, is a dark no-nonsense angel vamp. Her left hand with its red nails digs into her upper right arm, her eyes wing in the middle of a porcelain face, dark hair waving, thin cupid lips, the lower jutting. She'd be more Vallée's type, another Rudy with a V. But she would've eaten him alive, or rather, wouldn't have bothered.

As originally written by Nacio Herb Brown and Gordon Clifford in 1931, the song is sung from a woman's point of view, and indeed, Pola warbles it in *A Woman Commands*, revealing an attractive contralto. It is the story of a love "built on sand," melancholy, caught with nostalgic longing for a disappearing present. Time and tide are running out. Despite the assertiveness of the movie's title, the lyrics immediately assume a submissive tone: *"I'm just a wom-an,"* who will soon be looking for *"An-oth-er man to love."*

Russ dispenses with this prologue, switches the gender, and gets right to the clinch. He puts his arm around his once-beloved. *"We lived and loved, Our day is through,"* he admits, portentous chords doom-lading the entrance, but be he beggar or king, let's fling. A final moment to be together. To recall all we've meant to each other. It's over, but still not done.

He dims the light. Good night. He prepares the seraglio setting, arranging the paraphernalia of seduction like a *hashishin* slowly loading and firing an ivory hookah. The orchestra—three violins, cello, guitar, string bass, three saxophones, trumpet, and piano, under the direction of Leonard Joy—colors in the billowing draperies. A desert scenario. A tent. The flickering silent film, slightly out of sync with the movements of real life, like a flip book, faster or slower as an unseen forearm turns the crank.

Then she holds his hand. Then he understands. *"Then a hea-ven-ly kiss, could I re-sist?"* Then and then and then.

"And then he . . ."

"And then you . . ."

Croon.

HE CONTINUES the *dee-dah-dah-doo*s till a final chorus, where his voice solos with the orchestra. He scatting along with them, his voice like a violin, responsing, teasing the arpeggios; he sees Pola leaning back at her dressing table, cloth like a diaphanous drapery around her, jaw slightly slack, lost in reverie. At that moment Russ is as close to her as Valentino might have been. Under half-closed lids, weighted with their oily shadows, her eyes flicker and dart like a somnambulist's.

It's warm in the dressing room. She feels her head nod, rights it with a start, feels it sway again on the stem of her neck. Her thoughts mingle across the border of dream, sliding back to the sound of the bow and string, then back to the haze of her wandering mind. It's like a bath. Bobbing. Warm, moist. The enveloping. She drifts.

They don't have to talk. This is the silence of the silents.

DON'T THEY *understand we're trying to make a movie here?*

Pola is starting to steam up. She's trying to get in the mood for a love scene, entertained by a three-piece string ensemble in which that so-sweet Russell— *Rooo-gierr-oh*, she once cajoled him into revealing—was playing; and over the painted scenery on the other side of the set that sh-*it* girl Clara *Booo* was making some dreadful Charleston picture, all noisy jazz and raucous. Where does she get *oooff*?

Not off the boat, as Pola had, in the first wave of cinematic immigration. She was in the spearhead of the Foreign Legion, arriving in New York by boat in the fall of 1922 on the heels of the American release of *Madame DuBarry*, when they had all first emigrated to Hollywood from the European film centers, Ernst and Emil and Erich. There were no worries about an accent then; the mouth's movement signifies speech in most visual culture, and as actricians, they knew how to manipulate their bodies and expressions to get across their meaning, with the occasional inter-titled card to help.

Their arrival in mid-twenties America was not the best of times for the emotionally contradictory hero and heroine of the Euro cinema. Under the influence of the major studios, many found their personae flattened to the dimensions of predictable role-playing. Pola thought her character in her first American movie, *Bella Donna*, to be sinfully unredeemed, as if the English-speaking audience couldn't tolerate the idea of a woman who enjoyed the erotic two-step, and sometimes led. She fought back with the lacquered toe-nail and the Grecian sandal, gaining the admiration of newly enfranchised women, tipping the balance of the sexual frontiers.

Her *donna* became *prima*, the character she was portraying always dual, herself playing someone else, much more fun to enact than the ones she created on the screen having to listen to directors who did not understand her as had Lubitsch—"her pretty tricks and wild ways," Armand says of Madame DuBarry in *Passion*. She was reunited with Ernst for *Forbidden Paradise* in 1926. He made her a czarina.

The jazz band broke into shrill frenzy. It sounded as if the party scene had moved beyond the filmic. Clara was a pushy little b-*it*-ch. She didn't know how to respect her elders, though Pola realized with a start she had suddenly shifted herself a generation. It was like the time she had gone to pay homage to the great Italian actress Eleonora Duse, who had come to Los Angeles to appear in the local theater. She was said to be Bernhardt's great rival, and the one more genuinely humane. Her tragedienne's affair with the poet d'Annunzio had elicited widespread sympathy, given her a vulnerability and a melancholic resignation that expressed itself in shrugged wisdom. Eleonora knew of her work, though she recognized that Negri was not being given films of the breadth and scope of her earlier vehicles in Germany.

There was a canister of oxygen in the wings for La Duse's asthma. Pola thought there was an "invincible sublimeness" to her. She looked on in admiration as the actress saved her strength for the stage. It was 1924, and Eleonora would live only another month.

"I belong to the old world and you to the new," she said to Pola. "Your new art—it is of the future." Except for a single attempt in 1916, *Cenere*, La Duse had never made the transition from the stage to the camera. But, she warned with the air of one who still relived old hauntings, "the past is not dead, it only sleeps."

And the future never goes to bed, Pola fumed as she stormed off the set, tired of the syncopated clangor from the adjoining stage. Soon it would be called a soundstage, and she would come to miss the bustle and noisy uproar of a movie set that was the ironic working atmosphere of the silents as they were made movies. Soon it would be deathly quiet, and the camera would be confined within a soundproof box, constricting its angles. Soon she, once so eloquent in her movements, so expressive, she who felt more like a dancer than an actress, would begin to speak.

What would she sound like?

POLA RETURNED to New York on January 17, 1932, to answer that question, stepping onto the Grand Central platform with her hands on her hips and a rakish small-brimmed hat shading her right eye. Elbows jutted, a fur wrap tossed round her neck and encircling her wrists, a semicircular traveling suitcase by her well-planted feet, she was "too ill to think of love," though she did have a date for the premiere with Mayor James W. "Jimmy" Walker, who in his dapper leadership of New York bore more than a passing resemblance to his Scotch brother, Johnnie.

A *Woman Commands* was to open the following Thursday at the RKO Mayfair. Pola hadn't seen the movie yet; press agents circulated the story that she had wanted to see the picture in its entirety, but had been stricken with appendicitis during previews on the Coast. The air of suspense this tale was meant to engender, whether true or not, shows how much sound loomed as a make-or-break chasm to silent performers.

It was official now. There were no more silents. On October 20, 1931, *Variety* mourned the "Passing of Industry's Origin" amid somber *End of Silent Films* banner headlines. They survived only in "the most remote spots in the country." Within the year, no more silent prints would be struck. Obsolete.

That's what she would be if she didn't cross the great divide. But Negri had more working against her than the advent of sound; with the Depression, and with the subtleties of exposition that on-screen dialogue could evoke, the movies themselves were changing. A new breed of heroine, like that wisecracking Carole Lombard or the sneering Joan Crawford, was giving a grittier edge to screen women; the definition of "goddess" was undergoing renovation.

Faux royalty may have been over, but *A Woman Commands* scepters ahead nonetheless, the story of Queen Maria Draga of Serbia, whose King Alexander risks revolution to marry her. A last-minute shift to Basil Rathbone as leading man from Laurence Olivier (he had yellow jaundice) crippled the movie's tensile center; he was simply too reserved to make an impression on Pola. She had nothing to stimulate her.

Pianist Ignacy Jan Paderewski was in the glittering audience at the premiere, as was the Polish ambassador to the U.S., as well as Beatrice Lillie and Fifi D'Orsay, both then currently appearing at the RKO Palace, when Walker introduced her to the crowd, which had been held back and encouraged by police cordons. He handed her a bouquet, and Pola murmured a few words of welcome. She had gotten comfortable speaking declaimed English during a stint the previous season at the London Coliseum; when she returned to the movies, the only thing the director had to tell her was to speak more softly, because the microphones could hear as if they were in the front row.

She went back to her own front row seat for the entertainment. A young man came out from the wings to sing the love theme from *A Woman Commands*, "Paradise." There was a heightened undercurrent in the audience; Pola, attuned to adoring crowds, sensed their undivided attention.

He bounded onstage. Stepping to the microphone as the band swelled, he looked her way. Oh, it was Russell, after all. She had heard he was singing back east. Now she could see what all the fuss was about. Little *Rooo-gierr-oo*! Such a dear boy. She was happy he'd gotten out of Hollywood.

POLA IS going into vaudeville. She needs the money. On the circuit, each week a new town. Buffalo, Cleveland, New Orleans. Comedians appear on her bill: Milton Berle, Burns and Allen. *A Woman Commands* is not taking hold at the box office; Garbo and Dietrich have already stolen her exotic thunder, and it seems that the pub-lix, audience and studio, are not ready for more accents. There is an insular isolationism building in the country, fueled by economic calamity. Pola could feel it in her bankbook. She couldn't afford her lifestyle as a star. She'd even heard that Clara Bow had been given her bungalow at Paramount, as she herself had taken over Mary Pickford's.

She tries out the act at the Oriental in Chicago in early February. It is a five-minute playlet in which she is a woman of Montmartre. Brokenhearted. She strikes a reception pose as she enters without announcement, down a flight of impressionistic stairs. She'd had the set on her London engagement. Pola delivers a short soliloquy on love's foibles, sings a bit, and verbally spars with an unidentified "straight" man who seems to give her an excuse to exit with what one reviewer calls "a Pagliacci laugh." The audience is there to see her. She is heartened when a good portion of the crowd up and leaves when she finishes her turn. It will pay the bills.

In the second week of March she comes to New York to play the Paramount. Crosby has finally decamped, and the Paramount seems a bit lost as to what to do. They host a week with Mme. Luisa Tetrazzini, a former Metropolitan Opera star who sings "Caro Nome" from *Rigoletto*; another with Texas Guinan and Barbara Stanwyck. They book both Mr. and Mrs. Jesse Crawford at twin Wurlitzer organs. "Confusing," *Variety* called the stage show, with Boris Petroff producing a "Revue International" that was a hodgepodge of acrobats, dancers, accordionists, tenor solos (representing Italy, sung "before a gondola effect"), and "Miss Negri" (despite her previous marriages) making her entrance. She sings a torch song, caught by an overhead microphone and one at the apron, and then dramaturges a variation on a scene with an actor in evening clothes, discussing their love affair to no great audibility in the distant seats. It was disorienting going between movie set and Broadway theater; and she used to having no sound at all.

By the time she reaches Baltimore in the first week of May, at the amateur-hour Hippodrome, Pola is ready to pack it in. She tells the manager she won't be doing the six o'clock radio broadcast, nor the midnight performance. She is *s-e-e-k*. And tired. She finally agrees to do the remote from her hotel suite. The midnight show is a no-show and money is refunded. They never do give her the carpet she had requested from taxi to dressing-room door.

She'll cancel Washington, D.C., next. Back to Germany. *Auf Wiedersehen*.

"AUF WIEDERSEHEN, MY DEAR" is the opening song recorded at the April 6 session, at two o'clock on a Wednesday afternoon. It is Columbo's first time back in Studio 1 since the turn of the year. Because of his strenuous schedule at the Paramount, he'd had to come early in the morning then. Now he could afford to sleep later.

He was back on the radio. Three times a week—Wednesday, Friday, and Saturday—and NBC had given in to his refusal to try an afternoon schedule. What use was a crooner in the daytime? He needed the night-time slot; and they needed him more than he needed them. He'd proved that. After the Palace, he went on to Baltimore, the Keith's house, and took home a five-grand guarantee against 50 percent above average. Vaughn De Leath was on the bill, calling herself "The Original Radio Girl"; they watched each other work the mike.

Con was still trying to second-guess his business. NBC had gotten an offer from a panic-stricken Louis Lipstone at the Chicago Oriental who needed a name act in a hurry for mid-April. They sealed a deal with NBC for four thousand, but immediately got a call from Con not only demanding five thousand per, but an engagement of two weeks. Meanwhile, Publix, the theater owner, had been negotiating with NBC for Columbo separately in the twenty-five-hundred range. And Con said Russ wanted doubling privileges, perhaps a hotel ballroom for the late-night crowd. Earl Hines got the gig instead. Oh, well, there was always Philly later in the month. Didn't Con understand the meaning of the word "no"? That Russ had said they were through?

"Auf Wiedersehen" is another song of parting. You go your way and I'll go mine. Two lovers stand in the Viennese moonlight. *"Sweet violins were playing."* He steps to the microphone and asks her to come with him for one more stroll down lovers' lane. An imminent *soon we must say* hangs over their meeting. His heart will stop beating. Nearly every rhyme in the chorus is an *-ain*. *Refrain. Remain. Again and again.*

"*Sweet-heart, good-bye.*" Because it cannot beat until they re-meet, he will say goodbye to himself, love's suicide, noting his fading into memory, like Lubitsch irising the camera lens in on one character in a crowd scene, to provide exclamation. Here and gone. Lost yesterday.

He thought he could catch a glimmer of recognition in Pola's eye when he sang "Paradise" toward her from the Mayfair stage. She was all in white, trimmed in ermine, with a tiara. She would never acknowledge him; she was too regal for that. She might not even remember him, though his violin might remind her of the sound of her sorrow, his sympathetic strings, of when she had no time to say good-bye.

Now the script had changed. She was out of character.

He was in command now. A leading man.

GAMBLING

The game of chance. Over the county line, rolling the bones. Six sides, two of a kind, a gambler's dozen. Twelve, again.

Is there a skill in throwing the dice? Russ likes to think so. He has his own ritual of toss. He tumbles them in his hand, cups them in the hollow of his palm, blows hot breath on them, as if he's holding a microphone. Then he lays them flat between his palms in prayer. Right before he lets them go, he thinks of his mother who birthed him across the river.

He throws overhand, more a push, his hand flashing open, fingers spread, dice suddenly vanished, a magician revealing his trick. Now you see it, now you don't.

It isn't the random draw of a card, or the spin of a wheel. The die is cast in motion by your action, or even inaction. It's hard to imagine anyone who could pinpoint the dice with the horsehide control of, say, the Dean brothers, Dizzy and Dazzy, now playing for the St. Louis Cardinals and Brooklyn Dodgers, respectively, and they had the advantage of not only throwing but being screwballs.

Chance. Lady luck. The wooing that leads to winning. Or losing your pants. In *The Autobiography of an Ex–Colored Man*, James Weldon Johnson writes of men who would bet all their clothes after they'd run out of cash. As a callow youth, he visits a gambling den between Sixth and Seventh Avenues in Manhattan, on a West Twenties cross-street near the music publishing houses, where Johnson first hears ragtime. There, amid howls of "Shoot the two!" and "Shoot the four!" and "Fate me! Fate me!" he sees "perhaps a dozen men" wearing only "linen dusters . . . the men had lost all the money and jewelry they possessed. . . . Some of them were virtually prisoners and unable to get into the street for days at a time."

The vice of dice.

THEY HAVE their own dance, the dice. Seven come eleven or snake eyes, they skip down the green felt like a pair of Broadway hoofers, spinning and cavorting and bouncing off walls before coming to rest, breathing hard, accepting the hoots and hollers of the audience.

Five is fever. Six is sextra. Pair of twos: Little Joe. Pair of threes: six the hard way. Gain some weight. Lose some weight. Boxcars!

Russ is in the hole. He's digging it deeper by the throw. He's down more than ten grand and he's sure his luck is going to change before the night is over. Sure.

The Lanzettis are giving Russ the red carpet treatment. Tio and Ignatius, named after respective Popes, are from the old neighborhood. When they roll out the red carpet, you walk it. Like a plank.

UNTIL TONIGHT, it had been a grand homecoming. When he stepped off the train at Broad Street Station on Wednesday, April 13, at four in the afternoon, the girls were waiting for him. Alerted by yesterday's newspaper, they surrounded him in a half-circle, dressed alike in their long coats with the puffy fur collars, close-fitting caps on their head, clutching the photographs Con had handed out. Russ was holding his white hat, with a sporty black band, in his right hand, and wore a topcoat and scarf against the early spring chill.

He paid particular attention to a pair of lovelies, which caught the eye of the *Evening Bulletin*. "His arrival in Philadelphia . . . prompted two chic ladies to drape themselves for several minutes about the well-known Columbo neck." When asked about a romance, Russ demurred. "No." He winked. "Just a couple of old friends."

He still had family in town. He hadn't seen his eldest brother, Anthony, now forty-six and a machinist in the Erie Avenue engine house of the Reading Railroad, in seventeen years. Antonio was living at 2433 North Leithgow Street, having stayed behind when the family moved to California. Russ was still the "baby." "Marry?" he answered in response to the *Bulletin*'s prompting. "Well, gosh, I haven't really thought of it. You see, I'm the 'kid brother' — and I'd like to stay around the folks for a while." *Gosh.*

Yes, he preferred blondes. A girl ought to be intelligent and musical and pretty. Dorothy swam into his mind when he said this, and he shook off the thought, turning his attention back to the two girls who pressed against him as if he were the cheesesteak in their sandwich.

THE ENGAGEMENT started Friday, at the venerable Mastbaum Theatre at Market and Twentieth, part of the Stanley Warner chain. Taking over from Conrad Nagel, he was proclaimed "A New Thrill for Philadelphia! — the Idol of All America!"

The bill was typically local. Miss Rae Samuels was a red-hot mama ("she was red-hot when that brand of fire was known as a 'blue streak,' " nudged the *Philadelpha Daily News*), who handed the stage over to her tap-dancing protégée Eleanor Whitney, who performed routines lifted from Bill Robinson. Milton Charles sang "Wotta Life," imitating a trumpet, and "Mrs. Winchell's Boy." Willie and Joe Mandell did acrobatic comedy. David Ross and the Mastbaum Orchestra resounded the *William Tell Overture* and the Mastbaum Dance Ensemble took their ballet, while on the screen, Claudette Colbert and Edmund Lowe starred in *Misleading Lady*. A night out. Of town.

He introduced "I'm Sorry, Dear" at the lip of the stage. The microphone was "recalcitrant," according to the *Inquirer*. He went behind the curtains, only to reappear in a heart-shaped enclosure, singing "Guilty." Con came out to join him for "Now That I Call It Love" and "My Song." Con, in fact, was everywhere, handing out photos to patrons at the early show (40 cents before 1 P.M.). He even filled in for Russ at CBS outlet WCAU when NBC complained — they were out to get him, Conrad was sure — about a special, ballyhooed broadcast Con had set up.

On the road, Columbo was seeing what impact he'd made outside New York, on those to whom he was "Only a Voice in the Air" (as he'd write with Al Dubin in a song dedicated to all those disembodied "*Millions who lis-ten out there . . . gay songs of glad-ness / love songs of mad-ness*"). He could sense their uncertainty, not quite sure what to expect or how to react, their curiosity at his restraint, lost in the bow of his violin, a dreamy sit behind the piano; nuzzling the microphone. But once the spectators saw he didn't need the flamboyance of showmanship, they settled down with him, letting his seductive soothe scintillate their smolderings. One night a fire broke out in the backstage of the Mastbaum. Smoke billowed from behind the curtain. Before the crowd had a chance to panic, Russ began singing "You Call It Madness" even as the acrid air made his eyes smart, his tears beginning to flow. A man crying; the audience returned to their seats to see that.

Across town, Rudy Vallée was appearing in *George White's Scandals*, only he wasn't appearing the second week of the run, the same weekend of Russ's opening, because the Scandals had abruptly canceled due to poor sales. This was ridiculous, Rudy told the *Bulletin*. "Crooning," he said with a grimace, in his dressing room on what would be the show's last night; "it's 'soft singing,' I don't like the word and I resent its application. You ask me how long it will remain popular—well, this is my third year and I'm making more money than I ever did."

Once started, he couldn't stop his tirade, pouring out his heart to the *Bulletin* reporter while greasepainting in his dressing room at Philadelphia's Metropolitan Opera House. "I'm portrayed as a fellow without any sense of humor, because I talk about a few things close to my heart. I've hesitated about granting interviews after meeting so many people who were unfair and construed the things I said to make me appear very silly.

"After a while your attitude is not to see anybody. You don't want to be crucified or hurt. I'm serious by nature and when people expect me to wisecrack during times like this I can't.

"I don't need interviews anyway. I've got an audience of from 5 million to 15 million." He could do something besides singing, he reminded this captive audience, "something like Novarro did in *Mata Hari*." The reporter noted that Rudy referred to himself in the third person, as in "My first picture was just a stunt to get Vallée through to the public."

And what was Con's stunt? On Monday morning, he has Russ visit the youngsters of the Macfadden Free Clinic at the Osteopathic Hospital, treating them to ice cream. While Dr. Ira Drew, clinic head, proffers each child a cone, Russ cradles a baby, not quite sure what to do with it. He thinks of his mother, who birthed him across the river.

THE REDBRICK house that is the Quaker Outing Club stands in the shadow of the elevated, catty-corner to Market Street as it slips outside Philadelphia's city limits into Millbourne, Delaware County. The Sixty-ninth Street terminus is five blocks away. Surrounded by a low stone wall and atop a rise, its closest eastern neighbor is a Sears-Roebuck, on the west an automobile showroom. Number 6403.

A uniformed Negro takes your car. You go up the front stairs to a reception room with Oriental rugs and wood-paneled walls, where a young woman takes your hat and coat. From the second floor, there is the sound of a three-piece band. As your host takes your arm and ascends you, the stereo of the upstairs layout becomes clear. On the right, a dance floor surrounded by tables and chairs, a bar and a back office. On the left, the gaming room with a cashier and four tables: two roulette, one high-low, one craps. You're ripe for the taking.

Russ sits at the oblong craps table sometime late on April 20, after his last Wednesday evening show at the Mastbaum. The action is already well under way, and is being observed by Paul F. Cranston, a reporter from the *Evening Bulletin*, who has gone undercover to expose the post-midnight goings-on at "Millbourne's Monte Carlo."

Looking around the well-dressed room, he sees "two famous sisters, a singing team featured in the Scandals, with a well-known young actor." A prominent attorney is dropping $200 per play at roulette. The daughter of a theater owner rattles the dice.

"Seven! Oh, come on, you beautiful seven! If you can't seven, can you please come eleven, you bones!"

Russ hadn't been surprised when some of the local *goombahs* had visited backstage, remembering his father, or his school playmates. "Little Italy" had come out in force to see one of their own, the first in a long line of home-grown South Philly idols that, a generation later and under the patronage of *American Bandstand*, will result in such 1950s heartthrobs as Frankie Avalon and Fabian (Forte).

As in most Italian communities, the family clans of the home country divided Philadelphia's immigrant colonies much as Italy had been separate principalities before Garibaldi. The western Sicilians grouped around a *Castellammarese*, Salvatore Sabella, who ran the local Mafia franchise with a specialty in bootlegging. There was friction between the Sicilians and those from mainland Italy.

The Lanzettis were *Napoletani*. They insisted Russ come up to the club, do a few songs, drink champagne. Teo (Teodoro) was chisel-faced, almost wiry; Ignatius, who called himself Sylvester for short, had more oval to him. They were a third of a family of six: there was also Pius (he answered to Harry), William (Hugo), Lucien, and Leo, or there had been a Leo until his antics incurred Sabella's wrath. On August 22, 1925, Leo told his barber "Make me look good, Tony. This will be the last time." He then walked out onto Seventh and Bainbridge where four masked men driving a car with New York plates shot him twice in the head and once each in the thigh, chest, and face.

Columbo could hardly say no. Russ's family had lived only a few blocks from the corner of Eighth and Christian where most gang warfare was waged. When the Columbos had first come to Philadelphia, they'd moved the next block over from the Lanzetti homestead on Catharine. The brothers operated within a blossoming drug trade in morphine and opium and had a reputation as "protection engineers." By these standards, the Quaker Outing Club (overseen by the Duffy Gang) was practically legit. And besides, it was a very select spot.

The Millbourne police treated it as such, all three of them, each working a single eight-hour shift. Even with borough police headquarters located a mere hundred yards behind the house, there seemed to be no cause for suspicion. "At nights I myself have frequently walked near the place purposely to learn something about it," noted town burgess Franklin D. Edmunds. "But I could hear no noise. There apparently was no disorder, and no complaints from neighbors. It has been difficult to pin something on the place that will warrant a raid.

"Whatever noise might have come from the inside would be nullified, to a large extent, by the constant passing of automobiles on Market St. and by the elevated trains, which screech as they round the curve." And by the Lanzettis' way with a pocketed persuasion.

The brothers had an uncanny knack for getting away with, if not murder, then most other mayhems. Willie and Pius and Ignatius had served time for narcotics at Holmesburg Prison in 1924, where they went on a hunger strike, claiming the food was "inedible." It was about the last served time on the brothers' rap sheets. After Leo's demise, they assembled a well-lubricated system of payoffs and returned favors. Arrested again and again and again—"We have picked up the Lanzettis one hundred times!" complained Philadelphia police inspector John Driscoll—their "bail" was usually posted long before they arrived at the police station. It was a wonder they even bothered to show up at all.

I.O.U.

Russ wrote the amount on the receipt, wincing. Eleven thousand dollars. Almost three times what he was making at the Mastbaum this week.

I owe you. You owe me. Debt's power struggle; who is to hold the note of promissory?

Can you pay the cost? Take the risk? Borrow night's ink-black against the red ink of dawn, infiltrating the shaded windows, sending shafts of light through the slats on the blinds, the sudden glaring poured from the front door as it's opened to let another slightly askew creature stumble out into the pale light, squinting?

It was morning already. Con had no money; Columbo had hardly seen him since they walked in sometime last night. Russ looked down at the champagne glass, empty and tipped over on the table that ringed around the arena of the dice, painfully quiet, a Colosseum after the last gladiator had been dragged away.

He didn't have the cash on him. The Lanzettis each stopped by to smile and clutch him around the shoulder and say encouraging things like *We know you're not going to let us down* and *Hey, Teo, you remember Mario the Bacala? He thought he was a big-shot entertainer too; but he had a little trouble singing with no teeth.* They all laughed at that one, because nobody would do anything to Russ, would they? And they wouldn't. Russ would pay up, because he was from the neighborhood. He knew what family was about.

THE ONLY problem was that newspaper reporter. Now he had his angle. The Lanzettis could see the headlines, and in fact would, a day later: DICE AND ROULETTE BRING HIGH STAKES AT 64TH & MARKET. Front page. CROONER'S BIG LOSS BARES MILLBOURNE GAMBLING PALACE. And worse yet, 2 LANZETTIS HELD AS RUSS COLUMBO IS REPORTED $11,000 LOSER AT DICE.

Teo and Ignatius only wanted to continue a conversation they had begun with Paul Cranston earlier that evening when he had come to Russ's dressing room at the Mastbaum shortly after midnight. Columbo's last show was done and he was hurrying out the door, bodyguard by his side. Cranston had received a phone call from Russ about ten-thirty, saying he wished to talk about last night's incident. But when he got to the dressing room, there were four Lanzettis waiting for him.

"Without introduction they told me that as I was the fellow responsible for an article about gambling that would appear in the *Bulletin*, it was up to me to see that it would not be printed. I told them I couldn't kill it. I was told that if I was smart I would get on the telephone at once and have the story suppressed. They said it was much more a serious thing than I imagined."

They left other things to his imagination. "Blood will be spilled and you will be in the middle of it."

Paul told them that he would do what he could. He thought he might be able to keep the story out of the first edition. Teo and Ignatius rode him over to the Bulletin Building at the northeast corner of City Hall Square about 4:00 A.M. They had their girlfriends with them, Edith Martin and Helen Campbell. Cranston went upstairs to the editorial department while Teo waited on the first floor, and telephoned his city editor. "I'm on the spot," he said, waiting until the police came and took the Lanzettis and their dates into custody.

By the next morning, history was already rewritten. It wasn't Russ who had lost the money, it was "a member of Columbo's party" who wasn't able to cover the full amount. It had been paid in full the following day, the same day that Con Conrad made a special trip to the precinct while the Lanzettis were being interrogated by a Captain Malone. Teo and Ignatius were soon signing their own $500 bail bonds, leaving their lawyer to explain that the brothers had only tried to "induce" the reporter not to print an exposé of the club.

What club? When police finally arrived at the Quaker Outing Club on Saturday, they found no trace of the roulette wheels, nor the bar furnishings, nor the craps table where Russ had come a-cropper. "It is unexplainable how such a place could exist in Delaware County," thundered Judge Albert Mac-Dade, though several regulars made note that the club generally closed "during the summer months in former years while the sporting world has been seeking its pleasure at seashore and mountain resorts or the Eastern tracks where the annual meets are in progress."

The Lanzettis don't plan to stay out of gambling. They know better than to play by house rules. Not for them the vagaries of dice, or birdcage; their preferred wager is "Beat the Rap," and their luck could only hold out so long.

At four in the afternoon of New Year's Eve, 1936, Pius went into a delicatessen at 726 South Eighth Street, owned by Joe Grimm (real name: Joseph Giannini), who had been known in his boxing days as "the Human Punching Bag." He got a bottle of seltzer and sat down in a booth in the back room. Three men burst in, killing Pius and two bystanders. *Shoot the three.*

Pius had divided the numbers racket with John "Big Nose" Avena, found dead the previous August. *Crapped out.*

Three years later, Willie, long considered the muscle of the Lanzettis, earned his shroud of linen duster. Discovered tossed behind the stone wall of a social dowager's Wynnewood estate, wrapped in two burlap bags with his head "turbaned" in canvas, shot neatly behind the ear, he had returned to the city on business in February 1939 from the family hideaway down south. By summer he had overstayed his welcome.

He was stone broke as well. His widow had to take up a collection to pay the thirty dollars for the funeral, and only one car followed the body to West Laurel Hill Cemetery on July 5, 1939. In it rode his wife and his mother Angelina, who remembered the house in which all her boys were born on Catharine Street, between Tenth and Eleventh, and how she would visit church each day to pray for them.

Six. The hard way.

. . .

THE HIGHER the stakes, the more Russ finds himself thrilling to each cast of the die. Gambling has its own taut momentum. Once over the losing, or even the winning, it is the held-breath suspense that keeps him coming back for more. More. The more he loses, the more exciting it becomes. For him to turn his luck around, to snatch triumph from demoralizing disaster, will feel so much better than winning a few hundred lousy dollars.

Russ looks at the dice in his hands for a moment. They wink at him, catching the light, the snake eyes of a co-conspirator. Eve's temptation. *C'mon*, they seem to say. *What have you got to lose?*

A prayer and a breath. He gives the dice life. Shake it up, baby. Sends them on their way. Hoping for *buona fortuna*.

He releases them into the air, thinking of his mother, who birthed him across the river.

WOODMANSTEN INN

Abe Lyman and Joe Venuti take turns on the traps. B. A. Rolfe toots a trumpet. Carmen Lombardo strums a guitar while his brother Guy screeches a violin. Smith Ballew sits behind the piano. Freddie Rich. Joe Moss. Rubinoff. A jury of his peers.

It's a band made up of bandleaders. "Now all of you play the tune on which you're cut in," cracks the ceremonial master, comedian Jack Osterman, a pug chatterbox known as "the Bad Boy of Broadway," inviting the various celebrities to take a bow. He's aware that a good portion of the opening night audience are song publishers and pluggers, picking up the various tabs.

The Woodmansten Inn is just over the city line, off the Pelham Parkway at 1572 Williamsbridge Road. "Thirty minutes from Broadway," the ads proclaim, though it's not mentioned from where on Manhattan's longest street the distance is measured. Once a "Tavern," it has gone slightly upscale under the direction of "Christo of the Pavilion Royal." The owner is Joe Pani. It's not a speakeasy, per se, but no one's sniffing the drinks, either. The roadhouse circuit always does well in the hot months. Ballew is opening over at the Royal on Merrick Road next week, and places like the Glen Island Casino, on its own isle in the Long Island Sound, and the Lynbrook are preparing their summer season.

The bandleaders accept their accolades and the regular orchestra return to their places. Russ strolls among the crowd, violin tucked under his arm, greeting the à la carte dinner guests. He kisses Ethel Merman on her cheek; waves at Zelma O'Neill, Lillian Roth, Helen Morgan, and Lupe Velez. Jack Pearl,

Fatty Arbuckle, and Paul Yawitz are scattered among the tables. Fay Webb has arrived without Rudy.

Downtown, Harry Reser is opening at the Hotel Roosevelt Grill. He is also an NBC artist, which means that this Thursday evening of May 5, 1932, requires diplomatic shuttling on the part of those who are glad-handing and importuning; but Russ is clearly the draw. Even Con, sitting in a corner nursing his wounds over NBC's ascendance in Russ's career, has to admit the boy sounds good.

It's due in no small part to the round-faced intense young man with the wire-rim glasses who takes over baton duties for Russ as he works the crowd. Benny Goodman, with his alto saxophone and clarinet, has assembled this crew of white jazz veterans, all of them in their mid-twenties—Goodman is just shy of his twenty-third birthday. The prototypes and castings of what will become swing are being laid down. This is Goodman's first try as a dance-band leader, hiring and firing and driving a hard bargain on salaries. The boys were already complaining, though Benny knew from personal experience that right now the band members were grateful for a paying, somewhat steady job. The body blows of the Depression had knocked the wind out of the recording industry—with sales down more than a hundred million discs annually from a few years back—and vaudeville was reeling on the ropes, awaiting the knockout punch. It didn't look as if things were going to get better. Just this month, Publix announced the closing of ninety live houses, including seven in Scranton, Pennsylvania, alone, followed by four in Roanoke, Virginia, and three in Pittsfield, Massachusetts.

Benny was getting tired of the recording-studio grind. He'd been on nearly two hundred sides in 1931, mostly working with another Ben, this one the Selvin who contracted for Columbia. It was fairly predictable dance music, anonymous and blandly suitable for any occasion. It was beginning to grate on his nerves. He had realized just how much when he did a free-blowing session with Joe Venuti and Eddie Lang the previous October, along with the Teagarden brothers from Texas, Charlie on trumpet and Jack on trombone. Jack took the vocal on "Beale Street Blues" and Benny swirled around him with his clarinet, especially when they hit the line about New York may be all right but it's Beale that's paved with gold. They fit into each other's pockets, latticing free and easy, loping into their solo spots with a wink to the surrounding ensemble, playing for each other as well as the ubiquitous microphone. Lang's steady four-square inversions triangulated Ward Lay's bass and Neil Marshall's drums as each song dug deeper into the vein of chorus, Venuti urging them on with his raking violin through the full-throttle tempo surge of "After You've Gone," and the no-flam precision against-the-grain horn chops of "Farewell Blues," practically the first jazz Benny had ever heard, recorded and written by the Friar's Society Orchestra in 1922, later to become the New Orleans Rhythm Kings when Ben Pollack joined up on drums. "Someday Sweetheart" cooled them down. It was as if they wanted to remind themselves why they had begun playing music in the first place, goosing each other on the builds, playing for the exuberant joy of it. Goodman could only compare it to the tepid version of "You Call It Madness" he had cut the day before with Jerry Fenwyck and His Orchestra, or was it the Hotel Commodore Dance Orchestra, or Buddy Campbell and His Orchestra? The session went out under all three names. Now here he was conducting for Mr. You Call It Madness himself.

There hadn't been much work anyway. The record companies couldn't sell what they already had. He'd worked only once this year in the studios, playing some hot solos for Ted Lewis, of all people, on March 15 and 16, hoary groaners like "In a Shanty in Old Shanty Town" and "Sweet Sue—Just You," while Ted attempted to shake his bottom. Benny wasn't much of a dancer—his back was already starting to ache in odd places—but he knew he could do better than that.

The once and future King of Swing lifts his clarinet skyward, using it to count the band off. His brother Harry is on string bass (his original instrument, the tuba's "brass bass," has become irrevocably outdated, exiled from popular music into the cul-de-sac of large orchestras and marching bands); the elder Goodman has also mastered the more modern rhythmic movement of the straight four, the melody landing on each beat in the bar. It had long been two, with enough space between notes for the insistent rhythm to lose slack; now it's twice that, pre-programming the bass drum of acid jazz. Jazz for dancing; precisely arranged, yet framed to accommodate soloing. It splits the difference between the "hot" vs. "sweet" polarity of the twenties, as commercially popular as it is technically challenging, at least until bebop comes along to up the frenetic ante.

Benny is from Chicago, a jazz crossroads able to draw from heartland towns like St. Louis and Kansas City upriver from New Orleans. He knows trumpeter Jimmy McPartland from a high school jazz clique called the "Wild West Side Mob." The group—from Austin and Harrison—is, in Mezz Mezzrow's hemp-ridden prosody, "carried away by the tidal wave of hot music that was searing and singeing its way from the Gulf of Mexico up to the Great Lakes, cutting the country right up the middle with a smoky belt of jazz. These juvenile cats were gone with it. . . ." Severely underage, even in a town that was a wide-open Saint Valentine's Day Massacre cliché awash in bathtub gin (their type of music would invariably be scored to the scene in Dion O'Bannion's flower shop when a black car equipped with running boards and Thompson machine guns rat-a-tats past), the teenagers listen to Bailey's Lucky Seven and the New Orleans Rhythm Kings, go to Lincoln Gardens to catch Johnny and Baby Dodds with King Oliver's Band, and, in the case of Benny, absorb the role models of Jimmie Noone and the tragic Leon Roppolo. He admired Noone's control and technique, the Creole delicacy of his phrasing and his ability to be carried away by the music, though not so far as Roppolo, whom he heard at the Friar's Inn playing with the Rhythm Kings. In despair at his inability to play the music he imagined in his head, Leon would throw his clarinet into Lake Pontchartrain, finishing out his days in a mental asylum. Benny didn't want to sacrifice himself for his art. It was bad enough watching Bix drink himself to death last August. Such a waste. First Bix and now Tesch—fellow Chicago clarinetist Frank Teschemacher, who had been killed two months ago, on leap night, February 29, when he fell out of Wild Bill Davidson's car into the path of a taxi. It was enough to make a man feel the fragile puffing huff of his own mortality. Each breath expelled through his horn could be his last.

Drummer Gene Krupa had also come to New York from Chicago, from the Eddie Condon wing of the Austin High gang and under the spell of Zutty Singleton, as had pianist Joe Sullivan. Benny had met others in the ensemble, like tenor saxists Jess Corneol and Babe Russin, violinist Max Ceppos, trombonist Leo Arnaud (later Herb Winfield), trumpeters Bob "Bo" Ashford and Eddie Petrovicz and Jimmy McPartland, and guitarist Perry Botkin on the New York scene, moving in and out of ballroom bands as casuals, popping up in Broadway pits, backing up radio remotes and jamming late night in Harlem after-hours spots. When he got the call from Columbo's management, Benny simply went down to the coffee shop on Fiftieth Street where they all ate breakfast, and gathered them up.

Goodman took his musical directorship seriously. In fact, many of the boys were starting to feel that Benny took it all a little too seriously. As a musician, he was a stickler for preparation. He would rehearse them incessantly, including keeping them after the show, sometimes until 4:00 A.M. Benny felt he wasn't asking them to do anything he himself wouldn't do. They were supposed to be professionals. Even though Goodman could sometimes earn as much as four hundred dollars a week doing a variety of odd jobs, he still found time to set up his music stand and practice, practice, practice. That was how you got the all-important callback. He was always trying to shorten

BENNY GOODMAN AND GENE KRUPA, POST-RUSS

the time it took him to think of a phrase and convert it into melody with his arched, agile fingers. He knew how to follow the dots, and more important, he understood how to interpret the printed page. "You don't need the arrangements," he would tell the band at rehearsal. "Don't *read* the notes; *play* 'em."

The clarinet was a fleet instrument, piercing, with an element of Pied Piper. You couldn't miss its distinctive register, its clustering flurries of notes and daredevil swoops and shrill thrill. It was why he'd changed fingering when he was sixteen, from the simpler, more sonorous Albert system, with its warmth in the lower registers, to the brighter Boehm. He could be heard over the massed horns now, and the microphone caught the sharper attack of his instrument better, propelling it toward the front of the balance. He made sure to practice the new digital placements. He hated to make a mistake.

. . .

BENNY IS searching for the right reed. It eludes him, a peculiar grail for one so caught up in work ethic.

"I have still to find any particular kind that satisfies me thoroughly," he worries in the final coda of his autobiography, *The Kingdom of Swing*, written with Irving Kolodin in his thirtieth year. "Somehow they always seem to go bad just before I start work, or am getting ready to go on the air . . . and then the whole business of hunting and testing and swearing starts all over again."

Band rehearsals weren't much different. He'd fix you with the evil eye— "the Ray," as trombonist Murray McEachern is once said to have quipped, after the Paralysis Ray in *Little Orphan Annie*, and it stuck—if you slid your glissando into the afterbeat a bit late. He'd shift parts for the slightest infraction. Have a good night and you might pay for it the next day, accused of stealing the show. Benny could be a hard taskmaster.

He had picked it up from Red Nichols, who drilled his musicians until even their improvisations sounded rehearsed, fitting for a bandleader who left so little to chance that he wrote out his own solos in advance; and paradoxically, had left his first mentor, Ben Pollack, when he'd started acting more the big-headed boss than the drummer. But he could afford to demand; Goodman knew how good he was. With Nichols, he was fooling around, mocking the corny witticisms of a Ted Lewis when Nichols called him on it. "You know how I sound when I'm kiddin'?" Benny popped off. "Well, that's how you sound all the time." He was replaced by Jimmy Dorsey.

Benny was gaining a reputation for difficulty. Yet he remembered Red's attention to detail, the discipline with which he ran his bands, and applied his own methods of melding players, rehearsing each individual section, carefully adjusting intonation and blend, making sure it was a band that breathed together. Tight. Russ encouraged him. He'd had enough of Con hiring the first stray musicians he found on the union floor. Russ wanted the best, and he asked for the extra rehearsals, even if it meant a raise for the musicians. NBC had been complaining about the quality of Russ's bands, and now that they had put him back on the air three times a week, with a Sunday remote from the Woodmansten, he wasn't going to try to cut corners.

Benny had to be stern with his boys. He'd seen what happened when Fletcher Henderson had been too easy with his musicians; they were always late, out of tune, sloppy. They took advantage. It undercut the impact of Henderson's arrangements. A band was like a family. Everyone had to work together. When he was growing up in the airless tenements of the Maxwell Street ghetto, all twelve siblings of Benny's large clan had pitched in for the family's survival. It wasn't a luxury when he lied to get his union card as a musician, still in short pants; the family needed his paycheck. And he needed his paycheck to get out. His father had come home from the stockyards with animal offal crusted on his boots when he couldn't find work as a tailor. It made Benny not want to relinquish how he knew a band should be run. Dad let things happen to him. He never saw the car that hit him as he left the newsstand Benny and Harry bought for him in 1926. Benny was not about to be run over, left by the side of the road.

Perhaps he has to play it safe with Columbo. The last couple of years have been rough on Goodman. A virtual child prodigy, he had had youth on his side for a long time. Now he was no longer the hotshot young turk on the scene. In a music that was growing and reinventing itself every few months, he could hardly afford to stand still. He had gambled on the future when he went with the rhythmic excitement of jazz and blues and brought it to Broadway and Tin Pan Alley. As part of an immigrant family, he might have reclaimed his past, the clarinet a premier *klezmerim* instrument of the Jewish dance music that hearkened back to the old country. But Benny was now an American, and as he brought his varied musical energies into focus, trying to find a mixture that would cross racial and economic barriers, just as America itself promised crossover, he would come to represent a music that would soon unite the country itself.

Con had explicitly told him not to overshadow Russ, that Russ was a stickler for balancing his intimate vocal against the orchestra, that as a musician Russ had very high standards and knew what to expect. But it was hard for the band—especially for Krupa—to stay subdued for long. Could Benny help it if "Between the Devil and the Deep Blue Sea" got the people out of their seats? Who was the main attraction here anyway?

"We used to rock the Woodmansten Inn," Benny recalled years later, "and Con Conrad would get mad at us because we used to get a hand once in a while." Benny savored the time slide. "I had a little Ford roadster that I used to drive up all those roads in the Bronx, under the elevated, breaking my neck to get there. But I enjoyed it. It was my first job as a bandleader." Even then, he drove distractedly, pulling out to pass trucks, unconcerned with what might be coming from the opposite direction. He assumed he had the right of way.

Since he couldn't tell Con off, at least just yet, he tangled most with Krupa. Even their fights were like duets. When Goodman had been with Ben Pollack, they had gotten into horn-and-drum duels, the melody of rhythm and the rhythm of melody, trading licks for a dozen choruses on "I Want to Be Happy" (it was something he would recall for his and Krupa's 1937 showpiece of Louis Prima's "Sing Sing Sing"). He was a rhythmic player, and Gene drove him, not only musically, but crazy. There was something in the Krupa personality that was barely controlled; his enthusiasm irrepressible, his greased hair flopping over his brow when he leaned into the lo-hat. It was the first time a drummer had created such an unbridled stir among the ladies.

Benny looked down at his mouthpiece. *Damn,* he thought. He unloosed the screws of the ligature and took out the offending reed, inspecting it, holding it between his thumb and forefinger. He could see a hairline crack. It struck him as he looked at it what a primitive instrument he played, a slice of plant stalk clamped across a mouthpiece, life among the reeds, like Moses. Playing for the Egyptians. Slowly, deliberately, he closed his fingers together, bowing the reed between them until it splintered, cracking in half. He threw it on the floor and reached in the box for another.

RUSS THREADS his way through the throngs. Table-hopping. Strangely relaxed. Enjoying his own party.

It's a good gig for the time being. He has a deal with the Woodmansten for two and a half grand a week and a percentage of the food, steady work to focus and hone the band, and a summer resort to catch his breath. He's just rented a twelve-room house in Bronxville. It had been hardly a year since he and Con had stepped off the transcontinental train; he'd been up and down so much he felt like one of those rubber balls the kids played with in the streets, whacked by a piece of broom handle.

He needed to think about Dorothy. She wouldn't return his calls, though she did his flowers. A-voiding him.

He still didn't know what to make of her winter cold snap. Couldn't she see that Con was meddling in their affairs? By telling her that she stood in the way of his career, Conrad was implying that her career would also suffer. Dorothy didn't want to be shifted into house and home so quickly. She had hardly gotten out of the house herself, and it was enough her sister and mother had come up north to live with her. She had her own dreams. It was one thing to be "seen around"; it was quite another to settle down. She had known Russ was beginning to fall for her. That open-hearted vulnerability was what gave him his way with a song, that enabled him to capture his listeners' passions, including, she would often think, her own. Each felt the loss of the other.

His eyes grazed the room. He caught a glitter of blond at a table to the far right. Could it be? His heart jolted; there was a spurt in the pit of his stomach.

He could feel the blood drain from his face. Not here. Now. Dorothy. She turned to her escort and whispered before turning back to him and waving and smiling and putting on her public mask. He cocked his head, inclined his neck into a slight lean, and, catching his breath, started for her table.

The orchestra struck up "You're in Ev'ry One's Arms (but in Nobody's Heart)." Dorothy reached out her hand. "Oh, Russ, I'm so happy for you," she said, her voice oozing Mississippi Delta effluvia; there was a cold and clammy feel to her liquid vowels, a chill behind her feigned nonchalance. "You must be so thrilled . . . it's a lovely place."

"Yeah, it's such a lovely place it took me all day on the blower to convince her to come," came a gruff male voice. Russ started, turned to the speaker on Dorothy's right. He hadn't noticed him before, perhaps because he hadn't wanted to. He was a big burly guy, with a toothy smile, and Russ had never met him. But he knew him, like everybody knew him. The effect upon seeing his blunt features in person was like looking at a newsreel, suddenly in color. Russ had always loved boxing; and this man was the ex-heavyweight champion of the world.

Dorothy gave the man a reassuring squeeze on the arm. Jack Dempsey, newly single (WILL JACK DEMPSEY EVER MARRY AGAIN? asked a headline in the New York *Evening Graphic* two weeks before), patted her hand. The territorial look he gave Russ said that he knew all about their past, that he was next in line, and that he was the top hound now. *Want to make something of it?*

"Jack and I came down to wish you loads of luck, Russ."

Russ had a momentary urge to take his violin and smash it down on Dempsey's smug mug. That'd give the papers something to write about. Then he looked over at Dorothy, and Russ could see that as hard as she was trying, to act older and tougher and show he was just another passing fancy, he'd hurt her by not standing up for them with Con. She wasn't ready to forgive him for it. And she still cared. At a loss for words, he tucked the instrument under his chin and drew his bow over the strings.

The feint, bob, weave of shadowboxing. He circled the melody as in a canvas ring, searching for an opening in the rhythm. Right jab, left hook, the fingers skip ropes of string like fancy footwork. Bounce off the turnbuckle. There is no neutral corner when the long count begins to toll. A downbeat waits for no one.

Russ boxed his ears.

DREAMS

S urrealism begins in the mind's eye. We remember our dreams visually at first, the enhanced settings and stagings and sortings of our restless unconscious.

The cinema recognizes this. In the 1929 *Un Chien Andalou*, Salvador Dalí and Luis Buñuel slice a razor across an eyeball; even earlier, in 1902, Georges Méliès fires a groundbreaking space-flight bullet into the lunar eye in *A Trip to the Moon*, crossing an outer space of astral travel between earthly life and its imaginative counterpart in the heavens above, the roving inner dialogues of REM.

Dream sequence. Shut eyes, dissolving. Sleepwalking. A long night, last night. On the morning of June 16, Russ rehearses his orchestra in Victor's Studio 2 on East Twenty-fourth from ten to twelve-thirty, takes a short break for lunch, and then into Studio 1 for the session at one. The orchestra is there for nearly five hours—they finally break for a listen at 5:45, and get only two usable sides. Russ isn't finding it so easy leading a band: two violins, guitar, string bass, three saxes, two trumpets, a trombone, a pair of pianos, and a "trapman."

After six weeks to the day at the Woodmansten, the band is in live form, pulsed along by Krupa who cracks his brushes on the snare and pushes at the beat. Russ likes to slow it down, laze behind it. It is their tug-of-war, and it gives the music a strung rope of tightened balance, adding urgency to Russ's vocals, soothing Gene to the point of relaxed groove, placing him in the pocket behind the horns.

Benny hadn't lasted much past the first few weeks. Russ could overlook the usual band-room backtalk from the boys; he'd been there himself. They thought Goodman had gotten a big head, just like Ben Pollack when he walked out from behind the drums and started waving his hands in the air. Maybe he had. One night Benny and Gene had gotten into it over the brushes and that was that. "I'll never work for you again," shouted Gene, not for the last time, and Benny was out the door.

Then there was the missing money for the musicians' extra rehearsal time. Con swore he had given it to Benny; Goodman said he never got it. Between Con's reckless spendthrifting and Benny's cagey way with a dollar, it was likely they were both right. The union was still upset about missing payments from the two weeks' notice at the Paramount. Con said he'd taken care of it with NBC.

It wasn't about Gene and Benny anyway. Russ could tell that Goodman wanted the front spot. He liked leading a band too much. He was too good and too sure of himself, too cocky, and he had the chops to prove it. It was just that his clarinet was always getting into the violin's register, crowding him. He couldn't even *ba-da-dah* without Goodman surrounding him with his snake-charm tootle. He made Russ feel like he was the cobra in the basket. It was all too easy to fall under Benny's sway, move to his urgent rhythm. Russ knew Benny wanted to break out, jazz it up, swing it, as the musicians said. Well, let him. Him and his buddy Jack Fuckin' Teagarden. He had nothing against Teagarden, but he looked like Jack Fuckin' Dempsey, and he didn't want to be Jack Fuckin' reminded.

They start with the waltz first, Krupa pitter-patting circles with his wire brushes on the snare. "Makin' soup," as the colored musicians called it. The paired pianos ripple up and down the keys, a celeste rings like a door chime. There is an extended overture before Russ enters, the band playing through the entire sequence of composer Joe Burke's melody. Columbo doesn't step up to the microphone until the first minute has passed, and even then the band repeats his set-up and intro. Here he is, ladies and gents, a band vocal-ist again, awaiting his entrance instead of being the entrance itself. It's the price he pays to lead this session; back in the band.

Just Another . . . there is a shrug in Russ's narration of the song's particulars. He doesn't stick around for more than one full chorus before the band re-turns to dance mode, which it maintains gamely till the finale. Russ never re-turns to sing, not even to give a stray moan or two. It's probably the least singing he's done on a record since Gus Arnheim, but then, he's becoming Gus Arnheim.

He doesn't know how to take that. Crosby is on a train to Hollywood to make *The Big Broadcast* and Russ is dependent on Con to find him work. He'll be taking to the road this summer, the RKO circuit in Chicago and Cleveland and Boston, Atlantic City's Gateway Casino by the time August rolls around, a homecoming at the Paradise in New York as September begins. Only he doesn't have a clue to what might be happening after then. There is no movie waiting for him on the East Coast, and Russ can see everybody around him flocking to Hollywood, deserting the sinking ship of Manhattan nightlife like mink-coated rats. Con doesn't want to go back to California, because state law prevents him from taking more than 10 percent of Russ's income, instead of the 25 percent he could have anywhere else. Con thought Russ didn't know that, but Russ was learning fast. He chose to overlook it. Con's labyrinthine business dealings might be convoluted, but he had to admit that Con made things happen.

Con had found him the first song, "Just Another Dream of You," written by Conrad's old crony Benny Davis (with whom he'd co-authored "Margie") and Burke, who hadn't done too badly himself with "Tip Toe Through the Tulips with Me" and "Moon Over Miami," as well as the Villanova alma mater.

It is hardly hallucinatory; Russ is on overly familiar terms with "lovers in the moonlight," parting, roses, though he has a good turn-of-voice on the phrase "lay me down to sleep" before the trumpets overtake him. He's paying more attention to the band than to his vocal, and the dynamic's sudden push sweeps him under. The orchestra, full-voiced after so many weeks of playing at the Woodmansten, is eager, especially since they've spent all morning honing these songs. They haven't yet adjusted to the recording studio's subtler ambiance. The soup boils over.

It sticks to the pan for the next song, a fox-trot called "I Wanna Be Loved," adapted from the more euphonious Spanish of "*Quiero que me quieran.*" Even the repetitive romantic language wordplay is lost in translation. *I want that they want me*, emphasis on the third person and Cheap Trick, is perhaps closer, a more devouring, public desire. A lost song in more ways than one, "I Wanna Be Loved" is never released.

Russ couldn't say "wanna" anyway. Not his style.

THEY BEGIN the final song scheduled for the session with a sense of mounting unsettling. "Living in Dreams." Neither here nor there.

Is life a dream? The question is often asked in popular music, the dream state poeticizing the not-so-random minutiae of our detailed existence as song colors emotion. "Life Is But a Dream." "Dream of Life." "Dream Lover." "Dream a Little Dream of Me." Dream refracts reality, like a funhouse reflection. The Everly Brothers' "Dream" is underscored by their twin mirror image and the shimmer of Chet Atkins's vibrato guitar. Vibrato imbues the found note with what Chet, in his slowed southern drawl, might call the *sue*-real ("Wake Up Little Susie," exclaim Don and Phil on their followup hit, returning from dreamland—*"the movie wasn't so hot / It didn't have much of a plot, we fell asleep . . . "*—filming their own subliminal flicker in the deserted drive-in; their *"reputations are shot"*). The croon's flutter.

Are you a dream? When dreams reflect the real, does that make them any less a dream? Falling asleep, as shards and spikes of dream infiltrate normal thought, the closing of the eye's door on the outside world sparks one synapse to the next. Inside the enclosed universe of skull, the otherworldly becomes self-contained.

Memory and dream. They go hand in hand, ten fingers entwined, like tendrils. Where does one begin and the other leave off? We are at the borders of sleep.

"Living in Dreams" is an apt description of music's making. They've settled now, in Studio 1. The lights are turned down. Everyone's tired after a lengthy day, and there are four or five hours to go at the Woodmansten once they finish here. There's the long drive up to Westchester, and back to the city. It's hot in the studio. They can't put the fan on because of the noise, and the air is filled with cigarette smoke and the metallic tang of exhaled breath filtered through brass horns. They're seated on chairs, arrayed in volume order around the microphone, Krupa on his snare and bass drum (he was the first to bring a full-sized kit into the studio in 1927), both pianos arrayed so that stereo separation is achieved at least in the recording room, if not yet able to be caught by the stylus of the recording head. RCA has only just begun to experiment with two microphones and two turntables this month, cutting on shellac. The turntables have yet to sync up exactly.

Take one.

THE BRASS and reeds parry horn figures, three notes of the same and then a lunging forward up a third, down an octave, up a second. Up a fourth, down the sixth, up a third. They join for a suspended build, and Russ leaps in, glad to be at the forefront. The trotting fox begins its four-legged glide through the underbrush, tail swishing; Russ imagines the dancers settling in, joining the band as they pick up the beat, circling the floor at the Woodmansten.

His life seemed all wrong. He dreaded tomorrow. The sun, the moon, the stars, meant nothing in his life.

Now that's all changed.

You banish sorrow, and I'm living in dreams. Now we are one. The us of together.

This is the promised ideal.

The ear that will hear this proposal, sigh, and pick up the phonograph arm to replay the record again a month or two later is at this moment leafing through a copy of *Dream World* dated October 1931, while taking a lunch break from her job selling Maybelline eye shadow, eyelash darkener, and eyebrow pencil at a counter in Macy's. She had picked up the magazine, a Macfadden monthly (Bernarr Macfadden also publishes the *Daily Graphic*), at a newsstand on Herald Square somewhere about the time that Russ and Con passed by in the Lincoln headed downtown to their first recording session. On the cover is a painting by George Wren from an A. C. Johnston photo of Dorothy Flood of the Follies. He has adapted only her brown shoulder-length hair, pink face, and perfectly calved legs, draping the rest of her in a short Greek mini-tunic and setting her atop an Olympian mountain with an expanse of cloud and blue sky surrounding her, the sun a perfectly circular halo. Athena the acropalyptic.

True Stories of Love and Romance, swears the subtitle, and once inside, it does seem you've entered a universe where all roads lead to holy matrimony, though the emphasis is on insurmountable obstacles leading to blessed union rather than on love achieved. Few of the tales—"Shanghaied by Love," "Only the Moon Knew," "Stolen Happiness"—dwell on the after of happily ever. The dreamlike scenarios are heightened by Macfadden's photo-illustrations, meticulously staged dramas replete with painted backdrops and superimposition.

In "Fire of Passion," a young Italian girl allows her songs to be copied by a young composer. "I was singing as an encore a lullaby my grandmother used to croon to me. It must have been the eagerness of Roger's eyes which drew mine to him. When I looked I could not look away. When our eyes met, they seemed to form a bridge between us, joining us for all time."

Editor Macfadden disingenuously cautions his readers that "we can paint a halo around a mythical ideal that is inspirational to the last degree." But, he wags, "it is difficult, almost impossible, to approximate the perfection with which an ideal is environed." Hence, dream needs its own world.

One which Carole Lombard, the Hollywood actress, happily inhabits. In full portraiture across the page from Macfadden's "Inspiring Dreams," she is an embodiment of inspiration herself. She gazes delightedly upward, eyes affixed on the heavenly. She has just starred opposite Gary Cooper in *I Take This Woman*, which has led her to answering William Powell's popped question with a firm "I do." They have set sail for "a honeymoon in glamorous Hawaii." Her next film, the caption alerts, mistakenly as it turns out, will be *The Greeks Had a Word for It.*

THE ORCHESTRA has the last word. Russ runs through his two choruses, a quick verse, and another chorus, then turns things over to the band. There is no implied singing, no trace of croon. He doesn't join them; he has an arrangement to watch over.

The instrumental break keeps to the song form, the first two choruses a polite "after you" between trumpet mutes and saxophones, the verse banged out on the twinned pianos. The doubling clang of their higher notes glimpses a texture of what will be known as a "short" delay tape echo when country and blues fuse as rockabilly in the 1950s, an effect heightened by Krupa's leaning into his two-and-four, glad he has something to get behind and push, brushes or no.

Another round of saxophones, please, and then the orchestra moves in for the high-stepping dénouement, a wall of razzmatazz. Russ reenters on a high note. Living his dreams.

DOUBLE

Double or nothing.

Let's look at this other. The one you're not. Never will be. The altar ego, made to be worshipped from afar.

To see yourself without a mirror. It can't be done. What happens when the mirror starts reflecting not just you reversed? The part in your hair moves to the other side, but the style changes, slicked or bobbed or curled, a whirling Narcissean pool of water, uncharted fathoms amid sea and sirens.

THE OLD Italian guys are all that's left of the neighborhood, now gone to designer seed. They sit outside their social club by St. Anthony's and drink coffee and watch the cars change sides of the street as they have for so many years. Alternate days. Double parking.

Joe's last name is Russo. When he's in the eighth grade, he writes Russ a letter. He tells him he's Italian—his mother comes from Potenza, a Vesuvius stone's throw of fireball from Naples—and it's inspiring to hear an Italian singer. "He was my idol," says Joe. Columbo writes him back, a surprisingly long letter that's since gotten lost in Joe's fifty-four years on the block, and says how glad he is that an Italian kid has written to him, and he was going to appear at the Academy of Music downtown and he hoped Joe would come. There is a picture enclosed, a stock publicity shot (it will adorn the sheet music of "All of Me" and "Can't You See (How I Love You?)" and "Love Letters in the Sand" and "Was It Wrong?"—on which he's identified as *California's Radio Crooner*—and "Why Dance?" and "You Call It Madness," which tabs him as *Radio's Revelation*), signed in green ink, which he still has. *Best wishes.*

Joe's dad was laid off from the wooden-box factory. He couldn't afford to go out to Brooklyn, or up to the Palace. Joe could go as far across town as the Jefferson on Fourteenth Street or the Variety Photoplay around the corner on Third Avenue, where his father left him when he made the all-day journey to the Bronx by horse and cart, looking for work, while Joe went to the pictures.

He "played the hook" from P.S. 95 when Russ came to the Academy in February. Got an older couple to escort him into the early show, which started somewhere around ten in the morning with a movie. Cost a quarter. He's sitting in the back of the orchestra. The place is filled.

The drapes are drawn closed. From behind them come the strains of the onstage orchestra, striking up a familiar theme. A voice comes from behind the curtains — *"I can't forget the night I met you. . . . "* The audience is hollering, clapping. It's his voice!

The curtains part and reveal a twelve-year-old boy standing on a box, straining to reach the microphone. There is a moment of startle, and then the applause resumes with even more vigor. Even as Russ steps out from the wings, dressed in tuxedo and top hat, bringing his hands together, the boy keeps singing. Just like him.

CON IS thinking about the movies. He knows that *Wild Waves* has been retitled *The Big Broadcast* to take advantage of Crosby's radio popularity, that *Crooner* is on the verge of release, not starring Rudy Vallée, that the media are already starting to conflict their interest even as they compound it.

He calls up his old friends at Fox. One sunny day, shortly before it becomes clear that the Woodsmansten gig won't last the summer — Columbo refuses to take a cut in pay, and the Inn has no profit margin — he and Russ go out to Atlantic Beach, on Long Island's south shore. They're to film a short that will serve as a Movietone newsreel clip as well as a prospective screen test. Russ romps on the beach in a bathing suit, showing his muscular physique (something neither Crosby nor Vallée would be comfortable doing, he thought with some glee), singing "Between the Devil and the Deep Blue Sea" to an equally lithesome Billie Barber.

Despite the beach-blanket setting, the song is an impossible choice of opposites in attraction. I hate you, I love you. The extremities of emotion; a scarlet Satan, from a place of burning, and the drenching liquid aquamarine of a body's water. Deadlocked.

He looks strange under the sun, pale, as if missing a shadow of his former self. He has become night-dependent, not used to being so brilliantly lit. Just a pin-spot, please; he shrinks from the sun's unrelenting, overall glare. It's as if they turned the house lights on in a theater, the performers still onstage. All illusory mystery is vanished. The whole theater becomes the stage, whereupon it returns to real life, and that's not why the theater was invented. There needs to be a perspective; a way of looking at things.

THE WOODMANSTEN engagement closes on July 15, the same Friday that production on *That Goes Double* is completed at Vitaphone's Brooklyn studios. (Some of the film will be reshot the following January when problems with song publishing arise.) A twenty-minute short, it is both vaudeville showcase and technological gimmick. The Warner brothers are covering all past and future bets, using Russ as go-between.

He plays a dual role of mistaken identity, beginning as a shy, gum-chewing bookkeeper who bears an uncanny resemblance to "the King of Radio." When he walks into his office, wearing wire-rim glasses and a harried expression, a female secretary is declaring she's "just crazy about Columbo" to a male co-worker who rolls up a piece of paper into the shape of a megaphone and warbles. "Oh, pipe down," the UnRuss says, unwittingly echoing the words that frame his first screen appearance in *Dynamite.* "How do you expect a fellow to do his work with you howling like that?" "You dope! That's crooning," he is told, to which UnRuss, pulling on his bookkeeper's protective sleeves, an office affectation now long disappeared, disdainfully turns up his nose. "Well, I don't like crooning." Or Rudy Vallée, for that matter.

Told he looks like Columbo, the bookkeeper thinks of it as his cross to bear. "He's made my life miserable. When I walk down the street, people stare at me, ask me for autographs. Photographs." An o-graphic depiction of the celebrity life, as seen from without.

"I'd like to meet that guy face-to-face," he adds threateningly. "I'd tell him a few things."

He gets a chance to look in his mirror while watching the coronation ceremonies for Radio's King and Queen. The true Columbo is late, and the organizers spot the UnRuss in the crowd and have him dragged to the stage. He is standing there when the real thing arrives, in top hat and tails; the screen splits to show the two gaping at each other in amazement. "I'm not him, whoever he is," says the formal-wear Russ, proving his identity by singing "My Love." The UnRuss pretends uninterest. Tellingly, side by side, there is little difference in their respective body language. While one sings, staring off into space, only his lips and chest moving to draw in breath, the other watches him with the same hooded eyes and studied nonchalance, drawn into the melody's haunt. "He is murdering it," says UnRuss of the song, echoing the fears of entrenched musicality; Russ reaches for and rides a high note to climax.

The scene shifts to a sumptuous living room, where Charlotte Wynters plays a spoiled rich girl who will do anything to meet Russ Columbo. She is listening as Manny Stein, a fast-talking Jewish-inflected vaudeville agent striding dizzyingly around the room like a Groucho Marx (Con felt as if there was some familial resemblance to the Conrad family as well) goes into his *spiel.* "Shake the hand that shook the hand of Al Jolson," he cracks, speaking only in superlatives—"When Russ chirps a ditty, when he yodels a cadenza, when he gargles an obbligato, he's terrific, dynamic," etc. etc.—and promising to book him for her party. After all, Russ once dedicated a song to him— "Manny Happy Returns of the Day."

As a warm-up he introduces Berniece and Emily, a "terpsichorean" dance duo performing in perfect symmetry, faithful down to the synchronized cartwheel and stair-step somersault. "Is there a phonograph in the joint?" asks Manny before slipping a disc of their recorded musical accompaniment on the spindle. Canned music. It gets by the Musicians Union, which is already complaining about recordings taking away employment from their members.

Roy Smeck needs no phonographic assist. He has his ukulele. Another vaudeville agent brings over the "Radio Wizard of the Strings" to show off his bag of tricks, plucking and thumbing and swiping the strings at breakneck rhythms, tapping the neck with his strumming hand (a move that will rejuvenate metal guitar playing in the Eddie Van Halen era), blowing inside the sound hole, scraping the back of the body, waving it in the air to generate a phase. By the time he's done with his version of "We'll Meet Again," it's unclear whether he's speaking chronologically or repetitiously.

The Three Cossacks, a roller skating troupe, enter spinning rings around each other. "You ain't seen nothing yet!" promises the agent. We're ready for anything.

RUSS AND Unruss take each other's measure. How can they compare? The bookkeeper makes thirty-five dollars a week, "before the cut," while Russ has a lavish apartment and stands resplendent before him in a smoking jacket. UnRuss sits in a chair, crumpling his hat, hardly daring to look up. He doesn't even smoke.

Columbo offers him a hundred dollars a week to stand in for him at various functions. His tasks would include acting as a judge at baby parades and posing for a few photographs. And, oh yes, to go to a "pink tea" party thrown by a woman who writes to him every day, and wants him to sing for her. A social duty.

The UnRuss is easily co-opted.

He arrives at the party early and finds no guests, only his comely hostess; he's asked to sing one little song, for her alone. No wonder he nervously refers to "Prisoner of Love" as "The Prisoner's Song," the mournful Vernon Dalhart jail ballad. As the designated mirror, he moves to someone else's will.

He puts a phonograph record on to provide his musical backing, and palms a small handheld microphone—"I never sing without my microphone." Outside the window, an accomplice sets up another Victrola, playing the actual Victor recording of "Prisoner" while the UnRuss lip-synchs along. She sits at the piano and accompanies him, looking winsome. Sometimes he forgets to sing, entranced, almost believing the music is coming from his own mouth. The music starts to draw them together; eye contact.

Then, an unexpected cruelty. The real Russ strolls past the accomplice, removes the record, and puts on an operatic soprano. "I guess the wires must have gotten crossed," says a shaken UnRuss, spell broken. "And I've been double-crossed," the lady replies. Crossly.

It is unclear why Russ should play such a trick on his employee, the man who would be him. Maybe he's decided he wants the girl; maybe he's jealous of his creation.

"Which is which? Who is who?" she wonders, bewildered, confronting a personality in split.

"This imbecile is trying to take advantage of the fact that he looks like me," says Russ, even though it *is* him! "He didn't have me fooled for a minute," she says huffily, though we know that's not true.

The UnRuss seems disappointed that even their moment of togetherness is now rendered second-hand. "There are plenty of others just like you," she sniffs to the double, and as if to prove it, brings the real Russ over to the window. There, in each of several adjoining windows, can be seen a Columbo look-alike, serenading a lovely lass who can hardly tell the difference.

Reproducing, his voice on record, he can have many doubles now, can sing before the party starts to any desirous hostess, able to send his reflection into every home where there is an ear to hear him. Eventually, it won't matter if he's there at all. Transformed into whichever Russ is suitable for the occasion, glazed and silvered, he catches the lights as they're turned down low, his own illumination.

LAST VICTORS

And His Orchestra.

Russ takes the band into Studio 1 on August 3, 1932. He directs the session and they cut four songs in two hours and forty-five minutes, starting at 9:30 A.M. The constant playing and performance are paying off.

With a full brass section of three trumpets, two trombones, and a tuba, along with three saxes, a guitarist, a drummer, and two pianos, this is a lush thirteen-piece ensemble that reproduces how the Columbo Orchestra must have sounded in the midst of a busy summer of touring.

At Chicago's Palace, a show is added daily to "Accommodate Heavy Patronage." The Gateway Casino in Atlantic City "turns away two thousand people." There is "capacity business" in Boston, and a new house record is set at Cleveland's Palace. He comes into the Paradise in New York with the "largest house attendance since the inauguration of vaudeville."

To commemorate this high-grossing itinerary, "the Romeo of Song" takes a full back page ad in the September 12 issue of *Variety*. Russ extends appreciations to John Royal, George Engles, and Edwin Scheuing "for their heartiest co-operation during this, my first year" as an "exclusively" Victor recording artist under the wing of NBC Artists Service management. His radio, recording, and personal appearances are all gathered together under the Radio Corporation of America banner. Con's name is nowhere to be found, an uncharacteristically silent partner.

The session opens with "My Love," a Columbo original familiar from *That Goes Double*, distinctive as the only song in Russ's canon that he writes on his own (though Con Conrad Publishing does control the copy-right). He describes his intended in -able terms, *kissable* and *adorable*, and then at the tail of the chorus, makes a surprising self-reference: "*Some call it mad-ness and blame the moon a-bove. . . .*" Some? The third person is disingenuous.

There is a long instrumental stretch between two identical refrains—he skips the verse, more a shortcut to the chorus—and the band pads along nicely at *moderato*, a mid-evening dance tempo filling the interim between the getting-to-know-you icebreaker and the slow melt of the clincher. The orchestra plays its melodic understatement; even the saxophone "solo" is only a four-note repeated phrase. The song attains a mild crescendo with the alloy strike of tubular bells. Russ stands distant from the microphone, his voice within the band.

"As You Desire Me" is more to the point. Allie Wrubel's lyrics—he also writes the music, as well as such other songs that speak to the immediate as "Now You're in My Arms," "Zip-a-Dee-Doo-Dah," and the 1931 "I've Got a Communistic Feeling for You"—turn on destiny. The no-chance encounter. "*Some sort of Fate has laid its hand on me*"; Russ awaits his "*come what may.*" He gives in: "*I doubt not but you will do what you will with me.*" The horns rise triumphantly. "*Now at your mercy I must be.*"

He shifts focus, sees himself through her eyes. *How do you want me to be? Is that how I desire me to be?* The how-to of love; how two.

Russ's reading of the lyric is casual and once-removed; when His Orchestra storms in for the break it's as if they're trying to jolt the take into motion. Reentering in *la-da-dah-dee* mode, lilting the melody until he loosens his upper registers, he enters the song's spirit, skipping across the taglines until the final crooned flourish.

Con controls the publishing on the third number, "Lonesome Me," written by Andy Razaf and Thomas Waller along with Conrad; its stock imagery—empty arms and wasting-away charms—marks it as another workaday on Tin Pan Alley. Razaf was the son of a Malagasy nobleman who had a hand in Broadway shows like *Hot Chocolates* and *Lew Leslie's Blackbirds*, songs like "Ain't Misbehavin' " and swing radio themes like "Milkman's Matinee" and "Make Believe Ballroom." Waller was better known as Fats. "Lonesome Me" has the air of a secondhand song, a toss-off, which is how Con was able to snag a piece of it.

Lunchtime is nearing. "The Lady I Love" plays the chorus, bridge, and half-chorus before Russ steps out front, repeating the sequence. Old-time songwriter Joe Young ("In a Shanty in Old Shanty Town," "Rock-a-bye Your

Baby with a Dixie Melody," "Five Foot Two, Eyes of Blue") and newcomer
Bernice Petkere collaborate (she liked L's: another song of hers was "Lullaby
of the Leaves"). It's an agreeable enough turn, though his self-effacement
within the band will hardly enhance his recording profile. He robustly delivers the tagline while the piano ripples and Con hands him his coat. Conrad
suggests Luchow's down on Fourteenth.

COLUMBO COULD be content to be a bandleader, drawing half-circles with
the baton and coming in for the chorus, but that doesn't seem to be enough
these days. He'd read what Vanderbilt grandson and opinionated music
critic John Hammond had written about him—or rather about Goodman—
in the British music newspaper *Melody Maker*. Hammond had a sense of
mission about the music he loved, forsaking his privileged roots to become a
habitué of Harlem jazz joints, traveling in the rain to the Woodmansten only
to be disappointed. "We devotees of improvisation in 'jazz' were all excited
when we heard that Benny Goodman had organised a band. . . . Mr. Goodman, I fear, has forgotten all about the fact that there are actually individual
human beings in the band. The result is painful, and the band is merely
another smooth and soporific dance combination." Columbo was singled
out as an "irrepressible crooner. . . . All this goes under the name of 'com-
mercialism.' "

Russ bristled at the suggestion that it was Goodman's creativity at stake. It
was his music, and if Krupa had to play with brushes, or the musicians played
the arrangements as written, what of it? The song was the important thing,
and Columbo's place within it. This wasn't supposed to be a "hot" contest
after hours on Lenox Avenue or some late-night jam session, the pound-for-
pound jungle tom-toms that would become Krupa's showpiece with Goodman, "Sing Sing Sing." It was his orchestra. Even when a radio sponsor wants
to pair him with Vincent Lopez's Orchestra, he turns them down. He wants
to lead a band.

Yet Columbo would never be ready for the onset of swing, as Benny obviously was preparing. An instrumental virtuoso, Goodman was not without his
commercial instincts. When Hammond asked him a year later to record four
sides for British Columbia, he had to be talked into letting the arrangements
fly free. Assisted by Jack Teagarden, and Krupa—who broke his vow "never to
play for that son of a bitch again"—the selections generated enough acclaim
for Benny to be signed to a domestic Columbia contract by his old boss, Ben
Selvin. He would be continually encouraged by John to follow his more ad-

venturous inclinations, including playing with musicians across the color bar. His kingdom awaited.

THE MOVIE *Crooner* is released by First National & Vitaphone on August 18, 1932, starring Ann Dvorak and J. Carroll Naish, featuring songs by Cliff Friend and Irving Caesar like "Sweethearts Forever" and "Three's a Crowd."

The premise of the movie is enough to sink it, a romantic triangle in which the crooner of the title, played by David Manners, is odd man out. "Teddy Meyers" is a hopeless "prig," in the words of *Variety*, sure to repel any ticket-buying croon fans; they go on to say that the character plays as "a swell-headed impossible sapadillo." His appearance on-screen elicits a "Bronx cheer" from the theater audience. As for the singing, reviewer "*Abel.*" Green spares no salvos. "His . . . obvious inability to maintain any sort of tempo with the band and the tune he was directing evidences that they must have shot it cold and then dubbed in the fox-trot melody."

Bing has no such troubles with *The Big Broadcast* of that year. He's the star, playing himself. His name, as lead character, is mentioned twenty times within the film's first five minutes, usually without any surname attached, and its unique bell-like sound shows how large it looms in the creation of the Crosby identity. There are no other Bings. His first appearance on-screen, getting out of a taxi, mobs him with women; he's the object of every feminine affection. It's his showboat.

The Paramount film is Big Budget as well — Bing is to be paid $35,000 for five weeks' work — though there is no guarantee that radio stars will translate to the movies. Vallée is still recovering from *The Vagabond Lover*, and Amos 'n Andy have been disappointing in screen life. Bing will share top billing, hesitant to accept sole responsibility for the success or failure of any film (this stipulation will later be known in his contracts as the Crosby Clause), and is surrounded by the brightest stars in radio: Kate Smith, Burns and Allen, the Boswell Sisters, the Mills Brothers, and Arthur Tracy, the Street Singer. Cab Calloway and Vincent Lopez lead their orchestras, and Leila Hyams and Stuart Erwin support Bing in the acting sequences.

Crosby arrived in Los Angeles in mid-June, having left New York two months before. After still more headlining weeks at both Paramounts, he worked his way across country to the West Coast, stopping along the way in Detroit and Buffalo, the Metropolitan in Boston, the Paramount in New Haven, the Oriental in Chicago, the Minnesota in Minneapolis, the Ambassador in St. Louis. He continued to broadcast from each city, though his sponsorship with Cremo had expired. Once in Hollywood, he fulfilled his Sennett two-reeler contract with *Sing, Bing, Sing* and the delightful *Blue of the Night*, in which he impersonated himself, and began filming *The Big Broadcast* in early July.

Little remained of William Manley's original behind-the-scenes exposé except the radio-station setting. The play had attempted to cast a jaundiced eye (and ear) on radio crooners, but the movie took a more prosaic we're-show-folk-let's-put-on-a-show approach. Paramount bankrolled the short-lived theatrical production to obtain screen rights, giving it a Provincetown tryout the previous August, and were not about to undercut their gathered stars.

Everything builds to the Big Broadcast, which will save "WADX" from being taken over by its sponsor—a commercial fait accompli, even then—and give everyone a chance to brandish their specialty. Only Bing and Burns and Allen have made the trip west; the rest film their vignettes in New York. Guy Lombardo had been scheduled to appear, but clashed with Paramount over Bing's prominence in the movie. Two songs are filmed by each performer, but *The Big Broadcast* uses only one apiece; the rest are gathered together in *The Little Broadcast*, which circulates as a Paramount short. In fact, the whole movie seems like a strung-together short, like the competing Vitaphone *Rambling Around Radio Row* series. Except for the funereal "Here Lies Love," sung by a ghostly Arthur Tracy in a bar scene when Bing discovers he's been jilted, the chorus taken up by Bing when he considers consequent suicide, the music runs alongside the plot, rather than joining it. The novelty is in seeing these embodied radio voices. *Variety* predicts that the film will do better in the "hinterlands" where the audience isn't often visited by name performers.

The stars are introduced with a snatch of theme song, photos in a playbill come to life. There is symmetry to the casting: Bing and Kate reign as radio royalty, with sibling harmonies from the black-influenced Boswell Sisters and the white-influenced Mills Brothers, and the contrasting black and white orchestras of Cab Calloway and Vincent Lopez. Burns and Allen and the Street Singer provide comic relief (though in Tracy's case, unintentional). In an insider's nod, each will be welcomed to the microphone by the announcer from their own show. James Wallington brings on Vincent Lopez as he would from the St. Regis and makes way for Cab and the Harlemaniacs' *hi-de-hi* of the Cotton Club. For the acts with commercial affiliations, Norman Brokenshire bows the Boswells for Chesterfield, and Don Ball handles the Millses for Chipso. William Brenton nudges Kate into port.

And where is Bing "Hornsby," as he's referred to in the script? He's late, a mischievous boy-man who plays off his developing personality even at this early stage of his career. Rounding the corner of his first year of stardom, riding his own wild wave of personal appearances and films and radio broadcasts, he's mindful of showing up on time, poking fun at his early unreliability. They can't put on the Big Broadcast without him, and he knows it. He has just broken off negotiations with CBS for his contract renewal; his option calls for a raise when his contract expires on July 15, and CBS wants a 20 percent pay cut, on top of the 15 percent Crosby took with other CBS artists earlier in the year. He also objects to higher booking fees from the CBS Artist Bureau, and decides to go fishing off the Mexican coast for the duration of the dispute. He can be a no-nonsense negotiator, despite his easy demeanor, just as his air of on-screen insouciance can't seem over-rehearsed. He wants things one-take right, nonchalant, and he needs his golf.

There is something precocious about Bing at this juncture of man and medium. Women are lovestruck, like Leila Hyams, playing Anita, the secretary of the radio station, but he's a guy's best pal, too. "He's everybody's type, that's the trouble," says Anita when she learns of Bing's impending marriage. But Mona Lowe (Sharon Lynne) has given Crosby the go; her entrance is themed with "Moaning Low" in the background. When he meets Stuart Erwin's Leslie McWhinney at a speakeasy and the two share lovelorn tales, they repair to Bing's apartment. Over flickering candles, planning their suicide pact as if it were a deflowering, the innuendoes fly. "Maybe we both ought to." "Let's do it." They turn on the gas, lying down next to each other. "I've never done this before," says Leslie, though before they have their chance to go all the way, Anita arrives to save them.

She sleeps on the couch. Bing and Leslie wake the next morning in twin beds, newlyweds under the Hays Code. Mona arrives to make a mix-and-match foursome.

Crosby saves his true rapport for Eddie Lang. "Please," the second of Leo Robin and Ralph Rainger's songs for the movie, is done in simple duet, a rehearsal sequence with the camera looking over Eddie's shoulder onto the neck of the guitar. Eddie is turned away from the camera, the better to see his fingers arpeggiating and riffing, chiming the carillon of Bing's voice, leaning with him as he slides fore and aft of the beat. Bing whistles, *buh-buh-boos*, and tells him he'll see him at the show tonight. "Okay," nods Eddie, in his only known vocal.

Directed by Frank Tuttle, *The Big Broadcast* has its share of imaginative camera angles and stylish camera blocking, but it's all preamble to the performances. A rubber-legged Cab Calloway is seen "Kicking the Gong Around" complete with a "cokie"'s suggestive rubbing of his nose, while the Boswells show off identical spit curls in the triangulated harmony of "Crazy People." Donald Novis's high tenor climbs Joyce Kilmer's "Trees." Kate Smith, "the songbird of the South," takes a beautiful turn on "And You Were Mine." Vincent Lopez spotlights his percussionist in "I'm the Drummer," much like Bing scatting "Dinah" in his dressing room to the rhythmically rousing rag-mop of a shoeshine boy. The potentially demeaning racialism of such a scene is balanced by the Mills Brothers' lickety-split tempo on "Hold That Tiger," standing stock-still and self-possessed, making the swift pace look effortless.

The underplay is Crosby's secret as well. He involves even as he sublimates. "I want to kiss you because I love Bing," Anita declares to Leslie. Such are the powers of suggestion.

WHEN *The Big Broadcast* opens the week of October 14 at both Paramounts in New York, it's apparent that Bing has prevailed in the Battle of the Baritones, capturing both sides of the East River. Russ is consigned to the Loew's circuit, the Capitol and the State.

He starts at the Capitol, on Broadway and Fifty-first, in the first week of October, bringing his musicians with him, though to save costs he has them double as the pit band for the other performers. "*Abel.*," later to be *Variety*'s editor, wonders why he "needs the band," since "he could do just as well with a pianist, or accompanying himself." The orchestra, "competent enough and all that, is just a backer-upper." Russ plays piano and violin, and gives the band little chance to step out on its own. Dorothy Jordan, an MGM star who stands in front of her film clips and tells how it feels to kiss Clark Gable and Ramón Novarro, and songstress Irene Bordoni round out the bill. The Three Keys—a Mills-like black trio from Pennsylvania consisting of a hot guitarist capo'd at the fifth fret (Slim), a pianist (Bob), and a singer (Bon Bon)—take stage honors with their version of "Them There Eyes."

On the fourteenth, Russ moves down to the State, on Broadway at Forty-fifth Street, where, in an unusual billing, he shares the spotlight with Vernon "Lefty" Gomez, pitcher for the New York Yankees, who have swept the 1932 World Series from the Chicago Cubs. Gomez is not sure why he's onstage—"On the baseball diamond, I know my business. This isn't my racket," he repeatedly tells the crowd—except to stand around in uniform, complete with glove, though he isn't given a ball, or even much to do, and collect his five hundred dollars. It's a no-hitter with the crowd, who watch the slaphappy Mills, Kirk, and Martin comedy trio try to involve Lefty in a skit. He continually backs away from their knockabout antics.

The Friday night show is nearly filled, and despite Lefty's novelty appeal, the crowd is getting their money's worth. Acrobats Chapelle and Carlton roll up a flight of stairs supporting a young lady. The singing duo of Yates and Lawley hasten to grab an encore. June Carr, an "eccentric dancer," cavorts with Dan Harden, and tries to add a little sex appeal to the Gomez routine, but the crowd saves its ardor for ventriloquist Edgar Bergen. His dummy "virtually lives" and Bergen is no dummy himself, relying not on his voice-throwing so much as his exceptional material, which will bring him and "Charlie McCarthy" continual success all the way to the vaudeville that will be television.

It's a good show for Russ. He and the orchestra are in sync (if not -opation then -hronization), and he's "fast developing showmanship and poise," according to *Variety*. He even cracks a joke, referring to one song as "I'm between the Devil and NBC." Though perhaps the in-joke is on him. The company is moribund, despite the imminent opening of Radio City, and Victor doesn't seem able to sell any records. "As You Desire Me" had modest success (it was Victor's fourth-best September seller in New York and Los Angeles), but the relative numbers are way down.

The movie attraction at the State is *Life Begins*, featuring Loretta Young. He sneaks out into the audience and watches it one day, between shows, and feels a sudden yearning for her sister Sally Blane, and his old friend Lansing Brown, and his life in Hollywood.

VALLÉE IS also about town, and on the road. At Roseland, he personally autographs a "photo for each lady patron," and his Thursday Fleischmann hour is a resounding success coast to coast. The networks are moving to a variety show format with a permanent orchestra and M.C., instead of time-slotting music. They are asking performers to appear for free, "showings" that might gain them a program of their own. Vaudeville is turning to radio; the song publishers are turning to radio. And radio is turning to Rudy. The host. *Take of my body.*

At present, all appears calm with Fay—she was back from one of her numerous trips to Santa Monica—but he wasn't sure how long their reconciliation would last. He suspected something. Everything. It was probably this state of affairs (hers, he suspicioned) that shortened his fuse in Cleveland in early October, during a stand at the RKO Palace. Though it might have been a publicity gag, the press made merry over Rudy's threat to black the eyes of *Cleveland Press* reporter Anthony DeCola after he asked what "the Vagabond Lover thought of Russ Columbo." The ensuing rampage ended two days later when Vallée left town.

He had a temper, especially now that he wasn't the only romantic crooner vying for female attention. He'd blown up at Victor when Wayne King was given a song that Rudy had requested, and in January 1932 had signed a contract with Durium's Hit-of-the-Week label. Selling for fifteen cents, as opposed to Victor's seventy-five, these were one-sided cardboard records that attempted to capitalize on songs of the moment; Morton Downey, Nick Lucas, and Jan Garber's Orchestra were among the artists attracted by the novel format. Founded in 1930 and located at 160 West Thirty-fourth Street, the company also introduced four-inch discs, mailing out miniature Durium Juniors to advertise the new 1932 Chevrolets and Wrigley's chewing gum. The only problem was the discs' unfortunate tendency to curl, which meant they then had to be clamped to the turntable with a clothespin.

Despite a circulation claim of 300,000 for each weekly release, Durium records weren't selling either. By the fall, Rudy has switched over to Columbia, where he puts four songs on the September chart: "Maori," "Strange Interlude," "Have to Change My Plan," and, tellingly, "Same Old Moon."

IT SEEMS all of show business is barely scraping by. The chains are closing theaters by the hundreds; the Mastbaum in Philadelphia throws its final show in November, joined by most RKO outlets, and even top-tier houses like the Palace. Vaudevillians blame radio; radio blames high-priced stars. Movies seem to be flourishing, but Hollywood studios are skirting disaster. Fox is divesting, reorganizing. The Cohn brothers, Jack and Harry, are buying each other out at Columbia. Despite the success of *The Big Broadcast*, Paramount-Publix will go into receivership in the new year, suffering a severe shake-up that will exit Jesse Lasky. He tells *Variety* he is still convinced that "the future success of pictures lies in getting back to old silent techniques." He might have been talking about himself.

On the first of November, the NBC Artists Service doubles its concert booking commissions, from 10 to 20 percent, and raises its cut for theater, club, and private entertaining to 15 percent. Con refuses to go along, and starts casting about for ways to keep the orchestra working. NBC hadn't done badly by Columbo, meeting contract guarantees. Optimistically, Russ was on offer from the Artists Service for $2,500 a week for radio work and $4,000 for a theatrical engagement. Including band. Open to negotiation.

Columbo had spent two weeks at the Valencia, in Jamaica, Queens, the weeks of October 28 and November 4. With Stoopnagle and Budd, the Showboat Revue, June Carr. He was sliding down the scale, all right. Vallée was going into the Paramounts at the end of the month. Bing was on WABC with Leonard Hayton's Orchestra and a deal with Chesterfield. Russ was on Long Island. Con felt justified in asking for a release, even though there was another year to run on the contract.

Ed Scheuing's contretemps at the Artists Service weren't helping. When managing director Engles hired a head booker with twenty years' experience in vaudeville to cut salaries and offer artists on the cuff, Ed resigned. George refused to accept his letter and the matter was smoothed over. Scheuing had more than power struggles to think of; there were unacknowledged bonuses a grateful artist gifted his booker, like the ten-thousand-dollar check he once received from his good friend Rudy Vallée, "in appreciation for personal services." "This Damon and Pythias relationship came to an abrupt end," wrote *Variety* in its November 22 issue, when Ed tried to express his misgivings about Fay to a disbelieving Rudy. As for Con and Columbo, Conrad had decided they could do better on their own, at least for a while.

Russ's final Victor session takes place on November 23, 1932. Fred Erdman is there, as he was at Russ's first recording date. They talk about how much things have changed in the intervening fifteen months, that maybe Roosevelt will be able to turn the country around, that it's a sure thing Prohibition will be getting the heave-ho and maybe that'll help legit nightclubs stay afloat. People might go out more. Radio-listening is hurting the record business, not to mention sheet-music publishers, not to mention Victor.

Erdman was in charge of Victor's pop A&R; Eli Oberstein took care of the "hot dance" sessions, like those for Blanche Calloway and Her Joy Boys, Snooks and the Memphis Ramblers, Connie's Inn Orchestra (directed by Fletcher Henderson), Benny Moten's Orchestra, and Sunny Clapp and His Band o' Sunshine. Then there was Ralph Peer, traveling through the South making race and hillbilly records, transplanting Jimmie Rodgers and the Carter Family. These three men (among unsung others) did much to gather American music in the era of the great dissemination. No other record company would do more throughout the first three decades of the twentieth century to preserve a musical heritage than Victor (and not just in America— Victor had branches everywhere, their familiar Nipper logo astride many languages). The interdependent organism of their phonographs and radio sets and broadcasting was about to be subsumed by the Radio Corporation of America they had helped to create, better known as RCA.

If Columbo wasn't on the network, and he wasn't with the Artists Service, then why would Victor still claim him? Both knew it was over, but Erdman had always liked Russ. He'd heard his last recordings. He knew artists had a tendency to bury their solo, or vocal, within the ensemble. That was Erdman's job; to keep the artist out front, and that meant sales-wise too. You never knew where a hit was coming from. He had too much sense to second-guess his artists and audience. That was what made him a great A&R man.

The vocal is more prominently placed, though the orchestra marks considerable time surrounding his choruses, especially the opening "Street of Dreams," written by Sam Lewis and Victor Young, which begins the afternoon session. The lyrics come in short bursts, and there is a long instrumental stretch that meanders to the close. Erdman is concerned with the balance; he has his eye on the second song, "Make Love the King (Long Live the King)." Conrad has told him to take special care with it; Con had written the music with Bill Gasten, to lyrics by Joe Young (an ASCAP charter member, no relation to Victor).

Russ gives it a stately air, a hark and heraldry to the saxophones. It seems to take forever for him to stop steering the orchestra through their charts and enter with a slowed fanfare. Once he gets in range of the microphone, he's at his most appealing, reaching out and reeling in his notes, swirling them around his chest cavity. The tremolo in his voice is rapid, each note fluttering like a bird's wing. The orchestra ease their dynamic after he reaches his final *Kiing*. There are no solos, only displayed melody, and a solitary sock-cymbal crash.

"I Called to Say Good Night," which Con writes with Schubert, Young, and Bochmann, rises Russ to his tenor. The romancer returns. He plays innocent at first—he's come back for one more bite, uh, good night. "*As long as there's a moon . . . tomorrow the moon may not shine.*" Now or never.

The song modulates. The horns take turns following the melody line. He ripostes the ending, lazing it, sliding into the inflections of the croon without ever leaving the words. She can't turn him away.

But she does. The last selection strikes home. "Lost in a Crowd" (lyrics by Bob Hice, melody by Joe Krechter and—yes!—Con Conrad) walks him along his street of dreams, an urban *anomie* measuring him against the ignores and uncares of the city. He already felt like a scrap of yellowed newsprint tossed by a frivolous wind. "*No one seems to know / No one seems to care an-y-thing a-bout my song.*" The orchestra attempt to cheer him up, perkily foxing up the break. He still feels unrequited. "*All my hopes in vain,*" he vibratos, a death knell pre-echoing Robert Johnson. The end notes are among the most assured Russ Columbo will ever record, words blurred until they are stretched into the anthropomorphic sounds of *looose* and *youuuse* and *lawwsst,* music's pidgin lingo.

He will not record for a label again until August 1934. By then it's too late.

HANNAH

He puts on the sparring gloves for Battling Levinsky while the press photographers snap away. Russ wears his tight trunks well; there is no hair on his chest, and his body appears solid and muscled in a soft, inviting way, like a couch. At a hundred seventy pounds, he looks in much better shape than the former Barney Lebrowitz, a veteran of more than two hundred fights who took the light heavyweight championship from Jack Dillon in 1916, lost it to Georges Carpentier in 1920, and lasted three rounds with Jack Dempsey in 1918 before being knocked out. His final shot at the title was a loss to Gene Tunney in 1922. He hadn't fought since October 1930. Columbo throws a mock left into the Battler's midsection, and Levinsky *ooofs* for the cameraman, then poses with Russ and some dame and sings, his left gesturing like an uppercut.

They were all in show business. More than anything, they wanted to put on a good show, to keep the audience on the edge of their ringside seat. Like Russ and Con. They traded punches. In the end each respected the other for a good contest. He knew Con would usually win, but he didn't care. Con was the go-getter. Once Con got going, he never let go. From the get-go. He wore you down because he always came out like the first bell, ready to take the fight to the opposing corner. He had a right jab and a left hook, a not surprising combination for a piano player.

On Friday, December 9, Columbo's twenty-piece orchestra opened at the Park Central, much as Russ had moved into the Waldorf the previous winter. Eddie Cantor stopped by to introduce him, coincidentally plugging his new movie, *The Lady from Spain*. Signing for a ten-week stand, Columbo was payrolled at $3,500 a week; out of that he would have to furnish his own or-chestra and expenses, including opening acts the Girl Crazy Four and the ten-piece Casa Bella Tango Orchestra, and Jean Fay. Con had slipped Bob Royce, his latest singing discovery, onto the bill. The headlining girl singer, Hannah Williams, was nailing him for $750 a week. She was married to (though separated from) Roger Wolfe Kahn, and was used to a lot of money. Anyone built like her was bound to be expensive.

The Central (off the south rim of the park, at Fifty-sixth Street and Seventh Avenue) was one of the grand dance band venues; it was there, in November 1928, that gambler Arnold Rothstein was shot in Room 349, staggering down-stairs to expire in the lobby right under where Ben Pollack's band was per-forming and where Goodman tried to assume control of that same band in early 1930, a mutiny which Ben managed to nip in the bud. It was a New York kind of place.

So why not transform it? The Park Central had opened their enclosed-roof garden in October as "the smartest spot in town." Their concept, helped along by the opening bill of Harry Barris and Loyce Whiteman, was to bring an exact replica of the Cocoanut Grove, complete with palm trees, to Man-hattan nightlife. "Where Hollywood and Broadway meet," Con splurged in a full-page *Variety* ad ("Con Conrad Presents," it was headed, in case anyone had any doubts about who was straddling both coasts).

Everybody was hightailing it out to California, where the movies seemed to offer sky's-the-limit work, quick riches, swimming pools, and tans, all cur-rently in short supply on Broadway. It was said that the corner of Hollywood and Vine was awash with migratory vaudevillians, all trying out their act as they used to in front of the Palace. The time was ripe for a West Coast east.

ROSCOE "FATTY" Arbuckle is also given featured billing. The once-iconic film comedian has never fully recovered from the scandal that spread him across the front pages eleven years before, when he hung two juries and was found innocent of manslaughter by a third after a young girl died during a party in his San Francisco hotel room. There were allegations that she had been raped with a champagne bottle, or that Fatty's great weight had crushed her. This was juicier than any movie, and his shocked public was unforgiv-ing. He was no longer a surprisingly graceful and jolly heavyset man, but a debauched monster, a Hyde who could never go back to being Jekyll.

At this point in his career, he would've settled for Heckle. He has spent his last decade in a Hollywood wilderness, directing comedy pictures under the assumed name of William Goodrich, which he's borrowed from his father.

Now Warners has signed "Fatty" for a succession of two-reelers, twenty-minute specials with catchy titles like *Hey, Pop* and *Buzzin' Around*. The former has him befriending an orphan; in the latter, he swallows a bee, leading to a free-for-all in a china shop. There is no pie-tossing to speak of. With his career in free fall, Roscoe doesn't know what to do next, and so he tries vaudeville, and a nightclub act.

The thrush is another matter. Hannah Williams started as a duo with her sister Dorothy, but found a more rewarding partnership with Kahn, the millionaire bandleader, whom she married on January 26, 1931, in Woodbury, Long Island, at one of the family estates. His orchestra had a reputation as being the best that money could buy. Though this was often used to undermine Kahn's reputation, people often forgot that musicians are professionals who like to be recompensed, and Roger saw no worth in the self-righteous myth of the starving artist. Kahn's bands often featured top-notch talent, and he paid them what they were worth.

The Million Dollar Band, as it was unofficially dubbed, featured artists like Eddie Lang and Joe Venuti, trombonist Miff Mole, tenor saxophonist Babe Russin, early Jack Teagarden (on "She's a Great Great Girl"), and pre–Five Pennies Red Nichols. A Victor artist from 19616 to 21801 (his catalog numbers, translating annually into 1925–29), Kahn scored success with his first disc, "Hot-Hot-Hottentot," with his own compositions for the 1928 Broadway musical *Here's Howe*, "Crazy Rhythm" and "Imagination," and lighter fare like "Clap Yo' Hands" and "A Cup of Coffee, a Sandwich and You." Though he was a mere stripling of fourteen when he formed his first band, his musical career peaked with the twenties. He made a halfhearted move toward swing in the 1930s with Artie Shaw, but Roger knew he could never get free of his family connections. It was a twist on that old jazz musician joke, about the piano player who wins big at blackjack. *Guess I'll keep playin' till the money runs out.* There was no risk, and he needed to prove himself. He took to flight, the charged adrenaline drips of test and research piloting, where he finally emerged above the clouds of the Kahn fortune.

Hannah was dazzled by him. She knew about dance band leaders from her first husband, Charles Kaley, whom she'd married at sixteen; the marriage lasted long enough to be annulled. But she hadn't reckoned with Roger's family. His father was one of the richest men of the early twentieth century, a banker who knew his clients were enmeshed in his central nervous financial system. They'd let Roger's brother Gilbert play occasional banjo with Artie Hand's California Ramblers until the money had run out, and now he was down on Wall Street learning the family trade. And the mother . . .

The old man had his bevy of women, even the opera star Lydia Lindgren who, in September 1930, wanted half a million arias from him in a court action. All Mrs. Otto Kahn had was her resentment, and when she looked at Hannah, small, almost petite, exuding the kind of sizzle that made men drop their trousers and not about to stand for any rigmarole, she knew where to take it out. It became worse when the junior Kahns moved back into the family town house on Fifth Avenue after sailing off to Europe for their honeymoon. Roger had given up his apartment. They'd been away for over a year, hoping to ride out the financial upheaval that had overthrown the world economy and taken the dance band business into the red. Hannah wondered what the absence would do for her career.

She had been on the upswing when Roger swept her off her feet. Hannah worked in the Scandals after arriving in New York from Taylor, Pennsylvania, with her sister, but it was an early Billy Rose show, *Sweet and Low*, in which she began to attract attention. Fanny Brice, George Jessel, and Ted Healey were also on the bill, but her "Cheerful Little Earful" stole the revue. A dynamic brunette, only five foot four and barely more than a hundred pounds, she always captivated the pit orchestra with her vivacious turn onstage. They called her the Cheerful Little Rearful.

He didn't want Hannah to sing with him; he was still trying to become credible, to be taken as seriously as "a Jerry Kern," or a Gershwin. "I wish I could give it up," he moaned to *Variety* on returning to New York in May 1932, aware that most considered it a lark for him to continue. But it was all remotes these days, and the hotels referred him "to a radio station . . . the choicer spots state it's now out of their control, that they've leased the broadcasting wire privileges to NBC or CBS . . . just like a coatroom concession." He could find no place to hang his hat.

Kahn had been following Hannah's career since they'd had a chance meeting in Chicago, and asked the sisters to work in his Manhattan nightclub. After they were married, Roger spent more time taking her to the "21" Club and other nightspots than allowing her to sing in them. She welcomed the time away from her mother-in-law, who felt that her son was too good to be married to a theatrical performer; her father-in-law encouraged her to bring home any available showgirls for a weekend getaway in Woodbury. She was caught in the middle.

"Every time I felt good and wanted to sing, Roger would throw a fit," she remembered later for a *True Confessions* reporter. "He was a Kahn and wanted me to act like one. I must be dignified, he said. Why, if I so much as put on a bit of make-up in the daytime, his mother objected."

The final quarrel began when Roger wanted to go nightclubbing in Harlem. "I told him I'd rather go to a place where my friends went. I added that it was none of his mother's business if I wanted to use make-up or not." Mrs. Kahn had already made up her mind. She never allowed her daughter-in-law to call her "Mother." That was reserved for Roger. In May 1932, Hannah left the stone palace on Fifth Avenue with only a dollar in her purse and the clothes on her back, determined to go it on her own.

Roger responded by taking out an ad in a New York newspaper, claiming "Notice is hereby given that Mrs. Roger Wolfe Kahn . . . is not authorized to contract any obligation of any kind in my name or in my behalf on my credit or responsibility." The mother had always thought of her as a gold digger. Hannah refused to take one cent, much to the dismay of other divorcing prospectors. She hadn't married Roger for his money, and she wasn't about to start taking it now.

She would finance her own trip to Reno, so she thought, and after stints at the Central Park Casino and the State Theater, taking a turn with the Boswell Sisters, Abe Lyman's band, and headliner Lou Holtz, came to the Park Central.

"WHERE'S GENE?"

The band boy tapped him on the shoulder. Russ motioned toward the window. Krupa was outside on the fire escape, smoking his muggles, or reefer, or whatever they called it. The Chicago guys liked that funny tobacco. They got it from Mezzrow, or the coloreds uptown. Russ didn't want to get hooked, but around the last set, he always liked it when Gene laid into his snare and the dance floor came alive. Even Russ snapped his fingers.

He had other thoughts for the break. He was going to happen by Hannah's. *Hannah make me happy.*

They had been seeing each other for a month now. He knocked on the dressing-room door. She opened it a crack and peeked out at him, gradually opening the door, revealing her face, a dapple of red and black on white, like a hand of playing cards. Straight flush.

She swung her left arm grandly, in a flourish and welcome. "Come on in, Russ. I've been waiting to see you." She had on a dressing gown of dark blue, against which the blackness of her hair contrasted like a night sky. He reached around to take her shoulders, but she slipped to the side. She seemed nervous, unsettled. Preoccupied. She hugged herself, paced in front of the settee. She waved him off.

"Oh, I'm so worried," she said. "I don't want things to fall apart."

"Don't. Please don't. I can keep this show going."

"Oh, darling, I know. I believe in you. But you see what it's like out there."

"Business will pick up after the holidays. I know it will. When Roosevelt gets in office he'll lick this damn Depression. At least Prohibition will be over."

"And so will we. We can't stay here any longer. We have to get away. This town is in the doldrums. We have to go to California. To be together."

This script needs doctoring, Russ thought. Still, he'd been thinking of nothing else for weeks now. It wasn't getting any better for him in New York. Con knew it. That was the real reason Conrad had jumped ship three weeks into the Park Central engagement. Not the dollar cover charge, or the fifty cents from each dinner, or the payroll that was exceeding their guarantees.

It was no surprise they were suffering, with the radio wire going out over the tiny thousand-watt WMCA, a local station operating only part time. Con had blithely asked NBC to put a network remote into the hotel for Columbo, even after severing their relationship with NBC Artists Service, which was on its last legs anyway. Not surprisingly, they refused. In the new year, RCA would decide that "the orchestra booking business was impossible to sustain at a profit," and the bureau ceased operations. CBS had a remote deal with the hotel, but they had yanked their wire when Chesterfield complained that they had Crosby under contract and didn't want a competing crooner. Radio could afford to call the tune; only radio seemed to prosper in the "depresh," as *Variety* dubbed it. Even Columbo's records weren't selling. For the month of December, Leo Reisman was the top-selling Victor artist in New York with "Night and Day," and number one in Chicago with "Day and Night."

And where was Con? The chiseler had taken it on the lam. He was nowhere to be found. Leaving Russ holding the bag.

As long as he was holding it, he might as well pack and leave town. Hannah was off to Reno to get free of the Rajah. Russ would take the band across the country and hop over to L.A. at the end of the tour. Meet her there. Maybe his New York time had come to an end, in this sad replica of a joint where he'd begun, trying too hard to smile while he could hear the band breaking loose under him. Not that he wanted to go up-tempo.

He roamed his eyes around her dressing room, and then her. She assumed the shapeliness of her fabrics, the touch of fur, the bias cut. He wanted to change clothes. Step behind her screen and come out wearing something revealing.

Wearing her.

They continue at the Park Central until mid-January 1933, and then it's time to go on the road.

CROONING HAD settled into the country at large.

Should Crooners Marry? asked a Universal comedy short in March, in which a gout-ridden father has the double burden of "a sissy male secretary and a daughter who would go for a college crooner," according to *Variety*, adding "Subject is lower than second rate in every way." The crooner dresses as a butler, until he wins over the father. Nothing makes much sense, or as much sense as CROONER'S LURE?, a Cincinnati newspaper heading about a sudden crash interrupting the radio listening of the Melvin Garland family, when a car driven by William Blanton, sideswiped by a truck, plunges into the wall of their Eastern Avenue home, with "one front wheel almost touching the radio."

The croon had become domesticated. Over on the set of *College Humor*, Bing Crosby was returning to form with "Learn to Croon," his cheek in tongue when he came to the line about "you'll eliminate each rival soon," adding the *boo-boo-boo, boo-boo* that gave a knowing nod to his younger self. The song was written by Paramount staff writers Sam Coslow and Arthur Johnson, who also composed Bing's "Just One More Chance." Coslow soon showed up on Victor as the Voice of Romance: "Isn't It Romantic?" 'Tis.

3/33. The century is one third over. On the day Russ and his orchestra arrive in Harry Richman's home town, banks are just reopening from the holiday moratorium Roosevelt had declared when he was sworn into office earlier in the month.

Their week at the Cincinnati Albee is to run from March 10 through 16, following Ted Lewis, *"the rootin' tootin' syncopating swinging maestro of jazz. The high-hatted hit of happiness with a buxom bevy of hotcha-bent beauties."* With hoopla like that, it's no wonder Lewis attracts a fair $13,600 for the week in ticket sales; Russ can manage only a comparatively meager $8,500. *The Past of Mary Holmes* is the movie, with Eric Linden and Jean Arthur, about an opera singer who betrays her son for fame. It can't compete with *42nd Street* over at the Keith's, a photoplay that is its own stage show. *King Kong* is due to open this month as well; people are saving up their movie money in these hard times. The Albee will be dropping vaudeville after April 20.

After a warm-up date at the Two Two Club in Detroit, he's on the RKO circuit. Despite the economic gloom clouds, the tour gets off to a good start in Kansas City on February 11. The Mainstreet Theatre does respectable business, though the bill seems old-fashioned. A blackface comedian named Mel Klee struggles with the crowd before winning them over with some time-tested minstrelsy. Boice and Marsh are a female duo whose high point is the acrobatics routine Miss Marsh does while playing the violin. Bill Campo is a comedy dancer who pratfalls constantly.

Russ sings his favorites, including "Between the Devil and the Deep Blue Sea," "All of Me," "Paradise." "Several encores," deadpans *The Billboard*.

They move on week by week. Omaha. Minneapolis. Chicago during the first week of March. It's a good town for Russ. He played here only six months ago, and the Palace is respectably filled. Buster Shaver is back with his midgets; the Arnaut Brothers mix up their violins and their "bird language flirtation" routine; Vera Schwarz is a German opera singer who offers "The Blue Danube" and "Beautiful Lady," in German, no less; and the team of Douglas Leavitt and Ruth Lockwood gets the cherished next-to-closing spot, with a skit about two deaf people at the movies seguing into a whistling pianist and "a ventriloquial number." *Billboard* doesn't take sides.

Their Chicago correspondent, F. Langdon Morgan, is less happy with Russ's performance. The band "is nothing to rave over." Columbo is "stiff and has not yet acquired a stage personality." The set list is "How Deep Is the Ocean," "Say It Isn't So," an "I Got Rhythm" that gives the band a chance to work out, and then a flurry of "Night and Day," "Between the Devil and the Deep Blue Sea," and the *inevitable* "Brother Can You Spare a Dime." "He smiles but seldom and then as if he were doing the audience a favor. Act is paced too slow and needs showmanship. Good applause at exit." *Variety* agrees, saying that he was "diverting but missed fire as a distinguished entertainment." Critics.

It's true, he was distracted. There was something on his mind, and it was Hannah. She had been in Reno since February 19; she hadn't answered any of his telegrams. He ignored the rumors, that she was more than friendly with Goodman, or Tommy Dorsey, or that she was just using him like she'd used Roger Kahn. Only she hadn't used Kahn. So she said. He was getting confused. Russ couldn't be certain of anything until he was on his way to her, and right now the only way he was heading was to Cincinnati, which was in the opposite direction from Hannah. The tour had been booked in reverse, starting farthest west and moving east, which was not how he had planned to cross the country. No wonder he couldn't concentrate.

He lay back on the couch in his dressing room. He loved her, he was sure of that, and this time there was no Con to tell him what he should or shouldn't do. He was going to marry her after her divorce from Kahn was final. He could bring her home to Mama, who never liked New York much anyway. She could sing in the orchestra. They could take their shoes off and walk by the Pacific. They could make love every night. He was starting to sound like one of his songs.

Leavitt and Lockwood are lower on the running order than they were in Chicago, adding "Before and After Marriage" to their repertoire. The second-spot billing goes to Fritz and Jean Hubert, comedy pantomimists whose drunken imitations as "The Realistic Inebriates" are an audience-rouser. Larimer and Hudson's cycling antics open the entertainment, which is competing against local draws like the annual dog show, a civic flower exhibition, and the homegrown disaster of an Ohio River flood, bringing in sightseers from all over the state.

Russ is in his dressing room with the radio on while Fritz and Jean tipple about the stage. He's listening to Winchell's broadcast, half-hearing the machine-gun fire of Walter's style. His rat-a-tat delivery flattens the impact of each item even as it sensationalizes it; everything is earthshaking and trivial, here today, gone yesterday and tomorrow. Russ is not paying a lot of attention, though when Walter mentions Hannah Williams, he perks up, listens closer, waiting to hear his name. It's about time Winchell delivered his scoop, though Russ and Hannah had hardly been secretive in the weeks after the Central closing, or in Winchellese, fore-closing. The Cocoanut Grove had proved a costly affair.

This could be, too. Hannah wanted out of the Kahn family, and she didn't want Roger and his father's lawyers to make it harder than it had to be. It was tough enough to have to live in Reno for over a month, though she did like horses.

He tuned back in to Winchell, hearing him say something about Jack Dempsey getting hitched again and the girl who TKO'd his heart is a sweet little miss waiting out in Reno. The all-man from Manassas and the Willing Hannah. Wanna bet ringside bells turn to wedding bells?

Russ looks around for the referee. That was beneath the belt. He could feel the pain filtering up from his groin, doubling him over. He felt sick to his stomach. Queasy. The room was very hot. He didn't want to be here, he thought. He wanted to be away from here. He couldn't get away because he was sitting here with his shirt collar all done up and the band was waiting for him and he wanted to get away from here because the air was close and he had to get to a window *need some air it's so close in here* and he tries to get up.

He forces himself to stand even as the darkness closes in. He fights against the flashes of light behind his lids, yaws and tacks to the window, pulling up the shade. *Air.* He can't breathe. As if from far away, he pitches against the sill, hand grabbing for purchase, wobbling. It's two floors down to the back alley by the stage door.

"Somebody grab him," yells one of the musicians. "He's going out the damn window!"

Russ is just about to taste the cool air on his face when hands are grabbing for him, steadying his balance. His body feels swathed in a second skin, a damp and clammy sheen. He is wet all over. He fades back and looks around, uncomprehending. Déjà voodoo. Was this a dream? How had he come to be here, in this over-bright dressing room in Cincinnati, the guys in the band looking concernedly at him, a picture of a smiling brunette over by the flowers, time to go on? What was that he'd just heard about Jack Dempsey?

Over the crackling radio, Walter continues his parade of pronouncements, a wartime correspondent from the Broadway front, chronicling victory, defeat, casualty figures. The won-and-lost record.

JACK DEMPSEY had retired on March 4, 1928, a winter after he'd failed to regain the heavyweight title from Gene Tunney in the famous "long count" battle. Now he was preparing to take up life as a hand-shaker.

Five of Dempsey's fights in the twenties grossed more than a million dollars. He was the highest-paid athlete of 1924, and he celebrated this milestone—Dempsey had been born poorer than poor—by marrying a Hollywood actress, Estelle Taylor, the following year. It was a mismatch from the first, and no one took it harder than Doc Kearns, who had managed Dempsey from his brawler days, and found himself on the outs with the new bride. The marriage soured about the time that the Tiger lost his investments to the Depression: "My Rolls-Royce days are over," Jack said. "I'll just have to roll up my sleeves and go to work."

He took to the road, one-night stands of boxing exhibitions and refereeing, beginning in Reno in August 1931. Often he fought three one-rounders a day. It was a loss to another Levinsky, Kingfish Levinsky (a Chicagoan who grew up in the same Maxwell Street ghetto as Benny Goodman), in four rounds on February 18, 1932, that convinced him to hang up the gloves for good, though the tour kept going until March. The right hand that had terrorized opponents, bringing rivals like Jack Sharkey and Jess Williard and Luis Firpo to their knees, now extended itself in greeting. By 1938, he was averaging nine hundred how-do-you-do's a day, having just opened the Punchbowl, a cocktail bar at Broadway and Forty-ninth Street, to go with his restaurant on Eighth Avenue, the Dempsey-Vanderbilt Hotel in Miami, and properties in Ensenada and Los Angeles. Black Jack, indeed.

Hannah had met him for the first time as a fifteen-year-old girl, requesting his autograph at the stage door of a New York theater. He didn't remember. When she reminded him at their re-meeting, he wondered how he could ever forget.

RUSS GOT off the airplane and smelled the air. It tasted of baked aridity and desert dust, a scorched, bitter aftertaste. Reno: divorce capital of the western hemisphere.

It was March 27. He had canceled Milwaukee and the rest of the ten-week tour, sending the band back to New York. He had to hear the news from her.

Hannah was waiting for him at the dude ranch. When he burst into her room, she pressed her fingers to his lips.

Then she kissed him.

"You know how the press like to talk." She had her riding habit on. The black boots. Pants that flared out at the thigh. The crop.

Russ let himself be convinced.

THE DIVORCE came through April 4, on grounds of "cruelty." Hannah told the court that Roger was "impossible to live with any longer."

Then she told Russ about Jack, whom she would marry in nearby Elko, Nevada, in July, after he had established the required residency, registering at the hotel as Mike Costello and Jane Grey, though everyone knew who they were.

ALONE

A sucker. A *sap.*

He's sick.

In bed. A room at the Beverly Wilshire. A hundred-and-two-degree fever. Chills. Flu.

Flew. His little bird. *Away.*

THE WILSHIRE stands at the entrance to Rodeo Drive. Leon Belasco works there as musical director, and Russ doesn't know who else to call, where else to turn. His parents are still back east. Millie, his sister Carmella, is with them.

He's alone.

All one.

He's hiding out. He knows everybody knows. He and Hannah. Russ had been so sure they were meant for each other that he had allowed the NBC San Francisco office to submit a script to Standard Oil for a radio program entitled "True Romance," to star the both of them. *He and Hannah.*

He he. Ha ha.

WHEN THE fever takes over and he burns with an icy heat, he leans back into the pillow and closes his eyes.

He opens his ears. The surrounding sound has a physical presence. The rhythmic ticking of the clock, the wind rippling the filmy curtains, the foot-fall of the maid in the corridor outside his room set the air's vibrations shivering, rebounding off surfaces to spiral through the conch of his external auditory meatus, down the eustachian tube, striking the tympanic membrane, the inner drum that translates the soundscape.

He wants to slow the speed of sound. So he can appreciate each beat and pulse and cycle, make it linger and languor, to truly hear.

We see to confirm our senses, the tyranny of sight. Yet when the light wanes, the sounds come out to play. The musician's eyes close as the labyrinths of tone and pitch are navigated, the walls of an inner maze as much blind alley as convolution.

He'd been blindsided. Hannah had looped his loop, spiraled out of nowhere to knock him off his feet. He hadn't seen her coming. He thought about the chain of circumstance that had brought them together, only to split them apart. What were the odds you would meet the one you love? That she would love you.

That you could be two.

II

Love

*What is this . . . longing to break away from
the body and live sunken within the
veritable self?*
No other than the emotions of Souls under
the spell of love.

Plotinus, Ennead I, Sixth Tractate

CALIFORNIA RETURN

They're best friends.

Lansa is the enigma. You never hear much about him. He seems to be a man who lives in the shadows. With his parents. Over on North Lillian Way, near Beverly.

It's a modest house, number 584, one block west of Rossmore, a block and a half south of Melrose, a block from Cahuenga. The area is closer to downtown L.A. than Russ's neighborhood is, the bungalows bigger.

Columbo had dropped out of touch with Lansing Brown, Jr., when he was back east. Maybe it was because a phone call still cost a small fortune, no matter how much money you had, or maybe it was because Lansa hadn't really wanted him to leave L.A. Had told him so. In no uncertain terms: Con was a crook. Brown could be more like a big brother sometimes, overprotective and infuriating and blindly loyal, which was fitting because he'd been Fiore's friend before he and Russ hit it off.

Russ was only sixteen when Fiore brought Lansing to visit. Brown had taken a portrait of the older Colombo, staring sideways, his tawny skin set off by an open-necked shirt and rumpled hair. Fiore's movie career had never moved past the still picture. It was Russ who had the talent, Lansing recognized, to go along with his beauty. He looked like he sang. A photographer couldn't help but be attracted.

Lansa — it was Russ's pet name for his friend — was devoted, of that there was no doubt. And patient. Columbo knew Brown meant well; that Lansing would sacrifice their friendship if need be, if it meant that Russ no longer needed him along his path. But owing to his very steadfastness, it never came to that. He had become necessary.

Now that he was back, they'd fallen into their old, comfortable ways, riding around and talking about Russ's career or love life, Lansing patiently listening, offering his advice and rephrasings of what Russ had just said, enthusing and encouraging, content to drive until they'd missed the party they'd headed out for and wound up at the beach, or in the hills. "I'm always there for you," Brown had told him one night, before he left with Con, and Lansa was surprised to see how much he meant it two years later when Russ limped home, wounded. He picked up where they had left off, without a flicker of recrimination or told-you-so. It was like they hadn't been apart.

The lawsuits had started with Con. He wanted $66,000 from Russ, one third his supposed income. Winchell broke it to the world on July 16, 1933, when he said in his Monday hard-gossip column that "Russ Columbo and Con Conrad will tell it to a judge." But what would they say? That the party of the first part had screwed the party of the second? Both of them felt used, abused. Con-fused.

Russ knew whose side Walter would be on. He had signed on for Winchell's *Broadway Thru a Keyhole*, as, what else, a crooner. It was more than a cameo, though a lead role in a film in which Walter's milieu, however stylized (and to Winchell's credit, his was a triumph of style over portent, a poet of the vernacular), carried more cachet than any of the male leads. Still, Russ would have some dramatic moments, even if the Production Code was making the script more incomprehensible than Winchell's rambled summary to the actual scriptwriters, removing anything vaguely salacious, and nobody was sure who the female lead was going to be; he'd heard rumors of Ginger Rogers, Peggy Hopkins Joyce, or Lilyan Tashman. Mostly in Winchell's column.

He wished Sally Blane would take a crack at it. He'd really enjoyed getting to know her again, and she had proved a sympathetic ear when he talked about Hannah, and talked about Hannah, and helped him put the whole sorry business to rest. She was a good sport, and sometimes he felt like she'd be good for him. He knew she'd always had a soft spot for him, and they'd fooled around sometimes, flirting and tickling and thinking about it, though usually they just wound up laughing together. But you never went for what was good for you; love had higher standards than that. Sally understood. You had to have the unremitting desire, the self-abnegation that came with offering yourself up for consideration, laying yourself on the line. She didn't have the gumption for movie-making that her no-nonsense older sister had, whom she still called Gretchen behind her back; Loretta was the determined one. Miss Persistence.

THE SHADOW seems to embrace her, taller, muscular, encircling the slim waist where her hand rests on her hip, the billowed sleeve with its lace gather. Even the shadow appears to have a shadow. Lansa has taken great care with the lighting.

Luisa Espinel changes her position, preparing for the next pose. Her niece will be singer Linda Ronstadt, who will record an album *Canciones de Mi Padre* in 1987 (followed by *Mas Canciones* in 1991) that hearkens back to the music of her aunt's Hispanic American generation, the *latina* costuming she is showing off to Lansa. Brown adjusts the light, trying to blur the line between the shadow and his subject so that they merge.

"Head up, up, up . . ." he beckons with his right hand, coaxing her chin to rise imperceptibly, until he flips his palm over and motions her to stop. Luisa leans backward, widens her eyes, and smiles. At the moment when the light seems to burst from her, beaming toward his camera, Lansing takes the picture.

It's 1924, and he's arrived a few years earlier in Hollywood, from Courtney, North Dakota, parents in tow. He is apprenticed with Melbourne Spurr. Over the next few years, in his Wilshire Boulevard studio (variously located at 3305½ and 3719), Lansing Van Woert Brown, Jr., will photograph Norma Talmadge and Ronald Colman, Stan Laurel and Constance Bennett, and even Bing Crosby. He will especially train his camera on a young Russ Columbo, who seems only too willing to preen for him, and allow Russ to learn the camera's wiles, to look straight into the lens. Through it.

THEY ARE in profile, Russ and Sally, at the Brown Derby during the summer of '33. Her hair is a mass of curls resting on the base of her neck, like a bouquet; the rest of her blond halo lies close to her head, pulled back. There is a coffee cup in front of her. Russ still has his plate, his hand rests on the fork. There is a pin on his collar, under the tie. His nose seems somewhat slimmer; there are rumors that he's had it done. But he's eating again, and going out, and letting Sally's obvious affection make him feel like he wasn't such a chump.

Blane knew how your feelings could be hurt, especially when her father disappeared and her mother brought the four small Young children from Salt

Lake City to Hollywood in 1917. Born Elizabeth Jane on July 11, 1910, in Salida, Colorado, she couldn't bear auditions, or the pain of losing a part. Being rejected. Years later, Sally told a biographer—who, of course, was interviewing her about her sister—that "I'd be so crushed" over losing a role. "I can look back and remember wanting a part so badly that when I didn't get it, I'd get ill for two or three weeks."

Loretta "didn't take it personally." She acted the movie queen, even at home. Sally once put a star on her bedroom door, and teased her as "the Duchess" when she got too high-hat. But she couldn't keep up with Loretta's steely resolve, her Christian correction (Young would attend mass regularly, and frowned on the word "divorce" being used in her films). In 1933, Loretta starred in nine movies. She released four films that July alone: *Midnight Mary, Heroes for Sale, The Devil's in Love,* and *She Had to Say Yes.* Russ got used to escorting Sally to her premieres.

As for Brown, he was "the best friend a man could have. He has been my confidant, my adviser for ten years." Russ told Rilla Page Palmborg of *Motion Picture,* "I never make a move without first consulting Lansing." Born on August 24, 1900, Brown was seven years his senior. His mustache made him look even older.

"Lansing would never fail me." Not when entrusted with the most important supporting role of all.

CAROLE

The Prince. One popular version of their meeting has them at the Silver Slipper. Another says it was the Cocoanut Grove, Russ returning to where he'd understudied. But all agree that Carole Lombard met Russ while accompanied by screenwriter Robert Riskin, who had eyes for her, and hoped in squiring her away from the set of *White Woman* that he might pursue her, romantically and professionally, as if there was much difference in Hollywood. He was writing the script for Frank Capra's forthcoming *It Happened One Night* with Clark Gable and hoped she would be cast.

As it turned out, he was a bit early. This was the night, and then it happened.

What might have been.

HE SINGS to her even before he recognizes who she is. He's attracted by the flash of blond, the beyond-pale skin, the minus signs of color, as if she's subtracted. He sees her in the light, and the light brands his retina. When he turns to sing the next line to the other side of the room, she stays ghostlike in his vision, a seared silhouette.

He'd always been drawn to blondes. They were his type, though they weren't *his* type. That was the attraction; to love what he wasn't. Hannah was dark, and look what happened there. He'd gotten his nuts handed to him.

Russ knew of Lombard. She'd been friends with Sally at the Miriam Nolkes Dramatic School for Girls back when Blane had still been Betty Jane, and he remembered Lansing telling him that he'd photographed Carole's mother when Carole was still Carol, though after she'd been Jane Peters. In Hollywood, the changing of names was as much an indicator of age as the rings of a tree.

They had never met. As he sang, Russ kept revolving toward her table on the edge of the dance floor, teasing out a slight smile. He began to throw his voice toward her. Riskin tried to engage her in conversation, but Carole kept turning back to the crooner, enchanted by his attention. She had always been a beauty, but she liked to use her looks as an entrance, not an exit. And after more than two years of marriage to William Powell, dissolved just a month ago on the grounds of incompatibility and mental cruelty (he "displayed his temper repeatedly," she told the judge), Carole Lombard was enjoying being a single girl again.

She was no stranger to the Cocoanut Grove, or the Silver Slipper. As a teenager in the twenties, running with a frenetic, youth-driven crowd, Carole had frequented the Grove and was a regular winner of their weekly Charleston contests, usually competing against another ingénue, Joan Crawford. She had probably seen Russ as part of Arnheim's band, and though never formally introduced before, was surprised at how he'd matured. And he she. They were born the same year (her birthday was October 6), and both their careers had brought them a comfortable renown, though neither had ascended the first rank yet. If anything, Russ was better known, though Carole was on the cusp. Her breakthrough picture, *Twentieth Century*, was due to be released in 1934, and Lombard was about to start shooting a film with Russ's supposed rival, Bing Crosby, *We're Not Dressing*.

She and Bing had both worked for Mack Sennett in formative parts of their careers, Crosby in his song-oriented two-reelers and Carole as part of the ensembled bathing beauties. Though they contracted for Sennett at different times, it gave them an appreciation for comedy, and their scenes together in *We're Not Dressing* display a wry chemistry; they're lighthearted, with a bemused distance that is as much about entertaining the other as playing the part.

The movie was based on *The Admirable Crichton*, the same source material Cecil B. DeMille used for *Male and Female*. In fact, Carole and Russ might have met through DeMille in 1929 if she hadn't been fired from a juvenile part in *Dynamite* for not caring enough about the dialogue to learn it. In *We're Not Dressing*, the class warfare of the DeMille films is starting to transmute into gender warfare, the battle of the sexes that infused "screwball" comedy, the emerging genre Lombard would come to embody. It required a sass, a barely repressed energy that hovered just under the manic, and a salty disposition. She had to be one of the boys, and one of the girls; the thin frame and draping of a model, and a mouth that talked a blue streak.

It was Carole's manner. She could be ultrafeminine, born to the long gown and the perfectly drawn face, but she could be as tough as any guy, taking on all comers at tennis and famously sprinkling her conversation with profanity. She loved raising eyebrows, as madcap as her clippings. When making *We're Not Dressing* with Bing Crosby that winter on Catalina island, she came down to breakfast one morning inquiring loudly "Bing, dear, did I leave my nightie in your room last night?"

Carole learned that the practical joke was the best ploy of all. She sent Bing notes reading "Now?" several times an hour. She was going to preempt the situation, set the tone and level of respect, bring out the good humor. In a Hollywood rife with sexual barter, her mother, Bess, had taught her that it was the woman "who controlled the events," befitting a strong-willed matriarch who gathered her children and resettled in Los Angeles, far from Fort Wayne, Indian country, leaving her husband behind. Carole and her mother were great friends.

THEY HAD something to talk over immediately. She had two songs in *White Woman* and needed a vocal coach. Russ had seen rushes of his performance in *Broadway Thru a Keyhole* and thought he could use some acting tips. What better way to get acquainted than to take lessons from each other?

The next morning he sent her a dozen yellow roses. They were the closest he could come to her hair, her blond alight.

BROADWAY THRU A KEYHOLE

The left misses but the right hook scores, striking its mark. A head snaps back, a hat flies off, amid the bloodlust howling of the spectators.

It's boxing night at Hollywood Legion stadium. The movie crowd likes to unleash its pent-up emotions at the regular Friday bouts, only tonight, July 21, 1933, they get more than the pugilist's art. The action in the ring is superseded by the heavyweight showdown just at the edge of ringside.

Jolson sucker punches Winchell. An old-fashioned grudge match.

It's over Winchell's new movie, *Broadway Thru a Keyhole*. Jolie is defending the honor of his wife, the dancer Ruby Keeler, and her former association with the gangster Johnny "Irish" Costello, from whom he stole her. Walter says it isn't about her, or them, or even Russ Columbo, who is playing Clark Brian, the crooner that she falls for; but that's like saying Winchell's column isn't about the people he writes about. A bout. He's interested in the characters they have created, and how he creates them. Winchell doesn't have to make up his scenarios. He always draws from real life. You couldn't make this shit up.

Even the gals get into it. Winchell's missus, June, blocks Al's left so that he's forced to throw the right in desperation. She and Ruby exchange parries with their shoes, admiring the cut of the heel before using their soles to defend their men. In her haste, June clobbers Warners producer Hal Wallis, who is attempting to restrain Jolson.

Al hits him in the neck, according to Winchell. Jolson claims he smacked him "in the mouth," and then decks him with a second blow. The resultant publicity nets Walter another ten thousand dollars from Twentieth Century's Darryl Zanuck.

Boxing. Box office. Boffo.

HE IS a word-player. He could've been a great lyricist, but then he would've been just a songwriter. Walter wanted to call the tune.

In columns, radio broadcasts, headquartering at Table 50 in the Cub Room of the Stork Club, Winchell popularized a language that captioned the heightened onrush of media, their instant celebrities; a shorthand as sleight as it could be slight, or slighting; fame at its most rapid-fire.

Prince and Princess Matchabelli; Veree Teasdale; Kiki Roberts; Willie Hoppe, "the billiard wizard"; Nina Lee; Doug junior and Doug senior Helen Mack Ernest Schoedsack Ben Bard Skeets Gallagher. A *blessed expense. Alcoholidaying. Swelegant. Newsreel hocus-focus. Arm-in-army.* "Tomorrow will still be Wednesday whether you're a pancake or a hit," Blossom Seely tells the nervous ingénue backstage in *Broadway Thru a Keyhole.* "Fifteen years from now they won't remember you any more than they remember me, no matter how big a success you are." By Andy Warhol, the timeline was down to fifteen minutes, adjusted for inflation, encompassing the one-hit wonder of the three-minute single, the thirty-second commercial spot, the subliminal wink of an eye.

Jolson pitched his syllables to the cadences of the new media as well, one of recording's first consistent hitmakers, though he was always more acoustic than electric. His voice was designed to cut, to reach the far balconies, where his own kind sat. Superb as a singer, so-so as a dancer, his specialty—conveying the sentimental longing of his blackface—was the recitative imploring, on one knee, white-gloved hands clasped to his breast (Mickey Mouse would remember those hands, white on black), shouting out for the gal of his dreams. *My mammy!* His spoken plea was featured on most of his hits, and he willingly took on minstrelsy's mask for its dramatic and comedic exaggerations. When he debuted at the Winter Garden for the Shuberts in 1911, he hid backstage until it was time to go on, rehearsing in natural. Then he put on the burnt cork and wowed them. Minstrelsy was over, a low-class entertainment, or so the Shuberts thought. Jolson gave it a last hurrah, along with the rolling eyes of Eddie Cantor (still reprising the 1925 "Dinah" in the 1944 Hollywood production *Show Business*), and the pre–Hank Williams figurine of Emmett "Lovesick Blues" Miller, last and first, riding the minstrel train caboose.

Winchell and Jolson. They were more alike than one would imagine. Both

Joosh, as Winchell *brissed*, their voices pitched to rise above the *Yidiom* tumult that had deposited them on the streets of New York, projecting so loudly, so insistently, that it was easy to overlook their essentially minor keys. They'd bought a one-way ticket to the New World. "*Good evening, Mr. and Mrs. North and South America and all the ships at sea,*" Walter dot-dashed in his fake Morse code, a flat, wise-guy staccato that echoed Cagney and the Georges Raft and his old friend Jessel, beaming to all within his hemispheric radio beacon. "*Let's go to press!*"

Jolson incarnated the nineteen-twenties, a mixed breed whose role in *The Jazz Singer* offered assimilation amid the onset of the talkies, but at what price? He was bisected between church and state, between family tradition that would have made him a seventh cantor in a continuing lineage, and the lone-eagle flight that was America's symbol, summed up in the twenties by the original solitary bird, Charles Lindbergh. Lindy saw both sides of the decade, soaring high and then, in the midst of the Depression, an Icarus given retribution for his presumption by the kidnapping and subsequent media frenzy over his lost child. A private man turned inside out, he preached isolationism as Europe again broke into uncivil war.

Winchell didn't stick with show business for long. He branched out to the world, and the underworld; a self-proclaimed newsboy, he covered the Lindbergh baby trial, made friends with Roosevelt, and excoriated Hitler in an America that had yet to be convinced that Adolf was such a bad thing. He predicted the gangland slaying of Vincent "Mad Dog" Coll, toured Al Capone's Florida hideaway, accepted the surrender of Louis Lepke. They had as much right to celebrity as someone a press agent was getting paid to promote. Besides, he knew show business was fickle. Jolson may have had a few years' head start on him in vaudeville, but Walter was never able to rise above the deuce, the second act after the opening acrobats or jugglers. He first attracted laughs and attention as a backstage gossip, posting his *Newsense* on the call-boards, taking stints with the *Vaudeville News* as a stringer and ad salesman, and then becoming drama critic and pioneering scandal-seeker on one of the first tabloid papers, the *New York Graphic*. The newspaper reenacted "composographs" of crime scenes, clandestine assignations, and one bearing witness to Valentino dying on the operating table; movie stills.

Winchell adopted the showbiz slangese of Sime Silverman's *Variety*, abbreviating its sound-effect headlines into clipped, pungent sentences separated by three dots, as if punctuation would only slow his breathless gossips and jokes and *non sequiturs*. He made up words, pasted them together, caromed off their hard consonants and soft syllables, dangling and accessorizing and glitzing the news he was anxiously giving with a wink and a leer, as if it hadn't been the same yesterday, or wouldn't be again the day after tomorrow.

By the time he was hired by Hearst's *Daily Mirror* in 1929, positioned to compete with the Tribune syndicate's *Daily News*, he was better known, more feared, reviled, and loved, than most he wrote about. He was an inversion, the tables turned. He was the story. At least he thought so, and he was encouraged by the millions who read his syndication and tuned in to his radio broadcasts to hear gods make the same damn fools out of themselves as mortals, and then some.

He had pizzazz. A lot of nerve. Walter needed his thick skin and hard head to keep up the tap dance and patriotic song routine in some of the jerkwater towns he'd played on the grind circuit, a kid actor fresh from *Gus Edwards' Schooldays*, where his job was to run around and hit the other kids over the head with a rolled-up newspaper. He never lost his class-clown hyperactivity. A nocturnal creature, he couldn't sleep at night, cruising crime scenes after the clubs closed, bedding down chorus girls (*cho-rina!*), drifting past where he grew up in East Harlem and remembering his life when he had had nothing but his own pluck and desperation to rely on. "I'm the man who invented the low blow," he told one of his ghostwriters, Herman Klurfeld.

In 1933, he was riding as high as a newspaperman could headline. He had already appeared at the Palace, right underneath Harry Richman on the bill, his crowning vaudeville moment. On December 4, 1932, he'd gone on the NBC Blue network with a weekly Sunday evening spot sponsored by Jergens Lotion. And Zanuck had just offered him five thousand dollars for his initial "idea" for *Broadway Thru a Keyhole*, with another twenty-five grand to come when the screenplay was accepted. He didn't even have to do the writing.

A Universal short, released in February 1933, catches him at this apogee. *I Know Everybody and Everybody's Racket* guests the Whiteman Orchestra, fresh from a stand at the Hotel Biltmore, featuring Irene Taylor and Jack Fulton, and a few wave-ons from Ruth Etting and Arthur Tracy.

The story, written by fellow *Mirror* columnist Mark Hellinger, concerns a small-town newspaperwoman who comes to the big city in search of hot items. Winchell says he'll show her around, and gives the title as his calling card. After Whiteman's turn, he introduces her to some local gangsters; she goes off with them, and takes a powder with their dough. She's also lifted Walter's watch. The *cullud* doorman tells them she's the notorious Lancaster Sal. They ask how he knows. "Oh," says the doorman, "I know everybody and everybody's racket."

Even Winchell was not above a little minstrelsy.

. . .

A DISCUS of film. You can fit it in your hand. Sail it into the past, a long arc of sixteen millimeters. Boomerang it into the future.

I am going to see Russ move for the first time. Finally. The croon made celluloid, the flesh made motion. Three hundred feet, snared from some small-print collector in the back pages of a film magazine.

My filmmaker friend Stephen has a movie projector. No sound. He backlights it onto a white scrim, deep in the meat district with the Hudson lapping nearby. The silents. I bring along a soundtrack album with the song itself, so we can try and sync it up, a primitive talkies.

The clip cuts in on Russ, on the bandstand, finishing a number. He is not a showy singer. It's the drummer who is whisking his brushes in a wide arc, the violinist to his left turning the sheet music over. He mouths his words from the shoulders, turning his head slightly left and right, saving his best angle for the microphone. Sometimes he leads the band with a goofy smile on his face, looking a bit like John Travolta in *Saturday Night Fever*. Constance can't take her gaze off him; she does have large orbs, and without intending to, gives him a c'mon look. Russ arranges an introduction from her tablemates as they waltz by (he's done this before), and returns to his violin solo with determination, clenching the instrument between chin and chest, heavy on the finger vibrato.

He is casual, causing. When he goes to sit at her table, he borrows a convenient chair, twirls it so it faces the opposite direction, straddles it. He fondles, but doesn't light, his cigarette. There is enough smoky veneer in her eyes. I have no dialogue on my soundtrack. "Oh, you're a singer," I imagine them saying. Neither overplays the playfulness.

He calls her to the bandstand for "I Love You Pizzicato." It is this song that I sync up on compact disc (where it is misnamed "I Love You Prince Pizzicato," though he wears the royal allusion well), from a 1994 compilation on Take Two Records, the sole U.S. digital source for his greatest hits in the nineties, bridging technological breakthroughs on each side of the century. The song cleverly suggests a struggling show-business couple who speak to each other in terms of musical endearment. She plays to the crowd: he harmonizes her. They're both game, and for Russ, it allows him to loosen up to the point of good humor. The band rises section by section. The audience applauds. The track ends. Back to the silents.

He walks her outside, into the tropical night. He leans in toward her. The film stops, cutting them off in a midsentence I can't hear.

RUSS AS CLARK BRIAN IN
BROADWAY THRU A KEYHOLE

RUBY WAS "Irish" Costello's girlfriend when Al met her as a nineteen-year-old tap dancer in Texas Guinan's club. Jolson followed her to George M. Cohan's show *Rise of Rosie O'Reilly*, and courted her by standing up in the audience when she soloed with "Liza" in Ziegfeld's *Show Girl*, singing along. Ziegfeld offered to pay him if he'd duet nightly. From there, he leapfrogged to California, stopping in Chicago where he watched Keeler in *Sidewalks of New York*, and then to Los Angeles and Grauman's, convincing the Warner brothers to keep extending her engagement on the West Coast.

The only thing standing in their way was Costello, who had taken the young Keeler under his protective wing and even bought her a diamond engagement ring. He was so genuinely in love with Ruby that he let her go when he saw her attraction to Jolson. Besides, how could you go up against a mother-lover like Jolson? Irish's own mother would have killed him.

Al wed Ruby on September 21, 1928, in Port Chester, New York. Jolson had been married twice before, though his wives always seemed to stand in the shade of his theatrical ambitions. They would want children; he was still very much a child. He endeared himself to his audiences like a small boy wriggling and insinuating himself onto his mother's lap, wanting attention.

The feelings evoked in his best-loved songs, like George Gershwin's "Swanee" or "Rock-a-bye Your Baby with a Dixie Melody," attest to the virtues of home and hearth, if your home was a plantation and the hearth cooked meals beloved of the old country. Jolson was not a lover; he evoked nostalgia. He wanted to entertain you, win you over, not seduce or sexually suggest. Then he would go out to play, usually pinochle with the boys, or the horses. The stage catches him one foot over the threshold, leaving home. The question in *The Jazz Singer* is whether he'll look back.

In Samuel Raphaelson's stage play of *The Jazz Singer*, George Jessel returns to his faith and the "Kol Nidre," starring as Jakie Rabinowitz who has to choose between synagogue and sin-agog. On Broadway, that was as far as intermarriage could go. (Alternatively, the Yiddish theater row on Second Avenue offered a comforting cul-de-sac.) Jessel had been Winchell's boyhood friend. They'd begun in vaudeville together as two thirds of the Imperial Trio, anglicizing names as they all did. It wasn't surprising when Warner Bros. wanted to film *The Jazz Singer* and change the ending to one more secular. Jessel refused to go along, and they turned to Jolson.

Al had tried the movies a few years back, signing a contract and doing a screen test for D. W. Griffith for a proposed picture called *Mammy's Boy*. He hated the results, pulled out, and then was sued by Griffith for breach of promise. Even the court couldn't blame Jolson (David Wark G. collected only $2,600). Of any performer, he needed sound, and a live audience. He would perform anywhere, anytime, and seemed to come alive under the basking lights of an adoring crowd. He had leaped from success to success since his Shubert days, each new revue with its own instant standard: *Bombo* and "California, Here I Come," *Sinbad* and "Rock-a-bye Your Baby with a Dixie Melody." He owned his own theater on West Fifty-ninth Street. He toured the country, returned to Broadway, and in 1925 opened in *Big Boy*. It met with a deflatingly tepid reception. The soundies came along just in time to lift his career out of the imminent doldrums.

The story of *The Jazz Singer* is as much autobiographical as fanciful; little Jakie gives up a chance to be the fifth cantor in his bloodline and runs away from home to snag his big break in *April Follies*, a Broadway revue with May McAvoy, his *shiksa* sweetie. Opening night is on Yom Kippur, the most solemn day of atonement. Will he be forgiven? Will he be "the first Rabinowitz to fail your God" or disobey the cardinal show business commandment, "The show must go on!"

It's an agonizing choice between "giving up the biggest chance I have in my life, and breaking my mother's heart." We know how important the latter is because when he's offered his White Way salvation while on the road, he thinks *New York, Broadway, Home, Mother!* in ever-increasing inter-title letters.

For such a groundbreaking film, one of the surprising things about *The Jazz Singer* is how little it talks. There are only intermittent bursts of synchronized sound, very much like the Vitaphone short subjects that Warner Bros. was experimenting with in their Brooklyn studios. Jolson himself had made one in 1926, *A Plantation Act*, singing "When the Red Red Robin Comes Bob-Bob-Bobbin' Along" in the tatters of a black hillbilly. He recreates this performance in *The Jazz Singer*, exchanging his straw hat and rags for the garb of a well-creased city slicker, and another song that relies on repetition, "Toot Toot Tootsie," down to the *"wait a minute, wait a minute, you ain't heard nothin' yet!"* He begins with "Dirty Hands, Dirty Feet," a sentimental ballad about a father coming home to his son, a prodigal in reverse, and segues into "Tootsie," with a two-handed whistling solo in the third chorus. He has so much bubbling energy, so much *spritzvasser* effervescence, that he can hardly stay still, exuding an irrepressible sense of bravado.

There is also the celebrated scene where he sings "Blue Skies" at the piano to his mother; a moving rendition of "Kol Nidre" in the synagogue; and the stage finale, in which Al walks a million miles for one of his mammy's smiles in the front row. Each Vitaphone segment required a separate disc of simultaneous recording; beyond the music, the thrill was in the exchange of dialogue. Al steals a kiss from his mother, telling her that if he's successful in the show, he's going to move her up to the Bronx, take her to Coney Island, and buy her a pink dress to go with her brown eyes, and now he's gonna sing it jazzy, like he does on Broadway, syncopating and mugging and slapping at the keyboard. Eugenie Besserer, playing his mother, *kvells* on cue.

When Jakie Rabinowitz, now Jack Robin, comes bobbin' upon Cantor Josef Rosenblatt offering "sacred songs / popular prices" in a theater, he sees their aleph-bet similarities. A long scene in which Jolson pulls on his woolly cap and applies his blackface is a journey in transformation, his hands skilled at the corking, rubbing the black over and into his ears, down his neck. His mother hardly recognizes him when she comes backstage before he goes on in *schvartze*. "He looks like his shadow," she says. In rapprochement, he performs "Kol Nidre" for the congregation while his father (Warner Oland, whose skill at ethnic characters will extend to the detective Charlie Chan) expires within hearing distance, giving him the blessing to transfer his cantorial skills to the church of show business. In jewface, he is "a jazz singer, singing to his god."

Everyone agrees he has "the cry in his voice," like the Solomonic biblical wail of a baby for his mother.

NOW RUBY was a big star. *42nd Street* and *Gold Diggers of 1933* had made Keeler the best-known dancer in Hollywood. She was the one getting the plum roles, the offers for tours, the press attention. Sometimes, when they walked into a nightclub, he could see the *maître d'* nod respectfully to him, and then glow all over when he turned to Ruby. His Rubáiyát. She used to glow like that for him.

He hadn't planned on her prominence. Paul Yawitz, who by this time had taken over the Sunday tattle slot in the *Mirror* with his "New York Uncensored" column, reported on February 12, 1933, that Al was going to produce a picture for Keeler in which she would be his leading "gal." After that, Jolson grandly declared, "no more pictures for Ruby."

Evidently, Busby Berkeley didn't agree.

He didn't have it bad; he was still Jolson. But Al was smarting at the newer singers stealing his limelight. Those *fagellahs*. *Variety* had the nerve to insinuate in its August 18, 1931, issue that Rudy Vallée, "more than anyone else, brought to an end the epoch of raucous, vulgar mammy-shouting that ruined so many pairs of trousers at the knee in the old days." The *old days*? You ain't heard nothin' yet!

Al got his radio show, but he had to put on his glasses to read the scripts; the studio audience thought that funny. It confused him; he didn't know whether to play for the seven hundred ticketholders who had paid a dollar apiece to watch him speak into a microphone, or the vast faceless listenership who weren't able to let him instantly know whether he was being loved or not. He was doing well in the theaters, making twelve grand a week over the 1932 holidays in Chicago and signing up for a mid-February stint at the Paramounts. His "season's greetings" New Year's ad in *Variety* was nothing more than a white-on-black silhouette of outstretched hands, greasepainted mouth, and shirtfront; he hardly needed to autograph it.

Jolson timed his Paramount appearances to create interest for his latest movie, which opened with a gala premiere on February 8 at the Rivoli Theater, introduced by Will H. Hays of the National Board of Review, which might account for Al's neutered nature as the male lead. The occasion was to celebrate five years of talking pictures, and *Hallelujah, I'm a Bum* hoped to make a similar revolutionary impact. The film's gimmick, "rhythmic dialogue," allowing Richard Rodgers and Lorenz Hart to talk-sing conversation in rhyme and regular meter, was meant to be the motion-picture equivalent of operetta.

Al portrayed Bumper, the "bum" mayor of a hobo encampment in Central Park, sidekicked by Harry Langdon, whose job was to look tipsy, and Edgar Connor, whose dimunitive and impish stature enhanced the Pan-like qualities of his blackness. Al kept away from the charcoal, but still needed the foil of minstrel presence. The picture attempted to make light of the hobo jungles that had sprung up in the wake of economic ruin. Its scenes of displaced unemployed happily sleeping under the stars on the Great Lawn failed to provoke hallelujahs from ticketbuyers looking for more opulent escape. They could find that in a Busby Berkeley musical.

POETIC LICENSE, as in licentious.

It was one thing to take Jolson's own life and convert it into *The Jazz Singer* (and later, in the forties, *The Al Jolson Story*, bringing Al's mythos to a whole new generation). But as Ruby's husband, Al couldn't believe what he'd read in Louella Parsons's column about Walter's inspiration for *Broadway Thru a Keyhole*. If Ruby was upset when some columnist blabbed a pack of lies about Al giving her a million dollars to marry him, she'd hit the roof with this one. Al felt betrayed, humiliated, as if Walter had propositioned Ruby. He shouldn't have been surprised. Jolson had gone out of his way to buddy up to Walter, even forcing the Shuberts—who had banned Winchell from their productions—to let him attend the premiere of *Wonderbar* on Broadway. Walter gave it a bad review.

"I'm glad I socked him," Jolson said. "Winchell threw mud at my wife and me."

Walter was unflappable. "My story is about an actor, a chorus girl, and a Broadwayite who isn't a sissy. Mr. Jolson assumed that the story was about him, and that it is nasty. It isn't. It's a story about a murdered gangster and a woman now happily married to another man." As for the characterizations, "I play the part of a villain in my daily life, so I might as well cash in on it."

Broadway Thru a Keyhole ("Swinging down the straight-and-narrow into the crooked and Broad-way!" the ad copy winchelled) opened at midnight on November 1, 1933, at the Rivoli Theater at Forty-ninth Street along Walter's beloved Baloney Boulevard. The film's real hero was the intercourse (intersexion?) of Broadway and Seventh Avenue. "That little gulch out there," Paul Kelly muses as he taxis through the crossroads with his chorine in tow, "has got more personality, more character, more life, than any other spot in the world." A "chorus girl matinee" was promised at 3:00 A.M.: "They'll all be there!" The Winchell name was positioned possessively over the title, despite his distanced input. His only appearance in the movie was by association, a voice blaring over the loudspeakers of a *"Mirror-Journal"* truck speeding through the streets, or spieling over the radio.

Texas Guinan, playing herself as club hostess "Tex Kaley," complained that she hardly got any screen time either. Even Times Square got short shrift; a good portion of the movie took place in Miami, where Russ Columbo is a singer awaiting the arrival of his *inamorata*, and where his songs are waiting to win her heart.

The lead actress, Constance Cummings, had to cut short her European honeymoon to start work on *Broadway* when the production schedule was moved up, sailing back to America on the *Berengaria*. Twentieth Century wanted to get the picture into production before the public had a chance to forget the Jolson-Winchell punch-up. Only twenty-three, she came to Hollywood after understudying the juvenile lead in a Broadway play, *June Moon*. Her first role was opposite Walter Huston in *The Criminal Code*, and she would have a long career, still acting in 1996. "I never played any rubbish in my life," she told *People* magazine in 1979, the same year she won a Tony award for *Wings*, and ascribed this to a well-balanced marital arrangement where she spent six months of the year in England being Benn Levy's wife and the rest of the year in Hollywood pursuing her career. With reddish brown hair and deep blue eyes, she always wore strong colors, avoided "chiffon," and liked being described as "feisty." Once when her car was stolen in front of her, she jumped on the fender and rode along till the thief bolted.

Winchell is the keyhole's key, a Peeping Tom unlocking a vicarious realm which has already been romanticized into type: the good-hearted gangster, the vivacious and slightly naïve chorine, the cupid-struck crooner. It's a world of perpetual floor shows, cardsharps and horseplayers, and snappy dialogue, all spoken in a New *Yawk* accent. Winchell's nightcrawling buddy Damon Runyon further fictionalized the milieu, and was rewarded with *Guys and Dolls*, a Broadway play about his imagined Main Stem. He even had a columnist called Waldo Winchester populating Times Square. Winchell returned the favor by letting Runyon drink himself under Table 50.

Even if his snap-brim fedora doesn't figure in the film, his presence pervades it. It's like his Monday column, which delivers the hard gossip; the remainder of the weekly schedule ("The Column," he called it, chained to its tapeworm need to be nourished) shoveled in with collections of jokes and poems, musings, and fillers. He was almost like Leopold Bloom in his ramblings, as site-specific as Joyce's Dublin. Winchell had his rhythm, and whether tapping it out on a telegraph key, or shouting it into a microphone, or letting his typewriter click and clack, he put you in his world, motoring through late-night Manhattan, police radio band on to catch a crime in progress. *Broadway* begins when a black roadster shoots out of the darkness and rams a truck carrying chickens to the slaughterhouse, Winchell's imagination on the move. We're inside the office of Empire Poultry, a couple of racketeers talking protection: "The Koshers ain't gonna eat chickens that get killed in accidents . . . there's over a million Jews in this city, and if you lose their trade you're out of business." "Frank Rocci," played by a resolutely intense Paul Kelly, negotiates a half-million dollars a year for the Italians. The immigrants share and share alike.

New York crams its neighborhoods and ghettos so close together that their worlds can't stay apart for long. Soon they're "Doin' the Uptown Low Down," as Frances Williams puts it when the floor show begins at Tex's Club Kaley, the first of four Mack Gordon (music) and Harry Revel (lyrics) compositions to grace *Broadway Thru a Keyhole*, much as the pair scored Ziegfeld's *Follies of 1931*. Frances is her own uptown lowdown, dressed in a man's tailed tuxedo, tap-dancing (itself a crossover art, and one lost with the advent of drum machines), rhyming *Cinderella* with *high yaller*. She mixes it up with a fleet of chorines, a stag line in male drag.

It's a good time in Tex's club, and Tex is ever herself, a rawboned cowgirl named Mary Louise from Waco who found her Broadway reward as a *give that little girl a great big hand* hostess. Her character was a red-hot mama like Sophie Tucker, as much house mother as ill-repute madam, and she bordello'd more than a passing resemblance to Mae West, though the influence was probably mutual. Welcoming her *table d'hôte* "suckers," she knew men, and their weaknesses, and how to enjoy the bottoms-up of life's party. "I never heard of anyone dying from platinum poisoning," she tells Constance, who is the "ga-ga type." Her Chorus Girl, "Joan Whelen," is about to be plucked from the back line and exposed to the charms of "Frank Rocci." But her prurience has made our Gangster see the light. Texas's advice belongs to another era, when diamond baubles could be found secreted around backstage roses, virtue thus rewarded. The twenties are outmoded, the speakeasy and stock market, both with their champagne tinge of free-flowing wealth, sex, inebriation: gone. Texas Guinan would not live to see Repeal Night.

She exudes butter-and-egg charm for her swan song in *Broadway Thru a Keyhole*, though there are a few gratuitous barbs about face-lifts and broadening hips directed her way. It was Guinan's matronage that first secured

Winchell's position in Broadway society, and he returns the favor, at least until the plot moves to Miami. Her club puts on a good production, with an elaborate swirl from Constance and Eddie Foy, Jr., around "When You Were a Girl on a Scooter (and I Was a Boy on a Bike)," the camera mimicking Berkeley with its overhead shots and childhood props; Abe Lyman's orchestra; and an amusing dance routine by the Mutt-and-Jeff pair, Barto and Evans. Gregory Ratoff plays Max Mefoofsky, the show's heavily accented director, a role he will bring back for Zanuck in 1950 as Max Fabian, the impresario in *All About Eve*. He would also capably direct for Twentieth Century–Fox; a self-prophetic typecasting.

RUSS COLUMBO misses the first half of the film, waiting for a plane to carry Joan from Newark Municipal Airport to the ballroom of the "Rooney"-Plaza Hotel in Miami, where he fronts the orchestra as "Clark Brian." His is a name that goes both ways, linking the approaching love triangle. It is not only his relationship with her that concerns us, but the developing involvement of Clark with Frank, one of whom will have to make a supreme sacrifice to the other.

When we first encounter Russ, he is singing "You're My Past, Present, and Future." It is the set seen in the movie clip, palm fronds waving outside, white dinner jackets and a surrounding orchestra.

The Gangster has arranged for the Chorus Girl to become the Star of the show by buying Tex's nightclub. To show his affection, Frank hires Pierre, a pithy interior decorator, to decide on drapery colors for his apartment, a feminizing touch that complements Rocci's promises to change his ways for her. "Someday I'm gonna break loose from this racket." That was what Jolson was always promising his wives; that he'd spend more time at home. Winchell, too, for that matter. Sometimes they—wives and husbands—even believed it.

Is it love or gratitude? Rocci's attempt at togetherness is shattered by a spray of machine-gun bullets. When he looks at the mirror in which he'd envisioned them as a couple as he began his proposal, there are bullet holes shattering their reflections. Obviously, he's not ready to retire. He sends her out of town, to Miami, where she is smitten by the in-house crooner.

Russ is introduced by Winchell over the radio; "How's your New York and mine?" replies Russ as he assumes the bandstand. He hopes his song will "fall on willing ears," and since "You're My Past, Present, and Future" implies infinite inevitability, so it does. *This is even better than someone changing their life for you*, Joan must be thinking. *This is someone being you.*

She tries to back off when he invites her to join him on "I Love You Pizzi-cato." They're both nervous in the delight of duet. "I hope we all finish at the same time," he jokes. Come together, and make that *andante*.

He only sings these two songs in the movie, finishing out the film as a full-fledged *dramatis personae*. His performance is "fidgety," according to Kate Cameron of the *Daily News* who nonetheless gives the film three stars. His portrayed character doesn't help, a fearful hypochrondiac whose deep secret is he's "a coward." Far from putting off Joan, it intrigues her. "I hate men that talk big and ache with strength," she tells Russ as he lies on the beach with her, swathed in towels to protect him from the sun (a true creature of the night). She likes his vulnerability. It makes her want to shelter and care for him, much as Rocci wants to protect her.

Russ follows her to New York. "What's that crooner doing in there?" asks Frank when they all meet backstage in her dressing room after she's performed her version of "You're My Past, Present, and Future." He wants her to step outside so he and Clark can settle this, male to male, dual to duel. "I've heard you were a square-dealer," Russ begins in a long soliloquy, an extended apologia for love's transformation. "I love her more than my own life, and whatever happens to me doesn't matter if I can't have her." If *Broadway Thru a Keyhole* were a true musical, this would be a perfect curtain-raiser to a Clark and Frank patterned routine. *"You must not confuse gratitude with love. . . . Whether I live for her, or die for her. . . ."* Russ talk-sings, while the gangster skips a beat. *"Okay, just be good to her."*

In truth, they've both passed their trials by fire and proved their courage (and in Columbo's case, his nascent acting ability). Frank does truly change his life for her, eschewing violence. Clark discovers he is willing to risk the safety net of fear; he will give his life for hers. Constance can't lose. But on her wedding day, she is kidnapped by rival gangsters, and blood must be spilled to seal the bargain. Russ is roughed up, and Frank takes a bullet. *Flash!* Winchell reports over the radio that vengeance has been exacted on Rocci's rival.

Frank lies in his hospital bed. He asks for the lights to be turned out in his room, the better to look out the window at Times Square, its dazzle of beckoning neon, luring and alluring. *Flash! Flash!*

Russ gets the girl.

LOMBARD

She rotates the cap off the bottle, pours a splash into a tall glass, adds the ice, the lime. Swirls it around. She resists the urge to stick his finger in and stir.

It's a small party, by Hollywood standards. Twenty or thirty friends of the family; some all too recognizable.

Repeal Night in California is a surprisingly subdued affair. The Vendome shuts down at eleven on December 5, 1933. Though it's crowded along Hollywood Boulevard, sightseers thronging to catch a glimpse of the stars legally wining are disappointed with the turnout. Gus Arnheim draws only twenty couples to the Beverly Wilshire; the Ambassador and Roosevelt are similarly light. At the Colony, Nils Asther sits solo at the bar all evening, celebrating his divorce from Vivian Duncan, whoever they are. There is the curious sense that nothing has really changed.

It was California's fault. As the end of Prohibition neared, Utah checkmating the Twenty-first Amendment repeal of the Eighteenth Amendment, restaurants and hotels continued to offer elaborate under-the-table cocktail menus. But California law now stipulated hard liquor could only be consumed at a private club or private home; a nightspot's customers could only partially quench their thirst. All over town, stars were frantically constructing bars within their mansions.

Joan Crawford wood-paneled a wing of her house and added a tap system. Clark Gable hid his bar within a radio. Bing Crosby papered his walls with his sheet-music covers. Mary Pickford gave a bar to Douglas Fairbanks shortly before their separation.

In her new home, Carole Lombard had her watering hole done in matched Scotch plaid all the way down to the piano. It was Billy Haines's doing. A collegial actor turned interior decorator turned gossip confidant, he'd told her that deep red and green were festive colors, and he offset them with a zinc circular bar and seat covers of aquamarine. It sounded more unsettling than it looked, and with the lights turned down, the feeling was woody and masculine. Sitting on the couch made you want to smoke a pipe.

Yet it was also an extremely feminine house, with a velvet-and-damask drawing room in six shades of blue and furnished in Empire style (not State Building), accessorized in Wedgwood and Hepplewhite. It was meant for parties, and revelry, and Carole delighted in hostessing outlandish events. One time she rented a Venice Beach amusement pier, inviting not only the studio's stars, but the grips and script girls and riggers. She held themed soirées where you dressed as a barnyard hillbilly, or a Russian, or came to a re-created hospital, complete with bedpans for drinking glasses. Even when she was done with hostessing, later in the thirties, she brought a festive air wherever she went.

Tonight's occasion was more low-key, the drinking not enhanced by illegality. It was just . . . drinking. A fine Scotch, to be savored, not wasted on anything so plebeian as a drunk.

Carole had learned about single malt whiskeys from William Powell, who was Hollywood's idea of a most eligible bachelor when they were teamed in 1931's *Man of the World*. Powell, at that time best known as detective Philo Vance in the silent film series, lived up to the title, usually in a threesome with Richard Barthelmess and Ronald Colman, cutting a swath through Hollywood's upper crust. He insisted on the immaculate, endlessly fussing about the smallest detail of haberdashery, both on- and off-camera; but he was enough of a rake to pull it off, enhanced by a dry and resilient wit.

She had been in the movies for five years, if you didn't count a child's unbilled appearance in the 1921 *A Perfect Crime*, beginning as a Fox player in Westerns in 1925 starring Buck Jones. She had graduated to the Howard Hawks–directed *The Road to Glory* at the end of that year when the brakes failed on the car ahead of the Bugatti automobile in which she was a passenger. The car in front slid backward, shattering her windshield and severely slicing Carole's face along the left cheekbone. For an actress who was regarded by Fox as a "pretty face," the result could have ended her career before it had a chance to start.

She had to endure having her face stitched together by a plastic surgeon without anesthesia, lying immobile for a week and a half. Fox dropped her

CAROLE AND RUSS

even before they could see how the recovery went. Though the wound eventually healed with very little trace of scar, and that could be disguised by sympathetic lighting and makeup, it did cause Carole to reappraise herself at the critical age of eighteen. She resolved not to be as superficial as she might have been; to develop other elements besides her physical attractions. She would emphasize her positive energy, love of life, and unbridled spirit, and given the random, unexpected nature of the accident, to become fatalistic about the unforeseen, the plot twist that could change your life. Her mother believed in the cast die of numerology, the future read in mathematics.

Now "damaged goods" in the eyes of the major studios, Carole went to work for Mack Sennett, then coming to the end of his line as the king of silent comedy. He placed her in his cast of Bathing Beauties as the Cute One. Her apprenticeship with Sennett would go far in developing her sense of comedic timing, putting over a character whose pace was slightly accelerated, breathless, ever ready for a pie in the face, an anything-goes sportsmanship that would serve her in good stead as a comedienne, her forte.

She was a wisecracker. A firecracker; could cut and claw. If you wanted to get close to her, you wouldn't mind a few cuts and scrapes. Actually, it made things interesting, a tomboy who was a true girl.

Her advance through the studio system, first with Sennett, and then as a Pathé featured player on her way to Paramount, was born more of dogged re-silience than instant recognition. She was seldom challenged in her early ve-hicles, most of which required her only to show off her wardrobe and a winning smile. A random pick from the five films she worked on in 1929, *The Racketeer,* is typical. Pathé starred her with Robert Armstrong and a pre-gossip Hedda Hopper. As a society girl who has left her millionaire husband to take up with a musician, and then is taken under the wing of Armstrong's good-hearted gangster ("I've met many women at card tables," he tells her when he catches her cheating, "but never any like you"), her eyelashes look as if they weigh a pound apiece. She is visually stunning in a lounging robe with butterfly sleeves, or sprayed with orchids and ruffles, but the complexi-ties of her personality can only be glimpsed in a short scene in which she rides a horse and then runs; the young Carol (she had yet to add the "*e*") re-veals her coltish, athletic side. The movie was released in the midst of the col-lapsing stock market.

As a featured player, she slid comfortably into Paramount's movie-making factory (the company would release sixty-four features in 1930), churning out films and having her affairs; she had a healthy regard for making love. She was amorous with George Raft and publishing magnate Horace Liveright. One of her earliest assignations was with Howard Hughes, whose power was still such in 1976 that Lombard biographer Larry Swindell couldn't mention his name for fear of a libel suit; or was he just being coy?

That wasn't Carole. She laid it on the line. She could play the retiring type, but she was demanding of her men. De man.

Dat would be Powell. She was young enough to have swooned at the screen images of Colman and Barthelmess. William, nearly seventeen years her senior, was old enough to be the father (well, not quite) that she'd left be-hind in Fort Wayne. He thought he'd met his match. She was so excited to be playing opposite him in *Man of the World* that she forgot to act. He was all actor. On June 26, 1931 (the month Russ left for New York), after making a second movie together, *Ladies' Man,* they wed, announcing Carole's en-trance into Hollywood high society. Whether she could stay aloft in the social stratosphere was yet to be proved, just like her status in the movies.

The marriage to Powell lasted twenty-eight months. When Sonia Lee cor-nered her for *Motion Picture Story* in the spring of 1934, Carole ascribed their split to the artistic rigors of their profession, explaining that "a motion picture actress dares not permit herself to settle into a groove. She must be emotionally pliable." Marriage was outmoded, especially when it stood in the passway of a new ideal, the Career. Yet she admitted that "My present philosophy that marriage as it stands is all wrong for picture players may be delusion ... no woman can determine her emotions. ... Tomorrow someone may come along who will make her embrace [marriage] as with delight and with humility; embrace even its slavery and its difficulties, its destined monotony and its dangerous influences on an actress." Danger Russ.

As it turned out, 1934 would prove the breakthrough year for Carole Lombard. Though she lost Powell, she acquired his agent, Myron Selznick. He had taken over Carole's representation in 1931, renegotiating her deal with Paramount even as he moved William to Columbia, where Powell would have to wait for the late thirties and the *Thin Man* series to give him another aristocratic detective persona. Though the company was spiraling into financial difficulty, Paramount always stopped short of dropping her, and she did well on loan-outs to other studios, such as the 1932 *Virtue*, her cup-of-sugar to Columbia, where she met screenwriter Riskin. Carole, however, was always worried about impermanence. *Twentieth Century* marked more than thirty-five film appearances, not counting the fourteen shorts she made for Sennett, and she was still better known for her coiffures and glamorous fashions than her acting skills.

The Howard Hawks–directed comedy began shooting immediately after *We're Not Dressing*. The Crosby vehicle, with Carole's haughty heiress taken down a romantic notch after being shipwrecked on a Pacific isle, didn't ask more from her than to be dazzled by Bing's marooned croon. The difference between Crosby's casuality and John Barrymore's intensity was striking. The Great Profile hardly remembered screen-testing with her when she was with Fox (after a few preliminary passes that the seventeen-year-old Carole nimbly parried, he settled for kissing her in front of the cameras, though she was judged too young at the time to play romantically against him). Now she was older, wiser, and finally getting to complete a movie with Hawks. Barrymore and Carole were at improbably equal elevations on the Hollywood slopes, he on the dissolute downward tumble (usually recognized when a star player's billing topples under the film title, though he still precariously retained above-credit in *Twentieth Century*); she on the up-and-up, holding her own in the midst of an avalanche of failed dreams and disappointed would-be actors and actresses trying and failing to make the movie grade.

Ben Hecht and Charles MacArthur had adapted the script from *Napoleon of Broadway*, Charles Bruce Milholland's hit play. They wrote with Barrymore as a model; and when the comedic elements moved toward farce, Barrymore caricaturing himself, Carole remembered her Mack Sennett training and kept raising him, exchanging bons mots as if they were in a high-stakes poker game. The witty screenplay gave them each a good hand, and it was a frenetic toss-up to see who would get to the finish lines of the dialogue first.

Barrymore is disheveled, seedily elegant, shot through with a sense of his own greatness, both in character—an inspired director who can play all the parts, including a camel and Magdalene 'neath the Cross—and out. His performance has a confidence and passion that make him his own best subject. He jabs his lingerie-salesgirl discovery with a pin to find her inner scream, a symbol that returns to haunt her when she opens a keepsake case to see the pin and remembers her deflowering. He renames her "Lily Garland," and she follows the chalk lines Barrymore's "Oscar Jaffe" makes on the stage to find her own "passion, fire, everything! . . . I came to pay my respects to a great actress," he tells her after her opening-night triumph.

Carole is unleashed by his free-associating. He's like a Robin Williams filtered through Shakespeare, she a shrew untamed. Unhinged; the Un world. She gets to stamp her feet, shriek, kick her heels, say "phooey" with a flutter of her lips, all while dressed to the nines.

The layers are manifold. "We don't know anything about love unless it's written or rehearsed . . . we're only real between curtains," says Carole the actress as Lily the actress. Barrymore takes it more personally: "The sorrows of life are the joys of art." His career has turned baroque, soon to become rococo.

One of the most striking things about *Twentieth Century* is how much it resembles silent film, the over-the-top mugging and face-pulling, the melo-comic slapstick. Barrymore and Lombard are frenetic, histrionic, acting acting. Their madness is catching.

Twentieth Century was a highlight of 1934, along with another movie that helped establish the burgeoning concept of screwball comedy. An on-the-rise Clark Gable starred with Claudette Colbert in *It Happened One Night*, for which each won the statuette for Best Actor and Best Actress at that year's Academy Awards.

THEY CLINKED their glasses. *To you.*

She liked him a lot. She couldn't wait for the party to be over so she could invite him to help her clean up after the night, to step inside her bedroom with the windows draped in black lace, tied back with pale caucasian-colored satin bows, like a dressing gown asking to be undone.

The dress she was wearing tonight, fashioned by Lombard's favorite filmland designer, Travis Banton, was hardly more than a peignoir. Plunging backless, it revealed her shoulders and shapely arms. Though she was only five foot two, she looked longer, leaner.

She called him Ruggy for fun. And he was. She liked having him around. He was serious when he was with her, and that made her reflect his affection, because she wanted something that was more than an act, or the act. He had a crush on her, and she teased him about it, and that only got him in closer, and them warmer, and then he would wrap his arms around her slim contours and modulate her frequency until they vibrated together in a single wave. He would often hum.

He concentrated on her when they made love. Sometimes she found it disconcerting, when she wanted to go off her into own interior realms; but she appreciated the attention. It was involving. As an actress she'd always followed the lead of the actor she was paired with. It was how she'd fallen in love with Powell, and risen to Barrymore's slightly mad delirium. It was what the script called for.

Now she had a love scene to play. She didn't like a closed set. Russ made her feel as if they were alone, together.

She waved good-bye to the last stragglers, off to their cars and drivers, turning east on Hollywood Boulevard if they were heading downtown, west if they were venturing farther up into the Beverly hills.

She closed the door, leaned back against it. Slowly settling herself. Slowly opening her eyes to see Russ across the room. There was a fireplace; the blues of the room blended toward a dappled gray as she extinguished an electric light here, a candle there, until dusk had fallen over the remains of the party.

The fire flickered over him, made his skin seem in motion on his body. His eyes ducked in and out of shadow, watching her.

She could hear him creep up behind her as she leaned to right a glass.

"I think you need some help," he said, touching her on the flank.

"Kiss my ass," she told him good-naturedly, over her shoulder. He liked it when she talked dirty, and it was one of her favorite expressions.

Slowly he bent her over and slid his mouth down her bare spine.

DELL

Dorothy Dell arrived in Hollywood in November 1933.

She'd had a hard time of it those last months in New York. Louis Sobol saw her one after-hours night at the Ha-Ha Club, overweight and looking "slightly shopworn." Part of it was due to her injury the previous year. She had been riding through Central Park in a swain's car when a taxicab rammed them, breaking her wrist, her arm, her ankle. Just back from the road tour of the Follies, where she understudied Ruth Etting, Dorothy had been scheduled to go into Ziegfeld's *Show Boat*. The ship cast off from the Mississippi docks without her, leaving her as stranded as if she'd been back in New Orleans.

She felt robbed, dejected. She was able to get a song-and-dance act together for a supper club on West Forty-eighth, the Monte Carlo, but working in a restaurant was no good for her figure. And she was beginning to realize that she wasn't about to fill the void that Russ had left in her life so easily.

So Dorothy joined the great migration west, mother and sister in tow.

CAROLE COULDN'T say she was happy when she heard Dorothy Dell had joined Paramount's roster of New Faces, along with Elizabeth Young, Helen Mack, Evelyn Venable, Frances Drake, and Ida Lupino.

Sally Blane was one thing. She'd known Sally forever. Russ might take her to premieres, as he did last October when *The Bowery* had its debut at the Grauman, but it was obvious Blane's schoolgirl crush remained unrequited. Russ teased her, and if nothing else, Sally liked him as a friend, happy to spend time with him, entertaining possibilities that were indulgent and pleasant reveries, at least until Carole had come along. And Hannah. . . . Carole felt that anyone who would hook up with that big Manassas galoot didn't understand the subtler things in life.

No, the one who hooked Columbo was her. They were an item: "Carole Lombard saw *The Drunkard* the other night with Russ Columbo," revealed the *Herald-Examiner*, placing them in the audience of the long-running play at the Theatre Mart on North Juanita. Or "Jack LaRue and his 'heart' have gone Spanish, and are regular visitors with Carole Lombard and Russ Columbo at La Golondrina on Olvera Street." Sometimes they even were where they were said to be.

She'd heard about Dorothy, though not from Russ, how they'd broken up, and her blond youth. She was twenty to Carole's twenty-five, and in Hollywood, that made a difference. She noticed Russ had gotten flush-faced when she brought up Dorothy's name. In fact, Carole herself reddened when Paramount suggested, after they couldn't borrow Mae Clarke from MGM, that Dorothy replace her in *Wharf Angel*, the picture she had been scheduled to do for Paramount before Harry Cohn requested her for *Twentieth Century* at Columbia. It worked to Lombard's advantage. Blondes always looked good in red, as Betty Grable would prove in the next generation of actresses, type O legs and lips decorating B-52 fuselages and the hulls of World War II warships.

Carole wasn't sure she liked the idea that an actress newly on the lot could so easily be thought to replace her. Despite the high hopes that *Twentieth Century* would make her a major star, she knew that film studios were attuned to the bottom line, and it sometimes didn't matter whose bottom they were pinching. Especially Adolph Zukor.

ADOLPH PUT his arm around the blonde, in the same way that he was reasserting his control over Paramount.

It was his company. Stop, period. He was back taking command. He had begun Famous Players with four reels of imported Sarah Bernhardt as Queen Elizabeth in 1912, and then nurtured his own acting royalty with Mary Pickford. The foremost of the early silent filmmakers, he partnered in 1916 with Jesse Lasky, who built Hollywood's first studio, and they became, literally, Paramount. He was not about to see his city-state go under. They'd weathered the end of the silents; the Depression wasn't about to beat them either.

The company was still in deep difficulties, struggling to support not only its filmed product, but an empire of distribution and live venues, such as the flagship theaters in New York and Los Angeles. It was hard getting people to fill those seats when they could hardly fill their cupboards. The red ink had already claimed Jesse Lasky, and now Emanuel Cohen, consolidating and closing many theaters and even the New York studio, was having trouble meeting the loans due, the short-term interest. He had been appointed head of production from Paramount's newsreel department, and the news wasn't good. The picture division was in the hole to the tune of six million dollars, the theater wing had twice that much shortfall, and cost cutting was the rule.

The time wasn't right yet. Another year, maybe. Cohen had too many projects in the offing to pull his plug, but Adolph knew. He could feel it in his bones. He had come up in the fur trade; Hollywood, with its *ganefs* and connivers and chiselers, was nothing like dealing in animal skins. When they cut the fur off your body here, you were still alive. Only your career was dead.

In the meantime, let Manny take the heat. Adolph had the patience of a trapper. In the meaning of time, there were always starlets.

Seated in front of him are Toby Wing, Charlotte Henry, Gail Patrick, Ida Lupino. Standing are Gwenllian Gill, Barbara Fritchie, Dorothy Dell, Evelyn Venable, Elizabeth Young, Clara Lou Sheridan, and Grace Bradley.

Dorothy is wearing a frilly white blouse with ruffles. *Movie Classic* wrongly notes that the ivory blonde has been picked to star with Preston Foster in *The Man Who Broke His Heart*.

As the camera's bulb flashes, Adolph pulls her in closer, imagining her animal skin.

DOROTHY FEELS his arm tightening around her. She knows it's the same arm that hugged Mary Pickford at this stage of her career, and Clara Bow, and Gloria Swanson. Them all. And now her.

She was making friends out in California. The studio kept her on the go, and she felt as at home here as she had in Ziegfeld's organization. There was a sense of family, the pride of belonging: being a Follies girl or a Paramount ingénue seemed to suit her. And she still hadn't turned twenty-one.

After the Monte Carlo, where the main attractions were its table-to-table phones and a bill with fading film star James Hall, Dorothy had gone back to New Orleans for a couple of months to play the Suburban Gardens. It wasn't Times Square, but it gave her an opportunity to regain her confidence. Rather than returning to New York, she decided to try the movies, first screen-testing for MGM. Coming to California was the best thing she could've done. She'd immediately parlayed a part in a short, *Passing the Buck*, to interest Paramount in adding her to their roster.

At first they thought to cast her as a hootchy-kootchy dancer with Jack LaRue in *Good Dame*, but when Lombard dropped out of a movie that was first titled *The Man Who Broke His Heart*, and later *Down Home*, they moved Dorothy to star opposite Victor McLaglen. The focus of the movie even shifted to her. She was the *Wharf Angel*.

They started filming right after the New Year holidays in 1934, a tale of San Francisco docks-on-the-bay with Dorothy as Toy, the saloon girl who is pursued by sailor McLaglen and an on-the-lam Preston Foster. Directed by William Cameron Menzies, Dorothy felt confident enough on the set to pull a mock catfight with Grace Bradley, whom she knew from Broadway. Its thespian hair-pulling even fooled the crew, and made them respect her acting skills even more.

The film made little impact, but Dorothy had proved she could hold her own as a leading lady. Paramount was aware it needed female stars, especially in the niche once occupied by Miriam Hopkins. Even before *Wharf Angel* was released, the studio began filming her in a vehicle centered on their latest moppet, the precocious child star Shirley Temple, who seemed as self-possessed as any adult performer. She reminded hard-times America of the innocent hope and boundless wonder that children bring into the world. *Little Miss Marker* was the breakthrough picture for them both.

The Damon Runyon story is full of colorful underworldly types whose cards are about to be undercut by the opposite sex. Runyon's present-tense prose adapted easily to the movies, though Dorothy's character was not in the original "Little Miss Marker," which describes Shirley-as-Marky perfectly: "big blue eyes and fat pink cheeks, and a lot of yellow curls . . . fat little legs and a large smile." He leaves out the dimples. As practically the only women in the all-male world of poker players and cardsharps and bookies, Dorothy and Shirley have only to win at Hearts. A kid's game.

Shirley is an expert cajoler. Skipping over the mommy-mommy-look-at-me school of performance art, her acting has depth and resonance, role-playing that is not only adorable, but shows she means business. You can't say no to her cuteness. She's a tough cookie, and likes to get her way. By the end of the 1930s she will be the highest-paid actress in the country.

Dorothy's romantic interest in Adolphe Menjou, playing a bookie named Sorrowful Jones who is progressively softened by the willful winsomeness of Temple, is piqued more by his possibilities as a dad than as a lover. As Bangles Carson, Dorothy starts out as a "dame" who sings for her supper. She's

DOROTHY AND SHIRLEY TEMPLE

Big Steve's girl, a no-nonsense mama who reminds of Sophie Tucker and has some of the swing of her Louisiana cousins, the Boswells. When she sits on a piano for the drawled "I'm a Black Sheep Who's Blue," her silhouette seems more svelte than her. "She's a chunky little filly," says one of the horseplayers about Shirley when he picks her up; Dorothy might be her mare.

It's a fairy tale seen through Shirley's eyes, her version of Camelot with Dorothy as Guinevere, Menjou as King Arthur, and the Yeggs of the Round Table. She's the orphaned "Princess," a familiar tale of royal adoption, and in her fantasy, Dorothy and Adolphe stay together for the sake of the child. Her surrogate mom and dad betoken chivalric love. "Are you going sappy on us?"

They take to each other, sitting at a piano together to sing "Laugh You Son of a Gun" as America follows their bouncing ball. Shirley finds her mother, and Dorothy unlocks the mother in herself. Halfway through the movie, Dorothy is called to Shirley's bedside to sing her to sleep. As she southern-lilts a "Low Down Lullabye," both their eyes close, heads touching, dreaming: the before and after of woman.

. . .

PARAMOUNT ENCOURAGED her to get out and around, to enter the Holly-wood see-be-scene. To emphasize her Dixie roots, she held the first California "coon hunt" in early 1934 in a swamp near the Los Angeles harbor picturesquely referred to as Nigger Slough, complete with hounds, imported "coons from Al-abam'," and guests like Charlie Ruggles and Barbara Ritchie. The dogs snuffled their way through the marshy underbrush, chased by the assembled participants and Joshua, their Negro "lantern bearer." Dorothy led the charge, emitting blasts on the hunting horn she wore low-slung around her waist. They finally treed the animal on a nearby poultry farm, to the displeasure of the farmer. Also present was one Jay Henry, another aspiring actor from New York who, accord-ing to *New Movie*, had given her a bloodstone ring. Dorothy had to laugh when she heard that. The studios were always trying to couple you up.

So was her mother. She suspected Lilly was guilty of meddling in her af-fair with Russ. Everybody had meddled. Her manager, Martin Starr. Mr. Ziegfeld. Now Lilly was on her to go out with that doctor who was in all the papers, a witness in the Pasadena dentist murder mystery. He had been treat-ing her mother for a touch of pneumonia. He was nice enough, Dorothy thought, even dashing in his bedside manner. But she knew Ma hadn't come out here to marry her off.

She tried not to think about Russ. "I loved him but I guess he didn't love me enough," she told a reporter. It didn't help that she often passed Carole Lombard on the Paramount lot, knowing that she had Russ wrapped around her finger like a lovesick cur. Carole was friendly, always going out of her way to charm and disarm, but Dorothy could sense her guarded measuring be-hind the smile and the just-girls jokes.

Really, she didn't have time to worry about it. Nearing the end of May, she was almost done filming her third movie, *Shoot the Works*, another musical comedy. Directed by Wesley Ruggles, she was the dancer Lily Raquel (her mother was pleased with that, and told her so); her co-star was Jack Oakie. The movie also featured Lew Cody, and comic bandleader (and Winchell nemesis) Ben Bernie, making his picture debut.

Poolside in the Hollywood sun, Melville Shaver is giving a party for "Miss Dell" and other of Paramount's "younger players." Dorothy's not wearing a swimsuit. She curls her feet under her, dressed in a dark puffy-sleeved dress and a hat to match, in a fivesome with Phyllis Laughton (who resembles very much her father, Charles), Howard Wilson, Clara Lou Sheridan, and Gail Patrick in a rakishly tied bathrobe.

They play musical chairs, stopping only to be photographed. Dorothy leans against Phyllis and Alberta Vaughn. Alberta gets up and moves out of the frame, Phyllis goes back to mingling, making room for the host and Katherine DeMille. Dorothy keeps her shoes on. Her white handbag lies on the table next to her. She'll have to go soon.

The last shots are taken from the side. The three look at another photographer. It's a photograph of a photograph being taken, the snapshot capturing the procedure of portraiture, the subject's awareness taken by surprise.

Taken: the angle, the focus, the shutter speed. Release.

The light.

FAY AND FAYE

Rudy can't believe what he's hearing. The little *bitch*. That *hoo*-er. How could she?

It's Fay's voice, all right. "I just got out of the shower," she whispers in a low clandestine voice. "In fact, I am sitting here without any clothes on."

A male answers. "That must be a lovely sight."

It's not Vallée's voice. Rudy stares incredulously at the Dictograph. It's all he can do not to snatch the offending platter off the spindle and fling it against the wall.

He puts another aluminum disc from the pile onto the player. It's dated March 31, 1933. He had been tapping her phone all month, and this was the payoff.

The male voice comes on again. "You are speaking rather low."

"No," Fay murmurs huskily. "No, there is no one here at all. I am all by my-self in bed."

"That's swell," says the man, whose name is Gary Leon. "Hug the pillow for me, dear."

Rudy can imagine her slithering between silken sheets, her black satin nightgown sliding up her thighs, the wisp of undergarment. *His* silken sheets. "I wish you were here," she purrs to Leon. "It is nice and warm in a nice, comfortable bed. It is not very big, but big enough for two if you get close to-gether."

That was fucking *it*. He had her. Now the two-timing slut was caught with her hand down someone else's pants. Rudy imagined himself grabbing Leon by the collar and punching his lights out. Kneeing him in the groin. Teaching the palooka to screw around with his wife. Or Fay. He'd rip the clothes right off her and spread her out on that bed, make her cry and beg for mercy, give her a slap on her rear . . .

Rudy felt his erection on the rise. She could always entice him, his dark dream girl. She almost had him taken in. Just ten days before the Leon conversation, Fay had told him how much she loved him.

He'd asked her. "Oh, about fifty thousand billion billion billion trillion trillion times, around this world and all the other planets," she baby-talked to him.

"More than anyone in the world?" he continued.

She cooed. "More than anyone in the world. More than anything in the world. And I really mean it too, and I'll show you." She paused as if winking over the phone. "Now then, how much do you love me?"

Twice that, he assured her, as his brother William sat in a maid's room, holding a microphone to a secret extension speaker on the phone, recording the conversation. Twice that, for her two-faced lies.

She would pay. Or he wouldn't.

TEMPER, TEMPER.

In mid-August 1932, Rudy was at the Fernbrook Club in Wilkes-Barre, Pennsylvania, when a mug started razzing him, giving him the business. The large crowd of 3,500 dancers had paid a dollar each and here was this one guy getting his goat. "It would have taken the patience of a saint to withstand the taunts and insults of a florid, shiny-faced coal miner who stood there pouring it on for a little over an hour." Vallée was no Sebastian. He was off the bandstand, swinging wildly. On another night, he took on a Canadian "mountain man"; he told a drunk in North Adams, Massachusetts, that he would "knock his unprintable teeth down into his unprintable stomach." Once he leaped from the stage of the Twin-City Club in Winston-Salem, North Carolina, after he spied someone hitting on his girlfriend, administered a beating, and then climbed atop the bar to accept the crowd's plaudits. Host R. J. Reynolds, Jr., the tobacco scion, kept it out of the papers.

That was nothing compared to the way he ran his band. His run-throughs were punctuated by explosions and obscenities, as he dragged his musicians over the roadmap he meticulously typed one-fingered before each performance, with its stopwatch timings, key changes, mood swings. "When I walked into the rehearsal hall at Radio City I got the shock of my life," Adela

Rogers St. Johns reported in *Liberty* magazine. "The roof blew off. The amiable Mr. Vallée was transformed into something between a top sergeant and Cecil B. DeMille on one of his worst days."

Fay had put him over the edge, he was sure of it. He had tried to be a good husband to her, but she was having none of it. She hated New York—it was too cold, she told him from the outset, despite all the furs he bought her—and though he had decided to move to California, he still needed to work. He would go on the road, and she wouldn't go with him, staying in their apartment or traveling to Santa Monica to be with her father. He knew she wasn't listening to him on the radio. She hadn't even met him at the airport last year when he left the Scandals and flew to California to see her, costing him fifteen thousand dollars in lost work. Will Rogers was on the same plane, and his wife and children were there waiting for him. At least she could've brought their dog, Windy.

Fay really had it in for Alice Faye, his femme vocalist with the Yankees, and it wasn't just the similar name. A chorus girl in George White's 1931 Scandals when Rudy took an interest in her, Alice was a sixteen-year-old blonde who hadn't had to travel far to Broadway, having grown up in Hell's Kitchen. After hearing her sing "Mimi" at a cast party, Rudy invited her on his radio show. She went on the road with the Vallée band, including a series of one-nighters in January and February 1933 that took them through Florida and up through Georgia and North Carolina. They were in Memphis on Valentine's Day.

"Ours is a modern marriage," Fay declared, but Rudy was an old-fashioned guy. He wanted his wife home. "I was supposed to be the toast of New York. I was appearing in a Broadway musical, leading one of the most popular dance bands in the country at the Pennsylvania Grill and one of the nation's top radio stars—yet I was the most lonesome, unhappy person in gay Manhattan." Worse, when "my bride evidenced not the slightest interest in my work or anything that pertained to me, I naturally found it a bit chilling."

Fay had her own complaints. "I've put up with the weird hours his crooning demanded and the wholesale feminine admiration," she said, shuttling back and forth between coasts. "Life is just one railroad train after another." She even threatened to go to Reno, but the radio intervened; Rudy's lawyer had Vallée's Fleischmann Yeast Hour tuned in while Fay and her father sat in his office. They heard Rudy singing Irving Berlin's "Say It Isn't So," and in tears, postponed the separation. At least that's how Rudy told it.

But the undercover phone tap revealed the truth. The quality of the discs (played with wooden needles) was poor, but the incrimination was enough to send Fay back to her father for good, with only a hundred dollars per week to show for it. The Vallées separated April 4, 1933, the same week that Russ was shown the door by Hannah Williams.

Sheriff Webb and his daughter struck back in January 1934. In a twenty-one-page complaint, Fay alleged that Rudy had been continually unfaithful to her during their marriage, specifically naming two Jane Does and Alice Faye, who by this time had been signed to the Fox studios and was making the film version of *George White's Scandals*. In addition, she cited his "violent, vicious and ungovernable temper. . . . He repeatedly and on numerous occasions swore at, cursed and abused me, both when we were alone and when we were in the company of other people." He "indulges in blasphemy and uses intemperate, vile and vituperative language." She was asking alimony of $7,400 a month.

Well, perhaps he and Alice had been more than friends. You can see them cuddled together in a group photo taken at Rudy's 365-acre resort in the Maine woods in 1932. Vallée has scrawled "All My Gang at The Lodge" over the top of the picture, reminding himself and future generations of the occasion, a gathering of fifty guests and domestic staff. Of them all, only Rudy reclines, on Alice's lap, looking like a man well satisfied with his lot in life. He's drawn a circle around himself and Alice, and writes her name inside it. Fay is nowhere to be seen.

Thrown together on the road, he and Alice naturally confided in each other, offering a comforting shoulder to cry on, perhaps even falling in love in the way that proximity will breed intimacy. Long nights in a strange town lend privacy to any affair. After the show, in the bar, bargains were made. On tour, everyone got in each other's pants at some time or another, though sometimes it was just as a pain in the ass.

They had further tangled their destiny when Rudy's sixteen-cylinder car overturned, gashing Alice over her eye. She'd had to shave her eyebrows, penciling them in; the slanting look had the press calling her "the baby Harlow," which certainly didn't hurt her standing around the Fox lot. She was on the set doing a wedding scene for the Scandals movie with Rudy when the papers arrived from Fay's lawyer. He would have plenty of reasons for fisticuffs in the future. As the case wends its weary way through the courts, he'll take a swing at Fay's lawyer, and eventually exchange blows with George White after White asks the company of the 1936 Scandals to take a 25 percent pay cut.

He wondered who the Jane Does were. That he could wonder led him to believe she might have a case. He hoped she didn't drag Frances Langford

RUDY, 1932

into it. She was more Fay's type than Alice, a dark beauty with some of Fay's oriental musk and mystery. He had met her in 1932 in New Orleans and immediately invited her onto his radio show. Could he help it if he had an instinct for feminine talent, a divining rod, as it were?

Still, he had the recordings in hand, even the ones where Fay boasted to Leon that she was "stocking up. . . . Yesterday I bought five dresses and three pairs of shoes and three hats." Leon grunted his approval: "You're no fool." Fay was frantically claiming that Gary Leon was an old school chum from her hometown, and they were just playing one of their schoolyard games. Leon, an "adagio dancer," had gotten married himself at the end of 1933, and denied "misconduct . . . such a statement is deliberately falsifying." Though it was hard to refute arrangements to meet in a friend Jack's apartment on 189th Street, or an appointment for Room 825 of a nameless hotel on the March 22 night that Rudy has a show in Philadelphia, or a romantic ride around the park (Fay quelled his fears: "There are a lot of spies watching us, but my chauffeur is my chauffeur, see?").

The inevitable trial would be fought as much over geographic grounds as philandering. In California, Fay could nail him for a good portion of his income; he wanted a Mexican divorce, or to keep it in the New York courts, where the property division was more in his favor. When he heard that Fay's lawyers were attempting to serve him with a restraining order and tie him up in depositions, keeping him in California, he skipped out on his role as Master of Ceremonies at the Screen Actors Guild ball at the Biltmore and chartered a plane to take him to Needles, California, where he caught up with the *Santa Fe Chief* heading for New York.

As a consolation prize, the Club Richman in New York offered Fay three thousand dollars a week. "My deepest sympathy on your misfortune in failing to prevent your husband from obtaining divorce proceedings," manager Aaron Schwartz wrote to Fay in a telegram. "Would you consider an offer to return to the stage? Would like very much to have you and Gary Leon play as opposition to Rudy when he returns to the night club on Broadway."

Fay was thinking about it.

HE WAS in a foul mood when he got off the train in New York in the early morning hours of January 16, wearing a dark green felt hat, a dusky brown double-breasted suit with yellow stripes, a striped shirt, and a black-and-white tie. Eight hundred mostly female fans were waiting for him to enter Grand Central Terminal. Also greeting him and attorney Hyman Bushel were five girls, two blondes and three brunettes, carrying megaphones and dressed in white "duck" sailor pants with a blue stripe and white sweaters with a varsity-size "H" from the Hollywood nightclub restaurant where Rudy is scheduled to appear. For a second Vallée can't remember whether he's coming or going.

He hasn't had much sleep, and he *needs* his sleep, and his lawyer doesn't want any more bad publicity. There are already jokes about Rudy's new theme song, "My Time Is Two Time," in Ed Sullivan's column. Bushel told the Hollywood's owner, Mack Millar, that the display was "disgraceful" and "undignified." As the girls shivered in the damp trestle air, halfheartedly waving their megaphones, Rudy managed a sallow smile for the cameras before getting in his waiting car and driving over to his office at 113 West Fifty-seventh Street.

He spoke to the eager reporters there, sitting behind his desk, toying with a paper cutter. Over the course of the train ride, Fay had added another Jane Doe to the list, an assignation she claimed took place in Los Angeles on January 4.

They prodded him for details. He was only too happy to supply them with names and dates, from his "two thick volumes of typewritten transcripts."

There is the weekend that he goes to Albany on a Friday, to an auto show in Cleveland, and returns on a Thursday to find that Leon "had been in my house on the night I left home and remained there until six o'clock the following morning." And there were "some things which are too dirty and shocking to spread upon the court record."

No, he's not marrying Alice Faye. "That would be bigamy," he declared, "darned bigamy." The *Daily News* reporter makes mention of "a triumphant glitter of the eye" as he described how he made the recordings with his Speak-O-Phone. He's always loved a good gadget.

And then there was the money. "Prior to our marriage I never even had a maid for my household. To have had a butler would have been absurd . . . I certainly never taught her to want a retinue of butler, cook, maid, and chauffeur. I have no more need for a servant than for another nose." He wrinkled his for effect, pinching it as he would a penny.

"My marriage cost me a lot of money." He shrugged, remembering the ermine at $1,725, the mink at $3,500, the jewelry at $7,110. He even added in flowers, at a total of $67.20.

Referring to Leon, a reporter asked Rudy why he just doesn't "punch him in the nose."

"Lay off the baiting, now." The paper cutter looks as if it's ready to cut bait and fish. "We aren't schoolboys. A husband would be a fool to go out and poke a man."

He remembered the night he knew it was over. He had come back from the Black Cat Ballroom ("at the intersection of Routes 13 and 113") in Delaware on the thirty-first of March, 1933. His brother told him that shortly after Rudy left for Delaware at 5:00 P.M., his chauffeur drove Fay to the Bronx, on the Concourse near Fordham Road, to the Paradise Theater where Leon was appearing as part of the dance team of Taylor and Leon. DeMille's *The Sign of the Cross* played on the screen. Fay secluded herself in a dressing room with Leon.

April Fool.

MOULIN ROUGE

In the 1934 *Moulin Rouge*, released the week before Valentine's Day to take advantage of the scarlet splashes about town, two women become one.

"Two Constance Bennetts!" shout the ads. "Brunette by day, blonde at night." She might be a redhead, but the film is in black and white.

Of the three Bennett sisters, Constance is the oldest and most impetuous. Joan, the youngest (there is also the middle Barbara), will garner more renown as Bulldog Drummond's assistant, making movies with directors like Max Ophuls and Fritz Lang, but Constance didn't need the acclaim, having left silent films behind in 1925 to marry a captain of industry. She returned four years later after the demise of her liaison, finding the talkies suited her husky, no-nonsense voice and modest singing ability; she made three or four films a year into the late thirties, usually playing a fallen woman. As a comedienne, Bennett exudes savvy confidence in *Moulin Rouge*, though her French pronunciation owes more to Elmer Fudd than Maurice Chevalier. She's akin to the pre–*I Love Lucy* Lucille Ball, though not as zany. She's plucky.

The bookends of Constance's characters are the neglected and underestimated wife, Helen, who gets to double as the Other Woman, "that girl from the Moulin-Rouge," Mme. Raquel, with her cigarette holder accoutrements and notorious airs. They once played together in a sister act, Jackie and Jill; another game of doubles. The resident philosopher, Helen Westley's Mrs. Morris, calls it a "two-sided triangle."

"You want me to imitate you?" Constance asks Constance in trick photography, double exposure. Robert De Niro in *Taxi Driver* will make it simpler. "You looking at me?" Mirror, mirror; as the Spanish say, *mira, mira. Mirame,* look at me.

The third wheel is her husband, played by Franchot Tone. He hasn't got a chance. He'll be guiled by Raquel, but stay with Helen, not only because he realizes she is his true love, but she's got talent! By going on while Raquel is stuck in Atlantic City, Helen saves the play within the play, *LeMaire's Revue,* an insider's nod to *LeMaire's Affairs,* a stage show which stalled in Chicago in 1927 with Sophie Tucker and Ted Lewis. The musical sequences at the heart of *Moulin Rouge* are hardly on the grand scale of a Busby Berkeley budget (*42nd Street* set a high-water mark in 1933). What they lack in camera angle they make up in explicit tease, a line of chorines in see-through fabrics or dressed as schoolgirls, the Boswell Sisters wearing what look to be oversized plastic maids' uniforms, minstrelsy characterizing Connee in the broad Creole of her syllables when she takes her solo.

Russ enters with Constance, in performance. It's to be a duet, serving "Coffee in the Morning, Kisses in the Night." She sings her opening Al Dubin lyric in that *steak frites* accent, and he embellishes Harry Warren's melody, white hat in both hands, her ardent suitor. His pants are also white; his jacket and hair gloss black. He's come out of nowhere, the anonymous swain offering to be the father of her child, and after the Boswells' turn, it makes as much domestic sense as any for him and Constance to re-emerge through a schoolhouse backdrop dressed in academic robes and mortarboards to sing the final chorus to the assembled tap dancers. He even gets to take a bow at the end, emphasizing his guesting. He's hardly in the movie; he's part of the play.

What's all this got to do with *Moulin Rouge?* There is a tiny windmill decorating the last dance sequence, though "Boulevard of Broken Dreams" is introduced as "the Argentine number." The chorus girls unaccountably hold sombreros to their bosoms, baiting with their bare backs. The peek-a-boo continues *à la mode,* when Raquel *chansons:* "*Oh gay Pa-ree look what you've done to me. . . . I walk a-long the street of sor-row*"—she has trouble with the r's—"*You laugh to-night and cry to-mor-row. . . . Gig-o-lo and Gig-o-lette . . .*"

Raquel tells her tale, beginning in Marseilles with a French nautical twist, crêpe paper accordions and pom-pom berets, and then on to "the gay Paris that used to be, the Bar Tabaran, Maxim's, and the cafés on the Champs-Elysées." The girls roam a staircase in white feathered headdresses and not much else. They lie in a swoon as Constance ballroom-dances toward the song's reprise, her bittersweet stroll along the "Boulevard of Broken Dreams."

The camera close-ups on individual faces. Like Henri de Toulouse-Lautrec, who painted the demimonde of the original Moulin-Rouge, I regard them personally. What happened to the brunette lovely in the third row? The blond dancer stage left of Constance? The girl who turns slower than her neighbors, creating a ripple in the ensemble? Where did they go from here?

And there is further mystery. On the movie's advertising sheet, Connee (spelled "Connie") is billed "dancing—and singing 'The Song of Surrender' to Russ Columbo." In the film, Tullio Carminati overpowers it, singing at a piano while Constance and Franchot clinch in the next room. The song is tailor-made for Columbo's baritone, and as for a Russ-Connee duet, that would truly be a heavenly pairing, but Russ and Connee are nowhere to be found.

They are also absent from the caravan of red motorcars that passes through the Holland Tunnel at 8:30 P.M. on the night before Wednesday's opening. The passengers are Hollywood bit players, transplanted from Ireland, Sweden, and Spain, the easts and wests of small- and big-town America, eight chorines, and the silent comedian Ben Turpin. The procession stops at City Hall and is then escorted by motorcycle to the Hotel Roosevelt. On Wednesday, they dutifully troop over to the Rivoli for the premiere, then get back on the road for their next stop. *42nd Street* had commandeered a transcontinental train to announce the movie across America. Busby's bucks. Still, *Moulin Rouge* gets three and a half stars from the *Daily News*.

RED. THE color of blood; the color of love.

They share aspects other than tint. Both blood and love have to keep in motion, lest they harden, clot, and scab. Faster-moving hemoglobins blush and engorge, aiding the physical condition called *infatuation*, where the impulse races and unsteadies the nerves. Breath shortens and shallows. There is the snap of synapse, a switch thrown inside the skull, hardwired like a bull who aims his horns and lunges at the flap of red cape that conceals the toreador's sword.

You know how it's going to end. The bull is going to die.

Sometimes he takes the bullfighter with him. There are prices to be paid for participating in blood sport. Valentino is twice compromised in the 1922 *Blood and Sand*, caught between the sadistic lure of the bullring, in which he must kill, and the *masochismo* of his fall from erotic grace, for which he must enact self-sacrifice. Like the *corrida*, it is an unequal contest between man and his inner beast.

It must be a good challenge. The risk is balanced by the bull's valor, his noble courage, his instinct to charge even when the steel is in him. A bullfighter responds to inspiration, as a brave bull will rise to the heightened stakes of the matador's execution.

As *Blood and Sand*'s doomed toreador, Rudolph is tossed between the horns of Lila Lee's wifely L's and Nita Naldi's nocturnal N's, love and not-love. "It is torture to love two women," he cries at one point, echoing the bull's pain as the picadors pierce the animal. Sexual attraction is fraught with violence. When the aristocratic Nita seduces him, stroking a harp with her bare back to him, so like the bull's delicate *cruz*, where the bull's shoulder blades cross the spine, where the sword will enter if perfectly thrust, she breaks from his embrace to bite his wrist. He roughly throws her down.

"You snake!" He forks his tongue, smiting and smitten. "One moment I love you, the other I hate you." It is the split personality of a matador, who courts intimacy in the third and last act of the bullfight, so he can kill with *pundonor*, his honor intact, so he is not simply a butcher but a skilled lover.

They are together now, the only certainty is expiation in the hot afternoon sun, the red beach of the bullring.

The flourish of the *muleta*, the bull brought closer inside the embrace of the cape, turning him in circles, tiring even as he learns his mortal enemy. It is all a matter of placement. Rudolph raises his sword, and as he strikes home, the bull wets his horn in the man, gores him as Valentino's lifeline will be pierced a few short years hence. They trade entrances, the ripostes of the *paso doble*, when bull and man become one. In the film's last shot, Rudolph lies collapsed in Lila's lap, a rendered Pietà that allows for his absolution, her cape like the cloth of Saint Veronica wiping the sweat from Christ's eyes.

PIGALLE WAS Paris as it filtered from the city's ancient fortifications toward Notre Dame, the world's idea of a wide-open city, a potent symbolic mixture of easy sex and ab*sin*the with poetry and painters and pandering performers. *Cancan!* The mind unleashes whirling circles of skirts pulled high, legs a-shake in their petticoat layers, frilled underwear flashing, undulating the bared female body.

The musical possibilities are endless.

In the spring of 2001, a movie—accompanied by a fashion trend and a soundtrack album—made a significant impact on a culture not easily impressed. Eventually grossing over $200 million worldwide in its first year, a nominee for Best Picture and Best Actress at the Oscars, starring a freshly separated Nicole Kidman (from Tom Cruise, a sundering on the order of Carole

Lombard's split from William Powell, for those browsing in a far future when now-household names are encrusted in forgotten myth), and directed by Baz Luhrmann, it was heralded as a return to the movie musical, a form which apparently had gone the way of *Camelot, Oklahoma!,* and *South Pacific,* grinding to a halt sometime around *Grease,* not yet revived by *Chicago.* Music videos had taken over in the 1980s, dispensing with plot, cutting right to the song-and-dance.

The twenty-first-century version of *Moulin Rouge* borrowed liberally from the shuffled montages of the music video. In fact, the video reached more viewers, spread around the world by a linkage of music channels offering re-markably similar soundings, no matter the language or local attraction, a hit continent by continent, trailering the movie. The song was a remake itself, a cover version of a 1975 number one hit by LaBelle, "Lady Marmalade," or *"Voo-lay-voo coo-shay ah-veck mwah, seswah"* as it was better known, written by Bob Crewe, who knew the power of a good falsetto from working with the Four Seasons, and Kenny Nolan, once of Jay and the Americans. The Fran-cophone lyrics were sassily delivered by Patti LaBelle; she didn't even have to fashion a *belle époque* name, a "soul sistah soul" who pealed different types of religious fealty from "I Sold My Heart to the Junkman" to "You'll Never Walk Alone," flanked by the typographic triangle of *femme fatale* Sarah Dash and butch warrior Nona Hendryx.

Even those who don't speak French can answer the question. It's the clas-sic French phrase, *la tour Eiffel* of linguistic tourism. In our imaginations, it gives the French their *savoir-faire,* their *élan,* their *joie de vivre. La vie bo-hème.*

Mais oui? We may.

The cross-dress cinches the video's waist, garish and demanding, insistent in that nudging Hit way, in the air, wherever you turn. The Hit wants to dance with you. Pink, Mya, Lil' Kim, and especially Christina Aguilera (with her Spanish *lingua franca* flamenco on "Mi Genie Entrapado") are as much circus mask as Dee Snyder's Twisted Sister, mimicking the dead-on exagger-ations of the drag queen.

Dee-*vaahhs.* Women meant for worship.

Voo-lay-voo coo-shay ah-veck mwah, seswah? Who cancan resist such an in-vitation?

I SEE the post-mode *Moulin Rouge!* in a multiplex on Second Avenue. An in-scription of May 1926 dates the building's cornerstone, once part of the Lower East Side's Yiddish theater row.

Director Baz Luhrmann is a transplanter. He set *Romeo and Juliet* in the alternative-rock present (at least as it looked on MTV in 1996), and his version of *Moulin Rouge*, based on the Orpheus myth (but with Eurydice playing Orpheus), is timelined in a century-old "Summer of Love," poured like molasses over Montmartre. He wants to have his cake and eat it too, telling *The New York Times*: "Irony, to me, in the cinema or in the theater, means you can laugh and cry at the same time at the same thing."

This is a balancing act like no other, bridging emotional extremes. Select the sound track's dance card. The laser disc is set on random play. The performers are skilled in the art of juxtapose, from David Bowie and Beck to Fatboy Slim and Rufus Wainwright, deconstructing Sting ("Roxanne") and Eden Ahbez ("Nature Boy") and Madonna ("Like a Virgin"). Hearing some of the reconfigured songs is like seeing an old friend where you'd least expect, trying hard to recognize from which past life you know them.

In its set pieces—*Moulin Rouge!* is almost all set pieces—Luhrmann's film puts on the show it is putting on. The emphasis is on dazzizzying, a hallucinogenic swirl of colors and dissolves, Bollywood on parade (the Penniless Sitar Player first meets the Courtesan in the upper room of an elephant edifice. Ziegfeld would be pleased).

Nicole Kidman, as the heroine, Satine, takes to red very well. Her porcelain skin and chiseled bones set off her red hair, her red lips, her red dress. The glow of the Moulin-Rouge windmill that turns behind her is the infrared of a volcano. A tear has opened in the side of the mountain and rivulets of lava run down the slope, the gored skin of earth and blood. She-bull.

THE 1952 John Huston–directed *Moulin Rouge* is more the story of Henri de Toulouse-Lautrec than Satine's, acknowledging an I-like-to-watch quality that is an important attribute for any painter. Huston fought with Technicolor to mute their brash colorings and give him a color scheme that more suited Toulouse-Lautrec's palette. Henri himself was hardly toned down, torn bodi(ce)ly from the pages of Pierre La Mure's fanciful historical romance (he specialized in dashing artistic figures, fictionalizing Felix Mendelssohn in *Beyond Desire*, Claude Debussy in *Clair de Lune*, *The Private Life of Mona Lisa*). Jose Ferrer provides a Hispanic touch—Toulouse-Lautrec is apparently never "too Latin"—and the mad whirl of the Moulin-Rouge spatters around him as he tries to catch its perpetual motion with his brush.

Henri was unable to escape the long tail of prehistory. His twelfth-century ancestor, the Count of Lautrec, had been at the center of the Albigensian

Heresy in the Languedoc foothills of the Pyrenees, a loose collection of principalities isolated from the rest of what would become southern France by its Cathar culture. The Cathari preached a rigorous dualism in which good and evil were inextricably opposed, believing in reincarnation and elevating the feminine, and positing themselves against the Roman church, for which they were given the honor of their own Crusade and subsequent genocide.

Born the sole son of the Count of Toulouse-Lautrec in 1864, Henri grew to only four feet eight inches as a result of two falls as a child, a math made gematrial when he found refuge and acceptance in Montmartre's Latin Quarter when he was twenty-two. His was a most sympathetic eye in the moments before photography became portable, skilled in the imagistic poster that garnered him eminence throughout Paris. He spent hours learning and adapting his mass-production techniques, and his skill with the lithographer's stone helped him visualize his portraiture, the sketched black outlines, the attention-grabbing red slash of scarf in his heroic *Aristide Bruant dans son cabaret,* the colors that changed before the eye the longer one lingered.

His distinctive style advertised him as much as it did the Moulin-Rouge, which had opened on the fifth of October 1889, its garden containing a giant papier-mâché elephant left over from the Universal Exposition, its building on the Boulevard de Clichy topped by a windmill whose vanes gyrated like the dangling legs of dancers like La Goulue and La Mome Fromage. He was drawn to entertaining faces wherever he found them, in brothels and opera boxes, at horse races, or just sitting alongside him, ringing the floor, lost in thought, watching the passing parade. In the same place at the same time. A snapshot.

THE SCENARIO would reach the 1950s drive-in. *Ding Dong Girlies,* playing at the North 41 in America's upper Midwest, advertises itself as "A Night in the Moulin Rouge," starring Illona "The Bavarian Orchid" and Iva Pratt and the Red Mill cuties. Come-on and on. "The gay Red Mill at its gayest!" The S-curve lure of "Snappy, Saucy, Spicy." Girl power.

IT HARDLY matters from whose viewpoint the tale unfolds. Henri drinks himself to extinction. Satine will assume her deathly pallor. The Moulin-Rouge remains a test of life or death in the guise of love, a daredevil sport requiring as much courage as a race to the South Pole, or a solo flight across the Atlantic, both popular in these years. In the silent *Moulin Rouge,* a British production from 1928 directed by E. A. Dupont, Olga Tschechowa is Parysia, a revue actress whose daughter wants to marry André (Jean Bradin), an aristocratic auto racer. He decides the stakes aren't high enough for him; he has to risk all by falling in love with Olga. It doesn't help that the daughter (Eve Grey) is simple and unsuspecting, while Parysia sits around in various stages of undress backstage. He has to choose between mother and daughter; whose in-law will he be? Whose outlaw?

The movie is as much travelogue as plotline, with the camera going behind the scenes and in front of the footlights at the Casino de Paris, Paris by night, the "City of Temptation," already the stuff of tourism and caricature. It's as if Toulouse-Lautrec got a job working for the News Syndicate on a daily strip. *Moulin Rogues*, perhaps? No, the men are of little interest. How about *Nana Naughty*, recalling Nicole Kidman's transformative scene, in which, swathed in a fur rug, she rolls around on the floor at her first hint of Ewan MacGregor's sensitive side, slipping over the acting line to fall in love with her rapturous hooker who wants to be an actress, cuddling and hugging herself and giving little yelps and "naughty, naughty words!" and making me forget I'm notating a movie, word for word, Madonna as blushing bride, blood spotting the coverlet, a bedsheet waved out a window in triumph, the unfurled cape that signals the end of the passion play. *Olé!* Like a virgin olive oil.

The bull sees the dismounted man for the very first time in the ring. If trained properly, he has never before confronted a two-legged creature. The wedding night of beast and man.

THERE IS a trick conclusion to the *Moulin Rouge* of 1934. The husband tells the wife he knew it was she all the time. It's a familiar framing device; I've said it myself many a caught moment. A re-viewing shows he might be telling the truth, playing along with her ruse.

"You're a great artist," he tells Helen as Raquel aligns herself along a couch, as slinky as they come, both succumbing to the lure of artifice. "I've completely changed my opinion." Tone's impatient yet unhurried delivery reads both ways, a narrative layer twice removed, more apparent the second time around, like a windmill picking up speed as it's breathed on by the wind.

He is becoming who she wants him to be. He sees in her who she could be. He who she wants him to be is she who could be he.

A happy ending.

BING AND EDDIE

Out. Of nowhere, of the blue. Eddie Lang is vamoosed, vanished. Bing takes it badly.

He was the one who persuaded Eddie to have the operation. His tonsils, no big deal. He wasn't a singer. Bing assured him he would be unconscious for no more than two or three hours, and then he wouldn't have a sore throat anymore. He could speak without a rasp. It might be a good idea to have it done now, since he had a few lines in the upcoming *College Humor*. . . .

Eddie entered a New York hospital on March 26, 1933, right before he was due to head west with Crosby. He never awoke from the anesthesia. His last request to his wife, Kitty, was to bring him a racing form. Lang enjoyed gambling as much as playing guitar, specializing in poker, bridge, the angled geometries of pool. He often took home a chunk of the band's earnings, whiling away the time between sets or after the show.

The wagered game was akin to playing music for him, following hunches, weighing the odds, figuring the angles. Improvising. It was something he was good at, second-guessing the chord changes, and his ear was sharp. You needed courage and confidence to go with instinct, to let the song suggest your lateral movements across the frets, how long to hold or fold the note into the next hand. He liked the inside straight, the rhythm guitar of poker, along with the aces wild of taking a solo. As for the ponies, he'd bet the long shot on a muddy track, like when the band played "Dinah" faster and faster, *raggin' the scale* and *stringing the blues* and neck and neck to a photo finish. He and violinist Joe Venuti were always first across the line.

Kitty sits by his side, unbelieving, as the hours pass. She cries out when the nurse first runs from the room, and then finds she's unable to make a sound. Eddie's pulse has stopped keeping time; it's gone free, the arrhythmia of an embolism.

Bing arrives grief-stricken. "Kitty, he was my best friend."

He puts his head in her lap and cries.

EDDIE IS Bing's right-hand man. He makes it easy, the dips and swoops and comradely lean, the pick-fingered rhythms. He tries to be one step ahead of Bing, and simultaneously behind, giving Crosby room to breathe. His guitar is the bridge; a wooden structure strung in suspension, like J. A. Roebling's Brooklyn Bridge. And while we're on the span of fingerboard, let's call Eddie the Steve Brody of the guitar. He jumps off, and, at least on record, lives to tell the tale.

He's where twentieth-century guitar starts, the hundred years of which the guitar is perhaps its most signifyin' instrument. Strike the perhaps; I'm a rock and roller, and proud to play it.

What does Eddie do? For one, he pioneers its use as a rhythm instrument, almost single-handedly replacing the banjo as tempo scrubber and harmonic time-keeper. He burnishes the sound even as he moves it closer to the microphone, less snared and more brushed, a smoother percussion, there and not there. It can dip behind the insistence of the drums, or sidle in to bend a note, strike a harmonic. The guitar hasn't gone electric yet; Les Paul, listening to Eddie, is still looking at the telephone, the radio, and the phonograph in his living room, wondering how to bring their sound reproductions together. Lang's breadth of rapport will influence Les, and Charlie Christian, and Django Reinhardt (whose Hot Club Trio with Stéphane Grappelli is the same configuration as the uncanny interplays pioneered by Eddie and his old school chum Joe Venuti), and anyone else who picks up a guitar as the thirties plug in. His only real rival in the twenties is Nick Lucas, "the Crooning Troubadour," who will be remembered more for his version of "Tip Toe Through the Tulips with Me" than for his six-string skills.

For two, he is *the* jazz guitarist, rooted deep in the growth patterns of the music as it steps out from Dixieland, merging with the big bands to construct swing. He takes solos, flights of single-note fancy that cut like horns, suggestive melodies to support the soloist. His mobile bass-runs underpin the rhythm section, and he tops off their leading tones with broken chords and arpeggiations. He is the first-call guitarist of his era, and ever since Bing was able to form his own band, Lang has been by his side. They hear each other.

Lang trained his ear before he learned to play the guitar, which makes him different from most guitarists who followed him, attracted by the instrument's ease of play and accompaniment, its immediate strummability. *Solfeggio* teaches the do-re-mi of sight-singing and the principles of music theory before a hand is laid on a specific instrument; in theory, once you learn the proper hand-ear coordination, any instrument is a tool. Eddie could play guitar, mandolin, ukulele, and even violin, and he schooled himself in the classics as well as the sentimental Italian melodies that were neighborhood favorites.

It was all too easy to mail-order a guitar from Sears or Montgomery Ward, learn three chords, and head toward any stage (*hey, punk!*). Lang's musicality expanded the vocabulary of the guitar to play the most subtle of harmonic patterns, initiating the moving chords of comping, not unlike a piano's counterbalanced melodics. The physical contact with the strings via finger or plectrum gave a push to the chordal underpinnings, thrust to the solos. Dynamics could be moved from whisper-soft to brace-rattling loud, and the possibilities for inversion were obverse, even perverse.

For three, he was steeped in the blues, a genre in which the guitar was rapidly assuming the status of scepter. Lang had grown up in the same South Philadelphia neighborhood as Russ, a few years older, born October 25, 1902, starting out life as Salvatore Massarro. He was the youngest of ten children, and his father, Dominic, had been making guitars and mandolins since the family was still in Naples. Living across the river from the Victor complex in Camden, a voracious musical mind such as Eddie's surely heard guitar stylings come up from the South, the licks and tunings and finger-curls, the jazz harmonies of that period, and the articulations of black-derived music. He was fifteen when the Original Dixieland "Jass" Band cut "Livery Stable Blues" for Victor, "for dancing."

He met Giuseppe Venuti in the orchestra at James Campbell High School, where both played violin. By the early twenties, they were professional musicians, Joe in Atlantic City with Burt Eslow, Eddie working for Charles Kerr, a Philadelphia orchestra leader, playing mostly banjo, and some guitar. Lucas had pioneered the use of guitar in a non-string band with Sam Lanin, and by 1921 had recorded what are thought to be the first recorded guitar solos: "Pickin' the Guitar" and "Teasin' the Frets." Eddie began shifting between banjo and guitar, and even a banjo-tuned guitar (another guitarist named Eddie—Condon of the Chicago school—would keep his guitar at four strings in banjo tuning, because he preferred the way the chords fell under his fingers).

Eddie followed Joe to Atlantic City, then the most popular resort on the East Coast, with its Steel Pier and boardwalk, its streets soon to be immortalized in the 1930s' Monopoly, a board game devoted to the joys and jails of real estate capitalism. Over the summer of 1923, the bands at the hotels and clubs formed new liaisons, and Lang found himself attracted to a group of musicians from northern Pennsylvania whose ranks included the Dorsey brothers. By the beginning of 1924, Eddie was one of the Scranton Sirens, touring and playing in Philadelphia clubs like the Beaux Arts Café and the Pekin Café. Back in Atlantic City at the Folies Bergère that summer, the Mound City Blues Blowers asked him to make them a quartet. He recorded four songs with them in December of that year, including "Tiger Rag," and traveled to England in April 1925 for a two-month engagement. He played guitar exclusively for them, his texture warming the somewhat clackety comb-and-kazoo-based Blues Blowers.

Lang soon outgrew Mound City "hokum," and found himself in demand by a succession of bandleaders: Jean Goldkette, Roger Wolfe Kahn, Red Nichols (he was part of the Five Pennies), and ultimately Paul Whiteman, where he jammed with Bix Beiderbecke. Joe Venuti was on the same fast track, and they often hired together as a pair, in recognition of their shared past and musical versatility. Their compatible styles were in evidence on record as early as the fall of 1926, when Eddie and Joe recorded a distant-cousin version of "Tiger Rag" called "Stringing the Blues" for Okeh. They took three sessions to get it right, finally succeeding on November 8.

Eddie met Bing in the Whiteman orchestra. They became friends on and off the bandstand, attracted to the same mix of freewheeling scat jazz and a late-night good time. Their wives got along too. Eddie had married Ziegfeld dancer Kathleen "Kitty" Rasch when he returned from an English tour in 1926. On the road with Bing in the early thirties, Dixie needed a friend, already feeling a distance open up between her and Bing as his career skyrocketed and hers pointed to kids and home. Bing needed a friend, too, someone he could rely on. One of the guys; his accompanist.

Crosby knew how much he counted on Eddie. Early on, he wouldn't appear on radio without Eddie by his side. Lang traveled with him to California in the spring of 1932 and stayed with him there, earning a thousand dollars a week while performing live and written into Bing's Paramount contract at fifteen thousand dollars a picture.

For four: Bing wasn't the same without him.

Downbeat.

EDDIE LANG AND BING REHEARSE FOR
THE BIG BROADCAST

ON THEIR first trip to the West Coast together, stopping over in Chicago for the second time that spring, May 25 and 26, 1932, Bing and Eddie go into the studio. Pianist Lennie Hayton, who had worked for Whiteman, is also along for the ride, and leads the ensemble; the only other identified musician is Frankie Trumbauer on C melody sax. Bing feels particularly happy, caught in transit, left but not arrived, enjoying the present tense of traveling. He's been away from New York long enough to savor all he'd accomplished, and not yet in Hollywood, where his future career awaited. He would be making feature-length motion pictures; leading his own band; singing on radio and records; playing golf. What more could he want? It was always golf-playing weather in California.

It's a more informal occasion than his Isham Jones Orchestra sessions a month earlier, also in Chicago, when Bing let loose on "Sweet Georgia Brown." It was hard to choose between the two rollicking takes; in the end, both would make it to market. The only song of these Hayten-directed sessions to approach that level of foot-tap is "Some of These Days," a Sophie Tucker favorite and the last of the four they're cutting. Then it's Minneapolis, St. Louis, and out to L.A. for *The Big Broadcast*.

They're in a mind to whoop it up. Bing enters on a run, slips through the lyrics; he can't wait to get to the midbreak, where he scatters for two choruses.

Lang plays along with him as he used to with Venuti, giving Bing license to bounce each eighth-note on its line of staff, the music score's strung wire, five strings to Eddie's six. They set a fast pace. Lang's solo is more staccato than need be; he's pushing the L-5 to produce volume, and the notes don't have the sustain of electricity, which will prove as important as amplitude to the guitar's coming generations. Bing soars to the finish with a *tweet tweet tweet.* Birds of a feather.

LANG HAS his own minstrel mask: Blind Willie Dunn. Color-blind, more likely. His duets with Lonnie Johnson represent twenties blues as it moves from Dockery's plantation to the urban crossroads, Charley Patton to Blind Lemon Jefferson by way of Duke Ellington: sophisticated gutbucket; black and tan.

From New Orleans, Johnson had brought jazz with him along with skills honed on the violin, sometimes doubling his two top strings to create even more clang from his guitar. For his work with Lonnie, Lang stays in the engine room, supportive, feeding him bass runs and underlying chordal thrums as Lonnie trills and hammers-on. They record "Two Tone Stomp" in November 1928, drawing notice to their interracial alliance in a time when mixed bands are nonexistent. "Hot Fingers" features smears and slurs, stop-time and dizzying finger acrobatics on Lonnie's fretting hand. On May 15, 1929, they double-side an Okeh disc, "Guitar Blues" and "Bull Frog Moan." There are "Midnight Call Blues" and "Blue Room" and "Blue Guitars"; all shades, spectral blue shifts from light to dark and back again: azures, violets, and royals. Eddie liked his blues moniker so well that he recorded under the name of Blind Willie Dunn's Gin Bottle Four, with Tommy Dorsey on trumpet; sat alongside Johnson in the Clarence Williams Novelty Four, with King Oliver on cornet; and, along with Williams, backed Bessie Smith on "I'm Wild About That Thing" and Victoria Spivey on "Organ Grinder Blues." In a minstrel reverse, he accompanied one of the last blackface singers, Emmett Till, on "Lovesick Blues," later to be revived by Hank Williams.

He especially responds to the collaboration, the conversation, of playing with someone in duo. He can stand alone. "Prelude"—his version of Rachmaninoff's op. 3, no. 2 in B, transposed to E minor—is jewellike in its precision, showing Eddie's love for Andrés Segovia and his father's love of classical music; but he specializes in the shape-note encouragement of tandem. In his duets with Johnson (Carl Kress reverses the hierarchy, tossing Eddie accompanying chords in the way he will form a similar guitar partnership with Dick

McDonough), and even Venuti, Lang is the motor, the mortar. The mortal coil.

His last session with Venuti takes place in New York, on February 28, 1933. "Raggin' the Scale" allows them to cut a rug with their counterpointing counterparts (a Blue Three: Jimmy Dorsey on clarinet, Adrian Rollini on bass sax, and pianist Phil Wall). They fit together like another song at the session, "Jig Saw Puzzle Blues," the picture moving as fast as the music is played, a jiggling film. Eddie had come east with Bing the previous October, just in time for the opening of *The Big Broadcast*. They had performed at local theaters, playing the Capitol (where Bing traded jokes for the first time with an up-and-coming emcee, Bob Hope) and the Journal Square, in Jersey City (where a young Hoboken resident named Frank Sinatra was in the audience). They kicked off Bing's new twice-weekly radio series for Chesterfield on January 4, 1933. They were hoping to be back in Los Angeles by early April to begin *College Humor*. Bing planned to stay there, and "the girls" would meet them after going the long way around to California, by steamship. When Eddie went in for his routine tonsillectomy, Kitty opted to stay with him.

Eddie had a habit of ending his guitar pieces with a cluster of harmonics, glancing his finger off the strings on the fifth, seventh, or twelfth frets, the building blocks of the I–IV–V progression that underscores the Western tempered scale. The technique creates a pure bell-like chime along the octave that reveals a guitar's shimmering overtones.

Fingers touching lightly to the string, the ringing in the ears lasts long after the note has faded.

RUSS SIGNED a contract extension with Universal in June 1934. He wondered whether he'd made the right decision at the beginning of this year, when nothing seemed to be happening at all, but shooting was finally scheduled to begin on his new movie.

Carl Laemmle, Sr., had begun Universal in 1912, and though it specialized in low-budgets and serials and never had the cachet of the more sophisticated studios, still founded Universal City, a walled empire that became filmdom's most prolific factory. The Depression and changing technologies hit Universal hard, and while the elder Carl shuttled back and forth to New York to quell stockholder uprisings, his son took over the day-to-day helm. Carl Laemmle, Jr., promised forty-two features in the 1934–35 season, along with six Buck Jones Westerns and a new series of Walter Lantz cartoons about Oswald, the Lucky Rabbit, emphasizing quality films like *The Great Ziegfeld* with Billie Burke, Edna Ferber's *Show Boat*, and a film of Lloyd C. Douglas's bestselling novel *Magnificent Obsession*. It wasn't these worthy efforts that would save the studio, though. Universal's horror franchise—Frankenstein, Dracula, the Invisible Man, the Wolfman, and the Mummy—created a branding that would raise them from dead, pushing the company from the red of "I never drink . . . wine" into the black lagoon.

Laemmle junior assured Russ he was one picture away from stardom. The only problem was that while he was waiting to find the perfect picture, Bing Crosby had been making picture after picture. Columbo would never catch up that way.

Bing was out of reach. After the success of *The Big Broadcast*, Bing had signed a $300,000 pact with Paramount for five pictures. The first, *College Humor*, cast him not as a student but as a professor, even then attempting to distance him from a purely adolescent following. He gives his class a lecture on "Learn to Croon," complete with *buh-buh-buh*'s that wink at his heart-throb reputation. The *Broadcast* formula was turned sideways for *Too Much Harmony* (songwriters Coslow and Johnston even reprised their "Please" with "Thanks"), a behind-the-curtain musical that cast him as a theatrical singer caught between Judith Allen and Lilyan Tashman, in one of her last roles. On loan to MGM, he next progressed to a Marion Davies vehicle called *Going Hollywood* that included an impression of Russ (as well as Vallée and Kate Smith) by the Radio Rogues, and started the new year with *We're Not Dressing*. Any lingering animosity between him and Columbo was smoothed over by Carole, who held court on the Paramount lot.

By 1934, Bing was a well-established musical comedy star. He built a home in Toluca Lakes and had his first children—Gary on June 27, 1933, and the twins, Philip and Dennis, on July 13, 1934. He was managed by his brother Everett, and publicized by his brother Larry. His brother Bob was down from Spokane, now singing with Anson Weeks' Orchestra. It was all in-house. His records were steady sellers, and the year would produce such memorable performances as "Love in Bloom," the first of Crosby's Oscar-nominated songs.

1934 was also the first full year of Jack Kapp's Decca label. He had gotten funding from English Decca, though he never intended the company to be any less than his own vision. He had left Brunswick taking Bing with him, an association that would determine Crosby's musical directions far more than just label patron and artist. Kapp had an impatient way with a song, like most listeners. "Where's the melody?" was his favorite phrase. He didn't like a lot of decoration, the way jazz did. There were all kinds of musics; everyone had a favorite song. He had an unerring sense of the common denominator, and as the record business was built on fractions, the percentage points of the rack jobbers, the song publishers, the balance sheets of business and pleasure, he knew their bottom lines didn't have to be at odds. Kapp thought "crossover" before the word was invented for radio demographics and musical genre. Bing could be everybody.

And Bing had everybody's ear. He was prime-time radio. Though Cremo had withdrawn sponsorship of his original show after the initial six months' airing (Crosby's pre-dominantly female audience was not about to start smoking cigars), his CBS program merely switched tobaccos. Chesterfield was a cigarette. Now Woodbury Soap was about to soften his image further. A family man, he began to show a more adult side in his roles. The year 1934 placed him opposite such queen bees as Miriam Hopkins (in *She Loves Me Not*) and Kitty Carlisle (*Here Is My Heart*), as he begins to perfect his commoner guise, his ordinary writ large, worn as a boutonniere, like his crooner-waiter who seduces the hoi polloi, as much class comedy as love story. There is no doubt to what social rank Bing is aspiring. In 1934, he begins construction on a horse-breeding ranch north of San Diego, and buys a ten-thousand-dollar box at the Del Mar racetrack: the sport of kings.

Kitty came out to Los Angeles to live, to give Dixie moral support in her newfound motherhood and herself somewhere to be. Dixie had been the one to get Bing to stop drinking; he had. Now she was about to start.

RUSS WAS glad to be away from Twentieth Century. Zanuck had so little faith in him that he cut his singing verses out of "Boulevard of Broken Dreams"; originally he had been scheduled to sing two songs in *Moulin Rouge*. On top of that, his new manager, Jack McCoy, was trying to squelch Con's suit. Conrad wanted sixty-six grand in blood money, and it wasn't as if Con was doing badly. He had a couple of songs in the new Fred Astaire picture, the one with Astaire's new partner, Ginger Rogers. *"The Continental."* Russ drew on his cigarette, picked a piece of tobacco from his lip and breathed the smoke out in a wave. Change that *o* to a *u*. *Just like I did*, Russ thought.

Universal at first tried to convince him that he needed a nonsinging role. Russ didn't agree. He was a singer; his acting was that of the opera. He needed a song to advance the action, to sing his lines. In January, he fought against his inclusion in *Glamour*, which starred Paul Lukas, and his old *Broadway* love interest, Constance Cummings. Since it was taken from an

Edna Ferber story and directed by William Wyler, his decision seems wrong, in retrospect. He was then bruited for *The Bachelor Wife* in February, but that picture had already gone through two directors (the second, Lloyd Corrigan, walked out in twenty-four hours), and was being turned down by everyone. He was proposed for *Men Without Fear*, playing a "courageous" toreador. Too Valentino. By then he had been signed to Universal for five months, and still had nothing to show for it.

Russ was impatient. He couldn't wait forever. Everyone wanted a crooner. Bing's brother Bob had been offered such a role in Joan Crawford's *Sadie McKee*, until Bing and Everett thought it too close to home. Careers were built on sand. In Brooklyn, on May 11, Paramount had closed its vaunted namesake theater, promising vaguely to reopen in the fall. Russ couldn't afford to waste time. The Chicago World's Fair had just offered him $7,500 for a week's work. Where was the buildup he had been promised?

Finally, at the end of April, the first Russ Columbo picture at Universal is announced to the Hollywood reporters. *Castles in the Air*, once called *Love Life of a Crooner*, weathers the usual pre-production crises before it starts filming at the beginning of July. His co-star, June Knight, is hospitalized with "adhesions" after a tonsillectomy, which forces her to leave *Romance in the Ruin* and opens her schedule for the newly retitled *Wake Up and Dream*. A light comedy that will feature him performing three songs, it is to be his biggest outing to date. His first starring role. Russ can't wait.

THREE ON A MATCH

Once is an isolated occurrence. Twice is coincidence. Thrice reveals a pattern.

Actress Lilyan Tashman, only thirty-five, dies of cancer on March 21. Lew Cody, with whom Dorothy shared dialogue in *Shoot the Works,* is waked on May 31, the actor having expired suddenly in his sleep. "I wonder who'll be next," Dell remarks to friends in the studio commissary. She will have to redo some of her scenes with him. "They say those things go in cycles of threes."

It is her third movie. *Shoot the Works* sets her in the gambling den of vaudeville, where "the act" is the sleight-of-hand, a snappy patter aiming for "the big finish." The jackpot is when the "audience bursts into applause for five minutes." It means you might still be working next week. Jack Oakie is a fast talker but Dorothy runs rings around him, quips cut to the quick. She's honest, an aboveboard broad. The lyrics he's singing to "With My Eyes Wide Open I'm Dreaming" are bum; she can do the tune one better, and does, with the help of Gordon and Revel. Every time she presents him with another token of affection—a ring to pawn, their collaborative song, a promise for life—Jack gambles it away, to Lew Cody as the hard-nosed theatrical agent. The dice aren't kind to him. That's a pip, ain't it?

Oakie's world, his Nicky Nelson Enterprises, is carnival: he exhibits a whale, sponsors a flagpole sitter. He's still three rings and the medicine show. He'd walk the slack wire if he could; there are too many tightropers in this town anyway. You needed an angle.

And curves. Dorothy looks as if she's getting into fighting trim, her costume formfitting, curls and ruffles in a tight bounce. She draws comparisons in the press to Mae West, but it's only her knack for the sassy rejoinder. Not having a kid around allows her to vamp it up, but Dorothy's a good girl. She trusts him immediately. "You know your onions," she tells Oakie, though he hands her the old malarkey. She's been around enough to know a line when she hears it, that he won't admit he loves her until it's over.

Ben Bernie, a maestro of "the Joe Davis Orchestra," provides the slapstick novelty. A classically trained violinist (he had appeared at Carnegie Hall at fourteen playing Mozart), he quickly opted for vaudeville. He trades "yowsah, yowsah's" with a Winchell stand-in, "Larry Hale" (a pre–Fred Mertz William Frawley), a "Broadway Chatter" radio columnist who learns he's got to take the mickey as well as give it. In the press, Ben and Walter are each other's fall guy, exchanging insults as if they were buying each other drinks, all in slit-your-throat fun. Bernie will do anything for a laugh. He's Milton Berle without the jokes (or the legendary horse-hung member), but he's not really funny. He puts on yellowface for "A Bowl of Chop Suey and You-ey," recalling when Chinese cooking centered on the mandarin, clowning until the whole band collapses in a zany heap. *Yowsooey.*

The film is *Broadway Thru a Keyhole* with the eye looking back from inside the keyhole. She's the nightclub singer; when Dorothy duets with a male tenor, she takes the lower voice. It's a brass doorknob for the movie's theme as well. "With My Eyes Wide Open I'm Dreaming" is a hit, Dorothy the anointed singer. When she finally debuts the song with its sparkling new lyrics at a fancy nightclub, having lost Oakie to the flea-circus circuit when he tells her he's gambled their lives away, she spends considerable time on the word "illusion," vibratoing the *oo-oo-oo* in her silk shantung; the old bump-and-grind.

Nicky winds up on the outskirts of Brooklyn in the Gravesend sideshow district. He has won back her ring, and before he leaves town, comes across the river to see her and the song, now fully orchestrated, the applause tumultuous. Backstage he greets the band, dressed in Russian uniforms after previously donning collegiate garb and women's clothes. Bernie's "Merry Lads" are good sports, even when the clarinet player has to hang upside down from a trapeze for his solo. Supporting actress Arline Judge gives a winning performance as the perky sidekick, but it's Dorothy's arrival as a female lead that wins the picture. She has believability on her side; she's lost her southern accent, only barely detectable in her big dramatic scene, an "I'm going to be somebody" breakup with Nicky. He is convinced: "That girl's going to make something of herself. Someday she'll be way up on top."

Jack Oakie had been at the première of *The Bowery*, reading his radio speech too quickly off a slip of paper while the newsreel cameras captured his nervous, balled-up energy. Soon there would be another premiere, and Dorothy Dell would be walking down the red carpet aisle of the Grauman, to say-a-few-words to the Movietone audience.

Nicky and Lily clinch, kiss. *"I'm dreaming. . . ."* She can't get the song out of her head. She wonders *"if I deserve such a break . . . I can't believe that you're really mine."*

She has it all, she's become a star, and not yet twenty-one. The waking dream, its images seeping into the opening eyes, the round-trip return to aware, a where dream is real.

As Nicky, Oakie shakes the dice. He's got nothing left to lose. Where once he exhibited his Leviathan in a Forty-second Street arcade across from the Lyric Theater and the Republic Burlesque, his own Moby Dick on display, now he has thrown in his lot with Lily. "Shoot the works," he tells Lew Cody, who has this to say: "Just a nice little pair of boxcars."

DOROTHY AND the doctor start the night of June 8 with her meeting his mother. He drives her over to his home in Pasadena, at 48 Annandale Road. Dr. Carl R. Wagner is a surgeon, and Dorothy has finally acquiesced to her own mother's wish that she should see him.

Dr. Wagner had achieved some notoriety in the newspapers the previous December when a Dr. Leonard Siever, whose dental office was above his own in the Pasadena Professional Building, was found murdered. Mrs. Frances Coen Cooke had an appointment with Dr. Wagner on the afternoon of Dr. Siever's death; she was to meet Siever later, when he was to escort her to a party. Instead, the dentist had been shot on the night of December 12, 1933, and left in an alley next to the Pasadena Scottish Rite church. Mrs. Cooke was a divorcée; in a bizarre afterthought, a wristwatch belonging to Siever was sent to Mrs. Cooke in the mail. That was where the trail ran into a dead end, waiting for the invention of film noir.

He'd had to borrow his mother's sedan. It was a medical family. His father was a physician, and young Carl had graduated from medical school at the age of twenty-one. His sister, Louise, was also a doctor, and married to Dr. Joseph Szukalski, a surgeon at the Pasadena Emergency Hospital. There was no shortage of health care. Dr. Wagner wished it was as easy to get a good mechanic. He'd left his touring car in a garage on Thursday, and they'd had a fire there. His roadster had gone up in flames. *More bad luck*, he complained to friends, but perhaps fortune was about to smile on him. Dorothy was in the passenger seat, and they were on their way to the Marcell Inn, in the Altadena Hills.

She hadn't really wanted to go, but the doctor had been so kind to her mother, even donating blood when Lilly needed a transfusion. Mother had insisted. Carl was thirty-eight, far too old for her. And she didn't have time for romance: not with three films this year already. Paramount had given her a $2,500 bonus for *Shoot the Works*, and were preparing a star's contract; there was even word around the lot that she would be featured with Bing Crosby next year in *Mississippi*; you couldn't resist saying it was the role she was born to play. *Little Miss Marker* was two weeks into a box office sensation, and to open tomorrow at the Saenger Theater in New Orleans. She couldn't wait to tell Dottie Lambour, who was about to sign her own Hollywood contract! All the girls would be back together soon.

There was lots to celebrate: champagne, and an orchestra, and gay dancing. By the time she left with Dr. Wagner, about 2:00 A.M., she felt dazzled and shivery, like the night. The stars were hard pinpoints overhead in the sky; the chill expanse of open universe made her light-headed. Dorothy wrapped her black coat around her.

The doctor opened her door and, stepping up on the running board, she slid into the seat. He got behind the wheel, speeding off, heading south on Lincoln Avenue in Pasadena. The road swerved right. She remembered the taxicab in Central Park. Before she can warn him to slow, the car has already left the road, jumped the curb, sheared an eighteen-inch light pole, hit a large rock, caromed off a tree, turned over and over in a somersault and come to rest facing in the opposite direction. They have traveled more than a hundred feet from the road; the car's top is wedged in the tree's limbs. The auto body is crumpled, twisted.

Dorothy is pinned underneath, already lifeless. Dr. Wagner has been thrown clear, but the frantic efforts of his fellow doctors won't be able to save him. He lives until the next morning, never regaining comprehension.

The police don't know who the girl is with him. They ask his mother. "That's Miss Dell," she says, her horror growing at the extent of the tragedy. "She was at our house only last night."

LAST NIGHT. Last rites.

A private service is held in the chapel of the Pierce Brothers mortuary on West Washington. Only forty people are there on the Sunday afternoon at two, with Jack Oakie representing the film community, and Ruth Etting on hand to sing "The Rosary." Outside, hundreds throng, pushing against police to catch a glimpse of the proceedings. Dell has just begun to be a star, and the accident has made the front pages of the L.A. papers.

Both Dorothy's parents are there. Her sister stands between them, in a small alcove hidden from sight. They will all be leaving for New Orleans as soon as arrangements can be made. Dorothy's final resting place will be in the Metairie cemetery, lot 148, a one-room above-ground tomb that burial regulations will keep closed to other members of her family, including her mother. The monument, paid for by Paramount, is across from a mausoleum belonging to a Columbo family, though no relation to Russ.

He mourns and misses her, but it wouldn't be proper to attend. Her mother simultaneously blamed him and herself for their breakup, and he didn't want to risk a scene. He preferred to remember Dorothy as they were, the Romeo of Song and his own Follies Juliet, and the way she wiggled her head between his arms and upturned her face, poised for affection.

On an NBC radio remote with Hollywood gossip columnist Jimmy Fidler the night of July 1, Columbo performs "With My Eyes Wide Open I'm Dreaming" and "Stardust." They had been starry-eyed all right. He had opened his eyes on hers one night, while they were locked tight, and hers were open as well. They paused in their heavy breathings to look on the other, in wonder that they had come so close, their dreams forever entwined, their bloods transfused. He crossed himself in the familiar down-and-across motion.

"God will love her when He gets to know her," Russ said. Regrets and forgets.

THE NEWS is brought to Shirley Temple on the set of *Now and Forever*. The cameras are rolling on a domestic scene in which her father has lied to her about being a jewel thief. As they tell her of Dorothy's death, tears begin to slide down her dimpled cheeks; she's crying just like a little girl. The director signals to continue filming.

On the strength of her and Shirley's mutual affection, Dorothy had been proposed for *Now and Forever*, to star with Gary Cooper as the couple little Shirley will bring together. But Dorothy is already at work on *Shoot the Works* in April; there's no way she could be ready for *Now and Forever*, scheduled to start in late May.

In *Now and Forever*, Temple is her usual Cupid's bow, a matchmaker taking delight in being love's go-between, knowing she'll be included in the final clinch. Stay together for the child. It was to her irrepressible credit that the movie fared as well as it did. Shirley loved to play the game of moviemaking; in *Shirley Temple's Favorite Poems,* a 1936 collection, she leads off with Claudia Thorin's "Make-Believe Town": "*You can be what you will, from a king to a clown. . . .*"

Carole Lombard had a similar philosophy of unmethod acting. Though Fox had Temple's contract, Paramount had Damon Runyon's stories, and Fox knew that the *Miss Marker* role would make Shirley a star. Paramount had been shrewd enough to negotiate for two pictures, and *Now and Forever* needed to be made quickly. Paramount asked Carole to step in for Dorothy.

Dorothy and Carole and Shirley. Close cover before striking.

TOO BEAUTIFUL FOR WORDS

Jimmie Grier is waiting for Russ when he arrives to record the songs from *Wake Up and Dream.*

Columbo has known Grier a long time, since they were both in Arnheim's orchestra. Jimmie was Gus's chief arranger, a reed player whose easygoing personality well suited the Ambassadors' cut-and-tailored charts. When Gus left the Grove in 1931, Abe Frank asked Grier to take over the orchestra, but he didn't have the zest of a Phil Harris, who soon replaced him. Jimmie didn't mind. He liked the behind-the-scenes of radio and recording, and he found himself another residency at the Biltmore Bowl, another hotel ballroom.

There was plenty of work, and Jimmie took on all of it. He could be heard on radio in 1932, on the *MJB Demitasse Revue*; he backed Jack Benny and discovered Pinky Tomlin. He feuded with Jan Garber for sport, and settled it with a public peacemaking off Santa Catalina in which Eddy Duchin was referee. The yacht on which they shook hands was captained by Biltmore owner Baron Long. Everyone was doing well in Hollywood.

So was Russ. He bought the family a house on Outpost Circle, in the hills above the Roosevelt, a sprawling not-quite-mansion with five bedrooms and four and a half baths. Coved ceilings. A two-car garage. A large pool. A cabaña.

He and his folks and brother John ("Jack") had moved in on July 1 from where they had been staying, at 1019 Roxbury Drive, about the time filming began on *Wake Up and Dream.* The Spanish colonial house at number 1940 had been built in 1928. It didn't have much in the way of grounds, being carved into the foothills as Hollywood began its climb up to Mulholland, though it had a Mediterranean elegance, with half-oval doors and a cylinder of windows bulging around the inner stairs, an abundance of stained glass, and an intercom system. There were red semicircles of terra-cotta tiles on the roof, the pool with its diving board perched on a patio, Hollywood aglow falling away beneath the swimmers.

He finished filming *Wake Up and Dream* after a month of shooting. Everyone seemed excited about it. Now, on this summer's-end Friday, August 31, he was going to the preview at the Pantages tonight with Carole. Lansing had said he'd meet them there.

Russ was looking forward to working with Grier, though he did feel he was again trailing in Bing's wake. Jimmie had roomed with Bing for a time in the Arnheim days, when Bing was so poor he'd be constantly leaving IOUs in Grier's cash stash. In June 1933, and again in August, they had celebrated their old school ties by recording some of Bing's most exultant sessions for Brunswick, including "Learn to Croon." Grier had become virtual leader of the house band at the label's West Coast operations, and for a season, provided the musical accompaniment for Bing's Woodbury Soap radio broadcasts, though he had bowed out by the end of May 1934.

Bing recorded his last sessions for Brunswick in July 1933, with Irving Aaronson and His Commanders, performing the songs from the film *She Loves Me Not*. Kapp's new Decca label would be taking over his releases in the fall, and he first cut discs for this new affiliation on August 8, accompanied by Georgie Stoll. The premier Decca release backed "I Love You Truly" with "Just A-Wearyin' for You," and the next was a "Sweetheart" two-sider with "Let Me Call You Sweetheart" and "Someday Sweetheart." The choices were telling, a pair of turn-of-the-century chestnuts by Carrie Jacobs Bond, and the "Sweethearts" not much younger. Kapp had originally tried to convince Bing to record "semiclassical," by which he meant light operetta like Victor Herbert; Bing resisted, saying "that's for the high-class singers." Jack persisted; his quantitative instinct was that the highest-class singers were those that won the most hearts, sold the most records. To reach that many people you had to simplify. Overcoming Bing's misgivings, he told Crosby that he wanted to cut out the "frills" and turn down the heat, that Bing had the "opportunity to be the John McCormack of this generation." It would have profound implications for Crosby's future.

Kapp planned to battle the Depression in the same inverse way, boosting record sales by slashing prices, helped by the willingness of his artists— including Bing, Guy Lombardo, Isham Jones, and Glen Gray's Casa Loma

Orchestra—to help his fledgling label grow by accepting reduced royalties and advances for more turnover. He had kept an eye to the future when negotiating contracts for his former employers, keeping to the short term and leaving options open; Crosby's, for example, stated that his tenure with Brunswick could be terminated if Kapp left the company. Decca records cost thirty-five cents, compared to seventy-five cents for the big three: Brunswick, the nearly dormant Columbia, and Victor.

Now Russ was signed to Brunswick, his first coupling slated to be "When You're in Love" and "Let's Pretend There's a Moon." His contract called for 12 to 14 sides a year.

Yes, all appeared to be going smoothly. Columbo was back on the NBC red network as of June 10, a weekly fifteen minutes every Sunday night. A typical broadcast, on July 15, catches him in fine spirits, opening with a couple of songs from upcoming movies. *The Old Fashioned Way*'s "Rolling in Love" is as close as he comes to stepping out, surprisingly up-tempo. For once he seems informal behind the mike. *The Hollywood Party*'s "I've Had My Moments" is a maudlin look-back that has a sense of past-tense finality. He'd seen it all before: "*I sang of true love / I played gui-tar / Then found a new love . . .*" Her. His big moment.

Jimmy Fidler has the Hollywood gossip spot, leading with an item about Lupe Velez and Johnny Weissmuller's marital woes. "Lupe has turned her marriage into a three-ring circus," he moralizes, citing "extremely abusive remarks" to Tarzan by his Jane. Things hadn't changed much from *Wolf Song*, when Russ was the one doing the serenading, to no avail. Fidler runs through Miriam Hopkins, Garbo, the breakup of Ruth Chatterton's liaison with George Brent, Pauline Garrand, a star of "a few years back" who has been struck with "infantile paralysis," Gloria Stuart, Claudia Morgan, Robert Chipper the explorer, the known and unknown now. Jimmy's "Best Picture of the Week" is *The Barretts of Wimpole Street* with Norma Shearer and Fredric March. He plugs *Wake Up and Dream*, and the songs being recorded today. Russ ends with a trifle, "(I'm Not Lazy) I'm Dreaming," keeping to the somnambulist theme, before he croons his theme song. *La da dee da da.*

He was working hard, and it was paying off. Laemmle junior wanted him for *Show Boat*, to play the part of Gaylord Ravenel. And this was the weekend he was going to ask Carole to marry him. Again.

The only thing to mar his happiness was his mother's illness. They had taken her to the hospital yesterday. Poor dear Mama. She could hardly see him when he walked into the room, her heart struggling to keep up with her body. He cups his hands, blows warm breath between them, rubs the palms together, releasing his wishes for her good health and recovery. Then he turns his attention to the first song.

THE THREE from *Wake Up and Dream* go easily. After the nerve-racking stress of moviemaking, of remembering lines and blocking and reactions, the act of singing is a relief, like remembering to breathe. It's what he was meant to do.

Yet acting has trickled into his singing. He has acquired a third dimension, a thespian depth-of-field that enhances his vocal delivery. He is not as single-minded in his pursuit of the melody. Russ is defter; he slides between registers as if he's using hand gestures to help explain himself. His voice has entered its bronze age.

Grier is also cinematic. "When You're in Love" seems to suggest its own sound track. In the bridge, when the images turn to "traveling," he lets the guitar chug, the snare choo-choo. When Russ sings "hit you," a small bell punctuates in echo. The tempos ebb and flow.

Russ is a writer on all three songs, working the melody side of the credits, with the help of Grace Hamilton (on "Let's Pretend There's a Moon") and Ernie Grossman (the remaining two). Jack Stern takes the lyrics in hand, melding "exquisite" to "is it?" in "When You're in Love," the one most tied to film pacing. It has a nautical roll, parts fitting together in a slight incongruity, like the yachting cap Russ wears in one of the vaudeville skits. He will, however, have plenty of opportunity to be seen in his tuxedo.

When; not how or why. In love or out of love. There is the nagging self-doubt that it may not last. Or wonder that it's lasted this long.

Can it be captured in the bottled imp of language? Is love fiction, or fact? If you can measure its fleeting fancy, if only in poetry, does that diminish love? Can you read about it, and get the picture? Wake up and dream?

He is at the core. The birth of song. The en-core.

He moves from his viewpoint to viewing her. She is "Too Beautiful for Words." Once he might have taken this as a croon enticement, practically begging him to enter a more abstract realm of singing. Now he resists. He is too long the crooner. He wants to be more than a pretty song. As a writer, Russ knows he's *"not a Gershwin, or a Berlin,"* but they can't sing like him. His voice can make the *"moonlight serenade . . . a perfect rhapsody,"* to complement his sighing, gathering speed and then coasting, like a skater.

There is a moment in a dream when you try to remember where you've been when, what was dreamt, in the instant before awakening. You could explain the dream's logic, or try, only in day's light it doesn't make as much sense. Tell your dream to someone; they immediately stop listening, unless they're being paid to interpret.

In *Dream Days*, a collection of phantasmagoric stories from 1898, Kenneth Grahame tries on "The Magic Ring," a popular piece of jewelry in the approaching England of the twentieth century. You're either inside or outside the encircle. *En:* "Of certain supreme moments it is not easy to write. The varying shades and currents of emotion may indeed be put into words by those specially skilled that way. . . . But the sheer, crude article itself—the strong, live thing that leaps up inside you and swells and strangles you, the dizziness of revulsion that takes the breath like cold water—who shall depict this and live?"

He was taking a chance. He did worship Carole.

There is a hint of what his second voice might sound like, the one he holds in reserve for his lessons with Pietro Cimini, a flourish to round off the first verse of "Let's Pretend There's a Moon," a hint of grand operetta. Russ might be the one for Victor Herbert. He feints toward the croon but then dips back to the lyric chorus of "When You're in Love." He's bobbing around the phrasing, shadowboxing. He'd always loved boxing—until "my father gave me the worst beating I ever got in my life"—and is photographed in the backyard of Outpost Circle, wearing black swim trunks, sparring with his brother while his father referees. The family is happy.

They don't know what to make of Carole. If his parents hated the bright lights of New York, they might surely shut their eyes to this fluorescent beacon come into their close-knit family circle. But Lombard didn't give Mama time to dislike her. That wasn't quite the same thing as his mother accepting her as a daughter. In law. The Colombos were a Catholic family; Carole was hardly, and a divorced woman at that. She had been raised Baha'i—though unusual, the Iranian religion's credo of equality of the sexes and respect for other races and religions seemed to fit her and her mother's worldview. Russ didn't mind what she practiced, as long as one of his sons became a priest. He had never discussed this with Carole.

"Too Beautiful for Words." That was where it started going wrong. When you realized it was not just love, but compromise; two expectations merged into one and hoping there's enough left over for the explanations. If you have to talk it over, prove your point, convince and cajole or be your own alibi, it's already separated from the divine love that swallows you up, beyond argument or agreement.

Too beautiful. That moment when beauty overreaches, becomes aware of its finite impermanence. Then it might be described. But it is Too.

THIS IS getting dangerous. It's only a game, the actor's artifice. "Let's Pretend There's a Moon." It's not real. *"We don't need a moon to tell us when to kiss,"* but then why bring it up? She hadn't noticed until now. The movies have their own pretense. If he must play himself, at least he knows his lines.

He can stand on his own. *"The time and place are opp-or-tune,"* and he sings her that tune. *"Why should we be wasting time?"* Life is all too short. *"Who cares if there's no moon above?"*

He doesn't need the moon. The moon needs him.

THE FINAL song is postscript. In "I See Two Lovers," he is an afterthought: the eye as observer. A voyeur. It's their when, not his.

He feels isolated, alone by the *"moonlit"* sand and sea. He watches two lovers kiss, in *"a land apart."* Lyric writer Allie Wrubel tucks his rhymes within lines, while Russ lies in wait. The suspense of time. What next? How does this story end and song finish? The cliff-hanging *when.* He's impatient. Will she say yes, before Grier's orchestra takes a carioca around the *"heavenly music . . . voices of night, a silvery light, chasing the gloom"*? The instrumental break lets everyone have a dance while they think it over, before Russ is back in the "shrine of love." The whyne of love.

He's reached the tail chorus.

"I wonder when I'll find the trembling hand / Fate intended for me."

In reprise. He crescendos a fifth and holds on to the last word for dear life. *Meeee . . .*

He completes his body of work.

BEFORE HE leaves, Grier asks him what he'll be doing for Labor Day weekend. "I'm heading for Ensenada with some of the boys to fish. Want to come?"

Russ shrugs no. He's going with Carole up to Lake Arrowhead. Have a good time.

PREVIEW

I

n disguise.

Carole has on ZaSu Pitts's costume from *The Gay Bride*, which she's film-ing over at MGM, and a wig. Russ is done up like Sam Hardy, an actor in that movie, a gangster in a slouch hat. They don't want to be recognized at this preview at the Pantages, a dream theater even before the featured presenta-tion begins.

The Pantages is as much stage set as its entertainments. Like the other movie palaces along Hollywood Boulevard before stars were set in its sidewalk, it is a fantasy realm unto itself. Alexander Pantages hasn't spared the gilt.

Lansing Brown sits in another corner of the orchestra. He doesn't want to disturb Russ and Carole, or draw attention to them. He's understanding. They were a twosome, and he was the crowd. He'd been feeling left out re-cently, but that was to be expected. She was the one who knew about acting, who was teaching Russ the tricks of the trade, the one who had been married to William Powell and was so friendly with Billy Haines that she gave him the decorating job on her new house. She was the one who starred opposite Bing while remaining true to Russ, and convinced Hollywood (if not the picture-going public, for whom it was only a modest success) that she was a serious comic actress in *Twentieth Century*. She even had Fieldsie, her secretary, calling him, inviting him around, including him.

Brown couldn't be mad at her for taking up Russ's attention. Carole was a great gal, and Russ was great with her, and if that meant less time left over for him, well, he'd be great, too. When ever. Sooner or later, he knew Russ would want to talk over the movie, and ask him what he thought, and sit across from him at the table in his den. They'd close the door. Tell secrets. He wasn't going anywhere.

SHE PUTS her hand in his as the house lights go down, gives it a squeeze. She feels a distracted response, almost reflexive, and smiles. He's tense with excitement; his star is rising. She is anxious and happy for him.

Even though he had rehearsed this scene in his head for many years, Russ finds it hard not to be nervous. He looks around at the Friday night crowd, many of whom have stayed over from the feature attraction, *Million Dollar Ransom*, taken from a Damon Runyon magazine story, to see this "Major Studio Feature Preview." He was curious to what his reaction would be when he experienced *Wake Up and Dream* as more than just a jumble of disconnected scenes and take numbers. He had watched the dailies when he could, and a rough edit. It was nothing compared to the on-screen mirror of an audience, seeing yourself through their eyes, as they see through you.

He's set his alarm for this moment.

It rings in reverse. Wake up. *Dream*. He's like a hypnotist who snaps his fingers, lapsing his subject into unconsciousness, ready to bark like a dog, or feel warm, or investigate a past life. The REM of remember.

He enters the movie.

TOPPING THE screen credits, Russ Columbo is Paul Scotti, the sensitive one of a vaudeville two-guys-and-a-girl playing to empty houses five times a day in Atlantic City. His first scenes set the tone of "Merry, Modern Romance Pepped With Music Mirth and Melody" that Universal hooplas for *Wake Up and Dream*. In duet with June Knight, Russ wearing that goofy yachting cap and singing "Let's Pretend There's a Moon," the house rules are explained: she wants Russ, but as Toby, is pledged to Roger Pryor's Charlie, the act's resident tightrope walker.

Her voice is thin, but she has an appealing candor, and a resemblance to Dorothy Dell, another robust blonde. June had been a sickly child—diphtheria, a mastoid infection, double pneumonia—who built up her strength through dancing, so much so that she became a professional hoofer, appearing in the chorus of *The Broadway Melody* and standing in as a body double for Greta Garbo in the oriental sequences of *Mata Hari*. Though she sings in *Wake Up and Dream*, her part doesn't include dancing. June is already fighting with Universal about the quality of her roles, and would actually terminate her contract with the studio by "mutual consent" less than a week after the Pantages preview.

Columbo's first real acting comes with a mouthful of hot dog. The trio is having dinner, planning their next move. "How about the dough situation?" he asks Charlie, not referring to the bun, trying to chew and swallow and deliver his lines. Feigning casual. It's good he usually has something to do with his hands; his character smokes, inhales, his cigarette held between thumb and two fingers, blowing exhaust clouds out his nose. He is always seen dressed smart, his pleated pants riding high up on his waist, cinched by a thin belt, wide tie tucked into the waistband. The movie holds off the pleasure of viewing him in his tuxedo until the end.

He's concentrating on loosening up, but it seems like he's acting, while Pryor merges seamlessly with his character, a schematic double-talker who keeps the act alive by his brash anything-goes approach. When Charlie hears that theatrical impresario Earl Craft is losing patience waiting for his drunken star to show up, he has Russ audition. Columbo sings "Too Beautiful for Words," his paean to music's *"language heavensent,"* and the camera moves in for an indulgent close-up.

The "*song that can never be heard*" is the true star of the movie, inspirationally featured whenever there's a lull in the action. It is introduced as an instrumental theme over the title roll and has four separate appearances, including a scene in which Russ plays it himself at the piano. It is the only visual we have of his digits moving over the piano keyboard. He seems at ease, using more than one finger on his left hand, a proper pianist. He doesn't look at the keys when he sings to June. She in turn will accompany him when he performs it for Craft's show, and harmonize it in duet at "Nick's Roadhouse" on Hollywood Boulevard, where they come to "crash the pictures," though not when he pitches it to Hollywood actress "Marie La Rue" (an early appearance of Wini Shaw, an exotic half-Hawaiian beauty who will introduce "Lullabye of Broadway" in Busby Berkeley's *Gold Diggers of 1935*), as an honorable Scotti tries valiantly to turn his attentions away from Toby.

Wake Up and Dream has an overwhelm of characters, and the locales keep shifting as well, each stopover adding a zany new personality to the traveling band. The trio go to New York and are visited by Cellini, Scotti's guardian uncle from Italy, played by Henry Armetta, which gives Russ a chance to say a couple of words in Italian: *bambino* and *Com' esta*. On a Greyhound bus west, a dowager crystal-gazer (Catherine Doucet) and her bodyguard, Andy Devine (his gargle of a voice unique even then), attach to their party. Russ and June sing "When You're in Love" in a bus station in Santa Fe, though the final verses are stolen by Doucet and Armetta. There is a strange detective nosing about, a drunk played by Gavin Gordon, and a revolving door of producers that ends with a Hollywood magnate who signs Russ to his movie. As the cast enlarges exponentially, emotions and humor spread themselves thin. Russ gets less focal-length screen time. He's diminished by the hubbub. Even when he gives June a sultry stare and says "c'mere you," the film cuts to Cellini and Madame Rose in full histrionic. He can't compete; he's the only normal guy around, except when he sings "Too Beautiful for Words."

Except when he sings.

Too beautiful for words.

THE END.

He reprises the chorus to June one final time and kisses her. As the final credits roll ("A good cast is worth repeating!"), there is a moment of uncomfortable silence as the audience remembers they're in a theater. A clapping starts from the back of the house, a smattering of growing applause that lasts a respectable amount of time before stopping all too abruptly.

Russ could hear Lansing's cadence in there. He let out his breath, suddenly aware he was holding it.

Awake.

He felt like a phantasm in their midst. They didn't notice him, or Carole; or if they did, chose not to acknowledge their presence. It was the audience's part to play.

What did they think, or did it even matter? He knew what he thought. There might be a retake coming up this weekend, especially in the scene where he admits to Toby that "I just haven't met the right woman," knowing it's she. That whenever he wasn't singing, he was trying, and he'd have to work on that. Maybe Carole could help him.

He turned toward her, seeing her in costume, as if yet another strange character had entered the movie in its closing moments, a guest arriving after the party is over, the film continuing. He was still in costume as well. He had a sudden sense of camera movement.

"C'mon, you," she said. Her laugh was a tinkle. "I want to be the first one to fuck this movie star."

THE PARTING

She and he have been arguing for over an hour. Some of these making-their-points are on their third time around. The tenth. Weekly and daily. They were getting set in their ways.

He was ready to be married. Russ knew how much he adored Carole. He didn't need convincing, as obviously she did. He wanted her, and he wanted a family, before he was too old to be a grandparent, or his folks were. His mother was ill, and he wanted to make her happy.

She knew he was getting nervous. The *Hollywood Reporter* had been on the streets first thing Saturday morning with their review of *Wake Up and Dream*, calling the film "fair" and his performance "not as successful" as his singing. *They should've stayed around for the late show*, she thought.

It was a different Russ this afternoon. He seemed to need reassurance. Insecurance. He wanted to engage her, as soon as possible.

It was something to consider. When she was with him, she felt impelled by his obvious fixation toward her. She liked having him under her spell. He wanted to take care of her; it was a cliché, but she found herself considering it in spite of its ever-after fairy-tale ending. Flattery has its own seduction. That was what a girl was brought up to expect, to become a woman by having a man love and protect her. It was a survival mechanism, an ancient and instinctual biology, different from the adoration she found in her public. She was too practical to be that abstract. Even with her independent streak, she was lured by the prospect of finding the right guy and settling down. To settle, as she'd always been told, except by her mother, who had set her example.

If this hadn't been such a good year for her career, she might have thought

twice, even taken Russ up on his offer. But Paramount had sensed the unde-
niable maturity and, yes, charisma Carole had brought to her recent roles.
They were impressed with her toe-to-toe slugfest with the Great Profile in
Twentieth Century, her wisecrack reliability. In July 1934, the studio had rewarded her with a new contract, calling for three thousand dollars a week.
Even without a box office stunner, she moved through Hollywood earning
her keep. Lombard had proved herself no johnny-come-lately starlet, impressed to be sitting in some producer's lap; she had been around long
enough to come into her own.

Her screen life suited her, an embellishing character to her off-screen persona even as her Hollywood sociability added confidence and swing to her
acting. She was having a screw ball.

BESIDES, SHE knew Russ wasn't serious. Who was he kidding? His career
just getting off the ground, her career moving up a notch, the whirl of Hollywood around them. And children?

She wondered what they would look like. Her light translucence, his dark
eclipse, their shading grays.

He would want her to convert, and then there was the problem of her
divorce from Powell. What was he thinking? She saw herself among his swarthy
family, the one that doesn't belong, always an Aryan visitor. Russ desired her because she was different, the oppositional attract. She was uncertain whether
that helped or hindered. Do your differences keep you apart, or do they draw
you together? Would their moods and modes intermingle? Or maybe he was
just setting up a situation that couldn't succeed, because he knew that each of
them was too busy and didn't want to make the sacrifice for the other.

It was the tricky part of a relationship, she knew. Closing in on a year anniversary, it was time to declare yourself.

She had to get away, to turn down the flame on this runaway romance.
Anyway, she had been working much too hard, and the studio doctor had ad-
vised her to take a long weekend. She was going to Big Bear, a resort near
Lake Arrowhead, a little cabin, Fieldsie and the dog. Without him.

She told Russ she would meet him for a late supper at her mother's tomorrow night. She couldn't stand it when he got like this. So needy.

NEED. THAT'S why he sang. Because he couldn't be alone.

That was what his songs were about. The urge to couple, to find your self
in someone else. Within love.

His singing is transparent. You can hear through him, see yourself in the mirror behind his voice, and his desire to reflect. He's not selfless; far from it. He wants to absorb your light, like the dark star he is, a magnet's pull and gravity, to snap his centrifugal whip.

When a planet and a sun orbit around each other, who has the greater revolve, the planet or its phosphorescent captor? A solar system can't act alone; tides must be held in balance, along with the silhouette phases of the moon.

Russ could feel them waning. He and Carole had reached the inevitable moment when the expanding universe starts backtracking, contracting, when the earth of reality moves between sun and moon, creating unexpected shadows. Or could it go on forever? And ever.

He wanted to stop time. At the point of no return.

HE WAS going to the Brown Derby. He needed the solace and random noise of a crowd. This was supposed to be his triumphal weekend, and he was going to enjoy some of it. Let Carole go to Big Bear. He could use a break himself. He wanted to visit his mother tomorrow, and talk to Lansing, and get a chance to enjoy the new house on Labor Day. Take a swim. Practice his diving.

It's the first day of September. He remembers back three years. This was the week that NBC had given him the go-ahead for his radio show, when he cut his first records. When he became Russ Columbo for all time.

It was something to celebrate. Monday would be the third anniversary of his "You Call It Madness" session. Maybe he'd sit down at the piano and play it for himself, salute the wild ride he'd had. He thought of Carole. The song still held true. Two ways of seeing the same thing, and both right.

Love is madness.

Now can we move on?

LANSA'S

He tosses the Sunday *Examiner* into the backseat of the Packard, gets behind the wheel, and cranks the starter, heading for Lansing Brown's house.

The newspaper is folded to section V, page 8. A photo of Bing points a pistol across three columns to one of Russ kneeling in prayer, his hands clasped, eyebrows arched. Pleading his case for a stay of execution.

The accompanying stories, both written by the enigmatic Ray De O'Fan, are related by family tree. Crosby's picture goes with a nonitem about "the Kentucky Colonel from Los Angeles, Gustaphus Arnheim" returning to radio's *Hall of Fame* on KFI before setting off on tour, how "the men in the band prefer that I mount the rostrum" instead of hiding behind the piano. "They look to the baton for inspiration," says Gus. "I haven't been able to figure yet whether they are complimenting me or subtly giving me the 'works.' " Bing isn't mentioned, though his caption states that though he was "once a rival of Russ Columbo. . . . Today their difficulties have been patched and they once again are close friends."

There's friends and there's family. Russ wishes Carole could understand the difference. COLUMBOS ADORE BAMBINO his headline reads, subheaded "Baby of Family Now Topnotch Crooner." Wait until Mama sees her name underneath: "Papa and Mamma Live in Fine Home on Hollywood Hilltop." If only she could see. The article continues praising his generosity, that he'd helped his parents buy their own home and provided for his brothers and sisters. "Russ Columbo's last thought is of himself," it says; the youngest is "the apple of everyone's eye." He would take it over to her at Santa Monica Hospital after he finishes talking with Lansa.

He had tried to call Brown all night. He needed to discuss his dilemma with someone sympathetic. Carole had turned him down, *for the time being,* or so she said. *Pretty soon.* But what was she really saying? That she wasn't ready to be his wife? That she was less in love with him? That there was a limit to their love? He worshipped her, he had put her on a pedestal, and now she was stepping off her altar, threatening to walk out of the room.

He hadn't wanted to go home last night, to his father and Jack. He ducked in and out of nightspots, roaming Hollywood until it was time to make a break between night and day, to sleep fitfully. He has to talk this through. *Lansa is like a mirror,* Russ thinks, someone you can use to figure yourself out, from the perspective of their listening; audience participation.

The car drives itself to 584 North Lillian Way, while he smokes and turns the wheel and loses himself in thought. When he makes a right onto Lansa's block, he isn't quite sure how he had gotten there.

LANSING DRAWS aside the window curtains when he hears Russ's car pull up in the street. It's about twelve-thirty. He hasn't wasted any time getting here.

He must have something on his mind.

Brown had gone to photograph a wedding yesterday in Santa Barbara. He'd arrived in the afternoon, with the ceremony at seven o'clock, and didn't return to Hollywood until three in the morning. When he awoke at eleven the next day, his parents told him that Russ had been calling constantly. Lansing phoned him shortly before noon; Columbo asked if he'd breakfasted yet. Lansing had. Russ said he'd be right over. Lansing took out a cigarette, lit it. Russ would be here in half an hour. He needed time to gather himself. He could tell Russ was already disappearing from his life. He hadn't seen much of him in the past weeks, between the movie and Carole. He was starting a new life, and Lansing was being left behind. Again.

He'd been through this movie before. He knew what part he would play; the patient, understanding, loyal friend, in it for the long term. Always there. Russ was like a comet that visited his solar system every few years. Who knew when he would re-orbit into his life? Columbo's life was tumultuous, his affairs upheavals, and usually, Brown thought, over as soon as they started turning too serious. Lansing wanted to be a constant, to encourage him to keep singing. He had always loved Russ's voice.

A few weeks ago, Columbo had shown him the piece he'd been working on in his voice lessons, the "Prologue" from *I Pagliacci.* Written by his namesake, Ruggiero Leoncavallo, the opera concerns a strolling troupe of actors and musicians, a tragedy within an ostensible comedy. The "Prologue" is introduced by Tonio, a baritone clown: "*Our author tonight a chapter will borrow / From life with its laughter and sorrow.*"

His voice was tremulous. He was growing into his lower registers, Lansing noted with satisfaction as Russ sang. There seemed to be reserves of breath behind his notes. "*A song of tender mem'ries / Deep in his list'ning heart one day was ringing; / And then with a trembling hand he wrote it.*"

He can see Russ getting out of the Packard, shutting the door.

"*Ah, think then, kind people, when ye look on us, / Clad in our motley and tinsel / Ours are human hearts, beating with passion, / Since we are but men like you, for gladness or sorrow.*"

Lansing straightens up, shrugging his jacket over his shoulders. Russ is walking up the driveway to the small inset porch under the roof's overhang. Lansing hastens to meet him at the door.

"*Will ye hear, then, the story / As it unfolds itself surely and certain! / Come then! Let us begin!*"

THEY VISIT for a bit with Lansing's parents before retiring to his den. It's dark and cool in the room. The shades are drawn, and the redwood walls display some of Lansing's collection of armaments: a pair of cutlasses, an ornamental spear.

They sit on either side of a mahogany desk. There are a few scattered papers on the polished top, a couple of books and ends, a pair of Civil War–era dueling pistols Lansing had bought at an antiques shop next to his studio a few years back. There is an overhanging floor lamp on Russ's side of the table, and a mirror on the wall behind him in which the shade of the lamp can be seen reflected.

Lansing reaches in his jacket pocket for a pack of Luckies, offers one over to Russ. He takes a stick from a box of matches, scratches at the tip with his thumbnail, and watches it flare. Then he lights both their cigarettes, waving out the match and dropping it into an ashtray.

They are quiet for a moment. Finally, Russ breaks the stillness. "So . . . what'd you think the other night?"

"It was good," says Lansing, carefully choosing his words. "You have to remember that it's a start, that nobody is expecting you to do it all in one movie. I especially liked. . . ." Showing him the bright side, as always.

THEY SPEAK for an hour. Increasingly, Lansing realizes that it doesn't matter what he says. That Russ is intent on proving his point, if only to himself.

Talking about his voice is easy enough; Lansing thinks his singing in *Wake Up* is exquisite, that it's not important if his character seems naïve, a well-meaning *schnook*. When the camera fills the screen with his face, that's all that counts. His song is the important thing, and there is no question that "Too Beautiful" will be a major hit.

He should continue to work on his singing. Take advanced lessons. Practice more. Perhaps he could study with Marafiotti.

"You have ambition enough for the two of us." Russ smiles. Already Lansing's confidence is making him feel better. "Carole has been telling me the same thing. 'Russ, you can't go on crooning forever.' "

It's when the conversation turns to Carole that Lansing feels at a loss. What can he say? Love has to work in the real world, two lives into one. He wasn't ready. Or she.

Russ won't give it up, worrying at their relationship as a cat would a mouse, not ready to believe the fun is over once the prey is caught.

"Have you thought that Carole isn't quite prepared to become a mother?" Lansing looks around the desk for something for his hands to do. He picks up one of the dueling pistols, turns it absently over and over while he tries to think of the next thing to say.

"I'm not asking her to give up everything, but if we know how much we care for each other, we have to make a start somewhere." Russ shifts restlessly in his chair, leaning forward. "It's not just a whim on my part, Lansing. I've never felt this way about anyone."

Lansing purses his lips. How can he tell him? He twists the gun in his hand, tracing the line of its barrel, thumbing the hammer, stroking the wood worn smooth over the past threescore and ten years, a human life span.

AS NEAR as can be determined from a grainy newspaper photo, the pistols are anonymous. There might have been a manufacturer's name once etched along the six to eight inches of octagonal barrel, but for all we know they have been forged by a local blacksmith. No distinguishing marks. They are post-flintlock, belt-size, built somewhere in the mid-nineteenth century, a technology honed by a Civil War in a country built on readily available firearms, the home of the Second Amendment. The ramrod slides underneath the barrel, ready for reload. They are missing the percussion caps that would fit over the primer nipple.

They are exactly the same, yet different. In the chamber of one, among the residues of old gunpowder and dust and decayed cobwebs, someone

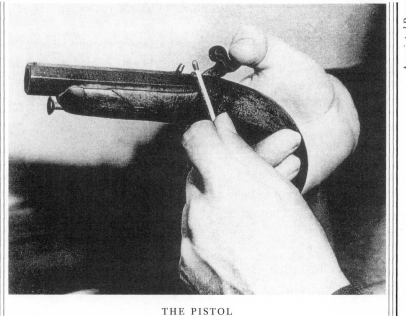

THE PISTOL

has taken the rammer and tamped down a small lead ball of .48 caliber, surrounding it with a measure of black powder. Forgotten, quiescent for decades, a patience born of ultimate purpose. Lying in wait.

LANSING SNAPS the hammer of the gun. A metallic clack punctuates Russ's musings.

"I'm really at a loss, Lansing. She never seems to make up her mind."

Click. The firing pin is raised. *Clack.*

"Do you think I'm being foolish? Selfish? She wouldn't have to give up everything, though certain adjustments might have to be made."

Lansing could fondle the other gun, its mate, but this one is closer. The grip is turned his way. Perhaps if he is leaning back in his chair he might run his fingers over his mustache, doodle on a scrap of paper. Study his reflection in the mirror behind Russ.

The gun asks to be picked up. It fits easily in his right hand. Lansing can hardly hear what Russ is saying. Columbo's voice is starting to sound to his ears like a foreign language, syllables separating from recognizable words, lost in translation, coming from afar. "It doesn't matter," he feels like standing up and yelling at Russ, shaking him by the shoulders, letting him know that friendship has its own passions.

He can't say that, of course. It has to be unspoken, open to interpretation. How can he say what he feels? He can't sing, like Russ. He has to gain control of himself. The only sign of his inner turmoil is a tremor in his palms, a twitch of the wrists. The pistol's grip, its seductive curves carved to hand. Thumb hammer, finger trigger.

Click. Clack.

His left hand holds a match. It's just there; he isn't aware of picking it up from the desk. Russ is talking fast, almost singing; an Italian lilt comes into his voice, the *verismo* of *I Pagliacci*, when Columbine of the play-within-a-play compromises the Harlequin: *"Till tonight, then: and forever I'll be thine."* It only remains for Canio to come out and address the audience: *"La commedia è finita!"*

Brown puts the match into the percussion pen. The barrel hangs toward the desk. Cocks the trigger. Lets go.

IN THE light flash he can see Russ bent over the desk, head slightly inclined to the right, midsentence. A shutter-speed blink, the imploding sound a heartbeat after, the shock effect of the movies no longer silent.

He thinks Russ is kidding when he keels over, hands clawing at his face, toppling backward off the chair.

He was getting to be a good actor, Lansing thought.

THE SHOT

Eight ball in the eye socket.

HE SEES it coming. There is no time to register its imprint on his consciousness, the approaching accelerate of infinity. His optic nerve registers the explosion, follows the round ball as it homes in on its target.

It looks him in the eye.

The imminence of impact.

IT'S A bank shot. Reverse English. The ball caroms, ricocheting off the table at a deadly angle, bouncing toward him. Speed, spin. The force of gravity. The occupied space. Metaphysics.

I AM *waiting for you. I have all the time in the world.* Until there is no time.

IN THE I

Consciousness. Un.
I am done and begun.
Be 'tween.

I KNOW—*what little I know*—*that my life is over. I'm a record pressed, a movie edited, a novel printed, awaiting release. I am awaiting release. To see if I'll be a hit.*

To enter memory.

I am marooned in this synapse of nerve, lines of communication cut, circuits destroyed. I'll never get back. Irreversible; time does not undo, though hopefully you get another chance. Not this time. Organ failure has started its reactive chain, burning my bridges, leaving behind a scorched earth. Nothing will grow where I've been.

My spirit in flight; my body shocked into stasis.

I am blind, beyond light. I cannot touch, because pain has nulled all receptors. The smell of decay, the taste of death.

There is silence. The negative decibels.

THE MEMORIES *revolve as in a dream, a random shuffle of the cards. It's not chronological. I'm standing on the stage of the Paramount and my brother Fiore dances past; I'm running down Catharine Street when Hannah steps out of an alley and pulls her dress up; I'm in Lansing's studio and Lansing has his arm around me and Con looks through the camera and Papa comes in the room and my little Ruggiero smiles shyly at his Mama and begins to play her favorite "Mattinata." Carole and Dorothy enter from each side of the stage and hold hands as they take a bow.*

I wave my hand at the orchestra leader, a tall gentleman with glasses—give Benny and the boys a round of applause! *Ziegfeld is up in his balcony; I tip my top hat to him, while Harry Richman fumes offstage. Winchell is there to take it all down.*

Bing and Rudy link arms with me as we step back into the ensemble, the whole cast come out to dance the finale. The camera pulls back; a chorus line of synchronized performers fills the screen as the camera cranes backward, in ever-growing numbers.

Good night, sweetheart, till we meet tomorrow . . .

Crosby's voice comes under mine, Vallée over. I take the baritone.

It's the final chorus. I tuck my violin under my chin and prepare for the obbligato.

Ah . . .

WOLF SONG

Carole knows from the moment she gets the call from her mother that something terrible has happened to Russ.

Fieldsie bundles her into the car, taking charge. Carole stares at the phone as if it had grown a head, trying to comprehend the extent of tragedy, while Madeline pulls her out the door. Then Fieldsie goes back for the dog and puts him in the backseat. She drives down the mountain to Los Angeles as fast as she can.

HE IS no stranger to the canine.

In *Wolf Song*, a 1929 Western starring Gary Cooper and Lupe Velez, "Russell Columbo" (the *Variety* reviewer notes a preponderance of "foreign names in the personnel") is Ambrosia Guiterrea. Paramount hails it as "the first musical film romance," starring Gary Cooper and Lupe Velez, in a Hispanic old-Sierra California setting that encourages serenading. Director Victor Fleming dwells on the languorous close-up; every kiss between Lupe and Coop is studied at great length. Gary is a fur trapper who answers to the "Wolf Song"; her mating call is "Yo Te Amo Means I Love You." Lash and Lola. Her father doesn't approve, they run away, there's a fight with "Injuns." Fleming close-ups Lupe's heaving bosom.

While they're waiting for the sound equipment to be set up, Lupe sometimes asks Russ to play "Yo Te Amo" on his *guitarrea*. They make jokes. They're both Too Latin; south of the border. They make jokes about that, too.

Columbo wishes he could do more than flirt with Lupe, but he doesn't dare. He's only just learning to croon, and he respects the pack order of a movie's hierarchy. She toys with him, but she's involved in herself, the dominant female. She's not looking for a rogue male.

He puts his tail between his legs while she sniffs at him.

He offers loyalty, unquestioning allegiance. To roll over and expose his belly to her teeth. To risk all in fealty.

That is what makes him such a devout singer, that he can become yours, and yours, and yours . . .

THE DOG stirs restlessly in the backseat, pacing back and forth, unable to settle. He whimpers, paws at the leather, puts his muzzle on Carole's cheek.

She looks at her watch. The pooch loves Russ.

He howls, a dog's croon, like a lone wolf silhouetted against the full moon. Were.

INQUEST

The immediate family begins to gather at Good Samaritan Hospital. His brother John. His brother-in-law, Joseph Benedetti. Carl Laemmle, Jr., by telephone. Sally Blane.

The doctor, a surgeon named George W. Patterson, doesn't offer much in the way of hope. The bullet has entered the orbit of the left eye, pushing through the soft tissue of the brain to fracture the rear of the skull. There is no exit. The ball remains lodged against the interior of the cranium. He is willing to try a risky operation, but at the moment Russ's condition is too delicate to embark on such surgery. Privately, he wonders how Columbo is still alive.

There was chaos at Lansing's in the moments after the gun went off. His parents were already at the door when he frantically rushed out of the den, panic-stricken. Beyond belief.

They rushed in to find Russ lying motionless on the floor, bleeding from a head wound. Lansing could only moan in shock and horror as his father called the police. An ambulance arrived to take Russ to Hollywood Receiving Hospital. There, Police Surgeon Malony realized that more than emergency care was needed. Accompanied by his brother, Columbo's unconscious form was rushed to Good Samaritan, where X rays revealed the hopelessness of his condition. Attempts were made to congeal the bleeding, to prepare for an operation, but there is little anyone can do.

Six hours after he is shot, at 7:30 P.M. Pacific time, Russ Columbo breathes his last and surrenders.

. . .

THERE ARE questions to be asked. Already the newspapers are hinting at a "pistols for two and coffee for one" scenario, along with an unnamed "mystery woman," but this appears to be wishful thinking. The detective lieutenants assigned to the case, J. L. Dwight, L. R. Patton, and Joseph A. Page, are inclined to believe Lansing's story.

He didn't know the gun was loaded. Classic. It could be a Victorian murder ballad, a cowboy lament. "*I took an old pis-tol / Of duel-ing de-sign / Stuck a match head in it, be-low the trig-ger.*" He snaps his fingers for emphasis. "*I was snap-ping the trig-ger / Snap-ping the trig-ger with-out think-ing.*" Trigger-snappy.

"I was pulling back the trigger and clicking it time after time," he said for the record. "I had just lit a cigarette and had the match in my left hand. When I clicked, the match head evidently caught under the hammer. There was an explosion. Russ slid to the side of his chair. I thought he was clowning. It was all mighty fast.

"I had never made an examination to see whether they were loaded because they were so old. I had no idea at all they were loaded."

Howard Nutt of the police research laboratory corroborates the ballistics evidence. In examining the antique cap-and-ball pistols, he finds the barrel of the death gun's twin to be similarly filled with black powder and paper wadding, easily ignited, but minus a leaden ball. There is no way to tell from the exterior of the guns whether or not they contain a charge.

Page escorts Brown to the Hollywood police station for questioning. Lansing, eyes downcast, avoids the lens of the photographer who snaps them walking into headquarters. He's not used to being on this side of the camera. He is bareheaded, in a dark suit and tie, and his left hand, the one that held the fatal match, is tucked into his pants pocket, as if hiding in shame.

THE COUNTY coroner's inquest is set for Wednesday. A jury will determine Lansing's culpability.

He is saved by the ricochet. Despite testimony attesting to Russ and Lansing's friendship, of their affection and warm regard for each other, it is only the two of them who could know what transpired in their sanctum. But the mahogany surface is scored, scraped, and cracked at the apex of its deadly triangle, the circumstantial geometry of Lansing and Russ and desktop. It's a trick shot, and Lansing is no Buck Jones.

There are eight men on Deputy Coroner Kane's jury who will stand in judgment. The case—dutifully reported in the newspapers—establishes subject when Virginia Brissac, Columbo's secretary, makes formal identification of Russ. She had seen his body in the morgue. Her hat has a floppy brim and she puts her purse primly on her lap when she gives testimony. "His name was Ruggiero Colombo, but they called him Russ Columbo. He was born in Camden, New Jersey, twenty-six years ago."

"You knew him then?" asks the deputy coroner. Virginia seems confused. She didn't know him then, she knows him now, her tears starting again as she realizes he is gone. "I was his secretary," she says, dabbing at her eyes. They dismiss her from the stand.

Lansing's parents follow. Lansing senior has a Plains-spoken demeanor, a wiry toughness, and his wife looks as determined, no-nonsense pearls strung around the base of her neck. There was never a quarrel. "I heard no loud talking and saw nothing to indicate my son or Russ had taken any liquor." They were in the kitchen when they heard the explosion.

The attention shifts to the inanimate. Ballistics expert Spencer Moxley demonstrates how the guilty pistol was fired, sliding a match behind the firing pin. He offers what-if's in the confluence of unforeseen coincidences. "If all the powder had been ignited by the sudden flare of the match when the hammer struck it, the bullet would have penetrated the tabletop between the two men, instead of ricocheting and striking Mr. Columbo in the head." There is also the maturing process to consider: "Powder grows more dangerous as it ages." When matter meets time, all theory is relative until you have seen the proof. Detective Lieutenant J. A. Page testifies that he has, in the "mark on the blotter and the desk where the bullet hit before it ricocheted into Columbo's brain." An audible shudder runs through the mostly female audience in the courtroom. None of Russ's family is in attendance.

Then it's Lansing's turn. He sits in the witness chair, his shoulders slumped, hands brought together in his lap, with Kane above his right shoulder, a spectator's partially bald head in the foreground. He hardly speaks above a whisper. "We were sitting in my den. Russ was doing most of the talking, telling me about the successful preview two nights previously of his new starring motion picture."

He'd had the guns for a long time. "I was fingering the old pistol. The pair of them—old dueling guns I had bought as relics seven years ago—always lay on my desk and I frequently fooled with them when my hands were idle. It was just a sort of habit.

"I had looked into the muzzle of the gun a hundred times, so had Russ. And I'd clicked the hammer thousands of times. I never suspected either of them was loaded.

"There was cobwebs in the barrels.

"I had an unlighted match in my left hand. I wasn't even looking at my hands at the time . . . just clicking the hammer aimlessly, listening to Russ talk.

"There was a flash of flame and a terrific explosion. I was looking at Russ at the time. I saw him slump down in his chair. I thought he was fooling . . . until the blood came."

At the time.

The jury retires to deliberate, but there isn't much discussion. "We find that Ruggiero Columbo, 26, came to his death Sept. 2 from a gunshot wound in the head inflicted at 584 Lillian Way by an old pistol in the hand of Lansing Brown Jr. We find the shooting to be accidental and exonerate Brown from all blame."

It's official. He did it, but he didn't do it.

Detective Page approaches him with the pistols. Lansing can have them back if he wants. Brown recoils, his own ricochet. "I never want to see those things again. Keep them!" Banished like Cain from his sight. Or, more properly, the weapon that fell to Cain's hand.

IN THE end, Russ is left with three women.

Sally rushes weeping from the hospital when Dr. Patterson comes out to break the news. She can't contain herself.

Her Russ.

She is forever to be the other woman. The one he didn't choose. Just a childhood crush, an adolescent game. Puppy love.

"Russ was my first boyfriend, but I'm sure he never knew it. I think he was the first boyfriend of a million girls who went to the Grove just to sit and stare at the boy whose soft voice made one dream.

"And then I met him. That was about six years ago. He was everything that an ideal should be." She is still his fan, star-struck.

"Our introduction grew into a warm and understanding friendship that I have prized more than any other possession. It is a tragedy that one so gifted, one so young and so capable of bringing happiness to so many millions of persons should be taken away like this."

At least Sally had been able to be there at the end, at Russ's bedside, before tearfully exiting the hospital. Carole, in transit, is denied his last moments, arriving to find Russ already gone.

She uses the word "shock" at both the beginning ("His death is a terrible shock to me, as it must be to all his friends and admirers") and ending ("His death shocks me beyond words") of her official statement to the press. Yet she senses an inevitability, as befits one who believes in predestination.

"Even though I have lost Russ," she tells Sonia Lee of *Movie Classic*, "I can't feel that life is at an end. For I have a peculiar philosophy. I believe that everything that happens is determined by an inflexible Fate.

"The whole tragedy seems to have been a chain of circumstances leading to death." For three weeks previously she and Russ felt "something cataclysmic hanging over us . . . a peculiar apprehension." She'd had a "horrible feeling the night before," a "frenzy of nerves," and couldn't sleep. "If it hadn't seemed so utterly stupid, I would have returned home early that Sunday morning. I tried to telephone Russ, but I couldn't reach him.

"If I had turned back to Hollywood, Russ would have been with me. If Lansing had been able to telephone him on Saturday, Russ would not have gone to see Lansing on Sunday. Yet, I am certain that no matter what we might have done, Russ would have died that day.

"I am convinced that if he had not met his death through that ricocheting bullet, he would have met it some other way—in an automobile accident, perhaps.

"His number was up."

In the meanwhile, she deftly turns attention away from herself to Columbo's popularity: "It is particularly tragic at this time, for I know that Russ was destined for the most successful year of his career. He told me of several new offers and he was scheduled within a few days to take up a new radio contract." There is no talk of an impending marriage. Her Russ. She calls them "just very good friends," and is purposefully vague about future plans to Sonia Lee, despite her descriptions of Columbo's ardor.

"His love for me was of the kind that comes rarely to any woman. I could never have expected to have such worship, such idolatry, such sweetness from anyone.

"He told you once that his love for me was the most important thing in his life. It really was paramount in his thoughts; it even dwarfed his desire for fulfilling recognition. He was completely content to sit on an evening and just watch me, without saying a word, hardly moving. He had no life apart from me. He was disconsolate when we were not together."

He loved her too much, she thought. "No woman dares to be the one goal in a man's life," but it was her own sense of independence she wanted to preserve. She'd had to fight hard enough for it.

It caused her to reconsider wedding plans. "When Russ would ask me: 'When will you marry?' I would always answer: 'pretty soon.' I was not afraid that marriage would in any way define or intensify my love for him: I was afraid that my love might stultify him with contentment." A clever parry. She wanted great things from him, for his film career, and his music, to take his place on the screen as an important actor. His voice should come first, his "beautiful poetry . . . sweetness and humility and the gift of a clean mind and heart.

"I loved Russ not only as a man, but as a mother would love her child." Her thoughts turn to Russ's mother, who still doesn't know, and can't be told, and wonders how they're going to keep the news from her.

HE'S HER Russ now.

Needing to spice up their stories, the newspapers resurrect the third female, and with her own recent tragedy in mind, reunite Russ and Dorothy Dell in the hereafter. The press fondly recalls their relationship, telling over and again how they broke each other's hearts, now united in life foreshortened. Together in dreams.

FUNERARY

Ruggiero Eugenio di Rudolpho Columbo has a proper Hollywood funeral, complete with fans craning to get a glimpse of the celebrity pallbearers, a flower-bedecked casket, and his sister Anna sobbing on the stairs of the church.

"He was just like a baby doll," she cries. "Nobody knows how we loved him." Russ's brother Alberto, down from San Francisco, wipes at his face with a handkerchief. Her screams and we-loved-him-so's recede into the nave of the Church of the Blessed Sacrament as she is ushered to her seat by John Columbo and mortuary director Delmar Smith, who is practiced in these matters. He grasps her left elbow to steady and comfort, touches his other hand to the small of her back, and deftly guides her to her pew as he would lead a dancer.

Also in the family car is a Dr. Harry Martin, escorting Carole. She hadn't wanted to be there, to expose her grief to the public. It blurred her self-awareness, took her outside her emotions; when she felt eyes on her, she entered the realm of performance. She gives herself a measure of privacy, shielded behind dark glasses, but she still has to sit in the front row, playing a wifely role. And motherly as well. Julia still hadn't been told. Her attending physician, Dr. H. H. Blodgett, thought it best not to shock her just yet.

Carole had sent flowers, a blanket of gardenias to cover Russ in his sleep. The Laemmles junior and senior supplied a cross of the same flowers. The Gethsemane garden of the gardenia.

The church is centrally located at 6661 Sunset Boulevard. The funeral is open to the public, and more than three thousand mourners crowd inside, while an additional thousand congregate in the street. It's Thursday, ten in the morning, and the Reverend Cornelius McCoy will lead a requiem low mass to usher Russ into the afterlife. Universal has decreed five minutes of silence, when all filming on the lot will stop, and then resume, life afterlife.

The hearse arrives, and the pallbearers take the bronze coffin in hand. Bing Crosby hoists Russ's earthly remains, as do Zeppo Marx (filling in for *Keyhole* director Lowell Sherman), Walter Wagner, Stuart Peters (Carole's

THE LAST PROCESSION

brother), Gilbert Roland, and Sheldon Keate Calloway. All wear matching white flowers in the buttonholes of their dark suits.

They place him before the altar, where the church aisles cross.

I am the Resurrection and the Life . . . A sprinkle of holy water amid the parch of *Remember, Man, thou art dust and unto dust thou shalt return.* . . .

Not quite yet. With Russ's brother Anthony and sister Carmela on their way from Philadelphia and New York, respectively, and the mother still not told, no decision has been made as to what to do with Russ's corporeal body. The remains will rest in Smith's mortuary pending final dispensation.

As for his soul, and the contracted salvation, the services are conducted in Latin, the formal tongue of Christian heaven. "Lead Kindly Light" is the chosen hymn, followed by the Lord's Prayer.

Frank Longo, who gave Russ his first job as a café singer, is in the hushed crowd, along with Dixie Lee and Everett Crosby, Ann Sothern, and the producer, director, and cast of *Wake Up and Dream*, still due to open at the Pantages on September 13, a week from today, billed with *Two Heads and a Pillow*. The perfect double feature.

LANSING MAY be legally innocent, but in his own mind he is forever damned, judged incriminate.

He watches the service from a back pew, kneeling all the while. He tries to pray, but it is too late for repentance. *Why?* This happened because of him. He had introduced the match to the firing pin: the matchmaker. If this was God's will, he felt used. An undeserving accomplice. *Whywhywhy?*

Carole comes by to solace him before she returns to the mountains, as do Virginia Brissac and Carmela. They all assure him that it wasn't his fault, that they understood his pain and despair. "Our one thought is to comfort Lansing," Virginia whispers to Rilla Page Palmborg when she comes for a journalistic visit. "He is still dazed. God help him when his mind returns to normal."

Carmela agrees. "Russell is gone and you must take care of yourself," she says to Lansing at his home, where he sits for hours, only drinking fruit juice and coffee, staring vacantly into space. "We need you now. That is the message our entire family sends you."

The Columbos want him to come up to the house, but he can't face them. He can barely sit here, in the den where it happened, in the seat where Russ sat, facing Rilla, the reporter from *Motion Picture* who had interviewed Russ only six days before the shooting. Columbo had spoken then of Lansing, of their friendship, and camaraderie in general.

"I am a friendly person, but I have few friends," Russ disclosed to Rilla. "The little taste I have had of popularity has taught me the difference between friendship and acquaintance. I had to have several experiences with so-called friends, using their so-called friendship with me to try to get into pictures or touch me for money, before I learned it." Russ thought of Con's entourage, his "stooges," and then of Con, recovering from a serious illness that had robbed him of his voice. Poetic justice.

"Lansing has never wanted anything from me, except just to help me. I don't know three people qualified to understand a friendship like ours. There isn't anything I can't ask of him or tell him. I confide my money troubles to him, my professional worries, and my personal ones too." Before she leaves, Russ asks her to use a photograph taken by Lansing with the article, and sends over a recent one the next day. "He has taken hundreds of pictures of me."

It is the final picture that Lansing will forever rue. "Russ and I used to do a pantomime when we heard an automobile backfire. We'd clutch our chests and exclaim, 'Ach, they got me.' I looked at Russ, expecting him to say it. Then I saw blood gushing from his eye. I screamed for Mother. You know the rest."

He's going to Santa Fe for a few weeks, "to get hold of myself." He shakes his head. He feels Russ's loss — "Russ got everything he ever wanted . . . how could a person with so many plans be gone — at twenty-six?" — and strangely, his comforting presence. "There is one thing I want to say," he begins haltingly. "Yet I hesitate. It sounds so theatrical. It is about the way I felt at the inquest. If Russ ever was with me, he was with me there — seeing me through."

He once again sifts the possibilities: "If all the powder had exploded, the slug would have pierced the desk and not glanced off here and struck Russ. If the bullet had struck Russ only a fraction of an inch higher, instead of penetrating the opening in his eye, it would not have been fatal. And why couldn't I have picked up the other pistol?"

This is where God's intention becomes omnipotent, unknowable. Who was really the gun? The shooter? "It just had to be," Virginia consoles Lansing. "There is a thread running all through this that we cannot understand. But some day, we will know why this had to be."

Lansing wishes he had such faith. Why? "I shall never understand," he laments, as he ponders the limits of mortal thought, a never-ending last chorus, no resolve. He felt like an instrument that had been forced into a particularly dissonant countermelody, in thrall to its musician. Perhaps he couldn't see his place in the orchestra, the sharps and flats of harmony as coloration to the piece as a whole. It was coupled with the fear that he had played the wrong note, been careless, broken a string or cracked a reed, fucked up. That he wasn't good enough. And that he had stilled the one pure note in his life, never to hear it again.

His is the coincidence; it is his cross to bear, nailed arms outstretched just as Christ found himself at the crossroads of two perpendicular wooden beams. Even as he looks for blame, or reason, he finds the fact of his complicity as hard to imagine as infinity, the random—or is he?—factor in this conjunction of collision, the unforeseen black cat that darts across your path at a frightening speed, out of control. No reverse. You can't get out of the way.

The following June, Lansing is walking across Sunset Boulevard in the wee hours of the morning. He's been drinking with a male companion, trying to forget and to remember who he'd been before the accident, looking downward, hands in his pockets, when a car driven by a teenager knocks him over, breaking bones, causing him to have an out-of-body experience in which he sees Russ. Two weeks later, beset by financial losses (he is the sole support of his family), he suffers a nervous breakdown, his recuperation made "possible through the charity of friends."

LANSING LIVES on, a reclusive figure by most accounts, rooming in a garage apartment behind a Victorian house at 637 South Lucerne Boulevard in Hancock Park, until he suffers a subarachnoid hemorrhage leading to a "cerebral vascular accident" at the age of sixty-one. He joins Russ on February 16, 1962. To find out for himself.

MEDITERRANEAN

He is sitting in a café by the Aegean. Writing a postcard.

He uncaps his pen and begins in the familiar fashion. *Dear Mama.* He leaves the point poised for a moment, lost in thoughts of her. The tip leaves a spreading blotch of ink. He turns the card over so he can look at the photo on the front. It is a hand-colored view of the White Fort overlooking the gulf that cradles the seawall of Thessaloniki. A squat column topped by a turret, it resembles the prison it would become in the eighteenth century, known locally as "the Bloody Tower."

There is a ship across the way, an old freighter, moldering and rusting on the dark olive-green water. Bobbing on the choppy waves, it is registered to a Colombo Shipping Co., and it wanders his mind.

The engagement goes well, he writes, a legible script that could be anybody's. *I have eaten the anchovies, the feta. I remember when you used to tell me that cheese is the mother's milk of cows, and goats, their gift to make us strong and grow.* His handwriting is not as flourished as his signature once was back in America. Sometimes he prints because he knows it's hard for her to read. *This seaside could be Santa Monica, near a Venice not our Venezia, home away from home. I think of you in this wind cooled by the sea and the promise of the Mediterranean.*

He signs it *Your Loving Son, Russ,* and wipes the tip of his pen on a napkin. He screws the cap back on again, a circular motion that slows to a stop like a record losing speed, sliding down the rpm's. He makes no move to put the pen away. His eyes blur. He hardly notices two girls walking by, arm in arm, exuding sensuality and animal gait, failing to divert him from why he is here.

. . .

HE FOLLOWS the curvature of the sea. One morning, after performing at the Teatro della Fortuna in Fano, Italy, he wakes restlessly at dawn to see the sky changing colors over the Adriatic, orange melding to deep gray above and blue speckled salt warm liquid below. When at last he crosses the peninsula, reaching the Tyrrhenian, a sea within a sea, watching the sun now setting over the surrounding Mediterranean as he arrives in Naples, he triumphantly writes her that he has tasted the roots of the pasta that always delighted him as a child, served with garlic, oil, capers, olives. Though he never liked olives. *Dear Mama. I have returned.* Turning again, like a tarantella. He breathes the Neapolitan air, moves northward through Ostia and the Tuscan hills, finally arrives at Milan where he becomes Jacopo in La Scala's production of *I Due Foscari.* Minor Verdi, to be sure, but he can feel her pride swell when he tells her of the ovation he received when the curtain opened for the second act. Jacopo is seated in a prison. A beam of light from a slit high up in the wall dimly illuminates him as he sings:

> *Notte! . . . perpetua notte, che qui regni!*
> *Siccome agli occhi il giorno,*
> *Potessi almen celare al pensir mio*
> *Il fine disperato che m'aspetta!*

Eternal night. Perpetual, as in perpetrator. The day shadows from sight. Can not the dark "hide from my thoughts / The terrible end which awaits me"? As he falls to the ground, bereft and hopeless, awaiting his wife Lucrezia, who wonders if she has been brought to witness his corpse, he cries out: "Away . . . horrible vision!"

When he is led away to the ship to meet his inevitable *exit,* Loredano, his captor, raises his mask, exacting his revenge. Russ/Jacopo retreats backward, shielding his eyes. "Heavens, whom do I see? My evil spirit!"

The paired Foscari of the title play out their genetic bonding, both aware of their ordained DNA—Duty, Negation, and the sacrificial bloodstained Altar—within the living death of banishment.

"Father, children, wife / A last farewell to you! / One day in Heaven we shall find / Mercy after such Grief." His parting words.

But it is the opening aria that resonates most within Russ's countertenor.

> *From farthest exile*
> *On the wings of desire,*

Often, swiftly,
My thoughts have flown to you.

He can't come home. Not yet. Not ever. The tour has been extended. He's been invited to stay at a villa in Rimini, the part of Switzerland closest to the Italian Alps. There is a benefit in Barcelona, an engagement in Lisbon. He must avoid the northern countries, because there will be war soon. Perhaps even now. And here. He writes from London. Paris. Amsterdam. When he is unable to write, others will write for him, and yet others will read to her. It is his way of keeping in touch.

HE IS sitting in a café turning the broadsheets of *Il Messaggero* when he comes upon news of Gabriele d'Annunzio's passing. It is March 1938, and the *Fascisti* are all about. He was stopped on a train yesterday, sliding along the Riviera, and asked to produce his *tessera*, his *carte di autorizzazione*. As if he wasn't Italian.

It was d'Annunzio who had written about The Flame: *Il Fuoco*. The consuming crackle of love's deep immolation. Only in d'Annunzio's fictions, the spark of lust and longing is posed in death's mirror, its fatal reflection. He serialized *The Triumph of Death* in 1893, foreseeing an existence enclosed in parentheses.

D'Annunzio duels, and often. In *The Triumph of Death*, his second, as it were, is Giorgio, who visits the bedroom of his uncle Demetrius, a recent suicide. As he opens a case containing a "violin made by Andrea Guarneri, dated 1680," Demetrius appears to him in a vision. The wraith plays, first a Mendelssohn motet, then an improvisation based on Tennyson: "*O Death in Life, the days that are no more.*"

Giorgio imagines himself in the hollow that Demetrius has left in the bed. He sees the dead man's face, covered with a black veil. "Through the linen wrappings, he believed he could see the ravages of the wound, the horrible ravage made by the explosion of the firearm, by the impact of the ball against the bone of the skull, against that brow so delicate and so pure." He opens the case carrying the dueling pistols. They rest on "light-green velvet, a little frayed at the edges of the compartments which contained everything necessary for loading them." One for you, one for me.

On the sixteenth of January, 1916, d'Annunzio is riding shotgun in a seaplane dispensing sheaves of propaganda and the occasional bomb over the Austrian front when he is knocked out of the sky over the Adriatic at Grado. Thrown against the machine gun when the pilot misjudges the refraction coming off the water and strikes a sandbar, severely damaging his right cornea, Gabriele is forced to lie perfectly still until the end of April if he hopes to regain his sight.

Gabriele writes his *Nocturne* on ten thousand *strisce di carta*, each complete sentence a strip of thought. His daughter shears each stripe of paper and places them in front of him on a table propped against his knees. It will take him five years to order the fragments he scribbles in phrygian pitch, considering the phantasms of his life, rearranging the narrative of *Il Notturno* like a musician ordering random notes to create a flowing composition. It is his game of solitaire.

His daughter, Sirenetta, tells him a story. She remembers "a night of full moon when she was a pupil at Poggio Reale, taken with several other girls to the observatory at Arcetri." There she hears "the world's most beautiful voice . . . a modest assistant, who while at the telescope spoke of the lunar mountains and valleys, of Saturn's rings and Mars' reddish glow. All the young girls hung from his lips, entranced by the spell of the full moon.

"The pure voice was like a note of the celestial harmony. And the crown of virgins pulsed like a humanized constellation, encircling the student of the stars."

Il Duce comes to visit d'Annunzio at his Villa Vittoriale hideaway in May 1925. Gabriele inscribes this over a looking glass in his sitting room to Mussolini: DO YOU BRING WITH YOU THE MIRROR OF NARCISSUS?

D'Annunzio's injury is Russ's mirror. Gabriele has shattered his right eye; sighting up from the pages of *Nocturne*, Russ feels the recoil spasm agony in his left, the light-speed reflection of word as it is sight-read and translated into the other senses. The port of entry.

LA MER. Debussy also has written nocturnes. For his third, *Sirènes*, he "describes the sea and its unnumerable rhythm; then amid the billows, silvered by the moonlight, the mysterious song of the Sirens is heard as they laugh and pass by."

IN THE FLAME, a "learned mystic" asks the d'Annunzio character if he's "ever considered that the essence of music might not be in sounds at all. It is the silence that precedes sound and the silence that follows. Rhythm appears and comes to life in those periods of silence. Every sound and every chord awakens a voice in the silence that can only be heard by our minds. Rhythm is the heart of music, but its beat cannot be heard except during the pauses between sounds."

To listen to the silence, that is his fascination now. To hear between the notes, and then listen until the silence gradates, forming its own notes, a ringing in the ears that is the diatonic dial tone of the universe.

Everyone else has gone to sleep. He's staying up all night.

O minus O. Subzero. Birthed from the whole and back again.

The silences get longer. Sometimes it seems as if he's between sound so long he hardly remembers what sound was meant to be.

Could be.

He suffers death's aloneliness. The one-on-one when you're not around.

HE IS sitting in a café. There is no one with him.

MOTHERS

She knows. A mother always knows. But she'll let them play their game, their reading-aloud of his letters, their tales of his wanderings in exile, because that's what being a mother is about. Shielding her kids from the no of hope.

Of course she knows. He's her *bambino*. Her Russ.

He's in London now. Spain. Even *Italia*. He and Carole will be home soon. Next Christmas. The following spring. By the summer, surely, but the Palladium or the Palais or the Palace want to hold him over, extend his engagement, keep him forever on the road. Here's the rent for the old house; sorry you have to move back there.

She remembered when Russell would call on the telephone from New York, all the way across the country. She would hear his voice on the radio. He would always stop by to speak to her, kiss her cheek, whisper words of affection.

Do they think she's deaf as well as blind?

She could tell something was wrong in the hospital. The choked voices, the false jollity, the uncomfortable silences. The whispers. It wasn't because she was ill. Something had happened.

At first they didn't get the stories straight. Russ and Carole had impulsively decided to marry. No, she had been called away to make a film overseas, and he followed. No, it was *he* had been called away. The only thing connecting them was the word: Away.

He could never go away for all these years and not let her hear his voice. Unless he was away, period.

She didn't want to know. She'd buried others of her children before, the ones who never had a chance at life, stillborn or caught in the draft of the ghettos, but not little Ruggiero, her sweet baby boy, the one who sang her lullabies back to her.

She could feel his loss, the break in their bonding, the hollow space in her belly when she thought of him, where he had grown and would always remain, an amputated limb of umbilical memory impersonating what was once within her. The momory. She missed him, the way he would squeeze her tighter a moment longer than necessary, a reassurance to let her know he was forever there. She had no favorites among her children; they all had their way. But Russ was her pride, her boy joy.

After a while, she grew to look forward to the charade. There was a comfort in having Russ's presence in the room, played like an old familiar melody. John would come and sit next to her chair in the living room, his voice at once hearty and heartbroken, as if he were cheering himself up. "A letter from Russ," he'd exclaim, overacting, and elaborately unfold and rattle the paper, so she might know it was a letter that arrived in the day's post.

"Oh, look at this," he'd say, though she couldn't, "Russ is on his way to Warsaw." He hummed a bit of Chopin prélude. "Imagine that," and she did, not listening to the words but letting their cadence create an image of Russ next to her, the prodigal come home to kiss his mama, so she would not outlive him.

MOTHERLY LOVE.

Mother songs make up a category all their own as the nineteenth century turns twenty, modern time no longer teenage. The kids are grown, or so they think. Between 1900 and 1930, thousands of sheet musics are imprinted with the eternal maternals of "Mother Is the Best Sweetheart of All" (1910), "Your Mother Is the Friend That's Always There" (1915), "That Loving Mother of My Own" (1920), and the ubiquitous "M-O-T-H-E-R," written by Howard Johnson and Theodore Morse in 1915 and popularized by Eva Tanguay and Sophie Tucker. The resurgence is encouraged by the success of Will Dillon and Harry Von Tilzer's 1911 "I Want a Girl (Just Like the Girl)," and inflamed by World War I, with its images of white-haired virginal Marys ("Mary Is My Mother's Name," from 1912) bidding adieu to their soldier sons destined for the gas-mask horrors of Verdun and Flanders. Harry Ellis and Lew Porter contribute to the war effort with the 1918 "Mothers of America (You Have Done Your Share)," while the 1917 "That's a Liberty Loan" — *"I'm giv-*

ing all I own"— contains a curious reference to a young soldier's dad falling at Gettysburg, in 1863, raising paternal questions that are better left unanswered.

War's filial sacrifice isn't new to the Great War. "Break the News to Mother," originally written for the Spanish-American conflict by Charles K. Harris, better known for "After the Ball," was resurrected to meet World War I demand. Even in the mid-nineteenth century, the Civil War had a long lineage of Mother songs to choose from: "The Blue and the Gray" (or "A Mother's Gift to Her Country") was enacted nightly by R. J. Jose at William West's Big Minstrel Jubilee. "Mother on the Brain," by M.F.H. Scott ("as sung by all the minstrel bands"), published in 1864, strung ten verses together from then-extant motherly song titles. At random, verse five:

> O *"Mother Dear Would Comfort Me," if only she were here*
> *"Fond Mother Thou Art Failing Now," "My Gentle Mother Dear,"*
> *"I Cannot Mind My Wheel, Mother," it must be I'm insane*
> *For "Mother Kissed Me in My Dream," with Mother on the brain*

Mother and home were inseparable. Does she never go out? Mother is always pictured in her rocking chair, knitting, her hair a snow bun, a blanket over her stooped shoulders and an aproned lap that invites snuggling, "Mother in the Doorway Waiting" (1881) patiently for her child to come home. Alice Hawthorne's 1854 "What Is Home Without a Mother"; Frank Drayton's 1856 "Mother Home & Heaven" (she is also fashion consultant in his 1882 "Mother Bids Me Bang My Hair"); "Mother, Queen of Home," a 1900 ditty with words by Raymond A. Browne and music by Charles Coleman, who also wrote "Always Remember Mother" and the 1914 "Your Mother Is Your Best Friend After All."

Pilgrimage must ever return to nostalgia's well: "In the Harbor of My Mother's Arms" (1918); "I Wanna Go Back to Dear Old Mother's Knee" (1919). "You're Always a Baby to Mother," suckles Jack Donnelly in 1926, while J. E. Dempsey hopes you "Keep a Corner in Your Heart for Mother"— *"No one will ever love you like your mother will!"*

Sometimes it's too late: Leo Corcorans's 1916 "I Lost What I Called Home Sweet Home When Mother Passed Away" appreciates her once removed. George H. Diamond warns in 1912 that "You Will Never Miss Your Mother Till She's Gone." Songwriters stand around her resting place, taking notes: in 1879, they are "Kneeling over Mother's Grave," then "Shedding Tears o'er Mother's Grave" (1883). Floral tributes pluck "A Flower from Mother's

Grave" (1878), "A Rose from Mother's Grave" (1879), "A Violet from Mother's Grave" (1881). "Mother Rests Beneath the Daisies" (1881), the aboveground of "Why Did They Dig Ma's Grave So Deep?" A popular trilogy from 1863 does better at riddle-me-this: "Who Will Care for Mother Now?" In ascending order, "I Will Care for Mother Now" and "Christ Will Care for Mother Now."

Pity the poor girl caught between a man and his mother. "You Remind Me So Much of My Mother (You Stole My Heart Away)" from Al Dubin and George B. McConnell in 1915; "You Are the Image of Mother (That's Why I Love You)" from Roger Graham, Marvin Lee, and May Hill in 1916; "I'm Looking for a Girl Like Mother" from Gus Kahn and Egbert Van Alstyne in 1916; and future comparisons: Joe Goodwin and Al Paintadusi's 1915 "What a Wonderful Mother You'd Be." There's also reverse lineage: "Grammy, You're My Mammy's Mammy," scribed by Joe Young and Sam Lewis, with music by Harry Akst, in 1921.

Mostly these songwriters respond to her voice, reminiscing, like H. Wakefield Smith in 1914, about "Those Songs My Mother Used to Sing." "The Song That My Mother Sang to Me" (1899) is "My Mother's Lullaby," a popular title that engendered variations-on-a-theme in 1883, 1915, 1917, 1923, 1929, along with "My Mother's Song" (1892), "My Mother's Rosary" (1915), and "My Mother's Evening Prayer" (1920). Francis Porteous's 1921 "Mother's Croon" is also a lullaby—"*Hush my dear! Mother is near. Hush! Hush!*" In "A Mother's Croon," written by Eldred Edson and Edward Walt also in 1921, a "violin or cello obbligato" is included, as if to provide a tune for the baby to accompany mother. "*My low croon, my soft croon / Tells all that's in Mother's heart.*"

Where it starts and unends. The first duet.

THE CARETAKING mammy of minstrel song is a stock, jovial characterization, love beyond the sensual. In the 1800s, E. P. Christy's Minstrels added "A Boy's Best Friend Is His Mother," "Mother Would Comfort Me," and "What Is Home Without a Mother" to their heartstrings repertoire, which also included Stephen Foster's famous "Old Folks at Home." This hindsight folksiness attempted to counter the sense of dislocation brought on by Civil War and racial brutality, the wear and tear on the family unit as a result of the creeping city, an "Ethiopian" fantasy world of pre-Emancipation plantations in which the horrors of the future had yet to happen. One could lose one's birthright. E. P. Christy showed how it could be done when he bought "Old

Folks" from Foster for fifteen dollars and declared himself the published author.

So goes "Sweet Southern Mammy o' Mine," sung by the all-white six-piece
Holly Moyer and His Orchestra in 1923, with music by a young Harry Barris
and lyrics by George E. Springer. *The sinking sun brings on the still of the
night / I'll be with you when the moon's shining bright. . . . How I long to
be / Back on your knee.*"

Al Jolson is back on his knees in 1930, starring in *Mammy*. The film
crosses the color line in more ways than one. With many of its sequences shot
in two-strip Technicolor, interspliced with black-and-white exposition, it presents racial blending as technical innovation. Mingling assimilation with maternal yearning is a role Jolson has perfected over the years, a mammy's boy,
and he never really does grow up.

The action is centered around a traveling stage troupe, Meadow's Merry
Minstrels. The enacting of its show within the movie is a surprising window
on traditional minstrel staging, depicted when its formalities and customs are
in twilight, nearly obsolete, gathered anthropologically like a forgotten rainforest tribe awaiting Tarzan (Elvis would've made a great Lord Greystoke).

There is the minstrel's triumphal entry march into town, clownish characters introduced by their instrumental names: Brudder Tambo, Brudder
Bones, joking "endmen" who sing sentimental favorites and crack pun-filled
jokes in dialect. "Endmen" are just that, as the blackened ensemble sit in a
patient semicircle around a white interlocutor, a master of ceremonies who
calls upon each to rise and do a turn. The second act presents the "olio," a variety show within the minstrel presentation. There is a ritual air, as if at a fraternal gathering, a Lodge or a Klan, a secret college society like the Skull and
Bones. *Mammy* is based on an Irving Berlin play, *Mr. Bones*; we are in the
elephants' graveyard.

"Let me croon a down home blues," pleads our Al. His supposed love interest isn't interested. She senses that her virtue will never compare to that of
his mother, to whom he's going back, as if being called home for dinner.
"Mammy Mine," he exults as he embraces Louise Dresser, repeatedly kissing
her on the lips. "I'm everything to my mammy! She's my girl!"

The truest of love. You choose your lover. You have no choice over your
mother. Always her child.

In the film, Al is convinced he has committed a crime, shooting the interlocutor in midshow. He doesn't know the gun he fires is loaded with a real
bullet. He has killed, or so he thinks; he pulled the trigger, didn't he? Someone has framed him, the old switcheroo. He'll give himself up, but first he has

to return home to say good-bye to his mother. What can he tell her? He knows he's going to jail.

He'll make her happy, that's what he'll do. She shouldn't worry. "Mama, Mama," he cries, wringing her hand, writhing around in his skin like an excitable little boy, plucking at her skirts. "Mama, I gotta go now!

"I'm going to Europe. London, Paris, Berlin . . . when I come back I'll be a big star! Mama!" He kneels, in reprise of *The Jazz Singer*.

"Three years will go awful quick." He hugs her. So that's how the Colombos got the idea.

She lets him convince her. She knows her child, and wants him not to worry. And he doesn't want to bring to her any more pain than that of childbirth. Anything but child-death.

REBELLION SET in during the 1950s and later for empeered teens testing parental limits. Mother's dicta were to be disobeyed, though usually, at the end of a Dumont-era TV sitcom, *Father Knows Best but Mother Knows Better*, she was proved head-shakingly right: Three Dog Night's "Mama Told Me (Not to Come)," the Shirelles' "Mama Said," Merle Haggard's "Mama Tried," Waylon and Willie's "Mammas Don't Let Your Babies Grow Up to Be Cowboys." Most of these mothers inveighed against the impolite virtues—masculine outlawry and tomfoolery. Only Smokey Robinson, he of the high, feminine falsetto, listened to his mother, who told him to "Shop Around": *"Don't be fooled by the very first one."* She wanted a girl for him as good as her. *"You better . . ."*

John Lennon's primal scream provoked the most anguished maternal singing yet experienced in pop music. On the rebound from the Beatles' breakup in April 1970, he read a book over the summer by psychologist Arthur Janov, *The Primal Scream: Primal Therapy: The Cure for Neurosis.* Janov theorized that one could release the repressions of parental abandonment by a primordial shriek. Janov counseled Lennon to reconcile with his son Julian, and connect with the pain suffered when his mother abandoned him to his aunt at a very young age, echoed in the raw shrill of the *Plastic Ono Band* album released that December. In a famous Annie Leibovitz photo taken toward the end of his Dakota years, John curls next to Yoko on a bed, naked, fetal, returning whence he came. "Just Like Starting Over," he sang to her on *Double Fantasy*, a shared dream squared, rebirthing after a pregnant pause in his creative life. Lennon was entrapped in maternal orbit, the goad behind his cheeky abandon and subsequent enshrinement as one of the most famous Buddy Holly imitators on the planet. He was a man at home within the double-track and the echoplex, reveling in the nonsense syllables of *In His Own Write* and the surreal seascapes of *Sgt. Pepper*, his sloganeering solo work as simple and direct and euphonic as a nursery couplet: "Oh Yoko." "Instant Karma." "Imagine" and "Jealous Guy." He's too human.

Mother, what can you do for me? What have you done to me? *"You had me but I didn't have you."*

The self-mutilation of Lennon's "Mother" is a caesarean wail too close for comfort, a smack on the bottom and a cry of separation sirening until it tires, subsiding into sobs and hiccups as a crying baby sleeps the heartbreak of rockabilly. *"Rockabye your baby to a Dixie melody."* In "Julia," on the Beatles' *White Album*, John sings his mother to rest. They are on a first-name basis. She is his "ocean child," the "morning moon." Is it morning, or does she mourn the moon's loss? Lennon's double meanings hide behind each other. The end of one verse overlaps the beginning of the next chorus, like lives crossing over successive generations. "Half of what I say is meaningless," Lennon evades. Which half? The one birthing or the one born?

Julia is the name of Russ Columbo's mother as well. He might have sung Lennon's words to her when he returned from Europe, if only she could have waited.

TUPAC AND Eminem never got to know each other.

Tupac Shakur is shot dead in Las Vegas on September 13, 1996, twenty-five years old, a few months before young Marshall Mathers makes a guest spot freestyling on an L.A. rap station and the word-of-mouth works its way to Dr. Dre. Shakur is too real, embroiled in a *gangsta* war that imitates in deadly fashion—and this *is* fashion—what happens when art steps in front of you with a pistol. Biggie gets it three months later; Suge goes off to prison; Snoop chronics and eyes the ladies; Puffy has a clothing line. East Coast, West Coast.

It's life inside a direct-to-video game, not only Suzuki squads and Kawasaki wheelies in Compton parking lots, '64 Impalas bouncing on their hydraulics, but an electron particle speeding through Times Square rush hour when *TRL* is on, a pick-pocketed sample, toasting and boasting quick violence and slowed sexual encounters, the codependence of vulnerability and revenge. Thuggery. It's video lifestyle, opulent jewelry and matching home team outfits, black-on-black tattoos, the brand-name champagne and exotic dancers and homies riding alongside just like they were in a chase scene out of *Mad Max 2*: Tupac's clip for "California Love." After the bomb.

In Detroit, in the nineties, the immolation is known as Devil's Night, set the evening before Halloween. An act of mass arson before drawing on its mask, the inner city enflames. Marshall watches downtown torching from his perch on the border at Eight Mile, and pulls down the night visor of his white underclass. He's Slim Shady; then he's "Eminem," star of MTV ("and it seems so empty without me"); then Jimmy in 8 Mile, playing a character not himself, but "like myself," as he tells the press when his first feature film opens in November 2002. He's created his own shadow, the black light.

Tupac comes up the hard way, a second-generation Black Panther (his mother, Afeni, is once part of New York's Panther 21, arrested for conspiracy; she carries Tupac inside her when she serves time in the Women's House of Detention). By the time he's shot five times in 1994, he has written himself into his own history. He's never believed anyone would try to kill him—"I didn't have to fear my own community," he tells the camera in Vs., speaking from behind bars—until he's shot again, this time fatally.

He's on the inside. Eminem needs a "ghetto pass" (in the movie, his friend Truth) to slip through the black door, though he's on his own once onstage, bound by the rules of rhyme. He masters the wordplay, the tongue twisters, the language as percussion and attitude. He constructs personae, wrapping himself in their character, the safety their distance provides, knowing that his whole appeal is how close he can come to narrowing the gap between his art and his existence without getting caught in the backlash.

When his movie opens, he's asked on TRL who he was on Halloween. "I went as myself," he answered. He has survived Devil's Night.

As might be expected, each appreciates his mother from a different perspective, a cogent commentary on the Mother song as it rounds off the century. On "Dear Mama," from 1995's Me Against the World, Tupac takes time to sing her praises, to tell her that he knows of the sacrifices she made as "a poor single mother on welfare" trying to raise two kids, forgiving her mistakes and acknowledging the values she instilled in him in the name of pride. "Even as a crack fiend . . . you always was a black queen," he affirms her, with tenderness. "Mama, I finally understand. . . ."

Eminem has no such compassion. "Cleaning Out My Closet" remembers a "poppin' prescription pills" mother and childhood abuse (the York Brothers get to Eight Mile Road first in 1948, when they record "Hamtramck Mama" for Fortune, though Em is from Hazel Park), turning a life of despairing privation into the need behind the words he compulsively scribbles anywhere he can make his mark.

It is a hellish existence, and he will exact his vengeance. He digs her grave, prevents her from seeing her grandchild, cursing her and cutting her off from her posterity. "You selfish bitch . . . I am dead, dead to you as can be."

Mothers. You can't live with them, he's trying to say. But you can't live without them.

SHE LIVES on without him, though the family's pretense keeps him ever alive. It breaks her heart sometimes, when John, or Nicola in his softly accented English, reads his letters, how much they want her to believe. How much they love her to keep on doing this, year after year. To take care of her so well, as she took their care, in the great circle of caring.

Caro mio.

The family Columbo.

CAROLE GABLE

Clark Gable is "a hit and run guy—a square shooter." Carole is a "livewire" librarian. He corners her in the stacks.

"Do your eyes bother you? . . . They bother me." The oldest lines in the book.

"You write the words and the music," she tells him, flippantly, knowing the score.

Carole is teamed with Clark Gable in *No Man of Her Own* in 1932. They get married on a coin toss. "I never go back on a coin," he says, a professional gambler leaving nothing to chance. Clark plays the kind of he-man who carries a spare deck of marked cards and his women to bed, a role he will perfect as the male lead in *Gone with the Wind*. And she's "met the guy I'm going to settle down with."

Off-screen, she was married, he was married. Nothing doing. At the end of filming she presented him with a smoked ham emblazoned with his pre-mustached likeness; he presented her with a pair of prima donna ballet slippers. Other than their palpable on-screen chemistry, there was nothing to indicate they would become Hollywood's most admired couple, a monarchical matrimony befitting the top billing of the movies' movie.

THEY WERE *Made for Each Other*. The day after she finished this 1939 weeper with James Stewart in March, about a couple's first year of marriage that culminates in the crash of a plane carrying their baby's emergency serum, she and Clark took advantage of a shooting break in his *Gone with the Wind* schedule to elope. Hidden in the backseat of a blue DeSoto driven by their best man, MGM staff publicist Otto Winkler, they drove to Kingman, Arizona, and tied the long-awaited knot.

She had been married before, and opted for a light gray flannel designed by Irene; he chose blue serge. The movies had turned colorful.

They would've made it official long before, but Clark's second wife refused to grant him a divorce. From a wealthy Houston family, Ria Langham had taken the gangling aspiring actor—still married to his first mentor, Josephine Dillon—to New York, where she supported him while he made the rounds of Broadway in the summer of 1928, and then moved him to Los Angeles and its screen tests. Clark's female co-stars were quicker to see his romantic potential than the studios were, and MGM was still tinkering with Gable's positioning in their firmament when he was paired with Joan Crawford in steam-heat radiators like *Dance, Fools, Dance* and *Laughing Sinners*. Their clandestine affair drew the attention and displeasure of Louis B. Mayer, who believed only the MGM publicity office should determine who would sleep with whom, and on what picture. To cool the growing scandal, Clark hastily married Langham in the spring of 1931, even before he was divorced from Dillon.

Ria hung on as they acrimoniously separated, wanting her due, as much for her own saved face as Clark's rising stature as the number one heartthrob (and box office attraction) of the movies. His rakish mustache and slightly formal mode of address toward women gave him a rough-hewn image (Clark took readily to such contact sports as hunting and fishing) as his big ears and slight clumsiness emphasized his simian vulnerability. He responded to older women, to independence and strong will; and that softened younger women to him. He meant well, in his unsubtle way, needing understanding, care, while evincing the rough generosity of a good man. He could never be cast as a villain.

Neither could Carole; it might well have been a white wedding. Gable and Lombard had met again at "The White Mayfair" on January 25, 1936, a formal ball held at Victor Hugo's in Beverly Hills with the trappings of a state occasion and more than three hundred glittering guests dressed all in white, stars and studio heads alike: Douglas Fairbanks, Jr., Henry Fonda, Gloria Swanson, Adolph Zukor, Bing Crosby, Norma Shearer (wearing, contrarily, red, a scene that would later inspire Bette Davis's scarlet entrance into the virgin ball in *Jezebel*), Lupe Velez, Harold Lloyd, Jeanette MacDonald. Carole was the hostess; her date was Cesar Romero. Clark was escorting Eadie

Adams, a singer from the MGM lot, though more table talk revolved about the presence of Loretta Young, who had gone into seclusion after making *The Call of the Wild* with Clark and was rumored to have birthed Clark's love daughter. It was theoretically possible. There would have been no question of abortion with Loretta; just as there was no thought of divorce from Ria, who sat across the room, glowering, as he asked Carole to dance.

"Who do you think you are, Clark Gable?" Carole joked to him when she took a break from the party by taking a ride in his Duesenberg. On the dance floor she made him do the rhumba. She had found a chink in his armor, the actorly distance between him and his persona, and she used the advantage to court and tease him. She sent him a pair of doves to fly around his bedroom the next morning, then a beat-up jalopy after he yelled at her for showing up at a party at his house in an ambulance and had herself carried in on a stretcher. She beat him at tennis.

Even in Hollywood's mid-thirties, "Unmarried Husbands and Wives" (as the January 1939 issue of *Photoplay* daringly blazoned in a story by Kittley Baskette) were still frowned upon, in Clark's case further compounded by his adultery. Ria put detectives on their trail, hoping to come up with legal evidence that would bolster her hold on his bankbook. She did have him by the balls; his womanizing was well known around the script-girl and understudy world, and proof of a liaison with Carole would surely sweeten the pot. He had known poverty when growing up, leaving the wing of his father, who considered acting for "sissies," and Clark was notoriously cautious with a dollar. He had no intention of splitting his fortune with Ria, who certainly didn't need the money. He did. Especially if he wanted to buy that ranch of director Raoul Walsh's that Carole had her eye on in Encino, twenty San Fernando Valley acres for fifty thousand dollars. Two and a half grand an acre, with a house and corral. It was Carole who eventually paid the whole sum. She was ready for cohabitation; all they needed was the piece of paper.

Matters came to a boil in mid-December 1938, when *Photoplay* sold out its print run with a national article on the lovers (placing them in the company of other notable Unmarrieds like Paulette Goddard and Charles Chaplin, or Constance Bennett and Gilbert Roland). There were such intimate details as the "hate hat" she wore when she was mad at him. He hates hats! How cute . . . and *married*. The Hays Office received numerous complaints about immorality from such bedrock defenders of the national virtue as the Daughters of the American Revolution and the National Catholic Legion of Decency. Louis B. Mayer (who had been secretly encouraging Ria, keeping Clark "available") switched sides to save the reputation of *Gone with the*

Wind (Scarlett could hardly be married to a philanderer, and Mayer did owe something to Carole for giving the part she desperately wanted to Vivien Leigh), and Ria relented. On March 9, 1939, she signed a divorce agreement attached to a hefty cash settlement. By the end of the month, on the twenty-ninth, Carole and Clark had come to Kingman. Kingman come.

Lombard did her best to see that all numerological portents were in their favor. When it came time to give her age on the wedding license, she penned "29," avoiding the three of her true age a year older, the ink splashing on the document as she wrote. Gable said he was thirty-six, and "an actor." No matter how she tried, she couldn't avoid the alignment of trinities.

HE CALLED her Ma; she called him Pa. But they had difficulties conceiving. They even tried to raise chickens on the ranch, marketing "the King's Eggs," but the venture fizzled. Maybe there wasn't room for children in between Oscar nominations and exotic pets and the war in Europe and the shrunken head he gave her one night that she finally buried in the backyard of an empty house to rid them of its perceived jinx.

Other than that, they were happy. She overlooked his peccadilloes; he took her on overnight camping trips with the boys. She always seemed to regard Clark with a raised eyebrow, as if she was letting him put one over on her. Carole had his number, and she counted on him.

In late 1941, she teamed with Ernst Lubitsch and radio comedian Jack Benny for a film that had the same black comic feel as Chaplin's *The Great Dictator.* Director Lubitsch "was tired of the two established, recognized recipes, drama with comedy relief and comedy with dramatic relief. I made up my mind," he told *The New York Times*, "to make a picture with no attempt to relieve anybody from anything at any time. . . . One might call it a tragical farce or a farcical tragedy."

To Be or Not to Be is set in Nazi-occupied Poland. Benny plays Jack Tura, an actor who imitates Hitler in a satiric stage play called *Gestapo* that is promptly shuttered by the German authorities. *Hamlet* is substituted and Carole—his wife, Maria Tura—invites her lover, a patriotic Polish aviator, to visit her backstage when Benny begins his famous soliloquy.

Lubitsch, a German-born Jew, poses Shakespeare's famous heads-or-tails as a morality play with fatalistic overtones, presaging Camus and the existentialism that went hand in hand with the World Wars: the ultimate soliloquy. Is life worth living? Is evil preordained? Is his portrait of the Nazis, for whom "brutality, flogging and torture have become their daily routine," a horrifyingly prosaic acceptance of the world at large? Is it even possible to influence the course of future events, to render their horror in the everyday, to reduce them in scale so they might be understood, empathized with, as the movies flicker reality on a rectangular screen in two dimensions, two passive senses of sight and sound, moving toward a cheery ending where Benny's Hamlet can recite his monologue in Shakespeare's home country? To laugh or not to laugh, that's Lubitsch's question.

Carole doesn't know the answer, but world events overtake her. In the midst of filming, the Japanese bomb Pearl Harbor, ending America's ambivalence about entering the war. By Christmas, Clark is named Chairman of the Hollywood Victory Committee, and filmmaking seems frivolous. Yet the cameras never stop rolling, preserving the movements and backdrops of history, newsreels now revealed on the Discovery Channel, the History Channel, Arms & Entertainment. Behind the movies.

This is that movie. Carole is in Indianapolis contributing her part to the war effort, waving to the crowd at Cadle Tabernacle. She is in black strapless and long gloves, returning to her home state like a reigning beauty queen. Miss In-Diana. Singing along to "The Star-Spangled Banner" on the pipe organ (preceded by "The Lord's Prayer" performed by a black choir; these are anthemic times), selling bonds and boosting morale, she has just raised over two million dollars, four times her hoped-for quota. At Clark's urging, she left L.A.'s Union Station on January 12, 1942, following the winter eastward through Salt Lake City and Chicago. She had forgotten how severe the Midwest freeze could be in a stark January, the first year of war.

So had her mother, accompanying her on this nostalgic return visit after being away for many years, to measure the distance from where they'd begun. Bess Peters wears an old-fashioned brooch in her dress, knowing she did the right thing by leaving. Carole doesn't want to stick around. She wants to get back to Clark. Instead of training it back to Los Angeles, with stopovers in Kansas City and Albuquerque, she decides to fly home. She's been gone long enough.

She's been getting jealous, and she doesn't like herself for it. She was suspicious of Clark's new leading lady; Lana Turner had just the right amount of *kitty kitty* for Clark to start scraping his litter box, and enough ambition for them both. She'd go crazy having to twiddle her thumbs on a train for all those hours, with the constant *clickety clack*, trying to study her script for her next movie, *They All Kissed the Bride*, and not being able to do anything, go anywhere, while he was tomcatting around. She was not someone who could sit still.

They'd been perfectly snippy with each other before she left. She didn't mind his dalliances, but she thought surely he could save it all up for her for the time being, until she got pregnant. That wasn't *too* much to ask for from the King from his "rancher's wife." Carole had certainly made him a home, as no other woman could. Mrs. Gable. Along with cows and chickens, she raised domesticity. Despite their words, she wanted to make him happy. She'd made sure to leave five letters for Clark with their secretary, to be given to him one each day she was away, and left a blond mannequin in her place in bed. She was no dummy.

Her mother didn't want to fly, had never, in fact, been in an airplane. Otto Winkler was again shepherding her for MGM, and he got airsick. But Carole was insistent, and to settle the argument, they decided to toss a coin. Heads/train, tails/plane. Tails.

Her mother was seeing three's everywhere. The plane was a Douglas DC-3. Flight 3. A party of three. Carole was thirty-three. When the plane landed in Albuquerque, it took on several army pilots returning to base in California. There were three extra. Carole, who felt she was working for the war effort, was not to be deterred, and didn't volunteer to give up their seats. Her mother was anxious enough about the flight as it was.

There was a stop for refueling in Las Vegas. The plane landed at 6:36 P.M. and took off at 7:07. You had to like those odds.

When Clark arrives on the scene, the fire is still glowing on the side of Table Rock Mountain, just where the plane had hit, resting like a spent bullet, embedded in stone. Rock, scissors, paper: they bring him the diamonds and rubies of the earrings he had given her for Christmas, though the matching ruby heart is lost. Missing. He watches the glow and flicker from his window at the El Rancho Vegas Hotel, and imagines his name writ next to hers, a brass plaque on the figured marble wall at Forest Lawn cemetery, when all their earthly cares are over.

RUSS KEEPS his distance.

He's got his eye on her.

Around the corner from where Clark and Carole rest side by side is the crypt of "Russ Columbo." It is a wall vault faced by a simple marble square in the Sanctuary of the Vespers, with only his birth and death years on the nameplate. Two bronze urns for floral offerings are filled with sprays of red and white wildflowers. There is still no one residing below him, though this cul-de-sac in the Great Mausoleum is well developed.

Through the years, she will remember Russ, sometimes surprised at how much he is still with her. In a famous off-the-record exchange discovered by Lombard biographer Lawrence Swindell, a journalist from *Life* magazine is asking her the love-of-your-life question. (Joan Crawford, Carole's old Charleston nemesis from the Cocoanut Grove, has answered it as "Clark Gable." This should be interesting, he thinks.) Like most entertainment-beat reporters, he already knows the response he is seeking. He's filling in the blanks.

She answers "Russ Columbo."

The reporter is taken aback. He had been hoping for a Perfect Couple. "Of course, you mean other than Clark Gable, don't you, Miss Lombard?" She is still Unmarried.

"Russ Columbo was *the* great love of my life . . . and that very definitely is off the record."

She looks at and then through the reporter, the line dropping to the cutting room floor, like the dialogue they excise from her last film. "After all, what can happen to a woman in the air?" She remembers love's float, its elevation. Clark was ground. Russ was flight.

Not to be.

AFTEREFFECTS

What you leave behind.

His Packard, night blue or emerald green, is out in New Jersey; some guy's brother has the bill of sale. The opal ring that Pola Negri gave him is hidden away in Queens. A collector in California has a bloodstained bow tie. Lansing's pistols find their way to the actor John Carroll. His ashes are scattered on eBay, an autograph surfacing here, a Woodmansten first-night invitation there: the reliquary. Russ is dispersed, like his recordings, reissued every few years when the formats change. He lingers in the recessive memory, not really remembered by the public, like a vapor trail dissipating in the light, or a wisp of fleeing dream at the end of sleep.

There is hardly any estate to go around. Along with a $49,000 insurance policy, counting the double indemnity, there is five thousand in cash; and that's it. The house on Outpost Circle isn't paid for, and will be sold for $25,000 to the actor Alan Hale, Sr., a veteran silent star whose specialty is the loyal sidekick (he will be Little John opposite Errol Flynn in the 1938 *Adventures of Robin Hood*), who will pass it on to his son Jr., the Skipper from *Gilligan's Island*. Once through probate, there's only enough left in Columbo's will to send his mother a check for $398 each month. It comes with his letters, which are unvaryingly cheery, brisk, and repetitive, in keeping with the reliable sum a good son unfailingly sends home. He takes care of his mother, who lives until August 30, 1944, three short days from the tenth anniversary of when Russ was called to Europe, sustaining her even after the death of Anna in 1940, and her husband Nicola in 1942, of which she is informed. Even from London, where he was doing so well, despite the German bombing raids, Russ always remembers Mother's Day.

There is the Columbo Stradivarius, though no physical trace exists of such a violin having passed through his hands. It can only be imagined, a lost example from the master's golden period, which began when Antonio Stradivari was in his mid-fifties; contemporary with the Dolphin (1714) or the Firebird (of 1718), though perhaps a bit earlier, since its one-piece back is slab-cut from an exceptional piece of maple Stradivari acquired in 1709, shortly after he made the Empress of Russia. Its pine belly is from wood grown on the southern slopes of the Alps, its fingerboard inlaid with mother-of-pearl cupids, like the quartet of instruments Stradivari constructed for Cosimo de' Medici in 1690. The strings are pliable in the middle register, a brushed and ambered varnish giving the instrument a golden hue, toning the wood's reverberation. It is a "long Strad," the nineteen-inch neck extended to fill the concert halls, attuned to the extremes of nodes and antinodes, the bloodrush of the bow. All the tempered pieces of Antonio's puzzle reverberate in harmony, the upper ribs absorbing the vibration of the belly, the wood tapped while being cut, listening for its major second or minor third, the body arched and resonant, balanced in the shoulder, braced by the perfect cylinder of the sound-post, the *anima*, the soul of a violin. Antonio the go-between. In the Italian tradition, he has not placed a head upon the scroll, but carved the wood in a tight spiral curl, like a galaxy.

Other "undisclosed assets" are also alleged to have been part of his estate, according to Albert (Alphonso), who sues to remove his brother John as administrator in 1946. It is a weighted task, chosen executor to the condemned after sentence has been passed, entrusted with the judgment of apportioning. Where should life's accumulations go? Among the supposed leftovers are a diary of Carole Lombard; a $750 gift ring from her to him; a $1,500 diamond-studded cigarette case; and clothing, including forty-five suits, ninety shirts, thirty pairs of shoes, and two hundred pairs of socks. John's tally of the estate's value comes to only $634. Albert, who reckons it's closer to fifty thousand, will die before the suit comes to trial. The case is closed a year later in Superior Court. Nothing is left of Russ but his memory.

THEY WILL want to make a movie.

In December 1955, *Variety* reports that a proposed "biopic" has reached a critical stage in its development deal. All parties are suing each other.

Maurice Duke Productions claim they paid $6,000 in 1953 to Russ's sister,

Carmela Tempest, for the rights to Russ's story. But now, two years later, Carmela has fallen under the spell of Johnny Desmond, who wants to make his own Russ movie, singing the songs made famous by Columbo. Louella Parsons has overheard Desmond saying "Either I do the picture or no one does." It's scotched one deal for Duke and his partner, Al Liberman, to sell on the rights to a group that includes the producer Howard Koch. It's already a pyramid scheme.

Johnny Desmond is known as "the Creamer." In July 1944, he was stationed in England with Glenn Miller's "American Band of the Allied Expeditionary Forces" and had his own radio show, *A Soldier and a Song*. Visiting Paris after the liberation, *Le Crémaire* took a café favorite he'd heard, "C'est Si Bon," and made it one of his biggest postwar hits, recording for MGM. He followed it with "C'est La Vie." In C'est.

He was another youngest Italian, this time of Sicilian descent: Giovanni Alfredo de Simone. Born in Detroit on November 14, 1919, he had a singing trio called the Downbeats when he was twenty. Bob Crosby changed their name to the Bob-o-Links and put them on his band bus, and by 1941 Desmond was on his own, singing at the Paramount with Gene Krupa's Orchestra. Then the war came, and everyone enlisted.

He might have been the "G.I. Sinatra," but even Frank was having his troubles in the postwar years, when the big bands foundered. By 1948, Johnny was a regular on Don McNeill's radio Breakfast Club. The only Columbo songs he recorded were "Guilty," during a brief span on Victor in 1947, and later "Time on My Hands" and "Sweet and Lovely"; he was too well rounded to specialize (his big hit in 1955 was "The Yellow Rose of Texas," and he recorded the "Battle Hymn of the Republic"). He looked as good as he gave, in a nondescript way, with a round face, a high pompadour, and a trim physique, five feet nine inches and 150 pounds, and Desmond transferred his charm to movies: *Calypso Heat Wave*, *Escape from San Quentin* (where he co-starred with Victor Mature), and *Fantastic Invasion of Planet Earth*; eventually he played Nicky Arnstein in the stage production of *Funny Girl*.

Maurice Duke's kind of productions. "If you wanna die, go ahead and die!" he bragged on the occasion of his seventy-fifth birthday. "Not me. Not the Duke. I'm still after the young broads."

Wearing leg braces (from a childhood bout with polio) and a blue baseball cap, clenching a cigar, jawing and jewing, Duke and other C-picture cronies could always be found at Nate 'n Al's deli in Beverly Hills, cooking up deals with the hot pastrami, the fried herring, the fruit soup. He cheerfully admitted he made bad movies, over a hundred before cashing in his sprockets in

1996. His worst—this said proudly, waving a Cel-Ray soda—was *Bela Lugosi Meets a Brooklyn Gorilla*, a 1952 thriller; *The Twinkle in God's Eye* in 1955 made the fifties his best decade.

The Russ story was a natural, and Maurice would have been producing it at the height of his powers, straight to the drive-in as tailfins came in. Desmond would have been great for the part. They could've worked together. Our loss.

JOHNNY'S NOT the only one who wants to be Columbo, to try him on for size.

Gordon Lewis is nowhere to be seen on the cover of his *A Tribute to Russ Columbo*, released by Ambassador Records, of 88 St. Francis St., Newark, N.J., a product of Synthetic Plastics Company. They have the raw material; now all they need is something to press.

Their Diplomat label is budget, one hundred and fifty–odd releases, smatterings of Broadway shows, television themes, pipe organ and percussion, twin pianos and polkas, *Lionel Hampton at the Vibes*, the travelogue hop-skip-and-a-jump-around-the-world of *Gaîeté Parisienne* and *German Beer Drinking Music* and *Folk Songs of Old Russia*, Sister Rosetta Tharpe's *Spirituals in Rhythm*, and Enzo Stuarti's *The World's Great Arias*. You can find your choice of aural backdrop on Diplomat, at a price anyone can afford, from Strauss waltzes to "Who Stole the Keeshka?" The only thing missing from their roster is rock and roll. You wouldn't know that at this moment in 1964 the British invasion of America is under way. For Diplomat, this is the year of *The Pink Panther* and "The Girl from Ipanema" and *From Russia with Love*. Russ is attributed to Gordon Lewis, following a *Tribute to Ken Griffin*, which follows a *Tribute to Glenn Miller* and a *Tribute to Mario Lanza*.

Lewis departs from the script early on, eager to try his hand at a solo career. Russ is praised in the liner notes ("And so legend passed before his time") as a "good singer of good songs," which presumably gives Gordon license (and mechanicals) to choose his own compositions, or old favorites like "In the Sweet Bye and Bye." These types-of-songs Russ might have sung, and Gordon's underhand swoop into his vowels, mark him in Russ's shadow. The only actual song of Columbo's is "(I'm Just a) Prisoner of Love." Lewis gamely tries to emulate Russ in his agreeable voice, though when he shifts ranges there is a slight hesitation in his transmission, as if he needs fluid, or to tighten his bands.

The during-dinner shuffle of "Prisoner of Love" is just shy of casual; he pours himself more into "Love Me and the World Is Mine" and "A Dream," and the curiously dashed "I—Love You Truly." If this is Russ's tribute, then Gordon Lewis does himself disservice by taking matters into his own hands; he's not a bad singer or writer. He could be himself. Then again, maybe he didn't have much of a choice. He wanted to be heard, like so many, and the Synthetic Plastics Company gave him a catalog number.

Paul Bruno sees himself more as Russ Columbo, the second coming. *The Russ Columbo Story*, released on Coral in the wake of Buddy Holly's death (his catalog number immediately follows *The Buddy Holly Story Vol. II*, in March 1960, leading to speculation on marketing and cross-promotion), sees Russ as "the personification of romance." Columbo outnumbers Bruno in front-cover photos seven to one, though Russ is in black and white, Bruno lit with the saturated reds and browns of an early Topps gum card. "Could he have stood the test of time?" wonders Burt Korall about Russ in the liner notes, and makes way for Bob Ancell, who tells us that Bruno, at twenty-six, and yes, the youngest of nine Italian children, is ready to take up where Russ left off. Gossip columnists like Hy Gardner, Herb Lyons, Robert Sylvester, and Louis Sobol concur: "*Bruno breaks through the rock and roll barrier. . . . A young man with a golden voice. . . . Good bet for a gold record-winner this year.*" The gold standard.

More than half the chosen songs are from Columbo's repertoire: "You Call It Madness but I Call It Love," "You're My Everything," "Goodnight Sweetheart," "Guilty," "Prisoner of Love," "Paradise," "Sweet and Lovely." The others are "identified" with him, and I must admit to a longing to hear even a faux-Russ sing "I'm in the Mood for Love," and "I'm Through with Love."

Bruno sounds nothing like Russ, except in his unhurried pacing. Each line is lagged into forgetfulness while the orchestra waits for him to catch up. The downbeat is vague. Bruno has little dynamic range and doesn't seem to care. Even when he moves from Russ to "Temptation," he seems swayed in the wind, distracted by the sound of his own voice. It's pleasant boudoir music; jerking on. He can snap to attention when the song slaps his face ("*Temptation. . . . I'm your slave*"), but he's more comfortable nuzzling next to his listener, a glassine murmur, slightly hoarse at this low volume, straining to be heard. You have to turn the record up. When the orchestra livens for the bursts of "If I Could Be with You (One Hour Tonight)," he steps out of the way. Maybe he's more like Russ than he imagines.

THERE ARE those who come to Russ from the other side of fame, illuminating him with their spotlight, rather than vice versa. Jerry Vale and Tiny Tim, an odd coupling in any paragraph, are *Tonight Show* veterans who each make their Columbo commemorative album, united in respect and admiration. Sing along with Russ.

In fact, it's the sing-along king, Mitch Miller, who first suggests to Vale that he make an album of Columbo standards for Columbia Records. *I Remember Russ* will follow up Jerry's successful *I Remember Buddy*, not referring to Holly, for this is April 1958 (Miller hates rock and roll, anyway), but Buddy Clark, the son of a Boston cantor who could *crescendo* to *diminuendo* in one phrase, and had his own ill-starred *decrescendo* in an airplane as the forties drew to a close, crashing on Beverly Boulevard in Los Angeles on his way back from an impromptu trip to the Stanford-Michigan game.

The fifties are a boom time for Italian singers, commensurate with the coming of age of the Italian third generation. The younger ones get diverted to doo-wop; teen streetcorner heartthrobs like Dion DiMucci of the Belmonts, Johnny Maestro of the Crests, the basses and tenors and baritones and falsettos of the Elegants and the Passions and the Mystics. For the older singers, on their way to the lounge, the smoky supper club, and the bachelor pad, Frank Sinatra provides the career model; though they don't underestimate Dean Martin and Perry Como, two performers whose softened edges are closer in style and mannerism to Columbo, at least as far as the croon is concerned. Frank is too angular, too sharp in his creased pants and insouciant hat; he's cocky. He wants to be inside the female, not have her inside him.

Martin is used to playing the straight man, after twinning with Jerry Lewis. In the face of Lewis's manic adolescent male energy, his sibling role is the big sister, prone to a crush and too pretty, a parent when she needs to be. When Dean goes solo, he perfects the art of the raised eyebrow, putting on his inebriation like makeup to loosen his audience, the way liquor enlivens a party, toasting emotion. The Rat Pack celebrates the mixed drink: "Go easy on yourself," Frank advises as he splashes in the soda, and they raise their glasses. Dino's best-known hit, "Everybody Loves Somebody Sometime," carries with it a reassurance of love's inevitability, that all will eventually partake of its joyful possibilities, and Martin's sleepy cuddling has the warmth and pull-up-the-covers of a good-night kiss. Sleep tight. *"That's Amore!"*

Only Como might have glimpsed Russ in person, when Columbo passed through Cleveland twice in August 1932, first at the RKO Palace, a large theater, and again on the last days of the month at the Lotus Gardens Café downtown. Perry was nineteen, singing with Cleveland bandleader Freddie Carlone, just out of the barbershop in Canonsburg, Pennsylvania. He never lost his touch with a soothing hot towel, and his voice had the comfort of a man you would trust with a razor at your throat. Como came up through Ted Weems—his closest competitors would have been Tommy Dorsey's Jack Leonard, or Jimmy Dorsey's Bob Eberly, who showed more pizzazz—and established himself in 1945 with "Till the End of Time," the A-flat major polonaise featured in the Chopin film treatment, *A Song to Remember*. His version of "Prisoner of Love," in 1946, could hardly hold a candle to Russ, but by then Como was heading for television, neutered.

Genero Louis Vitaliano is from the barbershop as well. Born the same month in which Russ made *That Goes Double*, Jerry Vale shined shoes up in Mount Vernon, New York, just above the Bronx, before heading to the Enchanted Room in Manhattan where Guy Mitchell ("Singing the Blues") recommended him to Mitch Miller. He started hitting in 1953 with "You Can Never Give Me Back Your Heart," and soon discovered his listeners had a soft spot for the same type of songs he used to sit around his grandmother's house on Sunday afternoon and sing to the family, the *bravissimo* tearjerkers that would remind them of the old country: "O Sole Mio," "Mala Feminina," "Non Dimenticar," "Anima e Core."

He speaks Italian "somewhat," he tells me on the phone one evening, though he's not a loquacious man. Even after recording an album of Russ songs, he goes no further than "If he had lived, who knows?" When I try to steer the conversation to the Italian character as exposed in song (like any entertainment beat reporter), he seems lost for the right catchphrase. "I can't put it into words," he trails off again and again. "I don't know how to say it." I shouldn't be surprised; that's why he sings.

Surrounded by the Cinerama orchestrations of Glenn Osser, strings laying gossamer sheets over bedded woodwinds while harps ripple and pillow, Jerry spends three days at Columbia's Thirtieth Street studios bringing Russ's best-known classics into high fidelity. Air is the spatial difference here, a world away from the cramped recordings Columbo made only six blocks and a quarter century downtown. The "Modern Arrangements" are written from the violins out, surrounding Vale's voice phrase for phrase; it's practically a collaboration. His confidence and breath control enable him to hold his own against their insistence, with his smooth epicurean thorax that intones as well as it projects. He is less nervous than in the *Buddy* sessions, and he doesn't sound at all like Russ—not surprising, because he is hardly familiar with Columbo's work when Miller suggests him, except through Como's recording of "Prisoner of Love," and "You're My Everything," which has become a virtual standard among Italian singers; he has to "research" Columbo. He is not as attracted to the man as he is to his songs, an old-fashioned biographic, seeing the artist through his work rather than his trials. "A good song will always have its appeal," Vale writes in the liner notes for the album's re-release in the year 2000, "and any rendition of it, as long as it is beautiful, will be in demand." He understands the remix.

He changes their sonority as well. His "You Call It Madness but I Call It Love" is pitched far above Russ's, allowing him to emphasize the second half of the equation. His timbre in 1958 is closer to Johnny Mathis than to other of his contemporaries, like Vic Damone, or Eddie Fisher (who has his own RussBingRudy moment on *May I Sing to You*, covering "You Call It Madness" and "Where the Blue of the Night" and "Vagabond Lover" on his way from Jolson to Sinatra and Cole, a man for all seasons). In the next year, Osser will billow his string arrangements around such Mathis classics as "Misty." Vale doesn't hold back—"Prisoner of Love" is hardly *sotto voce*—and color television is here. He remembers Russ, and Russ is remembered. Fair trade.

ON DECEMBER 17, 1969, in front of forty-five million viewers gathered for Johnny Carson's *Tonight Show*, Tiny Tim, thirty-nine, a fey and impish freak of good nature, married his Miss Vicki, a seventeen-year-old Italian girl from New Jersey. It was the crowning glory and fitting moral to the sixties mud wrestling that pitted Woodstock against Altamont, and an improbable apex of international celebrity and public fascination for one so uninhibitedly eccentric.

Tiny traveled the same rise to prominence from the bohemian Village to Times Square that Jean Malin traced. It was in Steve Paul's basement rock club, the Scene, located off Eighth Avenue on West Forty-sixth Street, a couple of blocks west from Symphony Sid's record shop where he was first introduced to Columbo's oeuvre, that Tim had started being regarded as more than just a freak. Strumming a ukulele left-handed, carrying his stage props in a shopping bag, hair falling below his shoulders in scraggly curls, and graced with a nose that might give Cyrano pause, he sang in a fluttering falsetto that cut through catcalls and queer-baiting abuse, throwing himself to the lions wherever he appeared. What saved him was his unswayable faith in the gospel he learned from scratchy 78s in his solitary bedroom up in Washington Heights, the transubstance of true romance (his stage name was once Larry Love). His world was of womanly virtue and chivalric respect for his musical elders. He had the sacrifical faith of a Christian, and he was taken

TINY TIM

for a lamb of God (albeit a born vegetarian, never having eaten meat or eggs) by a generation wearing the sandals and longhair-shirt of a wandering Christ in the desert. He starred on *Laugh-In*, their innocent savant. Unlike the Shangri-Las, there was never any good-bad in Tiny's world; only good.

And God, in His in-finite wisdom, saw that it was good, and granted him a hit record. Producer Richard Perry was dazzled by the purity in Tim's light-shine, his lack of guile and myopic pleasure in his performance art, and crafted an album around him, *God Bless Tiny Tim*. Thus, "Tip Toe Through the Tulips with Me," a smash hit for Nick Lucas in 1929, made a Top Twenty reappearance in the summer of 1968, with Tim's canarylike trill at the fore. "Bring Back Those Rockabye Baby Days," he pleaded in his follow-up, a time when pop was presumably more innocent, as pop is always more innocent in past tense. Then he proceeded to cover Jerry Lee Lewis's "Great Balls of Fire." Perry took him to London's Royal Albert Hall in October 1968, backing him with a full orchestra. Tim sang "Like a Rolling Stone" by a "Mr. Dylan" and the Rolling Stones' "Satisfaction," as well as Rudy Vallée's "Stein Song" and "I'm Just a Vagabond Lover." He showed no favoritism in his embrace of twentieth-century music, covering hits by Sonny and Cher ("I Got You, Babe") and Rod Stewart ("Maggie May" *and* "D'Ya Think I'm Sexy"). He saw no difference between them and an artist like Henry Burr, whose 1908 song "Beautiful Ohio" was the listening experience that deflowered him; or, in Tiny's case, flowered him. He was Flower Power's most exotic bloom.

Only good. But it was too good to last. Reprise, his label, dropped him after three albums, and the public soon moved on to other singing novelties (glam-rock was on the horizon). Ever keeping up with the hit parade, he tried AC/DC's "Highway to Hell" and Billy Idol's "Rebel Yell." By 1993, Tiny was putting out records on his own Toilet Records: "I Ain't Got No Money." He never stopped performing, however large or small the venue, and was especially beloved in Australia. Tiny Tim, who used to say of the singers he commemorated that "Their souls were living in me," died in December 1996 while tip-toeing at a benefit for the Women's Club of Minneapolis.

This might be the end of our tale, and no place here, were it not for Mark Robinson, who produced Tiny's final album, for Vinyl Retentive records, a label Tim shared with the suicidally extreme slash-rock of G. G. Allin. Ten Columbo songs were meticulously transcribed from their original arrangements by Clang, a band led by Paul Reller, along with additional musicians from the University of South Florida using vintage instruments. Over four days in September 1994, they reincarnated Tiny Tim as Russ. "I was in another world," said Tiny of the occasion. "I was in the twilight zone . . . in the world of spirits.

"I felt I was in Mr. Columbo's soul." His voice echoes this, gifted with a depth of baritone that is surprising. In the midst of straight-faced re-creations of Columbo settings, Tim is overwhelmed by Russ's emotive intensity. Tiny had made a career of performing outside his element, an odd duck out of water. Within the Reller arrangements, his séance of Russ allows him to sing full-voice, pulling Russ through the ether like a radio antenna, and it transforms this man whose emotion was never taken seriously enough; who is remembered as amusing, if not a joke. When he pulls on the mask of Russ, his sincerity convinces.

He doesn't try his hand at "You Call It Madness," though he had performed it live at the Royal Albert show. But on Russ's traditional canon, "All of Me," and "Time on My Hands" and a quavering, resolute "Prisoner of Love," Tiny pours out his be-longing, unlocking the cage of himself.

He's in his element at last. "You Try Somebody Else" opens the album; it's the Else that's spooky. Tiny has caught Columbo's vocal wavelength; you expect the falsetto and are given the baritone. If he overly tremolos as the song picks up confidence, it's the dawning on his part that he has been teleported. He's in the past, and his own future. Time is traversed, and he takes the exulting and turns it into a joyful cry.

He's true to all his dotted half-notes, dramatizing lyrics so they don't sound like empty promises or euphonia, and you begin to realize just how fine and underrated a singer Mr. Tim is, riding the inflections and curling cues that are the hallmark of late-twenties and early-thirties vocal performance, born natural within the arrangements. There is no irony; he could be the Street Singer. Maybe then his love of beauty wouldn't have been stunted, mocked, turned into sideshow. And then adored. Tossed aside. Renewed. Crush and heartbreak and salvation, "Paradise" and "More Than You Know" and "Save the Last Dance for Me." Love's lost and found.

I'M NOT immune to such temptations. The sensual attraction of the music whispers, like a silk excuse for a dress. The chords fall easily to hand, movable, walking the lyrics through their stately progressions while the song swirls around itself, liquor in a circling glass, wet rings on the bar top.

Me in a tuxedo shirt. Hair slicked back, fat guitar. Fretless bass. A slight vibrato on the Magnatone. Lights low.

Late show.

BING AND RUDY

They are their own trinity.

Bing is the universal dad. Rudy the misbehaving son. That leaves Russ. The holy ghost.

BING IS in eclipse.

Twenty-five years after Elvis Presley's death, pilgrims gather by the thousands in candlelight ceremony outside Graceland; through the crowds pass Elvis imitators, each capturing a different station of the cross: Sun Elvis, Sullivan Elvis, G.I. Elvis, Hollywood and Las Vegas Elvis and Comeback Elvis and "Elvis in Hawaii" Elvis.

For Bing's silver anniversary, two months later in 2002, the only scheduled commemoration is a three-day academic conference to be held in mid-November at Hofstra University, exploring "Crosby and American Culture," bookended by a Gonzaga gathering on his birth centennial a few months later. It's as if Bing has to be explained to the new century. Indeed, sparked by Gary Giddins's thorough, appreciative biography and the gracious charm of Kathryn Crosby, flashing the prominent cheekbones and radiant smile of the Texas beauty queen she once was and the stage actress she now is, it does seem as if a reevaluation is under way, though it's also amazing that such consideration is needed. Elvis's *buh-buh-boo* ("I Want You, I Need You, I Love You") is inconceivable without Bing; and even Eminem, a name that comes up at this conference as a mnemonic for modern music, shares a cross-cultural racial appeal in a way that implies first-name familiarity (see Jimi, Prince, Madonna). The conference explicates Bing's character in films (especially his turns as a Catholic priest and as Bob Hope's kick-side) and cartoons, his celebration of the American songbook, the tilt of his hat and the angle of his pipe and his conviviality. On more than one occasion, the "single most important musical influence in twentieth-century popular music" is posited from the podium, as is "invented the art of American popular song," and though such hosannas are dependent on birthdate and prevailing culture, exclusionary by nature, reliving his audio-video clips bears him up well under scrutiny. It's not just his encompass of every pre-rock genre, his spread over popular sentiment—Jack Kapp knew he could sing anything, because it would always be Bing first—and the consequent illusion of being everywhere at once. Even as his music develops over the thirties, on radio and filtered through his celebrity, enhanced and defined by *Kraft Music Hall* writer Carroll Carroll, who scripts an idealized Bing (he listens to Crosby's "cadence," the beats in his personality) and further blurs the lines between Crosby's privacy and publicity, which then carries over to his movie persona, he is only warming to his destiny. Though, counting movies and records, he is the biggest box office draw as the thirties close, it is the forties that iconize Crosby, as a wartime nation looks toward heart(h) and home and God's own American way and finds Father Chuck O'Malley opening the church doors, twinkling his bluer-than-thou eyes, and offering blessed *sanctuary.*

Bing is able to perform this miracle because of the rise of heartthrob Frank Sinatra, who heads the bobby-soxers off at the pass. Sinatra idolized Crosby, but he tried not to sound like Bing when coming up in the late thirties with the Hoboken Four on the Ted Mack Amateur Hour, or Harry James's band. Even his "Learn to Croon," an "old favorite" caught on a Tommy Dorsey radio broadcast on July 21, 1940, sounds impatient, and Frank drops the *buh-buh-boos* that Crosby poked at himself. Frank couldn't wait to get out on his own. By 1942, he'd bought his way out of his contract with T. Dorsey and created a solo sensation at the Paramount's Christmas holiday show. He was nervy, confrontational, pushy. Bing was no pushover, but he bent with the breezes. At a moment when a generational shift might have planned Crosby's obsolescence, much as Frank himself would go through a valley of popularity ten years hence, he retired from the game of foreplay, except for his omnipresent golf. Sinatra looked at the genial Crosby and saw there was no sense of living dangerously. Bing was unruffled, held himself in check, even when up to a bit of mischief. Frank liked to snap-the-whip of emotional turbulence, quick to insinuate and quicker to anger, and seemed to have more to lose. Italian. Like Russ.

They take up opposing positions around the libido. In a 1944 Looney Tunes directed by Frank Tashlin, *The Crooner Swooner*, caricatures of Frank and Bing serenade the hens. Frank gets them undulating and spellbound, but there's no eggs a-laying. Bing soothes them into shelling their yolks, a family man. When they sing together (as they often did as years went by, including a memorable television interlude in October 1957 on *The Edsel Show*, La-moured by Rosemary Clooney, in which they took off on each other's signature songs), they can even persuade farmer Porky Pig to start spouting omelets; over easy with sausage.

Bing is now free to put on the chaste collar, sing "White Christmas" for the troops (one of the stories at the conference recalls when Bing entertained twenty thousand tear-streaming G.I.s in wartime France, reminding them of Irving Berlin's assimilated American Dream). His Christianity plays softball with the kids, declares a holiday at the parochial school, and neo-platonically flirts with Ingrid Bergman, the sacrificial sister of *The Bells of St. Mary's*. Even as rapscallions of the *Road*, Bing and Bob Hope would rather play patty-cake than part over Dorothy Dell's best pal. More buddy-buddy than devoted romancers, their no-gals-allowed is the boys-only clubhouse of the priest-hood.

He's Joe Average, or so Bing will tell you. He's lucky, and yeah, you too could win the lottery, but luck has to be sustained by hard work and concentration and focus, and in that way he falls right into the myth of the common man writ large, a Boone or a Bumppo. He's the Great Plains, the midsection of the country, the last vestige of frontier that is Spokane before the Columbia Gorge rises to the Cascades and slopes down to the Sound. Frank is urban; Bing has his isolated Elko spread in Nevada, and he works it hard, like a cowboy. It's not a dude ranch—in a 1955 interview record for Decca, he says it's "a calf and cow operation . . . it's pretty lonely up there." He talks about it in ways that define his work ethic. "It's sixty miles from any town, and if they come up there thinking that they're gonna have jolly times and be cowboying every day and ridin' around the range singing 'Take Me Back to My Boots and Saddle,' why they're due for early disillusionment. . . . It's all work and, of course, the food is good." It reminds me of advice he gives to aspiring crooners in a radio interview with Jack Ellsworth around the time of his final New York appearances. "The competition is fierce," he admits. "Give it a whirl . . ." but if you haven't got what it takes, "drop it and get into something else." Don't keep betting hoping you'll recoup.

Not like the Las Vegas that Frank has come to embody in his stick figure, live at the Sands. That's about as close to *El Ranchero* life as Frank would admit, his life in the desert the hubbub and flashing lights and sexual tension of the slot machine. He carries his drink onstage; Crosby has to tuck it away, in his wall safe. Pre-dating Sinatra, Bing could have his Rat Pack. For Bing, it would be Louis Armstrong as Sammy Davis, Jr., Hope in the Joey Bishop slot, Rosie Clooney transposing Peter Lawford, and yes, if I had my way, Russ as Dean Martin. Set at the track; playing the ponies.

Bing never really transforms. The touch of Irish leprechaun that comes with his rendition of "Too-Ra-Loo-Ra-Loo-Ral" in *Going My Way* gives him an ageless quality, elfish and bemused, as his skin wizens and his hair thins further. Always in character, he is infinitely reliable, downbeat at nine on the one, casually dressed even in outlandish costume, a laconic guy content to let the world float. He goes fishin'. At least that's what he has Everett tell them when they call with offers that aren't up to par—he's a golfer in business too. He races horses, and bets on his own sure thing, first take, no over-rehearsal. Just enough, like when Seabiscuit goes up in match race against Ligaroti, an Argentine six-year-old from Crosby's stables, at the Del Mar track he helps build along the Pacific *Where the Surf Meets the Turf*. Seabiscuit nips Crosby's nag at the finish line by a nose. He loses the race, but the track's reputation is assured. It was why he always insisted on a co-star. He was in it for the mile *and* an eighth, and he wanted to finish in the money.

Just enough. The amount of tipple he would bring to the studio, three drinks' worth. Before, during, and after. He'd ask Les Paul, whose trio backed Bing on many classic records in the forties, if he wanted a nip, and Les knew not to say yeah, because Crosby had them measured out, not a drop more. Enough's enough, and it wasn't just drinking: he learned to turn off. Crosby would depart the movie set promptly at closing time, or waltz out the radio station door still whistling "Where the Blue of the Night," listening to the theme play out in his car on his way to the *solitaire* of the fairway. Even in a foursome, golf is one on one. Follow-through the bouncing ball. He worked hard at being a good golfer, just as he worked hard at singing, at his radio and then television appearances, his acting, his technical pursuits (he invested in magnetic tape and multitrack, though it would never change the way he made his own records, recording out in the room with the musicians, no isolation) and business interests, his family, his being Bing; and made it look a snap. He had impeccable timing, not just vocally. Despite appearances, he was a busy guy, and he had to ration himself. There are only so many beats to a measure.

On the same weekend that Russ is killed, Bing is promoting *She Loves Me Not*, which is to open on September 7. His co-star, Miriam Hopkins, is a murder witness who disguises herself as a man, causing hijinks for the "campus crooner," still Gonzaga at heart. But Crosby no longer wants to be the "first crooner of the land," as he tells Harrison Carroll of the King Features Syndicate (no relation to his future scriptwriter). "Boo boo pa doop songs won me my first reputation, but I believe my voice has developed since then." He's going "straight baritone." It's Miriam who cross-dresses. Filming is under way for *Here Is My Heart*. His Paramount contract is running out. Renegotiation is in the air. He's just getting started.

His movies in the thirties are formulaic in the way of his radio personality, almost as if his radio show is broadcast on the screen two or three times a year. He maneuvers through each vehicle with reassurance, increasingly himself, because he's Bing. It gives him a distance from his roles, to make the humorous aside, as a character in a movie might turn to the audience in the theater, stepping outside the film, a nesting of character. He reflects the light of his co-stars, using them to inspire his own performance. He has W. C. Fields to foil in *Mississippi*, Ethel Merman in *Anything Goes*, Andy Devine in *Doctor Rhythm*. Their exaggerated personalities set off his calming tendencies. He plays to them as much as to the camera, conspiratorial, sharing secrets. Bing is likable; the voluminous and star-studded guest listing for *Kraft Music Hall* as the thirties slide from Depression to depression testifies to his ability to make his guests feel more like themselves, witty and droll, prettier, more musical. He is disarming, like a friendly sheriff who doesn't want any trouble in town and asks you to check your guns at the door.

Guests come and go, but it is his own movie that people want to see, as if to figure out how Bing does it. He makes everyone at home, invitational. His geniality centers his films of the late thirties (nor did Paramount want to rock the casting boat), interchanging *Pennies from Heaven* and *Double or Nothing* and *Paris Honeymoon*. An exception is *Sing You Sinners*, where his performance slips below the surface to expose the self-doubt of a big-dreams garage mechanic who sings and winds up owning a race horse, winning the Derby. Well, maybe it wasn't much of a stretch at that. Bing stays in more jovial wardrobe through *The Starmaker* (1939) and *If I Had My Way* and *Rhythm on the River* (1940), always sniffing the finest songs, whatever the vehiculars, of songwriters like Cole Porter, Robin and Rainger, Johnny Burke, and James V. Monaco.

The country needs his comfort; his sense of permanent vacation. On a trip to Hawaii in 1936, he hears Harry Owens playing a song he wrote for his daughter, the delicate strains of "Sweet Leilani," and persuades Paramount to use it in *Waikiki Wedding* the next year. Hollywood has already seen a vogue for Island music in the twenties, the slack key and the lap steel, and vocals that move in and out of falsetto so quickly that they might be yodels, but Bing becomes an island refuge; something about his character lends itself to palms and sea. He's not without an awareness of a troubled world; and there is a wistful, lost innocence to "Sweet Leilani"—indeed, all Hawaiian music, with its glissandos and melancholic quavers—that makes prescient the coming of Pearl Harbor, when Hawaii is seen as a part of the United States, and must be defended, like a daughter's endangered virtue. Bing, too, is preparing the country for war.

He doesn't want to play a priest in *Going My Way*, but allows himself to be swayed by director Leo McCarey. The secular success of "White Christmas" from *Holiday Inn* in 1942 gives him leeway. Irving Berlin had originally written the song tongue in cheek—the verse, which is almost never sung, concerns a yearning swell in sunny Beverly Hills remembering the good old days back home, somewhat as Berlin must have looked through borscht-colored

BING AS FATHER O'MALLEY, STILL CROONING

glasses on the shtetl life he had left in Siberia while basking in the bright sun of America—before launching into the picture-postcard nostalgia of a rural Protestant New England Christmas straight out of Currier & Ives. The world takes on a blanket of white, once and again virginal; Bing plays it straight, in effect writing the verse out of history, his rendition solemn and gospel. His Catholicism has been tucked into the American dream of home ownership and a two-sleigh garage, a modern church, like these born-again movies Bing makes in the mid-forties that convert him.

Father Chuck is a new kind of priest, with the bedside manner of a psychotherapist, nodding and prompting, reacting more than agitating, gently steering his subjects to their own (his) conclusions. His plain demeanor undercuts the insular Church that provoked the Inquisition, forbade meat on Friday, and was about to decommission Saint Christopher. O'Malley's Father figure is knowing and forgiving, more compassion than Passion Play, displaying the Christian virtue of *apatheia* (as Dr. Elaine Phillips from Tennessee State University theorizes at the Hofstra conference) that emphasizes self-temperance and "moral probity." It is a very "masculine piety," she argues; he deflects desire. Yet he is willing to get his cassock dirty playing in the streets, sitting around a piano singing "High Hopes" with his *suffer the little* children. The penitences he hands out are lenient, absolving, and it is an image that will come back to haunt Bing later when his parental roles become confused in the public's eye; but mid-war, he assumes his vestments with the changing mores of the immigrant church, Irish and Italian and the fundamentalist crucible that is America. The Catholic Church has never pretended to be a democracy; now it meets a democracy that has become a church.

BING IS the quintessential American. He's an ordinary guy in an exotic locale, bringing his own bottoms-up view of democracy to the natives, usually represented by Dorothy Lamour, her hint of sarong—she has been typecast since her Hollywood debut in 1936 in *The Jungle Princess*—erotic enough for Hope and Crosby. They're on the *Road* a decade before the Beats put a permanent state of restlessness and present-tense living on the mythopoeic map, like the similar pairing of Kerouac's Sal Paradise and Dean Moriarty. It's a buddy movie, three steps removed from Huck and Jim, one from Stan and Ollie, sideways from Abbott and Costello, and leading to Martin and Lewis, Ralph and Norton, the Blues Brothers, Doug and Bob, Those Wild and Crazy Guys, Wayne and his World.

The *Road* patter of Bob Hope and Crosby has the crackle of grand improvisation. Bing's musicality and Bob's rhythmic fast-talk, convincing his own misgivings in its rapid-fire chatter, meet over the extended ad-lib that is these *Road* capers, a routine they have been honing since first meeting at the Capitol Theater in December 1932. Not all of it was invented on the spot and off the cuff—the two had radio scriptwriters working overtime to supply them with snappy comebacks and non sequiturs. These zingers were used like the practiced licks a musician brings to a jam session. They riffed, raffed, raffled, and Lamour could only look on in wonder, trying to slide her curves between the two, which was why they kept hiring her sequel after sequel; she was the straight gal. The other two were in love with each other. In *Road to Morocco*, each goes to kiss her mirage on the cheek; she vanishes, their mouths collide. *Eewwww*, they mock-grimace. Earlier, Bob taps Bing on the buttocks with his broadsword. "There's two sides to everything," he chuckles.

Like a pair of castaway Lawrences, they have arrived in the Arabia Deserta that is Hollywood *Morocco*. "What's that bulge in your pocket?" Bing asks Bob in their first roundelay, floating shipwrecked on a raft. Bing carries Bob ashore, as if over a threshold. A camel nuzzles them; they each think it's the other. Double-humped, they ride to Morocco, and walk into the casbah arm in arm. Bing sells Bob—"Why would a guy buy a guy?" Hope wonders. Springs eternal. It turns out his buyer is a woman: Dottie Love, bejeweled. They compete for her, a one-upmanship that often makes her seem beside the point. Their repartée is its own reward. Bing will win her, singing "Moonlight Becomes You" in her hanging gardens, *The Sheik* in reverse.

Morocco is the third of seven films they would make as fellow travelers. As the series went for baroque, the settings became increasingly outlandish and otherworldly; even Dorothy Lamour was reduced to a tourist attraction in 1962's *The Road to Hong Kong*, playing "Dorothy Lamour," before the two B's jet off Earth to visit their interstellar counterparts, Frank Sinatra and Dean Martin. Bob and Bing's palsy-walsy brotherhood is a constant, and innuendo aside, more a playful signifier than significant in these homogeneous mass-appeal comedies. Their sibling rivalry endures; Bing the older, ensnaring the younger and more impulsive Bob in his schemings. Wally and the Beaver. Kelly and Bud. Kelly and Jack. Family values.

It was a different relationship than he had with Frank Sinatra. Their rivalry was warily and warmly conspiratorial, a *High Society* showdown in 1956 that gave each his due, allowing them to work together, and more notably, to co-exist. It's Bing's world that Frank enters, and both realize it: "I'm scared, and I want to go home," his character, a scandal sheet reporter, says on entering the Newport world of the idle rich. He's not born to the manor, and has the required shoulder-chip. This 1956 remake of *The Philadelphia Story* has Grace Kelly remodeling Katharine Hepburn, a foreshadow of her impending royalty when she marries on-the-road-to-Monaco's Prince Rainier, while Bing renovates Cary Grant as a "juke box hero," a composer "who doesn't want to be serious." Frank turns his boudoir eye-shadows on Kelly, asking "Mind If I Make Love to You" in a way that melts the ice in her glass. But Bing follows with "True Love"—Cole Porter at his most Hank Williams. He's a "one-gal guy," and has even written her a love theme, which an orchestra led by Louis Armstrong choruses greekly. "Jazz Is King," Satch and Bing and Frank proclaim, though theirs is a jazz already wondering whether the big bands are coming back, hardly bebop or third stream cool. Crosby offers to soften her, to reveal her "frailty," to let her "tiara slip"; his persuasion works within. Frank's females learn the without. He's hard to pin down. He had given his all for Ava Gardner in their stormy few years together, when he left his first wife and scandalized the press; and here he was playing a snoop.

Sinatra was the opposite of emotional rectitude; he could bug out to extremes of character, verging on the psychotic. Though he tried on the guise of a soft-spoken coal-dust priest in the 1948 *Miracle of the Bells*, his character seems flat and glazed, unnaturally tranquilized. Frank is unused to turning the other cheek. He's more believable in *Suddenly* (1954) as a would-be presidential assassin, nervously wired like a time bomb whose clock runs fast and slow, so you never know when it's going to go off. His death scene as Maggio in *From Here to Eternity* was a career resurrection; his portrayal of a junkie's withdrawal in *Man with the Golden Arm* provided as much graphic gutwrench as William S. Burroughs. The closest Bing got to such searing portrayals was his role in 1954's *The Country Girl*, as an alcoholic actor who is guilt-ridden over causing the death of his son. For a moment his chasm opened, and one could see the distended strength that it must have taken to be Bing Crosby, the skirting of an emotional abyss in which his deceptively casual art found its grace.

But that's not how we remember him. The film preceding in his screenography is *White Christmas*, and every holiday season without fail we are reminded of Bing's greatest hit, the song and the VistaVision movie, entwined in the confluence that is Crosby. His numbers with Danny Kaye have the same sibling dynamic as Hope, only this time around they're "Sisters." Their love interests, Rosemary Clooney and the wasp-waisted dancer Vera Ellen, are the boyish, athletic ones. After *High Society*, and another priestly turn in *Say One for Me* (1959), Bing's themed variations overfamiliarize. He's a Disney character, a cartooned Ichabod Crane in *The Legend of Sleepy Hollow*.

He could be retired, though there were occasional films—including a supporting role in Frank's Rat Pack in *Robin and the Seven Hoods*, and television specials and, well, television specials, especially at Christmas. He side-stepped out of the popular time stream. Dean will have a number one hit in 1964 ("Everybody Loves Somebody"), as will Louis Armstrong ("Hello Dolly"), and Frank's appeal is given a *Playboy* buff-up by his pack-ratting, paired with daughter Nancy ("Something Stupid" reaches number one in May 1967, teaching those Haight-Ashbury creeps something about the sharkskin class of a fine-cut Italian suit), who has the kind of smoldering sexuality that Frank's namesake son never seemed to generate. Frank Jr. was the one kidnapped, held for ransom; Nancy Jr. wears the boots in the family.

Bing didn't seem to resent the lack of limelight. He had determined not to make the same mistakes he'd made with Dixie and his first set of boys, and he wanted more time to spend with his second family. It's the reverse of the plot of *High Society*; remarrying, it's his frailty he recognizes, and the second chance that comes with renewing your vows. He was a generation ahead of all his peers, probably ready to take it easy. He did like to take it easy.

Time took it easy on him. Until he fell into the orchestra pit of the Ambassador Theater in Pasadena, California, while taping a CBS television special in March 1977 to celebrate fifty years in show business, rupturing a disc in his spine and limiting his movements, he seemed remarkably preserved, ageless. He retained the easy step of a song-and-dance man who had started on vaudeville percussion, timing his vocal asides and wisecracks like a crash cymbal. He listened to the band, a fluid "chameleon" (a conference word) within the rhythm section; and tapped out the rhythm with his voice, all octaves in pretty good shape, all things considered, though he might choose a lower harmony for a couple of notes up top, in his supple, modulated tone that hardly ever shouted, at least on microphone. Crosby always entered a song with assurance, in motion and warmed up, as if he had already sung the first phrase.

He could be exacting, keeping himself at the ready. He demanded the same of others. He would arrive on the dot for recording sessions, as early as 8:00 A.M., pipe and racing form in hand, and if a musician made a mistake during the first take, it's likely he wouldn't be around for the next session. Arranger/producer Buddy Bregman says he got him to do more than one run-through for the cuts in the 1956 *Bing Sings Whilst Bregman Swings* where Bing lets loose; but that was a co-bill, and the good sportsman in Crosby liked a challenge as the fifties loomed, rising to one of his most driving, energized albums. He had no nervousness about the studio, liked to record seven or eight songs at a clip, and be out before the session moved into overtime. He preferred recording in the morning, before his voice had a chance to rise from its baritone. He liked the sonority, a *gravitas* that his otherwise slight figure might skip over in its rush to the driving range. Jack Kapp taught him to be open-minded about a song, and after Jack died, in 1949, Bing saw the world in the same public-friendly absolutes as Kapp, that he could make any song Bing. He bantered with the musicians and the control room, one of the guys. A well-circulated outtake has him singing the wrong melody while recording yet another version of "Wrap Your Troubles in Dreams," so he entertains the band as they wind the song down: *"They cut out eight bars, the dirty bastards, and I didn't know which eight bars . . . I'm going off my nut . . ."*

Sure, he hates rock and roll. Who wouldn't? It's "trash," he tells a Senate committee investigating a rival songwriting performance society, Broadcast Music Inc., in challenge to his American Society of Composers, Authors, and Publishers (ASCAP), where the "talented, dedicated songwriters" belong. Elvis? "He sings well enough, I suppose," but he hasn't "contributed a damn thing to music." There will be no duets. Still, you can't blame him. It's hard enough when generations transfer loyalties; but when it happens on the overnight shift, the talkies replacing the silents, animosity stirs. It's the mid-1950s when Bing starts to look backward, not that he lessens his reading ability, his acting-out of a song, his understanding of *the words*. Kids today *don't get the words*. His interpretation of classic material glows with the hard-won subtleties of older age. He knows his way, lasts longer, though there is a certain lack of suspense at the outcome. When Decca releases a five-disc *Autobiography* in 1954, Bing recuts his early catalog with Buddy Cole and his trio, including Perry Botkin in Eddie Lang's old seat. He introduces each track at his most deprecating—there's lots of oh-shucks like *journeyman sea level baritone* and *it may get a little dull* and *my thinning noggin*—until you realize that these are not just songs, but standards, outlasting the test of time, the sing-along still then, and it is usually Bing's version that is remembered.

He begins with the silt of "Muddy Water" and "Mississippi Mud" and sings straight through to 1934's "Love in Bloom," a verse and a chorus of the twenty-five best-known hits that comprise his early era, ending in the mid-thirties as the croon faded into innocuity, when he rose above mere romance. The easy sway of Cole's trio and Bing's well-worn acquaintance with the material are complementary, accomplished, reclined. "1931 was a halcyon year for me," he muses before singing "Out of Nowhere"; he might be singing about his own onrushing fame at that moment. He fits snugly around "Sweet and Lovely," "Paradise," "I Don't Stand a Ghost of a Chance with You," and

"Temptation," and sings "Stardust" with his own stardom reflecting: "it's a lit-tle rangy for my abbreviated vocal reach," but remains "my favorite song." Be-tween tracks, backed by Cole's sepulchral organ, he reminisces about the Rhythm Boys and Harry Barris, the Grove, *The Big Broadcast*, "the year Gary came along," his unwinding Road to Bing. Arrival.

Russ never had a chance. He's encircled by his era, like a child star who can't grow up. The song that carries his ASCAP royalties forward is "Prisoner of Love," and even Bing will think it Columbo's theme when he records it on an album titled *Songs That I Wish I Had Sung (the First Time Around)*. It's the opposite of Cole's album; and listening to him pronounce *pris-on-ner* with three beats instead of two, you can feel Bing making the phrase less wieldy, poking Russ in the ribs for taking a first crack at "Where the Blue of the Night." He writes in the liner notes, "I am sure if Russ had lived, he would have been a big, big star." Stardust to dust.

It seemed Bing could do no wrong, and even after his death, the sanctity of his reputation was inviolable for a time. He was the nice guy down the block, the good neighbor, the caring family man, the public private. No matter that Dixie Lee had abandoned herself in drink, or the children rigorously taught discipline and self-denial. He gave his first four boys "lickings" when they misbehaved, taking his leather strap off its appointed hook when they didn't toe the line, or act as they should, do their chores or play their part in the fam-ily business (even Bing's father worked as a bookkeeper for Crosby Enter-prises while his mother, Kathryn the First, remained the family matriarch). He brooked no nonsense.

Gary, the eldest, beset by his own alcoholism and self-destructive behavior, remembers his early life as one of having fights and being beaten, violences suppressed by the picture-book existence he was supposed to have been lead-ing as the Crosby firstborn. In 1983, when he's fifty, he tells all in a pri-male scream called *Going My Own Way*, where he bares his sense of being wronged by his father and upbringing, the fears and insecurities that Bing ex-acerbated in his desire not to spoil or incur laziness. The picture of Crosby as uncaring disciplinarian, belittler, and emotionally distant parent resounds within the popular imagination of a public hungry to see its idols brought low by scandal and malfeasance. If Bing really is Saint Everyman, he must learn the humility and the humiliation of the masses, the mortification of the flesh. The hard way, the way he teaches his children. If he won't give them dispen-sation, why should he himself receive doubt's benefit? The child will teach the father a lesson he won't forget. Fortunately, Bing isn't around to hear such backtalk; but it critically wounds his reputation.

Is it true? In late 1950, as Gary is nearing adulthood, he records with Bing (perhaps vice versa) a million-seller for Decca, "Play a Simple Song," and follows it with old warhorses on the order of "When You and I Were Young, Maggie." They exchange gibes; it's not a one-way conversation. In "On Moonlight Bay," Bing introduces his "associate in song," and Gary pokes fun at a younger Bing who *"acted so bad, just a regular cad / And this is the lad who wound up as my dad."* When Bing breaks into a bit o' "croonin' a tune," Gary groans. Bing tells him he shouldn't knock it: "It's kept you freeloading all these years." Gary improvises around Bing in the first verses; they seem relaxed, father and son, Bing giving a hand to his eldest, Gary taking it. But then Gary always seemed to get along with "Bing Crosby" when his father put on his public face. Being Bing. He could even sass him, at least in the script, and Bing would shake his head understandingly and tousle his hair. There was no "but" until after they left the microphone, the magnified mistakes (Gary would always focus on one flat note rather than the performance as a whole, classically self-destructive), bringing the disappointments and unfulfilled expectations of real life. The son's voice has more ragtime to it, an echo of the Dixieland that Bing's brother Bob will use to tinge his music in the Bob-Cats, a backward glance to separate from Bing's forward motion. Families can be very defining, not to mention confining. A Crosby first, a Gary second. Sometimes he can't stand it, and neither could Bing. He wanted his sons to be like him, and he didn't care whether they liked him. Opposites attract; likes repel.

When Dixie hit the bottle, Bing understood all too well, and not at all. He had given up drink for his career and, according to legend, for her. Why couldn't she do the same for him? Bing had the will, while Dixie wilted under pressure. If Gary blamed his father for his own drinking, he canonized his mother for hers, and when she died in November 1952, of cancer, just shy (and she was) of forty-one, he internalized her tragedy and desperate unhappiness. It was only Bing's Catholicism that was keeping him and Dixie together—that, and a potentially crippling financial settlement, and their family mythos. And the children.

By then, Gary and the twins and Linny were on their own, four boys estranged from their father. It was too late to make it up to them, and Bing desired to start anew. He wasn't about to change, but found himself a woman thirty years his junior who had the persistence and self-reliance to give his due breathing room. Olive Kathryn Grandstaff was feisty and determined, though not without a sense of compliance. Marrying Bing on October 24, 1957, after he had gotten cold feet several times, she understood how to play his lie, to be as indispensable as a caddy is to a golfing man, a helpmeet and confidante. She never took up the sport (she knew Bing liked to be out with the boys, somewhere *away*), but if need be, she could choose the right putter to go with his moods, roll with his green to supplement her sense of purpose (she would get her degree as a registered nurse, and continue her acting forays), and get along with Bing's mother—Dixie Lee could never face up to Ma Crosby. Kathryn held her ground where Dixie acquiesced, and her resourcefulness fed into Bing's desire to stay within the family circle, home more, especially when he settled into the routine of the Hillsborough mansion outside San Francisco and the remote second hacienda at Rancho Las Cruces, in Baja California, Mexico. They would have three children together, and Bing consciously tried to be less strictured. He'd made mistakes: "I guess I didn't do very well bringing my boys up," he admitted to AP reporter Joey Hyams, his first brood stunned to realize that Dad was actually admitting he was wrong. He gave them *too much:* "work and discipline . . . money" and *too little:* "time and attention." This from a man whose greatest gift in song was the balanced phrase, the baby bear–goldilocks of *just right.* Of his children with Dixie, only Philip seemed to emerge unscathed from an untimely, tragic end. He fares better with his next three, including the first girl, Mary Frances, but his original children never share a Christmas special with him again. Bing, too, is beset by a fantasy "White Christmas," the family at one around the fire, that real life denies him, a nostalgia for what was never.

But that's the man. Bing, the sound-effect creation of Harry Lillis, stands apart, as the son separates from the father. You can only be so responsible for your creation when it's all growed, given the keys to the car. It is to Bing's parental credit that he raises himself in his own image, a father now a son that will caretake the father. The song as singer. Reverse psychology.

In embracing all of American song, he has to spread himself so wafer-thin—his communion—that there is nothing left for the core of his personality except the easy stamp of his voice. He doesn't have a lot left over for small talk. Too many people want things from him. When he walks into a room, his keeps his eyes downcast, sits down, and reads a newspaper. It's as if he wears a Do Not Disturb sign. He disappears inside himself as he "disappears" those who don't see it his way, a chill distance that is a barrier to individual intimacy even as he opens his arms to all. Bing doesn't hug well, unless there's an audience. His emotions are held in reserve for their performance, spirits bottled and saved for a special occasion. On the Buddy Cole record, he returns to "Learn to Croon," and when he slides into the syllabials, a vocal insinuation, his tongue trips lightly; it's like a brogue, an overlay of language in which he was once fluent. You don't forget.

He is everywhere and nowhere, pervasive. It's hard to realize that he made very few truly public appearances after he crested in Hollywood, never concertizing, though he was always agreeable to a charity revue or celebrity golf tournament, or entertaining the troops. Where other performers made an A-line to the xanadu that is Las Vegas, he refused, saying he didn't want to have someone come see him and lose the family savings gambling. He hosts the *Hollywood Palace* variety series on ABC television, he tries his hand at sitcomedy with Beverly Garland as his wife for a single season, 1964–65. There is a lauded character role in a 1966 remake of *Stagecoach*, the drunken Doc Boone; and his last film, the 1971 made-for-television *Dr. Cook's Garden*, is a horror tale about a doctor practicing euthanasia on his sick patients. He makes a credible serial killer, but his fans want him to sing. They don't want him out of character.

After an operation in 1974 removes half his left lung, miraculously sparing his voice, he returns to the concert stage with *Bing Crosby and Friends* on Saint Patrick's Day, 1976, at L.A.'s Dorothy Chandler Pavilion, with Rosemary Clooney, celebrating his half-century of entertaining. The show is booked for a two-week run at the two-thousand-seat Uris Theater in mid-December 1976, the first time he's appeared on Broadway since his vaudeville days. Ticket sales sputter, down to half-capacity by the end of the run. Despite the disappointing turnout, he closes each night with a thirty-two-song medley of pure Crosby; sixteen bars here, eight bars there, led by pianist Joe Bushkin. It's condensed from an initial cull of eighty; maybe he is all the superlatives that are tossed his way, in his command of pure song. Bing doesn't miss a beat, comes in right on cue. Bushkin is amazed.

After Bing recovers from his fall, the show takes off for England, where on September 26, 1977, there is to be a repeat of last year's successful two-week season at London's Palladium. He closes on October 8, appears in Brighton on the tenth, and visits the BBC studios in Maida Vale on October 11, recording a few songs from the show with an orchestra led by Gordon Rose. "There's Nothing That I Haven't Sung About" is one of the sprightly numbers, and he's not just poking fun at his "vocal gadabout." He's done it all. In another BBC interview, recorded two years earlier with Michael Parkinson, he remembers "when I started, there was nobody. There was Vallée, myself, Columbo, one or two others . . . anybody who could carry a tune could get a job." He's still out there, singing flawlessly, despite the lengthy time he spends onstage during the show, and he closes the BBC broadcast with "As Time Goes By" and "Once in a While." Yesterday's memories: *"Will you try to give one little thought to me?"* He isn't bothered by a slight husk when he speaks, a remnant of the cold he shook off at the Palladium. Or maybe he's seventy-four years young. He enjoys the physical act of singing; it works him out, and he's hoping to take the show to Australia in the next month. Japan. They appreciate golf there.

He tapes his annual Christmas revue while in London, *Bing Crosby's Merrie Olde Christmas*, and it's decided to ask a contemporary singer to join him for "Little Drummer Boy." They find David Bowie, a young sixties mod who has transformed himself over and again, delighting in shock value and image manipulation. He has promised a "teenage moondream," has worn a dress, has taken on the guise of an alien, and in 1977 is a glam-rock graduate heading toward a Berlin hideaway that will palette some of his most austere music, the Hansa soundscapes of *Low* and *Heroes*. They are an unlikely couple, but their gracious respect for the performer's art—though Bing's current musical taste runs more to the Carpenters and Neil Diamond than Ziggy Stardust—makes for a professional exchange, a decorum. David's on his best behavior, offering his alto to Crosby's bari-quaver, more pronounced on the sine wave because he's learned to shout in front of a rock band. Bowie has picked up mime from Lindsay Kemp and showmanship from Anthony Newley; he takes the high part in "Peace on Earth." David responds, as do all Bing's guests, to Crosby's casual ease, that makes the theatrical less; at this point in his career, David is still relying on a good prop, an identity, and he enjoys the downplay. He lets Bing set the pace. Later for Tin Machine.

In the sketch, Bowie visits Bing, a "poor relation" staying at the home of the local aristocracy. "Are you the new butler?" David asks him. "It's been a long time since I've been the new anything." Bing laughs. David tells him he doesn't like only "contemporary" stuff; he also likes "older fellas" like John Lennon, Harry Nilsson. "I'm not as young as I look." They trade parenting quips, and Bowie speaks affectionately of his six-year-old son, Zowie, reassuring Bing he's just a regular guy, and Bing treats him like a son. They have fatherhood in common. A Christmas carol.

Then he goes to Spain to play golf for the last time. In Madrid, on Friday afternoon, October 14, he's paired with Spanish champion Manuel Pinero. After the eighteenth hole, carding an 85, he sinks his putt and walks toward the clubhouse, then turns and collapses, heart attacked. The initial BBC reports have it as the seventeenth hole, but Bing wants to finish the game. He's had a good round.

IT'S RUDY who has the last laugh. He retreats to his hilltop estate, Silver Tip, and becomes a comedian.

He has a lot to chuckle over, beneath a rooftop tennis court in an out-building where he keeps his files, his 78 records, his radio scripts and orches-trations, a walk-in scrapbook of his walk-through life, the docudrama papers and photos and clippings of his life and loves. He is a man who believes in credos, notes and reminders, aphorisms and nursed grudges, each cataloged in a separate folder, attentive to detail. There's a list of girls with whom he's dallied; he wants to write a book called *Dolls of the Vallée.* He only kissed Mary Healy "once"; he put Jean Harlow "in a cab and sent her home"; he ro-mances Lyda Roberti "in the wings just before I was to present her onstage." He would spend long hours behind an electric typewriter firing off letters, missives to any and everyone, scolding, advising, waxing eloquent on his views of life. He's not spoiled by fame; by now he's accustomed to it, enjoying his ephemeral relation to the culture, though he wishes it was easier to find work. In his second autobiography, *My Time Is Your Time,* written when he was sixty-one (there would be yet another, *Let the Chips Fall,* in 1975), he deprecates: "I don't kid myself that these rooms full of memorabilia mean very much in the march of history. My mission in life is to entertain, to pur-vey escapism." He still thinks of himself as a "wandering minstrel," inexorably becoming a "period piece" like the "vagabond lover" who steals away, tangled memories left in his wake. The one-career stand. Enjoy him while he lasts; he'll be gone tomorrow.

"Still, the fire horse never forgets, and the clanging of the alarm bells makes him yearn to be back in harness," he cheerily notes, a phrase already period-pieced, and unexpectedly reaches a whole new audience in 1961 with the Broadway play (and later movie) *How to Succeed in Business Without Re-ally Trying.* Now he has his finale, though he thinks of it as a second act.

Vallée had sustained his running-in-place with the radio Fleischmann Yeast Hour, which ran until 1939, and other radio endeavors. One of his most memorable shows was a live shortwave broadcast from England celebrating George VI's coronation in May 1937 ("We had a very pleasant crossing on the *Ile de France*" he tells his fans back in America, though he is piqued that George M. Cohan ignores him on board ship). He then spent World War II leading a Coast Guard band. The July 4 weekend before V-J Day found him in love, trailing the spoor of an adolescent Eleanor Norris around Kings Beach on Lake Tahoe. She is still riding her bicycle, sweet sixteen (or so), but Rudy is a diligent wooer; he knows he has met his Tinker Bell the first time he sees her in long fingernails, a Ceil Chapman satin dress, and four-inch heels (Rudy wears lifts in his shoes). She falls under the Vallée spell ("Rudy's libido was always in overdrive," Eleanor would remember. He tells her, "I knew you'd be terrific in bed . . . and it's going to get better now that I've awakened your sensuality") and they marry in September 1949, his fourth time—there had been a seven-month liaison with Jane Greer in 1943. She moves to Silver Tip with the poodles and the wine cellar and the 360-degree view of the southern California basin, a sunken living room and a fourteen-foot stone fireplace and a 125-capacity theater, where, on the natural rock patio, Rudy gathers in the twilight to sip rum 'n pineapple with his bride and recline against the city backdrop. He had bought the home in 1941 from Ann Harding. A king and his castle.

He wasn't taken seriously as a singer after World War II, his *vo-de-oh-do* archaic against the smooth supper-club dandies coming up, the Al Martinos, the Julius La Rosas, or pre-rock over-emotives like Johnny Ray. His movies were spotty, and he usually proved too headstrong to "get along with others," a lack-of-deportment that sometimes caused his contentious personality to bang his own head against the wall. Losing his temper and foul-mouthing and going after hecklers in nightclubs, at least he didn't hold it all in. Id. That was Rudy. *How to Succeed* slid him easily into the fussy, somewhat pompous character of J. B. Biggley; he had played roughly the same persona in *The Palm Beach Story*, a 1942 Preston Sturges comedy, only then he was a collegian turned talent agent, John D. Hackensacker III, the "richest man on earth." Sturges had inadvertently seen Rudy in *Time Out for Rhythm* (the Three Stooges are also featured in this 1941 comedy) and been impressed when the audience laughed at Rudy even when he was supposed to be serious. He thought him a natural comedian.

To hear Rudy tell it, he was on stormy terms with the play's producers, Cy Feuer and Ernie Martin, from the beginning. Despite all the backstage gossip, his how-to-succeed was in convincing them of his worth when they refused to believe he could project theatrically or take direction, or to let him invest in the show, which was nonetheless well received when it opened on October 14, 1961, at the 46th Street Theatre. Though the play boasted Abe Burrows's direction and Frank Loesser's musical numbers, and a star turn by a then-unknown Robert Morse as the window washer who becomes chairman of a wicket company, Rudy was a critical and popular surprise casting, and he made the part his own. The pinch of Bartleby's pince-nez was enhanced by Rudy's codger-y reputation as a penny-pincher ("I'm frugal, not stingy," he would say), and his "love interest" is invariably poured into tight satin dresses, a Miss La Rue to his La Rudy.

How to Succeed is a morality tale, set in a world where sexual roles are formalized: the women are secretaries, the men wear suits. The joke is that

Morse is *really trying*, relentlessly charming his way up the corporate ladder, his naked ambition like a topless song-and-dance. He won't stop till he gets over-the-top. Rudy respects his sense of how-to; it's not unlike the set lists and rules he once delivered to the Connecticut Yankees from on high, his manual for winning the game. He delivers his big number with gusto when he thinks that Morse is a college alumnus, a fellow Groundhog. "Stand Old Ivy" they sing, Vallée's voice roughened and burred, marching about the office like drum majors. His last song echoes his first. Back to school. In the 1967 film version, after he and Morse have done the Groundhog leap in tandem, he turns and smiles. For a moment he's not JBB, but Rudy, enjoying the grand time of himself.

His gift for comedy is not surprising, given *Is This Your Rudy Vallée?*, a live album recorded at the Anaheim Bowl in California somewhat contemporaneously in late 1960. The cover sports Rudy in his undershorts strumming a broom, wearing a top hat and sock-garters (the photo is from 1938), and the album is released by Crown, a budget label owned by the three Bihari Brothers, R&B entrepreneurs whose Modern and RPM imprints explain why Rudy's labelmates include B. B. King, Elmore James, members of the Goodman and Dorsey orchestras, and George Liberace, who is not his famous brother.

He's undeniably funny in stand-up, with a knack for delivering punch lines, along with blue limericks and song parodies and jokes that start with "An old lady goes to confession . . ." or "A drunk goes into a bar. . . ." He medleys his best-known classics, and wants the music to be played "not too slow or fast. . . . sort of halfast," closing with "The Stein Song" written by Frank N. He takes his wife on an airplane: "We wanted to fly United but the hostess wouldn't let us." "Some girls get minks the way minks get minks." He's an "old goat." Teenagers think of him as the "Pat Boone of the Stone Age."

But self-satire goes only so far. His song is not taken seriously anymore. An "ex-crooner," as Vallée refers to himself, he is the man with the megaphone, a lifetime caricature on the verge of becoming an institution, unable to outrun his nostalgia. He has to laugh; life's been good, a bowl of cherries, and he knows his wife is a virgin. He lives it up, traveling and giving out souvenir pens (*"Gratefully yours—Rudy Vallée"*) and coming up with schemes that he is outraged are called "comebacks," which, of course, they are. In the end he is as interred as Russ, a relic of his era. He may not want to be regarded as an old-fashioned singer, but he is always thinking in terms of a career retrospective. As late as 1984, he writes to Frank Sinatra, telling him he has a "gold mine" of thirty-four hits culled from his sixty years of performing, and wonders if Frank could help him find a recording deal. "Today's recording guys aren't panning for gold," Frank tells him, deadpan. He assures him he "will drop kind words should the occasion arise."

Instead, Rudy settles for Richard Nixon, Ronald Reagan, fellow Republicans, though he is against the Vietnam War and pro labor unions. He goes to the Desert Inn in Las Vegas in the 1970s for a *Newcomers of 1928* show with Paul Whiteman, Buster Keaton, Fifi D'Orsay, Billy Gilbert, and Harry Richman. He is supposed to share a dressing room with Harry, but the quarters are cramped, too small for the both of them. They remember all too well when they didn't have to share the fame. The last stand doesn't last long.

Sometimes people visit him in his aerie. Tiny Tim might come to pay homage, or a party of ad agency execs proffering potato chips. He invites them all to dinner, a main course of memories along with the *sole amandine* and turkey soup. Great or small, known or unknown, Rudy then graciously takes his guests on the guided tour of who he's been, where he lives now. He has it down to a patter. It's almost like his one-man show, and he's a showman.

If you ask—or even if you don't—he'll set up the lights and sound system and take you into the Silver Tip theater and tell the story of his life; a slide projecting, a song distorting from the cassette player, a serenade, a bit of soft-shoe comedy. His tale relives it for himself, like his life flashing before his eyes in the moment before his passing on another July 4 weekend, 1986, after a series of strokes. He picks up his saxophone, silhouetted in the light gels, colors blurred, sepiated. Dick in his mouth.

THE WANDERING CROON

Some sound like Bing, capturing his mannerisms and phrasing, the flattery and good business sense of imitation. The Eberle Brothers, Bob (with Jimmy Dorsey) and Ray (with Glenn Miller; he's the younger, distinguishes himself as Eberly). Dick Haymes. Bob Carroll (even to the initials), who holds his larger-than-life voice in check working with Charlie Barnet, and whose Bingisms come to the fore in his 1942 cover of "White Christmas" with Gordon Jenkins. Internationally, there is a French Bing (Jean Sablon) and a Brit (Denny Dennis).

Charlie Palloy doesn't just sing like Bing. He plays guitar like Eddie Lang, and his label, Crown Records, believes in offering two-for-one. Their advertising slogan is "Two hits for two bits."

There is nothing known of Palloy before he cuts "It Don't Mean a Thing If It Ain't Got That Swing" on January 10, 1932, with a similarly anonymous house orchestra, making just over twenty appearances for Crown spread over eight sessions in the next year and a quarter. He makes his last recording on April Fool's Day, 1933, then disappears from sight—after returning for an encore with Meyer Davis's Orchestra on Columbia, "On a Steamer Coming Over," on November 23, 1933—never to surface again. He still outlives Lang, perhaps a moonlighting musician with a need for anonymity, making records on the cheap. Or somebody else.

He's earnest, professional, and occasionally inspired, especially when he sits back with his guitar. His April 1 song is "You'll Never Get to Heaven That Way," one of his most relaxed performances, backed by a solo piano and trading arpeggios and bass runs. He accompanies himself as a singer, double-timing his own bridge, and his keen sense of transposed melody and scale helps him circumnavigate a tune. Playing the guitar, an instrument with the chords-and-single-note possibilities of a piano, no hammers but a hands-on stringing, he simultaneously leads and sits back with the boys in the band, his musician cronies, the workaday AFM camaraderie of the Local 802 exchange floor.

On the Ides of March, 1933, Charlie records "Learn to Croon" with a piano and violin (Crown still calls his combo an Orchestra). He starts right in with the ba-ba-ba-ba; he's so anxious that his voice grasps for pitch. He's not a teacher advising, like Bing. He's the pupil. He guitar tandems with the violin, and then Charlie takes his final exam. He emphasizes the "b sound": *bi bi bee bah bah.* B plus.

In the same session, he cuts "I've Got to Sing a Torch Song," the feminine counterpart, her side of the story. The masks of comedy and tragedy: "*I could never croon a happy tune / Without a tear.*" He concludes the session with "We're in the Money," bluesy guitar solo and all—take two choruses and a verse and call me in the morning. Then he disappears, the next day of a one-night stand who doesn't phone.

"THE BLACK BING" was a category all its own in the mid-thirties. Harlan Lattimore, the best known, was born in Cincinnati the same year as Columbo. He worked mostly under the imprimatur of Don Redmond's Orchestra, which also took on the name of the Connie's Inn Orchestra, a Harlem musical landmark, when they proclaimed "Got the South in My Soul," at a session in June 1932. It must have been a doozie, since they also scratched a match on "Reefer Man" and "Chant of the Weed" that New York day. Lattimore quickly went on to the harder stuff, and by 1936 was pretty much gone.

But the baritone had been opened to blacks. A love song might be delivered seriously, without the slapstick comedy of whiteface. Herb Jeffries went from vocalizing with Earl Hines's band to being "the Bronze Buckaroo" in a series of black Westerns (*Harlem on the Prairie*) to recording a hit, "Flamingo," with Duke Ellington in the waning days of 1940. Around the same time, beginning in 1937, Nathaniel Cole caught the freeway jazz of Los Angeles with the King Cole Trio, his café au lait voice gliding like his long, bony fingers over the raised black-and-white plains of the keys.

Billy Eckstine had not only Crosby but Columbo in him. More the latter, even, since Eckstine was confident enough in his vocal abilities to defer to Bing only obliquely. It is Russ who gives Eckstine his intense romanticism. Mister B's vibrato is the insistent tongue of a Gaelic kiss; deep throat, a ladies' man.

He's not unaware of his debt to Columbo. In the fall of 1945 he records both "Prisoner of Love" and "You Call It Madness" in a big band that features Fats Navarro and drummer Art Blakey and will at other times include Dizzy Gillespie, Gene Ammons, Sonny Stitt, and many other luminaries of bebop to be. The big bands are going under at this unfortunate time, and Mr. B has to wait until the 1950s and life on MGM to find his crossover audience. Early on, his orchestra could pass for rhythm and blues, his permissible sensuality ahead of his time. It would take until the 1950s to finally breach the color line within popular commercial music, "race" records integrating the pop water fountains, the 1954 of *Brown v. Board of Education* opening up public schools in the same year Elvis recorded "That's All Right Mama."

The height of crooner romanticism in the 1950s is Johnny Mathis, a name synonymous with make-out music, a voice in the nether region between male and female, the will-she-won't-she of sensual grapple. "Chances Are," he sings, and everybody takes them, though birth control and the sexual revolution are still a few years in the future. That's too cut-and-dried for Mathis. In the end, he's in it for the seduction, the act implied.

He's more jazz when discovered at Ann's 440 club in San Francisco by George Avakian of Columbia Records in 1955. 440: Johnny did have perfect pitch, and breath control, a track-and-field star at San Francisco State College who thought of trying out for the 1956 Olympics. Mitch Miller had it in mind to get Johnny the gold medal in soft ballad singing. Mitch had a Midas touch, as he proved with his 1955 pyrite choral version of "The Yellow Rose of Texas." But these are not Mitch's sing-alongs. Nobody could sing with Johnny, because no one had a voice like Johnny's, the torch and croon combined.

"Mathis Magic" is the advertising slogan, and Johnny agrees that his voice "seems to float a few inches off the ground," the weightless hang time of the high jump and the long jump and the pole vault. Defying gravity, he's "as helpless as a kitten up a tree," "Misty" a time-hoared classic in 1959 that he makes definitive, at the peak of his allure. He could be cared for, nursed, held to a bosom. And yet he's unreachable, too swish and too sultry, pushy and pussy, a future sex.

WHISPERING CHET. Poor doomed Chet, though his sepulchral features and horn which seemed always on the verge of drawing its last breath take up more acreage in the jazz bins than most, right up there with Coltrane and

Davis, the first tier of legends. Chet Baker is the subject of elaborate picture books—a craggy visage that such as Bruce Weber have iconified—and myth, his struggles with drugs and privation as they carve their furrows along the saintly features of his facial geology. It looks good on him. I once saw Chet in the mid-seventies at a basement jazz room on West Eighty-sixth. He was hardly breathing; every note examined, turned and inspected, as he took his time, slowing the moment. It made his life seem longer.

My Funny Valentine, from 1954, takes standards (there is a sequel in 1956, and a more elaborate *Chet Sings with Strings* in between) and lets Baker remove their clothes. He goes directly to the melody, which makes him a funny kind of jazz guy. His version of the title tune—*"Don't change a hair for me / Not if you care for me"*—is plaintively unadorned, each note and word sung as Rodgers and Hart intended. There is no mistaking what he's asking for. Stay; even if he's not going to be around for long. The after time of "Time After Time." His trumpet solo, "Moon Love," from October 1953, is filled with the sadness of knowing it's over before it has a chance to begin; he records "Moonlight Becomes You" in December, on the lunar dark side. He chooses notes carefully, economically, which is not how he spends his life. The profligate son, he has the unenviable ability to turn triumph into scarred defeat. He is in Paris two years later when the gifted twenty-four-year-old pianist in his Quartet, Dick Twardzik, succumbs to an overdose. Chet figures, *what's the rush?*

Dean Martin might have agreed. The lazy insouciance of his voice, the happy-go-lucky go-fucky that he made into a stage show. He's good-looking and he knows it, like Russ. Elvis, too, for that matter, that lazy southern drawl and a lifestyle built on plush, the eye shadow and the hip swivel. Though he too could be considered a Colored Crosby, Elvis is eventually more like Sinatra, too hopped up ever to really unwind. He picked up where the screams left off from Frank; if he had been a true crooner, the gals would've been moaning.

The croon disappears into the onomatopoeia of vocal group harmony, an *ooh wah* chord that rides the exhale like a wind chime. The Harptones, the Flamingoes, Nolan Strong and the Diablos. Heard on a million street corners, the Slow side, leg slid between hers pulled close hand slipping down her waist fingers a soft outward curve, eloping, a developing enveloping. Necking, petting, parking ("Petting in the Park" is the fourth song in Palloy's mid-March session), each small permission, to part and depart her. Going pinned steady engaged all the way. Finger ring. Wear my ring around your neck, the encircling O sound.

Two oh's.
Oh-oh.

IGGY POP, né Stooge, lies on the floor of Ungano's on West Seventieth Street, Manhattan, the early seventies, down the street from the horticulturally inclined Continental Baths, where later Plato's Retreat will locate a multisexual paradise. He's wearing long silver opera gloves, singing "The Shadow of Your Smile." He's in the lower registers, the horse latitudes of melody. I recognize the Sargasso Sea from Jim Morrison: "*Before you slip into unconscious / I'd like to have another kiss. . . .*" The first song the open Door writes with Ray Manzarek after they meet on the beach is "Moonlight Drive." He will rise to fame with "Light My Fire," enter the back door and come to the room where his mother is and send her a cry from beyond "The End." We have seen these images before.

Glam-rock is good for the croon. Bryan Ferry, who plays a lounge lizard looking for his heat lamp within Roxy Music starting in 1971, records an album in 1999 that takes a heart-on-his-sleeve approach to some of the grander hits of the pre-rock era. "There's something feminine about this music," he tells *Time Out.* "Throughout the years, women seem to have gravitated to it in a romantic way that men haven't allowed themselves to. Maybe I'm a bit of a sissy."

No stranger to the cover version (he is as much interpreter as originator, and has often gone to the classic well of Bob Dylan and Wilbert Harrison), he leads with "As Time Goes By" and bye-bye, properly nostalgic for the black tie and supper club. Unfailingly polite, he possesses the discreet forgetfulness of a "Where or When," his women draped over a fashionably illustrated *Town & Country* divan. "Sweet and Lovely" may four-march to no apparent reward, but his turn on another Columbo touchstone, "Time on My Hands," slinks, properly oiled. He has the reckless jade of the landed gentry, a hint of getting down with the help when he sings and dances, one of them by being them. Even the upper crust suffer heartache, he says, loosening his tie, indulging his loss.

The formality extends to Bowie, and so does the gender play. As in his duet with Bing—David remembers that Bing's eyes were distant, and that he shut off the moment he left the set—the Thin White Duke is able to croon his way into being the progenitor of the New Romantics of the mid-eighties, going as far east as Goth (there is something vampiric about his aristocracy at this time), when a new generation of girlish boys grow their hair big and apply the eyeliner, and west, like the pretty-boy metal and waving butane lighters that are Poison's "Every Rose Has Its Thorn." It wasn't just dress-up: Boy George broke through—was taken seriously—when "Do You Really Want to Hurt Me?" plaintively asked if he could be loved. *Really?* The girlish heart responds.

You find the croon in odd places. Chris Isaak wraps himself around Helena Christensen on an MTV beach in "Wicked Game." Ray Price places Russ next to a classic Nashville writer like Harlan Howard in his *Prisoner of Love* collection. Nick Cave recites an old murder ballad and turns it into a love song; his 2003 album is called *Nocturama*. Craig David talks about the week it takes to create an affair in "Seven Days," and "we chilled on Sunday." A creation myth, lovemaking as that old-time religion. Any time you want to play the game, I'll be at the flea market. I like to look.

IT'S THURSDAY in Hollywood's Magic Hotel, underneath Russ Columbo's final home. I'm on the block below Outpost Circle, some seventy years later. The terrace door is open to Franklin. The night sounds whoosh by in a furl of cape, like the poster on the wall in which Howard Thurston is preparing to make a lady and a horse vanish in one go. I can feel Russ's shadow hovering, as it has these past few years in the midst of his life and mine. I'm drawn to him, I'm drawing him, and I'm trying to figure out why.

His chord sometimes resolves, and sometimes its tension leads sprung-wire to the next. Sometimes that chord is not the one you're awaiting. Could be an unexpected augmented; a demented.

He comes out of the great age of magicians in the twenties. There is something of the Houdini in him, the hocus-pocus of an escape artist. *Now you don't.* He's always just beyond my grasp. Every time I think I have him, he peels off another layer of tangent with a stripper's coax. He reaches into the dark recesses of his top hat and pulls out a squealing ball of fur. He saws a woman in half; he sticks swords within the cabinet where she is confined.

"He's a master of illusion," I'm told by one collector who has spent a lifetime inspecting 78 records for signs of the anonymous Russ, when he might have been pulling a Charlie Palloy, earning a few bucks on the side for a couple hours' work. He and another acolyte have amassed a boxed fifty-one-song set of Russ's supposed appearances. While there are Russ obscurities (an alternate version of "Too Beautiful for Words," with Russ on accordion), and could-be's ("Patch Up My Heart" and the western horse-behooves of "Rollin' Plains"), most allegeds are Harlan Lattimore. Les Reis and Jack Fulton also make appearances. There's an Al Bowly track, and someone, maybe Mr. B himself, doing "Until Eternity," Eckstine's set opener and a Columbo compositon, which wasn't recorded until the 1950s. Columbo Colored.

S. KAYE. That's the one that blows me away.

I'm in L.A. On the loose, living in this kidney-shaped pool of stars on the walk and smooth operators who operate out of police precincts and old cars preserved in the Neapolitan clime, and not thinking about the S that stands for separation, the first initial of my first wife's first name. S; in my alphabet it's next to Ex. Are we? Come together or stay apart? Do you ever?

It's in the *Herald* on September 8, 1934, attached as an afterthought. DEATH MAY END LAWYER'S SUIT ON FAMOUS SINGER. It goes on to describe how a nonpayment suit had been brought against Russ by an attorney, Irving D. Lipkowitz, contending that he hadn't been paid over a two-year period, and wanted his dough. Rather than be his own client, he opted to assign a plaintiff to stand in for him.

Named S. Kaye.

Let me think about this.

A stand-in. Lipkowitz stood behind S. Kaye. Stand-in Kaye.

Living in someone's skin, but looking out with your own eyes. The Biography channel.

They're all vanished, a puff of smoke and a flourish. A lifetime away, stored behind the curtain of memory. The separating, the distance between now and when. You're still here.

Take the bullet. Be the body double. Cut the scene and get a stunt man to recoil with the shot, sprawling in shock on Lansing's floor. The hero has to live, here in the movie's epicenter. There's a sequel somewhere.

Russ was contesting the suit. Scheduled to go before Judge Marshall of Superior Court the week after he was killed, Russ had previously declared that he was "without sufficient information" to reply to the allegations, and issued a general denial.

Case dismissed.

RUSS FOLLOWS me.

From out of the airwaves I can hear his voice, singing through the crackle, faraway, a station out of reach.

I go into a record shop of my acquaintance. Today I'm on the prowl for

Rudy Vallée. I find a reprocessed stereo *Best Of* on RCA, black label, his voice hollow and ghostly in the echo; and a fifties Capitol ten-inch 33⅓ of his *Greatest Hits*, with new orchestrations by Billy May. Rich, the dealer, wants fifty bucks for the latter. Too much. Instead I opt to listen to it there, hearing Rudy as he knowingly comments on his younger self, a shade too heavy on the *vo-de-oh-do*. His own impression of himself. I pass. Keep the stereo, if only to compare with an original 78 mono.

He's hot to play me something. I know Rich from deep in the record-collecting underworld, when Slim used to run Times Square Records in the subway arcade at Sixth and Forty-second, eternally searching for "Stormy Weather" by the Five Sharps on Jubilee. He's unearthed an old R&B vocal group piece. Nobody else knows of it. When he plays it for me, he drapes a handkerchief over the turntable so I can't see the label. He wants me to guess, or maybe he doesn't want me to search it out ahead of him, flood the market. At least I know it's a 45.

The lead voice is teen, delicate. Black. The croon goes on around him, the *oohs* and *aahs* of doo-wop before it turned white and had a name. I pick 1952 out of the air. He says it's from 1960 but sounds older.

Much older, for me. It's "You Call It Madness," softly and sweetly sung by a group called Merdist.

I'll never hear it again.

ACKNOWLEDGMENTS

At this remove, the era of the croon's popularization is a life span past, long enough to be hearsay, forever a secondary source—a newspaper clipping, a photo, a recording—away. That is why I am so grateful to have had the opportunity to share the living memories of Celia Trovato, Joe Russo, and most especially Virginia Biddle-Bulkley, who allowed me to be her last stage-door Johnny.

Even recent history can be tantalizingly out of reach, subject to myth and modulation. As I progressed deeper into the mystery of Russ Columbo, gathering in Bing Crosby and Rudy Vallée and all manner of tangential byways, I was guided by keepers of the flame. Max Pierce took me around Russ's holy sites in Hollywood, and helped me obtain his movies, none of which are commercially available. Tony Toran unearthed arcane facts and provided hours of surmise. Al Gianetta showed me the archives he and fellow Columbo enthusiast John Liquori had amassed throughout the seventies. All shared their knowledge with a sense of honoring the man who would be Russ. I postponed reading the two biographies of Columbo that came out during the concluding stages of my writing, not wanting to compromise the streams of my own serendipitous research, interpretations, or improvisations; but in the light of day, I can wholeheartedly recommend the investigative work of Lou Miano, whom I met once in that great-but-no-longer-research-archive the monthly St. Andrew's paper collectibles market in Manhattan, run by the Gallagher family, a noted name in New York periodical preservation; and Joseph Lanza and Dennis Penna, who have gathered a treasure trove of Russ memorabilia, including diaries and love letters. It is good to have Russ remembered in this new musical century.

The music of the 1920s and 1930s has to be heard to be appreciated, preferably long enough to listen past the initial scratch of the 78. Rich Conaty's *Big Broadcast* over WFUV on Sunday nights caused me to be glued to the radio much as I might have been in September 1931, when dueling baritones ruled the airwaves. Closer to home, Numa Snyder of WESS reacquainted me with the wonders of the pre–rock and roll era, and showed me many byways of style, repertoire, and vanished personality.

Jeff Roth and Anthony DiFlorio III located elusive and long-buried circumstantial evidence. Jennifer Barton took me up to the top of the Victor tower in Camden, Russ's birthplace, where the light streamed in through the stained glass of Nipper. Barbara Dell Glass led me on a guided tour of New Orleans through the eyes of her aunt Dorothy. Vince Giordano, Jerry Vale, Sandy Marone, Whit Smith, Les Paul, Nils Hanson and the Ziegfeld Club, Janet Wygal, Adam Korn, Carole Lowenstein, and Emily DeHuff shared their *rubato* time and perspective.

My editor, Bruce Tracy, allowed the story of the croon to unfold in any key it wished; we were introduced by my agent, David Gernert, who is a lover of music, as we all are. That I get to play the music is my own madness, shared with whom I play: Patti, Tony, Oliver, and Jay Dee.

My wife, Stephanie, and my daughter, Anna, as all ways.

LENNY KAYE
Oct. 25, 2003
Eddie Lang's 101st birthday

BIBLIOGRAPHY

SELECTED BOOKS

Atkinson, Brooks. *Broadway.* New York: The Macmillan Company, 1970.

Baral, Robert. *Revue: The Great Broadway Period.* New York and London: Fleet Press, 1962.

Barr, Steven C. *The Almost Complete 78 RPM Recording Dating Guide (II).* Huntington Beach, Calif.: Yesterday Once Again, 1992.

Basinger, Jeanine. *Silent Star.* New York: Alfred A. Knopf, 1999.

Bidou, Henri; translated by Catherine Alison Phillips. *Chopin.* New York: Tudor, 1936.

Black, Shirley Temple. *Child Star.* New York: McGraw-Hill, 1988.

Bookbinder, Robert. *The Films of Bing Crosby.* Secaucus, N.J.: Citadel, 1977.

Burk, Margaret Tante. *Are the Stars out Tonight? The Story of the Famous Ambassador and Cocoanut Grove.* Los Angeles: Round Table West, 1980.

Carpozi, George, Jr. *The Fabulous Life of Bing Crosby.* New York: Manor Books Inc., 1977.

Carter, Randolph. *The World of Flo Ziegfeld.* New York and Washington: Praeger, 1974.

Chauncey, George. *Gay New York: Gender, Urban Culture, and the Making of the Gay Male World 1890–1940.* New York: BasicBooks, 1995.

Colin, Sid. *And The Bands Played On.* London: Elm Tree Books, 1977.

Collier, James Lincoln. *Benny Goodman and the Swing Era.* New York and Oxford: Oxford University Press, 1989.

Condon, Eddie, with Thomas Sugrue. *We Called It Music: A Generation of Jazz.* New York: Da Capo, 1992.

Connor, D. Russell. *Benny Goodman: Listen to His Legacy.* Metuchen, N.J., and London: Scarecrow Press & Institute of Jazz Studies, 1988.

———, and Warren W. Hicks. *BG on the Record: A Bio-Discography of Benny Goodman*. New Rochelle, N.Y.: Arlington House, 1969.

Conway, Michael, and Dion McGregor and Mark Ricci. *The Films of Greta Garbo*. New York: Cadillac Publishing Co., 1991.

Coslow, Sam. *Cocktails for Two: The Many Lives of Giant Songwriter Sam Coslow*. New Rochelle, N.Y.: Arlington House, 1977.

Crosby, Bing, with Pete Martin. *Call Me Lucky*. New York: Simon & Schuster, 1953.

Crosby, Gary, and Ross Firestone. *Going My Own Way*. Garden City, N.Y.: Doubleday, 1983.

Crosby, Kathryn. *My Life with Bing*. Wheeling, Ill.: Collage, 1983.

Eells, George. *Ginger, Loretta and Irene Who?* New York: G. P. Putnam's Sons, 1976.

Everson, William K. *American Silent Film*. New York: Da Capo, 1978.

Ewen, David. *The Life and Death of Tin Pan Alley: The Golden Age of American Popular Music*. New York: Funk & Wagnalls, 1964.

Finck, Henry T. *Chopin and Other Musical Essays*. New York: Charles Scribner's Sons, 1890.

Firestone, Ross. *Swing, Swing, Swing: The Life and Times of Benny Goodman*. New York and London: W. W. Norton, 1993.

Fréches, Claire and José; translated by Alexandra Campbell. *Toulouse-Lautrec: Scenes of the Night*. New York: Harry N. Abrams, 1994.

Friedwald, Will. *Jazz Singing*. New York: Da Capo, 1996.

Gabler, Neal. *Winchell: Gossip, Power and the Culture of Celebrity*. New York: Alfred A. Knopf, Inc., 1994.

Gelatt, Roland. *The Fabulous Phonograph 1877–1977*. London: Cassell, 1977.

Giddins, Gary. *Bing Crosby: A Pocketful of Dreams 1903–1940*. Boston, New York, and London: Little, Brown & Co., 2001.

Gilbert, L. Wolfe. *Without Rhyme or Reason*. New York: Vantage Press, 1956.

Glenn, Susan A. *Female Spectacle: The Theatrical Roots of Modern Feminism*. Cambridge, Mass.: Harvard University Press, 2000.

Gracyk, Tim, with Frank Hoffmann. *Popular American Recording Pioneers 1895–1925*. New York, London, Oxford: The Haworth Press, 2000.

Hadlock, Richard. *Jazz Masters of the Twenties*. New York: Collier, 1965.

Hall, Ben M. *The Best Remaining Seats: The Golden Age of the Movie Palace*. New York: Da Capo, 1988.

Harris, Warren G. *Gable and Lombard*. New York: Simon & Schuster, 1974.

Hellinger, Mark. *Moon over Broadway*. New York: William Faro, Inc., 1931.

Hemming, Roy, and David Hajdu. *Discovering Great Singers of Classic Pop*. New York: Newmarket Press, 1991.

Herr, Michael. *Walter Winchell: A Novel*. New York: Alfred A. Knopf, 1990.

Higham, Charles. *Ziegfeld*. Chicago: Henry Regnery Company, 1972.

Huisman, Philippe, and M. G. Dortu; translated by Corinne Bellow. *Lautrec by Lautrec*. New York: Viking Press, 1964.

Jasen, David A. *The Composers, The Songs, The Performers and Their Times*. New York: Donald I. Fine, 1988.

Kallberg, Jeffrey. *Chopin at the Boundaries: Sex, History and Musical Genre*. Cambridge, Mass.: Harvard University Press, 1996.

Kanter, Kenneth Aaron. *The Jewish Contribution to American Popular Music 1830–1940*. New York: KTAV Publishing, 1982.

Keepnews, Orrin, and Bill Grauer, Jr. *A Pictorial History of Jazz*. New York: Crown, 1966.

Kinkle, Roger D. *The Complete Encyclopedia of Popular Music and Jazz 1900–1950, Vols. 1–4*. New Rochelle, N.Y.: Arlington House, 1974.

Klurfeld, Herman. *Winchell: His Life and Times*. Praeger Publishers, Inc., 1976.

Lamour, Dorothy, with Dick McInnes. *My Side of the Road*. Englewood Cliffs, N.J.: Prentice-Hall, 1980.

Lanza, Joseph, and Dennis Penna. *Russ Columbo and the Crooner Mystique*. Los Angeles: Feral House, 2002.

Macfarlane, Malcolm. *Bing: A Diary of a Lifetime*. Gateshead, England: International Crosby Circle, 1997.

Marks, Edward B., as told to Abbot J. Liebling. *They All Sang: From Tony Pastor to Rudy Vallée*. New York: Viking Press, 1935.

Matzen, Robert D. *Carole Lombard: A Bio-Bibliography*. Westport, Conn.: Greenwood Press, 1988.

Mezzrow, Mezz, and Bernard Wolfe. *Really the Blues*. New York: Random House, 1946.

Miano, Lou. *Russ Columbo: The Amazing Life & Mysterious Death of a Hollywood Singing Legend*. New York: Silver Tone, 2001.

Mitgang, Herbert. *Once upon a Time in New York: Jimmy Walker, Franklin Roosevelt and the Last Great Battle of the Jazz Age*. New York: The Free Press, 2000.

Morello, Celeste A. *Before Bruno: The History of the Philadelphia Mafia (Book 1 1880–1931)*. Philadelphia: Morello, 1999.

Morgereth, Timothy A. *Bing Crosby: A Discography, Radio Program List, and Filmography*. Jefferson, N.C., and London: McFarland & Co., Inc., 1987.

Negri, Pola. *Memoirs of a Star*. New York: Doubleday and Company, 1970.

Oberfirst, Robert. *Al Jolson: You Ain't Heard Nothin' Yet*. San Diego: A. S. Barnes and Company, Inc., 1980.

Paris, Barry. *Garbo: A Biography*. New York: Alfred A. Knopf, 1995.

Parish, James Robert. *The Paramount Pretties*. New Rochelle, N.Y.: Arlington House, 1972.

Pitts, Michael R., and Frank Hoffman. *The Rise of the Crooners*. Lanham, Maryland: Scarecrow Press, 2002.

Russell, Tony. *Blacks, Whites and Blues.* New York: Stein and Day, 1970.

Rust, Brian. *The American Dance Band Discography 1917–1942, vols. 1 and 2.* New Rochelle, N.Y.: Arlington House, 1975.

———. *The Complete Entertainment Discography from the Mid-1890s to 1942.* New Rochelle, N.Y.: Arlington House, 1973.

———. *Jazz Records 1897–1942, vols. 1 and 2.* London: Storyville, 1969.

Sallis, James. *The Guitar Players: One Instrument and Its Masters in American Music.* New York: Quill, 1982.

Sanjek, Russell. *American Popular Music and Its Business.* New York and Oxford: Oxford University Press, 1988.

Shepherd, Donald, and Robert F. Slatzer. *Bing Crosby: The Hollow Man.* New York: St. Martin's Press, 1981.

Snyder, Robert W. *The Voice of the City: Vaudeville and Popular Culture in New York.* New York and Oxford: Oxford University Press, 1989.

Sobol, Louis. *Along the Broadway Beat.* New York: Avon, 1951.

———. *The Longest Street.* New York: Crown, 1968.

Souhami, Diana. *Greta & Cecil.* London: Flamingo, 1996.

Steiger, Brad, and Chaw Mank. *Garbo.* Chicago: Merit Books, 1965.

Stewart, Lyle. *The Secret Life of Walter Winchell.* Boar's Head Books, 1953.

Swindell, Larry. *Screwball: The Life of Carole Lombard.* New York: William Morrow and Company, Inc., 1975.

Thomas, Bob. *Winchell.* New York: Doubleday & Co., Inc., 1971.

Thompson, Charles. *Bing: The Authorized Biography.* London: W. H. Allen, 1975.

Tosches, Nick. *Dino: Living High in the Dirty Business of Dreams.* New York: Doubleday, 1992.

———. *Where Dead Voices Gather.* Boston, New York, London: Little, Brown & Co., 2001.

Ulanov, Barry. *The Incredible Crosby.* New York: Whittlesey House and McGraw-Hill, 1948.

Vallée, Eleanor, with Jill Amadio. *My Vagabond Lover: An Intimate Biography of Rudy Vallée.* Dallas: Taylor Publishing Company, 1996.

Vallée, Rudy. *Let the Chips Fall. . . .* Harrisburg, Pa.: Stackpole Books, 1975.

———. *Vagabond Dreams Come True.* New York: Grosset & Dunlap, 1930.

———, with Gil McKean. *My Time Is Your Time.* New York: Ivan Obolensky, Inc., 1962.

Van Hoogstraten, Nicholas. *Lost Broadway Theatres.* New York: Princeton Architectural Press, 1997.

Walker, Alexander. *Rudolph Valentino.* New York: Stein and Day, 1976.

Walker, Leo. *The Wonderful Era of the Great Dance Bands.* Garden City, N.Y.: Doubleday & Company, Inc., 1972.

Walker, Stanley. *The Night Club Era.* New York: Frederick A. Stokes Co., 1933.

Whitcomb, Ian. *After the Ball: Pop Music from Rag to Rock*. New York: Simon & Schuster, 1973.

Wilder, Alec. *American Popular Song: The Great Innovators 1900–1950*. New York and Oxford: Oxford University Press, 1972.

Winwar, Frances. *Wingless Victory: A Biography of Gabriele D'Annunzio and Eleonora Duse*. New York: Harper, 1956.

Woodhouse, John. *Gabriele D'Annunzio*. Oxford, England: Clarendon Press, 1998.

Zeidman, Irving. *The American Burlesque Show*. New York: Hawthorn Books, 1967.

Ziegfeld, Richard and Paulette. *The Ziegfeld Touch: The Life and Times of Florenz Ziegfeld, Jr.* New York: Harry N. Abrams, Inc., 1993.

MAGAZINE AND NEWSPAPER ARTICLES

Fan and collector publications are often where the cognoscenti gather to swap the microcosmic details that thrill a biographer's heart. I have spent many hours within the subcultural corridors of *Bingang* (the official publication of the Club Crosby, now folded, the U.S. fan club merging with the International Crosby Circle), *78 Quarterly*, Len Kunstadt's long-departed *Record Research*, and *New Amberola Graphic*.

In addition, chronological runs of *Variety*, *The Billboard*, *Radio Guide*, and the daily newspapers of New York, Philadelphia, Los Angeles, and other major cities were consulted during the relevant time frame, providing a wealth of background detail, contemporary opinion, and minutiae. I would generally peruse their pages on microfilm, a cumbersome format, often badly photographed and blurrily focused, and so would recommend Nicholson Baker's *Double Fold: Libraries and the Assault on Paper* (New York: Random House, 2002) as a warning to those who would dispose of their original newsprint copies in the name of "making space" or preservation. Though a poor second-generation copy is preferable to none at all, it's foolish to entrust our priceless resources to a swiftly outmoded technology, especially in light of today's digital scanning abilities, and the future's ever increasing capacity to store and sort data.

Libraries are a most important resource for our collective (un)conscious. I would especially like to thank the New York Public Library for the Performing Arts at Lincoln Center. To paraphrase Harry Richman, "No minute spent at a library is wasted."

"Boat Blast Burns 3 of 'Follies' Cast," *The New York Times*, July 27, 1931.

Borg, Sven-Hugo. "The Private Life of Greta Garbo," *Film Pictorial*, 1932.

"Brandwynne Succeeds Columbo at Waldorf," *Radio Guide*, February 4, 1932.

Brookhouser, Frank. "The Brief, Lurid Lives of Three Brothers in Death," *Philadelphia Evening Bulletin*, March 9, 1969.

"Brown Freed of Blame in Russ Columbo Death," *Los Angeles Examiner*, September 6, 1934.

Calhoun, Dorothy. "Carole Lombard's House Is a Background for a Blonde!," *Motion Picture Story*, May 1934.

Chapman, John. "Palace Becomes Radio Studio as Ether Stars Act," New York *Daily News*, March 14, 1932.

Churchill, Edward. "America Discovers COLUMBO!," *Screenplay*, December 1933.

"Columbo Estate $54,000," *The New York Times*, September 21, 1934.

"Columbo Killed by Wild Bullet," *Philadelphia Evening Bulletin*, September 3, 1934.

"Con Conrad, 45, Composer, Dies on West Coast," *New York Herald-Tribune*, September 29, 1938.

"Con Conrad Turned Popular Song Writer to Pay for London Trip," *The Telegraph*, December 27, 1925.

"Conquest: The Amazing Love Story of Jack Dempsey and Hannah Williams," *True Experiences*, February 1939.

"Crash Kills Screen Star," *Los Angeles Times*, June 9, 1934.

"Death Takes Dorothy Dell," *Los Angeles Evening Herald*, June 8, 1934.

"Dice and Roulette Bring High Stakes at 64th & Market," *Philadelphia Evening Bulletin*, April 22, 1932.

"Duke-Johnny Desmond Bout to Biopic Columbo Reaches Litigation Stage," *Variety*, December 22, 1955.

"Echoes from the Explosion on Harry Richman's Yacht," *New York American*, December 27, 1931.

Elman, Frank. "The Bullet That Killed the Crooner," *New York Enquirer*, July 25, 1955.

"End of Silent Films," *Variety*, October 20, 1931.

"The Face on the Ballroom Floor," *Motion Picture*, February 1929.

"Family's Tender Deceit of Ten Years Ends as Late Russ Columbo's Mother Dies at 78," *The New York Times*, September 1, 1944.

"A Film Star Arrives," *The New York Times*, February 2, 1930.

Fletcher, Adele Whitely. "At Last! The Truth About Fay and Rudy," *Radio Stars*, May 1934.

Foster, Jack. "Stooges Dog Heels of Radio Celebrity Wherever He Goes," *New York World-Telegram*, October 24, 1931.

"Fox's First Piano Player Now Writing His Song Hits," *New York Evening World*, March 2, 1929.

"Friend Kills Russ Columbo with Accidental Shot Fired from an Old Dueling Pistol," *Los Angeles Examiner*, September 3, 1934.

"Girls Weep as 3000 Jam Russ Columbo Funeral," *Los Angeles Herald Express*, September 6, 1934.

Goodman, Peter. "Singing Bing's Praises: Being Bing," *Newsday*, November 12, 2002.

Grant, Jack. "Dorothy Dell Had Premonition of Her Death in Auto Accident," *Movie Classic*, August 1934.

———."How Hollywood Likes Its Legal Liquor," *Motion Picture*, March 1934.

Hall, Warren. "Follies Beauties Burn in Richman Yacht Blast," New York *Daily News*, July 27, 1931.

———. "Kept Alive by Conspirators," *The American Weekly*, October 3, 1944.

Hellinger, Mark. "Goodbye to a Pal," *New York Daily Mirror*, July 29, 1934.

"Hollywood Mourns Death of Noted Singer," *Los Angeles Examiner*, September 7, 1934.

Holusha, John. "A Theater's Muses, Rescued," *The New York Times*, March 24, 2000.

"Is Rudy Vallee Slipping?" *Radio Guide*, October 31, 1934.

James, Rian. "Names Make News!: Harry Richman," *Brooklyn Eagle Magazine*, September 13, 1931.

———. "Names Make News!: Russ Columbo," *Brooklyn Eagle Magazine*, November 29, 1931.

Kenny, Nick. "Getting an Earful" column, *New York Daily Mirror*, 1931–32.

Lahr, John. "Sinatra's Song," *The New Yorker*, November 13, 1997.

Lee, Rosemary. "The Tragic Love Story of Dorothy Dell and Russ Columbo," *Movies*, November 1934.

Lee, Sonia. "Carole Lombard Tells Why Hollywood Marriages Can't Survive," *Motion Picture Story*, May 1934.

———. "We Would Have Married—," *Movie Classic*, December 1934.

Lewis, Lloyd. "Portrait in a Café: Hasty Sketch of Richman," *Chicago Daily News*, date unknown.

Liebling, A. J. "Russ Columbo, 'Slob Ballad' Singer, Is 'Something Like Vallee, but Lower,' " *New York World-Telegram*, September 22, 1931.

Madden, Muriel. "Russ Columbo Fatally Wounded in Odd Accident," *Movie Classic*, November 1934.

Mainwaring, Dan. "Crash Kills Film Star Dorothy Dell, Doctor," *Los Angeles Herald-Express*, June 8, 1934.

Mantle, Burns. " 'Follies' Gorgeous in Flesh and Picture," New York *Daily News*, July 2, 1931.

Matthews, Francis Barr. "The Story Behind Russ Columbo's Death," *Movie Mirror*, November 1934.

Miley, Jack. "Rudy Vallée Elopes; Weds Movie Actress," New York *Daily News*, July 9, 1931.

"Miss Larrimore and Con Conrad Wed 18 Months," *New York Tribune*, June 11, 1924.

Mortimer, Lee. "Harry Richman As Seen Under the MIKEroscope," *Radio Guide*, July 7, 1934.

"New Listerine Program with Russ Columbo," *Radio Guide*, December 8, 1931.

"Night Fire Wrecks the Club Richman," *The New York Times*, September 23, 1929.

O'Fan, Ray De. "Arnheim on Air Lane Again," *Los Angeles Examiner*, September 2, 1934.

———. "Columbos Adore Bambino," *Los Angeles Examiner*, September 2, 1934.

Paikoff, Herman. "Jack Kapp, the Most Successful A&R Man of His Era," *New Amberola Graphic*, Spring 1993.

Palmborg, Rilla Page. "Just Friends," *Modern Picture and Golden Screen*, December 1934.

"Passionate Pola," *Picture Show Annual*, 1927.

Phillips, Ruth. "Richman Saves Beauty as Yacht Burns, Sinks," *New York Daily Mirror*, July 27, 1931.

Pierce, Max. "Russ Columbo: Hollywood's Tragic Crooner," *Classic Images*, April 1999.

"Prelate Hits Air Crooner," New York *Daily News*, January 11, 1932.

"Radio Crooner Sued," *New York Herald-Tribune*, February 14, 1932.

"Radio's Valentino: Russ Columbo Now First in Hearts of Women Fans," *Radio Guide*, December 5, 1931.

Ramsey, Walter. "The Tragic Death of Russ Columbo," *Radio Stars*, December 1934.

" 'Romeo's' Story of Success," *New York American*, December 13, 1931.

"Rudy Doesn't Like His 'Crooner' Title," *Philadelphia Evening Bulletin*, April 13, 1932.

"Rudy Vallée in N.Y. Discusses Marital Woe," *New York Herald*, January 17, 1934.

Ruhlmann, William. "Swingin' (on a) Star: The Road to Bing Crosby," *Goldmine*, December 24, 1993.

"Russ Columbo Dies from Accidental Gun Wound," *Los Angeles Times*, September 3, 1934.

"Russ Columbo Fatally Wounded as He Examines an Old Pistol," *The New York Times*, September 3, 1934.

"Russ Columbo Inquest Slated for Tomorrow," *Los Angeles Times*, September 4, 1934.

"Russ Columbo Sued," *New York Sun*, February 13, 1932.

"Russ Columbo's Mother Dies in Belief He Lives," *New York Herald Tribune*, September 1, 1944.

Sealander, John. "My Dinner with Rudy," 1995 (available at www.sealander.com).

Shilkret, Nat. "Modern Electrical Methods of Recording," *Phonograph Monthly Review*, June 1927.

Skolsky, Sidney: "Shot Stopped Columbo's Rise to New, Greater Fame," New York *Daily News*, September 4, 1934.

———. "Tintypes: Harry Richman," New York *Daily News*, October 2, 1930.

———. "Tintypes: Russ Columbo," New York *Daily News*, January 18, 1932.

Sobol, Louis. "Snapshots at Random!," *New York Evening Journal*, December 21, 1931.

St. Johns, Adela Rogers. "The Private Life of Rudy Vallée," *Liberty*, April 7, 14, 21, and 28, 1934.

Town, Eleanor. "When the Flying Beauty Jilted the Love-sick Composer," *New York Journal*, August 18, 1926.

Townsend, Lee: "Newcomers Today—Stars Tomorrow?," *Motion Picture Story*, April 1934.

"The Tragedy of Russ Columbo," *Tower Radio*, November 1934.

"The Truth About Jack Dempsey and Hannah," *True Confessions*, October 1941.

"Two Lanzettis Held as Russ Columbo Is Reported $11,000 Loser at Dice," *Philadelphia Daily News*, April 22, 1932.

"Univ.'s 'Dream' Just Fair," *The Hollywood Reporter*, September 1, 1934.

Vallee, Rudy. "Night Clubs of New York," *Radio Digest*, February 1931.

"Vallee Airs 'Love Plot,' " *Los Angeles Times*, January 15, 1934.

Wald, Jerry. "How Columbo Discovered America and Vice-Versa!" *Modern Screen*, December 1933.

Washburn, Mel: "The Story of Dorothy Dell Goff's Star of Life, Burning Dimly, Brightly, Then Quenched," *New Orleans Morning Tribune*, June 10, 1934.

"Who's Who on the Radio," *New York Sun*, September 26, 1931.

"Why Should I Talk of Love? I Am Going to Work." *New York Evening Graphic*, November 10, 1924.

Yawitz, Paul. "Hollywood Called It Madness but Columbo Called It Luck," unknown magazine, 1932.

———. " 'Crooners' War' Built Columbo," *New York Daily Mirror*, September 6, 1934.

———. "Business Broke Russ's Romance," *New York Daily Mirror*, September 7, 1934.

———. "Bunko Love for Publicity Dogged Russ," *New York Daily Mirror*, September 8, 1934.

SELECTED DISCOGRAPHY

Ambrose and His Orchestra. *London 1927–1935* (Pavilion PAST 9713; CD).

Armstrong, Louis. *The Complete Hot Five and Hot Seven Recordings* (Columbia Legacy C4K 63527; 4 CDs w/ booklet).

Arnheim, Gus. *Echoes from the Cocoanut Grove* (Take Two TT410; CD).

Austin, Gene. *A Time to Relax* (Take Two TT414; CD).

Baker, Chet. *My Funny Valentine* (Pacific Jazz 7243 8 2826 24; CD).

Boswell Sisters. *That's How Rhythm Was Born* (Columbia Legacy CK 66977; CD).

————. *The Boswell Sisters* (CSP/CBS P3 16493; 3 LPs).

Bruno, Paul. *The Russ Columbo Story* (Coral 57327; LP).

Columbo, Russ. *A Legendary Performer* (RCA CPL1-1756(e); LP w/ booklet).

————. *The Complete Studio Recordings* (Taragon 83785-11032; 2 CDs).

————. *The Films of Russ Columbo* (Golden Legends 2000/2; LP).

————. *Love Songs by Russ Columbo* (RCA Victor LPM-2072; LP).

————. *Prisoner of Love* (ASV AJA 5234; LP).

————. *Russ Columbo* (Sandy Hook 2006; LP).

————. *Russ Columbo on the Air* (Sandy Hook 2039, Totem 1031; LP).

————. *Save the Last Dance for Me* (Take Two TT409; CD).

Condon, Eddie. *Eddie Condon 1928–1931* (Timeless CBC1-024; CD).

Crosby, Bing. *Bing: A Musical Autobiography* (Decca DL 9054; LP).

————. *Bing! His Legendary Years, 1931–1957* (MCA D4-10887; 4 CDs).

————. *A Bing Crosby Collection, Vol. II* (CBS CSP 059; LP).

————. *The Bing Crosby Story, Volume I: The Early Jazz Years 1928–1932* (Epic E2E 2020; 2 LPs).

————. *Bing: The Final Chapter* (BBC 22398; LP).

————. *Centennial Anthology of Decca Recordings* (MCA 113 222-2; CD).

————. *Classic Crosby Vol. I* (Naxos Nostalgia 8.120507; CD).

————. *Der Bingle* (Columbia CL 2502; 10" LP).

————. *Going Hollywood, Vol. I (1930–36); Vol. II (1936–39).* (Jasmine 108/09, 113/14; 2 CDs each).

————. *In Hollywood, Vols. I and II, 1930–34* (Collectibles 6805-6; 1 CD each).

————. *Lost Columbia Sides 1928–1933* (Collector's Choice A2 53123; 2 CDs).

————. *My Favorite Irish Songs* (MCA D-21048; CD).

————. *Songs I Wish I Had Sung the First Time Around . . .* (Decca DL 8352; LP).

————. *The Voice of Bing in the 1930s* (Brunswick BL 54005; LP).

————. *Where the Blue of the Night Meets the Gold of the Day: The Original Sound Tracks from Bing Crosby's Early Films (1930–1931)* (Biograph BLP-M-1; LP).

————. *Wrap Your Troubles in Dreams* (RCA LPV-584; LP).

————. *Young Bing Crosby* (RCA Victor LPM-2071; LP).

————, and David Bowie. "Peace on Earth / Little Drummer Boy" (RCA BOWT 12; LP).

————, and Buddy Bregman. *Bing Sings Whilst Bregman Swings* (Verve MGV-2020; LP; also Verve 314 549 367-2; CD).

————, and Bob Hope. *Hit the Road with Bing and Bob* (Jasmine 127/8; CD).

Duchin, Eddy. *Dream Along* (Columbia CL 1432; LP).

Eckstine, Billy. *Mr. B. and the Band: The Savoy Sessions* (Savoy 2214; 2 LPs).

Edwards, Cliff. "Ukulele Ike." *Singing in the Rain* (Audiophile ACD 17; CD).

Etting, Ruth. *The Original Recordings of Ruth Etting* (Columbia ML 5050; LP).

Ferry, Bryan. *As Time Goes By* (Virgin America 48270 2; CD).

Fisher, Eddie. *May I Sing to You* (RCA Victor LPM 3185; 10" LP).

Goodman, Benny. *The Complete Benny Goodman: Vol. I (1935); Vol. 2 (1935–6)* (RCA Victor AXM2-5505, and AXM2-5515; 2 LPs each).

————. *A Legendary Performer* (RCA Victor CPL1-24701e; LP).

————. *A Jazz Holiday: The Early Benny Goodman 1926–1931* (ASV CD AJA 5263; CD).

————, and Jack Teagarden. *B.G. and Big Tea in NYC* (Decca GRD 609; CD).

Horowitz, Vladimir. *Horowitz Plays Chopin* (RCA Victor LM-2137; LP).

Jolson, Al. *The Essential Recordings* (Stardust CLP 0759-2; CD).

Lang, Eddi, and Joe Venuti. *The Classic Columbia and Okeh Recordings of Joe Venuti and Eddie Lang Sessions* (Mosaic MD8-213; 8 CDs w/ booklet).

————. *Jazz Guitar Virtuoso* (Yazoo 109; CD).

————. *Stringing the Blues* (Columbia C2L 24; 2 LPs w/ booklet).

Lewis, Gordon. *A Tribute to Russ Columbo* (Diplomat 2331; LP).

Lown, Bert. *Biltmore Hotel Orchestra* (The Old Masters MB 105; CD).

Martin, Dean. *The Capitol Years* (Capitol 9777 7 98409 2 2; 2 CDs).

————. *Love Songs by Dean Martin* (Ranwood 82592; CD).

McDonough, Dick, and Carl Kress. *Guitar Genius in the 1930s* (Jazz Archives 32; LP).

Mills Brothers. *Chronological Vol. 1* (JSP 301; CD).

——. *The 1930s Recordings: Remastered and in Chronological Order* (JSP Jazz Box 2; 5 CDs).

New Orleans Rhythm Kings. *The Complete . . . Vol. 1 (1922–23)* (King Jazz 109 FS; CD).

Palloy, Charlie. *Vocals and Guitar* (The Old Masters MB 118; CD).

Paul, Les, and Mary Ford. *Time to Dream* (Capitol T802; LP).

Price, Ray. *Prisoner of Love* (Justice / Buddah 74465-99705-2; CD).

Richman, Harry, and Sid Garry. *Vocalist's Showcase Vol. 9: Radio Favorites 1927–1931* (Vintage Recordings; CD).

Selvin, Ben. *The Columbia House Band* (The Old Masters MB 102; CD).

Sinatra, Frank. *Love Songs* (BMG 09026-68701–2; CD).

——. *The Voice of Frank Sinatra* (Columbia Legacy CK 62100; CD).

——, and Tommy Dorsey. *Learn to Croon* (Buddah 744659601; CD).

Smith, Kate. *Emergence of a Legend 1930–1939* (Take Two TT401; CD).

Tiny Tim. *Prisoner of Love: A Tribute to Russ Columbo* (Vinyl Retentive 005; CD).

Vale, Jerry. *I Remember Russ* (Columbia Legacy CK 63549; CD).

Various Artists. *Art Deco: The Crooners* (Columbia Legacy C2K52942; 2 CDs).

——. *The Big Broadcast* (Soundtrak ST-101; LP).

——. *Black Secular Vocal Groups, Vol. I (1923–1929)* (Document DOCD-5546; CD).

——. *Broadway Through the Gramophone: Vol. I (1844–1900); Vol. II (1900–14); Vol. III (1914–20); Vol. IV (1920–29)* (Pearl GEM 0082-5; 2 CDs each).

——. *Chicago* (BBC 589; CD).

——. *College Rhythm: Hot Dance Band Classics: 1927–1934* (Memphis Archives 7021; CD).

——. *Early 1900s Whistling Songs Vols. 1 and 2* (Old Time Victrola Music; CD).

——. *The First Crooners: Vol. I (The Twenties); Vol. II (1930–34)* (Take Two 411 and 418; 1 CD each).

——. *Gone: But Not Forgotten . . . Russ Columbo* (The Russ Columbo Archives Inc. ALG 11408; 4 LPs).

——. *Great Virtuosi of the Golden Age, Vol. II: Violin* (Pearl GEM 102; LP).

——. *La Grande Époque des Crooners* (Best of Crooners 23; 2 CDs).

——. *The Music of Broadway 1930–1936* (Box Office ENBO-CD2 9/94; 2 CDs).

——. *Silly Songs 1922–1934* (BBC 652; CD).

——. *They Called It Crooning* (ASV AJA 5026; CD).

——. *Those Wonderful Thirties: The Stars of Broadway, Nightclubs and Vaudeville* (Decca 7-2; 2 LPs).

————. *Those Wonderful Thirties: The Stars of Radio: The Great Bands, the Great Vocalists.* (Decca DEA 7-3; 2 LPs).

Vallée, Rudy. *The Best of Rudy Vallée* (RCA Victor LSP 3816(e); LP).

————. *Is This Your Rudy Vallée?* (Crown 5204; LP).

————. *The Voice That Had Them Fainting 1929–1937.* (Take Two TT405; CD).

LINKS

www.earlyrecordings.com (the home page of Old Time Victrola Music).

www.kcmetro.edu/~crosby (Steven Lewis's comprehensive Bing "Internet Museum").

www/lrbcg.com/pogo/MAPS.html (headquarters of the Michigan Antique Phonograph Society, a worldwide organization dedicated to the preservation and dissemination of early recorded sound).

www.nfo.net ("Big Bands Database" assembled by Murray L. Pfeffer, centering on musicians and songwriters of the pre- and post-swing era).

www.russcolumbo.com (the unofficial fan site; Max Pierce, webmaster).

www.vintage-recordings.com (rare CD transfers of early vaudeville, blues, comic songs, ragtime, and jazz).

INDEX OF SONG AND ALBUM TITLES

INDEX

Moore, James, 108
Moore, Pryor, 17
Moran and Mack, 98
Moreno, Antonio, 208
Moreschi, Alessandro, 138
Morgan, Claudia, 345
Morgan, F. Langdon, 269
Morgan, Helen, 59, 107, 117, 118, 120,
    124–25, 146, 165, 230
Morgan, Helen, Jr., 146
Moriarty, Dean, 417
Morricone, Ennio, 170
Morrisey, Will, 90
Morrison, Jim, 435
Morse, Robert, 428, 429
Morse, Samuel, 130
Morse, Theodore, 385
Moskowitz, Mrs. Henry, 120
Moss, Joe, 230
Moten, Benny, 259
mothers, 385–92. *See also specific person*
Motion Picture magazine, 23, 280, 376
Motion Picture Story (film), 301
Moulin Rouge (film/musical), 123, 306,
    319–26, 335
Moulin-Rouge (Paris club), 325
Mound City Blues Blowers, 330
Mourning Becomes Electra (play), 204
Movie Classics, 307, 372
Movie Weekly, 209
Moxley, Spencer, 370
Moyer, Holly, 388
Mozart, Wolfgang Amadeus, 171, 338
Mr. Bones (play), 388
MTV, 324, 436
Muir, Florabel, 190
Munn, Frank, 178
Murray, Billy, 28, 169–70
music videos, 323
Musicaladers, 90
Musicians Union, 88, 105, 140, 164,
    240, 248
Musso, Joe, 17
My Time Is Your Time (Vallée), 53, 68,
    427
Mystics (singing group), 405

Nagel, Conrad, 26, 208, 223
Naish, J. Carrol, 253
Naldi, Nita, 24, 322
Napoleon of Broadway (play), 302
Nate 'n Al's (Beverly Hills deli), 402

National Catholic Legion of Decency,
    395
Navarro, Fats, 433
Nazimova, Alla, 24, 211, 212
NBC
    and Columbo, 7, 48–49, 65, 88, 128,
        131, 136, 140, 142, 177, 180, 182,
        199–200, 202, 205, 219–20, 231,
        235, 240, 250, 257, 258–59, 267,
        273, 341, 345, 356
    commissions at, 258
    Conrad fills in for Columbo on, 223
    and Crosby-Columbo rivalry, 142
    headquarters of, 48
    and Kahn orchestra, 265
    lawsuits against, 205
    and Parade of Stars broadcast, 165
    and quality of Columbo bands, 235
    and Reser, 231
    Tonight Show on, 405, 407
    and Vallée, 43, 44, 62, 75, 259
    and Winchell, 287
Negri, Ada, 207
Negri, Pola, 207–9, 211–12, 213–19,
    220, 400
Neilan, Marshall, 60–61
Nelson, Ozzie, 48–49, 72, 75–76
New Amsterdam Theater (New York
    City), 109, 112, 142
New Moon (play), 161
New Movie magazine, 310
New York Daily News, 140, 200, 201,
    287, 297, 318, 321
New York Graphic, 36, 57, 136, 194, 238,
    243, 286
New York Mirror, 68, 72, 75, 78, 136,
    189–90, 287, 292
New York Morning Telegraph, 34
The New York Sun, 5, 35, 200
New York Theater (New York City), 112
The New York Times, 324, 396
New York World-Telegram, 140
New Yorker magazine, 71
Newcomers of 1928 (revue), 430
Newley, Anthony, 426
Nichols, Red, 91, 92, 235, 264, 330
Nijinsky, Vaslav, 212
Nilsson, Harry, 426
Ninotchka (film), 191
Nixon, Richard M., 430
No Man of Her Own (film), 393
Noble, Ray, 150
Nocturne (d'Annunzio), 382

ABOUT THE AUTHOR

LENNY KAYE is an acclaimed music writer whose work has appeared in *Rolling Stone, The Village Voice, Creem, Hit Parader,* and *Crawdaddy!* He has been a guitarist for poet-rocker Patti Smith since her band's inception thirty years ago and serves on the nominating committee for the Rock and Roll Hall of Fame. He is the co-author of *Waylon.* He lives in New York City.